Essential
Japanese
Vocabulary

T0161103

Essential
Japanese
Vocabulary

AKIRA MIURA

Professor of Japanese, Emeritus
University of Wisconsin, Madison

Foreword by Wesley Jacobsen
Harvard University

TUTTLE Publishing

Tokyo | Rutland, Vermont | Singapore

"Books to Span the East and West"

Tuttle Publishing was founded in 1832 in the small New England town of Rutland, Vermont [USA]. Our core values remain as strong today as they were then—to publish best-in-class books which bring people together one page at a time. In 1948, we established a publishing outpost in Japan—and Tuttle is now a leader in publishing English-language books about the arts, languages and cultures of Asia. The world has become a much smaller place today and Asia's economic and cultural influence has grown. Yet the need for meaningful dialogue and information about this diverse region has never been greater. Over the past seven decades, Tuttle has published thousands of books on subjects ranging from martial arts and paper crafts to language learning and literature—and our talented authors, illustrators, designers and photographers have won many prestigious awards. We welcome you to explore the wealth of information available on Asia at **www.tuttlepublishing.com**.

Published by Tuttle Publishing, an imprint of Periplus Editions (HK) Ltd.

www.tuttlepublishing.com

Copyright © 1983, 2002, 2011 by Akira Miura
Foreword copyright © 2011 by Wesley Jacobsen

Library of Congress Cataloging-in-Publication Data

Miura, Akira, 1927–
Essential japanese vocabulary : learn to avoid common (and embarassing!) mistakes / by Akira Miura : foreword by Wesley Jacobsen.
    320 p. ; 23 cm.
Includes bibliographical references and index.
ISBN 978-4-8053-1127-1 (pbk.)
1. Japanese language—Conversation and phrase books—English. 2. Japanese language—Glossaries, vocabularies, etc. I. Title.
PL539.M48 2011
495.6'83421--dc22
                        2010027441

ISBN 978-4-8053-1127-1
ISBN 978-4-8053-1821-8 (for sale in Japan only)

Distributed by

North America, Latin America & Europe
Tuttle Publishing
364 Innovation Drive
North Clarendon, VT 05759-9436 U.S.A.
Tel: 1 (802) 773-8930; Fax: 1 (802) 773-6993
info@tuttlepublishing.com
www.tuttlepublishing.com

Japan
Tuttle Publishing
Yaekari Building 3rd Floor 5-4-12 Osaki
Shinagawa-ku, Tokyo 141 0032
Tel: (81) 3 5437-0171; Fax: (81) 3 5437-0755
sales@tuttle.co.jp
www.tuttle.co.jp

Asia Pacific
Berkeley Books Pte. Ltd.
3 Kallang Sector #04-01, Singapore 349278
Tel: (65) 6741-2178; Fax: (65) 6741-2179
inquiries@periplus.com.sg
www.tuttlepublishing.com

First edition
26 25 24 23   10 9 8 7 6   2312VP

Printed in Malaysia

CONTENTS

Foreword

As most adult learners can attest, classroom study is by itself rarely enough to gain true proficiency in a second language. Time spent outside the classroom using the language in the real world is crucial to the process of trial and error that allows one gradually, sometimes unconsciously, to adjust one's knowledge of the language to match more and more closely the knowledge of native speakers. The valuable feedback one gets in this process of trial and error can come at the cost of some pain, but pain that can be relieved with laughter. This is illustrated by the experience of an American having lived a short time in Japan who, unable to bear any longer the constant staring he was subjected to in public, burst out on a crowded train, "**Jirojiro miru na. Watashi datte ninjin da yo**," intending to say, "Stop staring! I'm a human too," but in the process mixing up **ningen** "human" with **ninjin** "carrot."

Japanese language teachers are often asked what it is about Japanese that poses the greatest difficulty for native English speakers. Various characteristics of Japanese are typically given in answer to this question. Its grammar is, at least at first glance, quite different from English, putting verbs last in a sentence rather than immediately after the subject, conjugating verbs into long, sometimes complex forms, and marking nouns with particles that distinguish subtly different shades of meaning. Its writing system is a tedious one, requiring long years of schooling even for native speakers to master. And it is a language sensitive to fine nuances of interpersonal relationships that do not always match the social intuitions of native English speakers.

One hears less often, though, about the challenge posed by vocabulary—that is, just plain words—in learning Japanese. We tend to think of words as atomic units that express inherently simple ideas and to assume that all one needs to do is memorize these, leaving the difficult work of arranging them into meaningful sentences to the rules of grammar. But experience shows that, in getting one's meaning across in a second language, insufficient grasp of vocabulary is actually a greater obstacle than insufficient control of grammar. Even if the grammar—the word order, for example—isn't perfect, one's meaning can usually be understood if key vocabulary items are recognizable but not the other way around. Research in second-language acquisition shows that control of vocabulary is in fact a fairly reliable predictor of one's overall level of proficiency in a language: the more words one knows, the more likely one is to be proficient in other areas of the language, including grammar. These results bear out the observation made by Akira Miura in his preface to this volume that, from his experience, errors of vocabulary are as prevalent among the overall errors made by English speakers learning Japanese as are those of grammar.

What is it about vocabulary that poses such a challenge? Apart from issues of pronunciation that led our American friend astray in the story related earlier, at least two basic reasons can be given. The first is the tendency to assume incorrectly that words in a second language cover the same range of meanings as corresponding words in our native language. If we think of meaning as a kind of space that words divide up into distinct chunks, different languages tend to divide up this space in different ways. To take liquid H_2O as an example, the English word "water" occupies a meaning space that in Japanese is divided in two, depending on the temperature of the water, as expressed by the distinct words **mizu** "cold water" and **yu** "hot water." It is therefore an oxymoron in Japanese to say ****atsui mizu** "hot **mizu**." Similarly, Japanese has two verbs covering the meaning space of English *help*, one (**tetsudau**) referring to help given by doing the same thing as the person helped, the other (**tasukeru**) referring to help given by doing something different from the person helped. Helping someone wash dishes, for example, would be expressed by **tetsudau**, but helping a person in financial distress by lending him money would call for **tasukeru**. This explains why, if you were drowning, you would want to cry out **Tasukete-kure**! rather than **Tetsudatte-kure**! as the latter would, if taken literally, lead to fatal results.

A second reason that vocabulary poses a particular challenge to the second-language learner is that vocabulary and grammar are not as easily distinguished as commonly thought. Many important words, such as verbs and other predicates, in fact carry grammar with them. Part of understanding the meaning of a verb in Japanese is to know how many and what kinds of nouns go with the verb for it to make sense, and what the particles are that express the role played by each noun. So to understand the meaning of **taberu** "eat," you need to know that it takes two nouns, one expressing the person or thing that eats (marked by the particle **ga**, often replaced by **wa**) and another expressing the thing eaten (marked by the particle **o**), as in **Kyaku ga soba o taberu** "the customer eats soba." Every verb or predicate carries with it a grammar like this—although that grammar is often co-vertly present rather than overtly expressed, and it may or may not behave as one might expect from its English counterpart. The verb **au** "meet," for example, takes an "object" marked by the particle **ni**, not the normal object marker **o** as one would predict from the fact that "meet" takes an object in English (e.g., **tomodachi ni au** "meet a friend"). And there are times when a given verb in one language corresponds to two different verbs in the other, as with verbs like English "open" that have two distinct counterparts in Japanese, each with their own separate grammar (**aku** and **akeru** in the case of "open").

For reasons such as these, numerous pitfalls lie along the seemingly straight path to acquiring Japanese vocabulary at the beginning and intermediate levels, and it is just such pitfalls that this volume is designed to help learners avoid. In it Akira Miura distills the wisdom of a distinguished career of thirty-five years teaching Japanese in American universities to target more than five hundred words and expressions that are most likely to give beginning and intermediate learners difficulty, whether or not they may be aware of it, as they venture out of the classroom into the real world of Japanese. In the process he brings to bear not only his formidable classroom teaching experience but also his skill as a linguist and his trademark love of humor in language that has so endeared him to his colleagues in the Japanese teaching profession. Both teachers and students of the Japanese language will find here explanations that are clear, accessible, hands-on, and oriented to actual situations of daily life that are most likely to be encountered by beginning and intermediate students. Interspersed among the language explanations are numerous points of commentary on Japanese culture that make this volume equally suited to being read for pleasure as to being used as a reference tool. Though it may not guarantee that you will never encounter a situation like that of our American friend who described himself as a carrot, this volume will bring a heightened awareness of the pitfalls in using Japanese vocabulary that will greatly decrease the likelihood of you finding yourself in such a situation. At the same time it is certain to add colloquial spice to your expressive power in Japanese, and, last but not least, to add hours of enjoyment to your study of the language.

WESLEY M. JACOBSEN
HARVARD UNIVERSITY

Preface

I taught Japanese to Americans for more than thirty-five years. During that time I observed a large number of errors in Japanese made by my American students. Most of those errors were due to the students' insufficient mastery of Japanese grammar (for example, their inability to inflect verbs correctly or to use appropriate particles), but there were also at least as many errors that are basically attributable to vocabulary problems.

When the American student of Japanese first comes across a new Japanese word, it is usually introduced with an English translation, which is considered the "equivalent," e.g., **atatakai** 暖かい is matched up with "warm." The student is therefore very likely to conclude that there is in fact a one-to-one correspondence between the two words, and he or she does indeed start using **atatakai**, for example, in all situations where "warm" would be called for in English. The student might thus say to a Japanese friend in the middle of summer, with the mercury hitting the mid-eighties, **Kyō wa atatakai desu nē** 今日は暖かいですねえ "It's warm today, isn't it!" That would really baffle the poor Japanese friend because, in Japanese, temperatures that high are not **atatakai** but **atsui** 暑い "hot." **Atatakai** most aptly describes a nice spring day that arrives after the cold months of winter.

Essential Japanese Vocabulary combines the two volumes of my *Japanese Words & Their Uses*, which were originally published separately. It is designed to provide help for American students, especially those at the elementary and intermediate levels, by explaining approximately five hundred Japanese words and phrases and their usages. It explains not only how they are used but also how they should *not* be used. Whenever possible, I've contrasted Japanese terms with their English counterparts. Many of the errors cited in this volume were actually committed by my own students (although they are not always quoted verbatim).

There are just as many synonyms in Japanese as there are in English, and they also may create problems for students of Japanese. For example, both **binbō** 貧乏 and **mazushii** 貧しい mean "poor," but they differ in usage. In this book, I have included a number of synonyms like that, with sample sentences as well as explanations of their differences.

If American and other English-speaking students of Japanese can find solutions to some of their problems in mastering basic vocabulary with the aid of this book, I will be more than happy. It is also my hope that teachers of Japanese working with English-speaking students may find the explanations and examples helpful for their own classes. I would like to express my appreciation to the Australian National University, which awarded me a research grant that enabled me to continue writing the manuscript. Thanks are also due to my wife, Charlotte, who proofread the final draft for me.

AKIRA MIURA

Explanatory Notes

ARRANGEMENT OF ENTRIES

The main text of this book consists of a list of more than 500 Japanese terms. Each entry heading gives the term in romanization and in Japanese kanji (ideographic characters) and/ or kana (syllabics), then one or more English "equivalents." The kanji are limited to those widely in use. The heading is then followed by a detailed explanation of the term's usage.

TERMINOLOGY

Since this book is meant not as a scholarly treatise but rather as a reference book for elementary- through intermediate-level students, the number of technical terms has been kept to a minimum.

I-Adjectives. These adjectives are inflected words that end in **-ai, -ii, -ui**, or **-oi**. Hayai 速い "fast," **ōkii** 大きい "large," **furui** 古い "old," and **hiroi** 広い "wide," for example, are **i**-adjectives. The **-ku** form of an adjective (e.g., **hayaku**) is referred to as the adverbial form.

Na-Adjectives. Na-adjectives are so called because when they are used to modify a noun, they require **na** な, as in **kirei na hana** きれいな花 "a beautiful flower" or **iya na hito** いやな人 "a nasty person." Na-adjectives are sometimes called **na**-nouns by other authors for they behave like a noun in that they may occur with **desu** to form complete sentences. Other examples of **na**-adjectives are **genki** 元気 "healthy" and **shitsurei** 失礼 "rude."

Nouns. Japanese nouns are noninflected words that can occur before **desu** to constitute complete utterances. **Hon** "book," **eiga** "movie," and **gaijin** "foreigner," are nouns.

Particles. Japanese particles are uninflected words that occur within or at the end of a sentence. They generally do not begin an utterance. When they occur within a sentence, they relate what precedes (whether a word, a phrase, or a clause) to what follows. (For this reason, particles are sometimes called relationals.) Examples of this type are **wa** は, **ga** が, **o** を, and **to** と. Particles that occur at the end of a sentence are called sentence-final particles, and they make the sentence interrogative, exclamatory, emphatic, etc. Examples of this type are **ka** か, **nē** ねえ, and **yo** よ.

Verbs. Japanese verbs are inflected words that take **-masu** in the formal nonpast and **-mashita** in the formal past. **Iku** "to go," **kuru** "to come," and **taberu** "to eat," for example, are verbs.

Potential forms of verbs. Potential forms are forms that mean "can do such and such" or "such and such can be done." **Yomeru** 読める, for example, is the potential form of **yomu** 読む "to read" and means "can read" or "can be read."

Punctual verbs. Verbs representing actions or occurrences that take place without duration over time are punctual verbs. **Shinu** 死ぬ "to die," **tsuku** 着く "to arrive" and **kekkon-suru** 結婚する "to get married" are examples of this type.

Stative verbs. Verbs that express states rather than actions are stative verbs. **Iru** いる "(someone) is (somewhere)" and **aru** ある "(something) is (somewhere)" are examples of this category.

JAPANESE ACCENT

Accent marks are used in this book. They are, as a rule, used in the entry headings only, e.g., Ō⌐KI⌐I.

Unlike English, which has a stress accent, Japanese has a pitch accent. In Japanese words, each syllable is spoken either high or low. If the first syllable is low, the second is always high, and if the first syllable is high, the second is always low. In this book, the mark " ⌐ " indicates a rise in pitch, and the mark " ⌐ " indicates a fall in pitch. The syllable followed by " ⌐ " is always the accented syllable. For example, Ō⌐KI⌐I, a four-syllable word, should be pronounced low-high-high-low, and KI, the last syllable before the fall, is the accented syllable. Some words are left completely unmarked, e.g., KIMONO. Unmarked words are accentless (or unaccented) words, i.e., words that do not have a fall in pitch. In accentless words, the first syllable is always low, but the remaining syllables are all high, and there is no fall in pitch even when the words are followed by a particle. For example, **kimono wa** is pronounced:

> **mono wa**
> **ki**

Words that end with an accented syllable (e.g., A⌐TAMA⌐) have the same accent pattern as accentless words when pronounced by themselves, but when they are followed by a particle, a difference emerges. For example, A⌐TAMA⌐ (accented) and KIMONO (accentless) have exactly the same pitch pattern when pronounced alone, but when followed by a particle (e.g., **wa**) they are pronounced differently, as follows:

> **tama**
> **atama wa** → a   **wa**

> **mono wa**
> **kimono wa** → ki

Note that **wa** in **atama wa** is low while **wa** in **kimono wa** is high.

ROMANIZATION

The system of romanization used in this book is the popular Hepburn system. There are, however, some differences that should be mentioned. In this book, ん is always written **n**, even before **m**, **p**, and **b**. When **n** should be pronounced independently of a vowel or *y* that follows it, an apostrophe is inserted to indicate the fact. Long vowels are generally shown with macrons. Long vowels, however, are not indicated in the proper names that appear in the bibliography.

OTHER CONVENTIONS

An asterisk is used in this book to mark incorrect utterances. A question mark at the beginning of a sentence indicates unnaturalness or awkwardness.

Essential
Japanese
Vocabulary

Abiru 浴びる *to take a bath, shower*

Japanese people who have spent a number of years in English-speaking countries such as the United States often end up having their spoken Japanese affected by English. One example of this that I once heard was ***Mō shawā o torimashita ka** *もうシャワーを取りましたか, a direct translation of "Have you taken a shower yet?" In authentic Japanese, the sentence should be **Shawā o abimashita ka** シャワーを浴びましたか, using the verb **abiru** 浴びる rather than **toru** 取る.

"Take a bath" also can be **furo o abiru** 風呂をあびる, although another expression, **furo ni hairu** 風呂に入る, is probably more common.

EXAMPLE:

Nihonjin wa furo o abiru (or furo ni hairu) no ga hontō ni suki da.
日本人は風呂を浴びる(風呂に入る)のが本当に好きだ。
The Japanese really love taking baths.

Abunai 危ない *dangerous*

Abunai 危ない most often means "dangerous, risky, hazardous."

EXAMPLES:

(1) **Yopparai-unten wa abunai.**
酔っ払い運転は危ない。
Drunk driving is dangerous.

(2) **Kodomo no matchi-asobi wa abunai.**
子供のマッチ遊びは危ない。
Children's playing with matches is hazardous.

Abunai! 危ない! may be used as an exclamation in situations where "Look out!" or "Watch out!" would be called for in English. For example, if you see someone walking into the path of an oncoming car, you shout out, **Abunai!** Other examples of adjectives used to give warning are **Urusai!** うるさい! and **Yakamashii!** やかましい! (lit., "[You are] noisy!"), both meaning "Be quiet!" or "Shut up!" (see URUSAI).

A⌈chi⌉kochi あちこち *here and there*

Achikochi あちこち, short for **achirakochira** あちらこちら, looks very much like English "here and there," except that the order is reversed, i.e., **achikochi** literally would be "there and here." Although **achikochi** and "here and there" are quite similar in meaning, there is a slight difference. **Achikochi** seems to cover a wider area than "here and there," as in the following example.

EXAMPLE:

Achikochi sagashita keredo mitsukaranakatta.
あちこち捜したけれど見つからなかった。
I looked far and wide but couldn't find it.

There is another variant, **atchikotchi** あっちこち, which is a little more colloquial than **achikochi** あちこち.

Agaru 上がる *to go up*

The basic meaning of **agaru** 上がる is "to go up."

EXAMPLE:

(1) **Mata gasorin no nedan ga agatta.**
またガソリンの値段が上がった。
The price of gasoline has gone up again.

Entering a Japanese-style house as a guest is also **agaru** 上がる because it is an act of "going up." When you enter a Japanese home, you first step into the **genkan** 玄関, or vestibule. There you take off your shoes and *take a step up* to the floor level of the house. The act of stepping into the vestibule is **hairu** 入る "to go in," but the act of stepping up to the floor level of the house is **agaru** 上がる "to take a step up." That is why the Japanese host says to a visitor:

EXAMPLE:

(2) **Dōzo oagari kudasai.**
どうぞ お上がりください。
Please come in (lit., step up).

Sentence (3) below therefore sounds extremely strange.

EXAMPLE:

(3) ***Nihonjin wa ie ni hairu mae ni kutsu o nugimasu.**
*日本人は家に入る前に靴を脱ぎます。
The Japanese take off their shoes before going into the house.

Agaru 上がる has to be used in this context. Otherwise sentence (3) would describe someone taking off his shoes outside the front door!

A⌈isu⌉ru 愛する *to love*

The noun **ai** 愛 "love" and its verbal counterpart, **aisuru** 愛する "to love," are both written expressions. Although some young lovers nowadays may use such words of endearment as **Aishite-iru yo** 愛しているよ (men's speech) and **Aishite-iru wa** 愛しているわ (women's speech) to mean "I love you," such sentences still sound stilted because the verb 愛する **aisuru** is rarely used in speech. **Kimi ga suki da** 君が好きだ (men's speech) and **Anata ga suki yo** あなたが好きよ (women's speech) also mean "I love you." The versions containing **suki** 好き (see SUKI) are more conversational and are perhaps more frequently used in speech than the versions with **aisuru**. As Donald Keene (p. 156) wisely points out, however, the most typically Japanese expression of love has been silence (although, in the rapidly changing society of contemporary Japan, this tradition too may be on its way out).

A⌈ite⌉ 相手 *partner, opponent*

Aite 相手 means someone with whom one does something. Depending on the activity, therefore, **aite** could be either one's partner or competitor.

EXAMPLES:

(1) **kekkon no aite**
結婚の相手
marriage partner

(2) **ashita no shiai no aite**
あしたの試合の相手
the opponent of tomorrow's game/match

A⌐kachan 赤ちゃん *baby*

Akachan 赤ちゃん is normally a word for someone else's baby.

EXAMPLE:
(1) **Otaku no akachan wa hontō ni ogenki sō desu nē.**
お宅の赤ちゃんは本当にお元気そうですねえ。
Your baby really looks healthy, doesn't he/she!

Although some Japanese, especially women, use the word to refer to their own babies, the practice, in my opinion, is in poor taste. The word to be used in that case is **akanbō** 赤ん坊.

EXAMPLE:
(2) **Kyō wa uchi no akanbō no tanjōbi na n desu.**
きょうはうちの赤ん坊の誕生日なんです。
Today is my baby's birthday.

A⌐kema⌐shite o⌐medetō gozaima⌐su 明けましておめでとうございます
Happy New Year!

When a New Year draws near, English speakers still new in Japan often ask their Japanese friends how to say "Happy New Year!" in Japanese. The answer is almost always **Akemashite omedetō gozaimasu** 明けましておめでとうございます (or its equivalent **Shin-nen omedetō gozaimasu** 新年おめでとうございます). Having received this answer, these English speakers practice hard to memorize this long salutation and, after finally learning it, they try it on their Japanese associates—most likely toward the end of December. Unfortunately, this Japanese greeting may not be used until New Year's Day since it literally means "[The New Year] having begun, this is indeed a happy occasion." This contrasts with the English salutation "Happy New Year!," which is an abbreviation of "I wish you a happy New Year" and may therefore be used before the arrival of the New Year. The expression to be used before the old year expires is **Yoi otoshi o omukae kudasai** よいお年をお迎えください "May you see in a good year!" However, this is a rather formal salutation and is rarely used among close friends. There is regrettably no informal equivalent, except for the shorter form **Yoi otoshi o** 良いお年を, which is sometimes used.

In America, New Year's wishes are exchanged with vigor at the stroke of midnight among those present at New Year's Eve parties. After that, however, "Happy New Year!" is, as it were, put away in mothballs fairly quickly in my experience. In Japan, **Akemashite omedetō gozaimasu** is heard at least through the first week of January and sometimes as late as the middle of the month.

Amai 甘い *sweet*

Amai 甘い primarily means "sweet in taste."

EXAMPLE:
(1) **amai kēki (chokorēto, kyandē, etc.)**
甘いケーキ(チョコレート, キャンデー)
sweet cake (chocolate, candy, etc.)

Used figuratively, **amai** 甘い can mean "indulgent, lenient" or "overly optimistic."

EXAMPLES:
(2) **amai oya**
甘い親
indulgent parents
(3) **amai ten**
甘い点
lenient grades (or marks)
(4) **amai kangae**
甘い考え
an overly optimistic view

Unlike English "sweet," **amai** 甘い cannot mean "amiable" or "kind." In English, calling someone a sweet person would be complimentary. In Japanese, on the other hand, **amai hito** 甘い人, if it means anything at all, can only be interpreted as either "an indulgent person" or "an overly optimistic person."

Amari あまり *too, excessively*

Amari あまり means "too" in the sense of "excessively." The word mainly appears in negative sentences.

EXAMPLES:
(1) **Kyō wa amari samuku nai.**
きょうはあまり寒くない。
It is not too cold today.
(2) **Koko wa amari shizuka ja nai.**
ここはあまり静かじゃない。
It is not too quiet here.
(3) **Watashi wa amari nomimasen.**
私はあまり飲みません
I don't drink too much.

Amari あまり may be used in the affirmative if it appears in a dependent clause.

EXAMPLES:
(4) **Amari nomu to byōki ni narimasu yo.**
あまり飲むと病気になりますよ。
If you drink too much, you'll get sick.
(5) **Kami[noke] ga amari nagai kara, katte-moratta hō ga ii yo.**
髪(の毛)があまり長いから、刈ってもらった方がいいよ。
Your hair is too long; you should get a haircut.

(6) **Koko wa amari shizuka de sabishii-gurai desu yo.**
ここはあまり静かでさびしいぐらいですよ。
It's so quiet here that it almost makes one feel lonely.

The following sentences, which are independent affirmative sentences, are ungrammatical.

EXAMPLES:

(7) **Anata wa amari nomimasu.*
＊あなたはあまり飲みます。
You drink too much.

(8) **Kaminoke ga amari nagai.*
＊髪の毛があまり長い。
Your hair is too long.

(9) **Koko wa amari shizuka desu.*
＊ここはあまり静かです。
It's too quiet here.

To express the ideas of the English translations of sentences (7) through (9) above, use **-sugiru** すぎる.

EXAMPLES:

(10) **Anata wa nomi-sugimasu.**
あなたは飲みすぎます。
You drink too much.

(11) **Kaminoke ga naga-sugiru.**
髪の毛が長すぎる。
Your hair is too long.

(12) **Koko wa shizuka-sugimasu.**
ここは静かすぎる。
It's too quiet here.

Amari あまり may be used in combination with **-sugiru** すぎる words also, without changing the meaning.

EXAMPLES:

(13) **Anata wa amari nomi-sugimasu.**
あなたはあまり飲みすぎます。
You drink too much. (same as 10 above)

(14) **Kaminoke ga amari naga-sugiru.**
髪の毛があまり長すぎる。
Your hair is too long. (same as 11)

(15) **Koko wa amari shizuka-sugimasu.**
ここはあまり静かすぎます。
It's too quiet here. (same as 12)

Anmari あんまり is a more colloquial version of **amari** あまり. There is no difference in meaning between the two.

A⌈na⌉ta あなた *you*

Anata あなた "you (singular)" has a very limited use. In fact, long conversations between two people may be carried on without **anata** being used even once. In contexts where it is clear that the speaker is talking about the hearer, no verbal reference to the latter is usually made.

EXAMPLE:
(1) **Ogenki desu ka.**
お元気ですか。
Are you well?

Even when reference to the hearer is verbalized, **anata** あなた is usually avoided. The speaker is much more likely to use the hearer's name with **-san** attached.

EXAMPLE:
(2) **Tanaka-san wa mō ano eiga o mimashita ka.** (speaking to Tanaka)
田中さんはもうあの映画を見ましたか。
Have you (lit., Mr./Mrs./Miss Tanaka) seen that movie yet?

If the speaker is lower in status than the hearer, he uses the latter's title as a term of address.

EXAMPLES:
(3) **Sensei wa kōhī to kōcha to dochira ga osuki desu ka.** (speaking to one's teacher)
先生はコーヒーと紅茶どちらがお好きですか。
Which do you (lit., teacher) like better, coffee or tea?
(4) **Kachō wa ashita gorufu o nasaimasu ka.** (speaking to one's section chief)
課長はあしたゴルフをなさいますか。
Are you (lit., section chief) playing golf tomorrow?

Anata あんた is perhaps used more often by women than by men. Women say **anata** あなた, for example, to their husbands or close friends.

EXAMPLE:
(5) **Anata dō suru.**
あなたどうする。
What are you going to do?

Anata あなた has a more informal and less polite variant, **anta** あんた. It is wise to avoid using this altogether since it is difficult, especially for nonnative speakers, to determine when it can be safely used. (See also KIMI. For a detailed discussion of Japanese terms of address, see Suzuki, ch. 5 "Words for Self and Others.")

Ane 姉 *older sister*

Ane 姉 is a generic term for older sisters. It is used by adults, especially in writing, to refer to older sisters in general.

EXAMPLE:
(1) **Nihon de wa ane wa imōto yori meue da.**
日本では姉は妹より目上だ。
In Japan, older sisters are of higher status than younger sisters.

This use of **ane** 姉, however, is generally restricted to written Japanese. In conversational Japanese, **onē-san** お姉さん is the norm.

EXAMPLE:

(2) **Nihon de wa onē-san wa imōto yori meue da.**
日本ではお姉さんは妹より目上だ。
(same meaning as 1 above)

When talking to an outsider, an adult refers to his own older sister as **ane** 姉.

EXAMPLE:

(3) **Kinō ane ga kekkon-shimashita.**
きのう姉が結婚しました。
My older sister got married yesterday.

An adult talking to an outsider about the latter's older sister or someone else's uses **onē-san** お姉さん.

EXAMPLES:

(4) **Kinō onē-san ga kekkon-nasatta sō desu nē.**
きのうお姉さんが結婚なさったそうですねえ。
I hear your older sister got married yesterday.
(5) **Yoshida-san no onē-san wa eigo no sensei desu.**
吉田さんのお姉さんは英語の先生です。
Mr. Yoshida's older sister is an English teacher.

An adult also uses **onē-san** お姉さん in addressing his own older sister or in talking to his family about his older sister.

EXAMPLES:

(6) **Onē-san, chotto matte.**
お姉さん、ちょっと待って。
lit., Big sister, wait a minute.
(7) **Onē-san doko.** (speaking to one's family)
お姉さんどこ。
lit., Where's big sister?

(In corresponding situations in English, one would of course use the sister's given name.)

The use of **ane** 姉 is restricted to adult speakers. Children say **onē-san** お姉さん in referring not only to older sisters in general or someone else's older sister, but to their own as well, whether they are talking to an outsider or a member of their own family.

Onē-san お姉さん has variants such as **nē-san** 姉さん, **onē-chan** お姉ちゃん, and **nē-chan** 姉ちゃん (the last two being used mainly by children). **Ane** 姉 also has a variant (though perhaps not a very common one), **aneki** 姉貴, which is used by young men in informal conversations, primarily with outsiders.

Since **ane** 姉 sounds very similar to **ani** 兄 "older brother," the two words must be pronounced carefully and distinctly to avoid confusion. **Ane** is accentless while **ani** is accented on the first syllable (see A⌐NI. For a detailed discussion of family terms, see Suzuki, ch. 5 "Words for Self and Others").

A⌐ni 兄 *older brother*

Ani 兄 "older brother" is the male counterpart of **ane** 姉 "older sister." What can be said of **ane** (see ANE) on the female side, therefore, can be said of **ani** on the male side. One should remember the following parallels: **ani** corresponds to **ane** in usage; **onii-san** お兄さん corresponds to **onē-san** お姉さん; **nii-san** 兄さん, **onii-chan** お兄ちゃん, and **nii-chan** 兄ちゃん correspond to **nē-san** 姉さん, **onē-chan** お姉ちゃん, and **nē-chan** 姉ちゃん, respectively; and **aniki** 兄貴 corresponds to **aneki** 姉貴 (though **aniki** 兄貴 is much more commonly used than the latter).

A⌐o⌐i 青い *blue*

The adjective **aoi** 青い and its nominal counterpart, **ao** 青, cover a wider range of color than does "blue," since the Japanese word may also refer to the range of color that one would call "green" in English. Though **aoi** normally means "blue," it can indicate "green" in reference to a limited number of items (though **midori** 緑 "green" is also acceptable), especially vegetation, as in **aoi shiba** 青い芝 "green grass," **aoi kusaki** 青い草木 "green vegetation," and **ao-shingō** 青信号 "green traffic light." Centuries ago, according to Ikegami (p. 16), the use of **ao** for green was even more extensive than now; nowadays, however, in the sense of "green," **midori** is becoming more popular.

　Aoi 青い also means "pale" in reference to a person's complexion.

EXAMPLE:

Suzuki-san dō shita n deshō ka. Aoi kao o shite-imasu yo.
鈴木さんどうしたんでしょうか。青い顔をしていますよ。
I wonder what's happened to Mr. Suzuki. He looks pale.

In this case, no other color word may replace **aoi** 青い.

Are あれ *that*

In Japanese, there are two words corresponding to the English demonstrative "that" as in "That is a park." They are **are** あれ and **sore** それ. The difference between these two Japanese demonstratives when used with reference to visible things is that **are** is for something removed from both the speaker and the addressee while **sore** refers to something removed from the speaker but close to the addressee. Suppose you are talking to Mr. Suzuki and want to refer to a book that he is holding in his hand. Then use **sore**, as in

EXAMPLE:

(1)　**Sore wa nan no hon desu ka.**
　　それはなんの本ですか。
　　What book is that?

On the other hand, if you and Mr. Suzuki want to talk about a building seen in the distance, you use **are** and say, for example,

EXAMPLE:

(2)　**Are wa nan no tatemono deshō ne.**
　　あれはなんの建物でしょうねえ。
　　I wonder what building that is.

When **are** あれ and **sore** それ are used as prenoun modifiers, they become **ano** あの and **sono** その, as in **ano pen** あのペン "that pen" and **sono hon** その本 "that book," but the semantic difference between **ano** and **sono** remains parallel to that between **are** and **sore**.

Since, in Japanese, words normally do not differ in form whether they are singular or plural, **are** and **sore** can mean "those" instead of "that." The same is true of **ano** and **sono**.

With reference to something that is not visible to either the speaker or the hearer at the time of speech, **are** and **sore** are used as follows. **Are** is used "when the speaker knows that the hearer, as well as the speaker himself, knows the referent" whereas **sore** is used "either when the speaker knows the referent but thinks that the hearer does not or when the speaker does not know the referent" (Kuno, p. 283). Compare the following examples:

EXAMPLES:
(3) A: **Kinō Sutā Wōzu to iu eiga o mimashita yo.**
   きのうスターウォーズという映画を見ましたよ。
   Yesterday I saw a movie called Star Wars.
 B: **Are** (not ***Sore** それ) **wa omoshiroi eiga desu nē.**
   あれは面白い映画ですねえ。
   That's a fun movie, isn't it?
(4) A: **Kinō Roshia-eiga o mimashita yo.**
   きのうロシア映画を見ましたよ。
   Yesterday I saw a Russian movie.
 B: **Sore** (not ***Are** あれ) **wa donna eiga deshita ka.**
   それはどんな映画でしたか。
   What kind of movie was that?

In (3), speaker **B** has already seen the movie, so he refers to it as **are** あれ. In (4), on the other hand, speaker **B** does not know what movie speaker **A** is talking about, so he uses **sore** それ instead.

A⌈ri⌉gatō gozaimasu ありがとうございます *Thank you*

The Japanese equivalent of "Thank you" has variants depending on the tense. If you want to thank someone for something that he is doing, is going to do, or repeatedly does for you, you say **Arigatō gozaimasu** ありがとうございます. To thank someone for what he has already done for you, however, you say **Arigatō gozaimashita** ありがとうございました. For example, if someone has just invited you to a party that is to take place next week, you say **Arigatō gozaimasu**. After the party, however, you say **Arigatō gozaimashita**, meaning "Thank you for what you did for me." Likewise, as you accept a present from someone, you say **Arigatō gozaimasu**, but next time you see him, you thank him again by saying **Arigatō gozaimashita**. The difference in usage between these two forms remains even when **dōmo** どうも "very much" is added for emphasis. **Dōmo arigatō gozaimasu** どうもありがとうございます functions like **Arigatō gozaimasu**, and **Dōmo arigatō gozaimashita** like **Arigatō gozaimashita**, except that the versions with **dōmo** are more polite than the ones without.

The informal version **Arigatō** ありがとう (without **gozaimasu** ございます or **gozaimashita** ございました) may be used regardless of the time of the event for which you wish to show gratitude. This version, however, cannot be used when speaking to someone higher in status. Since it is difficult for nonnative speakers of Japanese to determine who is higher or lower than they are, the safest thing would be to use **Arigatō** only when talking to a child.

Otherwise, use the full form **Arigatō gozaimasu** (or **gozaimashita**) ありがとうございます (ございました), or simply **Dōmo** どうも.

Unlike "Thank you," **Arigatō gozaimasu** ありがとうございます and its variants may not be used in response to compliments. If someone compliments you for your "excellent Japanese," for example, say **Mada dame desu** まだダメです "It's still no good." Thanking someone for a compliment, to the Japanese way of thinking, is like admitting you deserve the compliment; it is therefore an act of conceit.

A⌐ru ある、在る *to be;* 有る *to have*

Aru ある means "to be" in the sense of "to exist." As a rule, the verb is used with inanimate subjects (including plants).

EXAMPLES:
(1) **Ishii-san no ie wa Nagoya ni aru.**
石井さんの家は名古屋にある。
Mr. Ishii's house is in Nagoya.
(2) **Go-gatsu no dai-isshū ni wa kyūjitsu ga mik-ka aru.**
五月の第一週には休日が三日ある。
There are three national holidays during the first week of May.

Aru ある may also be used with reference to animate beings, particularly family members, or other humans comparable to family members, e.g., friends and guests. **X ga aru X** があ る in this usage is very much like **X o motte-iru X** を持っている "to have **X**" in meaning, as in the following examples:

EXAMPLES:
(3) **Watashi wa kyōdai ga go-nin aru.**
私は兄弟が五人ある。
I have five siblings.
(4) **Yamamoto-san wa kodomo ga san-nin aru sō da desu.**
山本さんは子供が三人あるそうです。
I hear Mr. Yamamoto has three children.
(5) **Ii tomodachi ga aru kara ii desu ne.**
いい友達があるからいいですね。
Isn't it good that you have nice friends!

Although to signify the existence of animate beings, **iru** いる (see IRU) is the verb that is usually used (e.g., **Asoko ni inu ga iru** あそこに犬がいる "There's a dog over there"), **aru** ある is sometimes used, especially (a) if the subject is not a specific person or a specific animal, (b) if where the subject exists is irrelevant, and (c) if the noun signaling the subject is preceded by a relative clause, as in

EXAMPLE:
(6) **Yoku benkyō-suru gakusei mo aru shi, asonde bakari iru gakusei mo aru.**
よく勉強する学生もあるし、遊んでばかりいる学生もある。
There are students who study hard and there are students who fool around all the time.

There is another important use of **aru** ある: to refer to happenings or events.

EXAMPLE:

(7) **Konban hanabi ga aru sō da.**
こんばん花火があるそうだ。
I hear there will be fireworks tonight.

In this case, **aru** ある does not indicate existence but rather refers to an event. When a location is mentioned, therefore, the particle **de** で (not **ni** に) is required.

EXAMPLE:

(8) **Konban Ryōgoku de hanabi ga aru sō da.**
こんばん両国で花火があるそうだ。
I hear there will be fireworks at Ryogoku tonight.

Compare this with sentence (1), where **ni** に is used to indicate location.

A⌐ru⌐ku 歩く *to walk*

Aruku 歩く means "to walk."

EXAMPLE:

(1) **Ano hito wa aruku no ga hayai desu nē.**
あの人は歩くのが速いですねえ。
He walks fast, doesn't he!

When the destination is mentioned, the particle preceding **aruku** 歩く should be **made** まで "up to." When **e** へ or **ni** に, both meaning "to," is used, the verb is changed to **aruite iku** 歩いて行く (lit., "to go walking") or **aruite kuru** 歩いて来る (lit., "to come walking").

EXAMPLES:

(2) **Itsumo gakkō made arukimasu.**
いつも学校まで歩きます。
I always walk to school.

(3) **Itsumo gakkō e (or ni) aruite-ikimasu.**
いつも学校へ（に）歩いていきます。
I always go to school on foot.

When the place along or through which the act of walking takes place is mentioned, **aruku** 歩く is preceded by the particle **o**.

EXAMPLE:

(4) **Asoko o aruite-iru no wa dare deshō.**
あそこを歩いているのは誰でしょう。
I wonder who that person is who is walking over there (lit., along that place).

Other verbs of motion such as **iku** 行く "to go" and **kuru** 来る "to come" are also used with **o** in comparable situations.

When walking takes place up or down a steep incline (e.g., stairs), **aruku** 歩く has to be either replaced by another verb (such as **noboru** 登る "to climb up") or changed to the **-te** て form and followed by another verb (e.g., **aruite noboru** 歩いて登る). In the following example (5), therefore, (a) is incorrect while (b) and (c) are correct.

EXAMPLES:

(5)	**kaidan o** 階段を	(a)	*__aruku__ *歩く	
		(b)	**noboru** 登る	*to climb* (or *walk up*) *the stairs*
		(c)	**aruite noboru** 歩いて登る	

Unlike "walk," **aruku** 歩く is normally not used in the sense of "to take a stroll." Sentence (6) is therefore wrong for the meaning intended.

EXAMPLE:

(6) *__Kyō wa tenki ga ii kara issho ni arukimashō.__
*きょうは天気がいいから一緒に歩きましょう。
Since it's such a beautiful day today, let's take a walk together.

Arukimashō 歩きましょう in this case should be replaced by **sanposhimashō** 散歩ましょう "let's take a stroll" (see SANPO).

A¹sa 朝 *morning*

Asa 朝 begins at daybreak and ends at midmorning. This is in contrast with English "morning," which begins earlier and lasts longer. Eleven A.M. is still morning in English, but in Japanese **asa** does not normally refer to such late hours. Eleven in the morning is **gozen jūichi-ji** 午前11時 "11 A.M." rather than *__asa no jūichi-ji__ *朝の11時 (lit., "11 in the morning").

A¹sa-go¹han 朝ご飯 *breakfast*

In English, breakfast is always breakfast, and there is no other word that can take its place. In Japanese, however, there are at least four words meaning the same thing: **asa-gohan** 朝ご飯, **asahan** 朝飯, **asameshi** (also written 朝飯), and **chōshoku** 朝食. **Asa-gohan** probably is the most common term, **asahan** is slightly less common, **asameshi** is used only by men in informal situations, and **chōshoku** is the most formal of all. All these words come as part of sets representing the three main meals of the day, as follows:

Breakfast	Lunch	Dinner
asa-gohan 朝ご飯	**(o)hiru-gohan** お昼ご飯	**ban-gohan/yū-gohan** 晩ご飯/夕ご飯
asahan 朝飯	**hiruhan** 昼飯	**yūhan** 夕飯
asameshi 朝飯	**hirumeshi** 昼飯	**banmeshi/yūmeshi** 晩飯/夕飯
chōshoku 朝食	**chūshoku** 昼食	**yūshoku** 夕食

These sets require different verbs meaning "to eat." To mean "eat breakfast," for example, one can say **asa-gohan/asahan o taberu** 朝ご飯/朝飯を食べる, **asameshi o kū** 朝飯を食う, or **chōshoku o toru** 朝食を取る, switching from one verb to another, depending on which noun for "breakfast" is used.

A⌐shi⌐ 足 *foot, leg*

In English, "foot" and "leg" are two different words, but in Japanese, **ashi** 足 might mean either of them or both. **Ashi ga itai** 足が痛い may therefore mean "My leg hurts," "My legs hurt," "My foot hurts," "My feet hurt," or some combination thereof. It really doesn't matter since the person who feels the pain is likely to point to the painful spot anyway to indicate where he is hurting. Moreover, if it becomes necessary to be more specific (e.g., when one has to explain one's ailment to a doctor over the phone), there are words for parts of legs and feet, e.g., **momo** 腿 "thigh," **hiza** 膝 "knee," **sune** 脛 "shin," **fukurahagi** ふくらはぎ "calf," **ashikubi** 足首 "ankle," **kakato** 踵 "heel," and so on.

A⌐shita⌐ あした *tomorrow*

The word for "tomorrow" is most often **ashita** あした(明日), as in **Ashita wa ame ga furu ka mo shirenai** あしたは雨が降るかもしれない "It may rain tomorrow." In fact, that is the only word children use to mean "tomorrow." Adults, however, also use two synonyms for **ashita**, **asu** あす(明日) and **myōnichi** みょうにち(明日), though not as frequently as **ashita**. **Asu** is more formal than **ashita**, and **myōnichi** is even more so. **Ashita** may appear in either informal or formal speech, while **asu** is more likely to appear in formal speech, and **myōnichi** is used only in very formal speech, as in **Mata myōnichi ojama-sasete-itadaki-masu** またみょうにちお邪魔させていただきます。"I shall pay you a visit again tomorrow."

Just as **ashita** あした has its formal counterparts, other temporal expressions have their formal counterparts. For example:

Usual	Formal		
ototoi	issakujitsu	おととい/一昨日	*day before yesterday*
kinō	sakujitsu	きのう/昨日	*yesterday*
yūbe	sakuban, sakuya	ゆうべ/昨晩、昨夜	*last night*
asatte	myōgonichi	あさって/明後日	*day after tomorrow*

Asobu 遊ぶ *to play*

The verb **asobu** 遊ぶ means "to play."

EXAMPLE:
(1) **Kodomo-tachi wa niwa de asonde-imasu.**
子供たちは庭で遊んでいます。
The children are playing in the yard.

Asobu 遊ぶ, however, cannot be used in reference to sports, whether sports in general or specific sports such as **yakyū** 野球 "baseball" or **tenisu** テニス "tennis." Sports require **suru** する "to do" instead. In (2) below, therefore, **shimashita** しました must be used.

EXAMPLE:

(2) **Kinō wa ichi-nichi-jū yakyū o shimashita** (not *asobimashita 遊びました**).
きのうは一日中野球をしました。
Yesterday I played baseball all day.

Playing games also requires **suru** する.

EXAMPLES:

(3) **Toranpu o shimashō** (not *asobimashō 遊びましょう**).
トランプをしましょう。
Let's play cards.

(4) **Yūbe wa ichi-ji made mā-jan o shimashita** (not *asobimashita 遊びました**).
ゆうべは1時まで麻雀をしました。
Last night we played mahjong until 1 o'clock.

Playing musical instruments requires different verbs, depending on the kind.

EXAMPLES:

(5) **Piano o hiite-kudasai** (from **hiku** 弾く**).
ピアノを弾いてください。
Please play the piano for me.

(6) **Toranpetto o fuite-iru** (from **fuku** 吹く**) **no wa dare desu ka.**
トランペットを吹いているのは誰ですか。
Who is the person playing the trumpet?

Asobu sometimes means "to be idle, to be out of work, to be not in use."

EXAMPLES:

(7) **Ano hito wa daigaku o sotsugyō-shite kara, shūshoku-shinai de ichi-nen asonde-shimatta sō da.**
あの人は大学を卒業してから、就職しないで一年遊んでしまったそうだ。
I hear he has idled away one whole year without getting a job since graduating from college.

(8) **Katta tochi o asobasete-oku no wa oshii desu yo.**
買った土地を遊ばせておくのは惜しいですよ。
You shouldn't leave the piece of land you bought unused.

A very common idiom involving **asobu** 遊ぶ is **asobi ni iku** (or **kuru**) 遊びに行く (or 来る), meaning "to pay a social call."

EXAMPLE:

(9) **Dōzo ichi-do oasobi ni oide-kudasai.**
どうぞ一度お遊びにおいでください。
Please come and see us (not *come and play) *sometime.*

A⌐tama⌐ 頭 *head*

One puzzling expression for English speakers might be **atama o karu** 頭を刈る, which literally means "to clip one's head," but actually is another version of **kami[noke] o karu** 髪[の毛]を刈る "to give someone a haircut, to get a haircut." We often use **atama o arau** 頭を洗う (lit., "to wash one's head"), too, to mean 髪 **kami[noke] o arau** [の毛]を洗う "to wash one's hair."

Two very common expressions containing **atama** 頭 are **atama ga ii** 頭がいい (lit., "the head is good") meaning "smart, bright, intelligent" and **atama ga warui** 頭が悪い (lit., "the head is bad") meaning "stupid, dumb, dense."

EXAMPLE:

(1) **Ano ko wa atama ga ii kara, nan de mo sugu oboeru.**
あの子は頭がいいから、なんでもすぐ覚える。
That child is so bright he learns everything quickly.

A student of mine once wrote ***Ii atama ga arimasu** *いい頭があります to mean "someone has a good head." In normal Japanese, however, one would say **daredare** ("so and so") **wa atama ga ii desu** 誰々は頭がいいです instead. In fact, this pattern "**A wa B ga + adj.**" is commonly used to describe a person or a thing, the most famous sentence being **Zō wa hana ga nagai** 象は鼻が長い "An elephant has a long trunk (lit., As for an elephant, the trunk is long)." Other examples would be:

EXAMPLES:

(2) **Ano ko wa me ga ōkii.**
あの子は目が大きい。
That child has big eyes.

(3) **Tōkyō wa hito ga ōi.**
東京は人が多い。
Tokyo is heavily populated.

Atama 頭 and "head" do not necessarily refer to the same part of the human body. While "head" refers to that part of the body joined to the trunk by the neck, **atama** refers to the portion of the head roughly from the eyebrows up, plus the whole of the back of the head.

A˥tataka˩i 暖かい *(pleasantly) warm*

Atatakai 暖かい (or, more colloquially, **attakai** あったかい) is almost always translated in English as "warm," but, unlike "warm," **atatakai** always carries a connotation of pleasantness. When we have a nice warm day in the midst of winter, or when winter gradually gives way to pleasant spring weather, we use **atatakai**. We do not use **atatakai**, but **atsui** 暑い "hot" instead, if, in the midst of summer, the mercury reaches, for example, the mid-80s Fahrenheit, although in English one often says "It's very *warm* today," on such a day.

Atatakai 暖かい may be used with reference not only to weather but to liquids and solids as well. Study the following examples:

EXAMPLES:

(1) **atatakai tenki (haru, hi,** etc.)
暖かい天気 (春、日, etc.)
warm weather (spring, day, etc.)

(2) **atatakai nomimono (gyūnyū, misoshiru,** etc.)
温かい飲み物 (牛乳、みそ汁, etc.)
warm beverage (milk, miso soup, etc.)

(3) **atatakai tabemono (te, gohan,** etc.)
温かい食べ物 (手、ご飯, etc.)
warm food (hand, rice, etc.)

(See also ATSUI "hot" and NURUI "lukewarm.")

A⌐to あと *after*

The following sentence represents an oft-committed error.

EXAMPLE:

(1)   **Benkyō-suru ato de terebi o mimasu.*
   *勉強するあとでテレビを見ます。
   After studying I watch TV.

If one wants to use a verb before **ato** あと, one must use the **-ta** form, whether the event reported is a past event or non-past event, as in (2) below:

EXAMPLE:

(2)   **Benkyō-shita ato de terebi o mimasu.**
   勉強したあとでテレビを見ます。

Also, the verb must directly precede **ato** あと. Since **ato** functions as a pseudo-noun, there is no need to use **no** の, as in (3).

EXAMPLE:

(3)   ***Benkyō-suru no ato de terebi o mimasu.**
   *勉強するのあとでテレビを見ます。

A⌐tsui 厚い *thick*

Atsui 厚い meaning "thick" requires a kanji different from the ones for **atsui** 暑い meaning "hot" (see ATSUI "hot"). This **atsui** is used in reference to flat objects.

EXAMPLE:

(1)   **atsui kami (hon, ita**, etc.)
   厚い紙 (本、板, etc.)
   thick paper (book, board, etc.)

We also say **atsui ōbā** 厚いオーバー (lit., "a thick overcoat"), focusing on the thickness of the material, whereas the English speaker would speak of "a heavy overcoat" with the weight of the overcoat in mind.
   Although, in English, "thick" may be used in reference to cylindrical objects as well as flat objects, as in "thick thread," "thick fingers," etc., that is not the case with **atsui** 厚い. **Futoi** 太い is the correct adjective then.

EXAMPLE:

(2)   **futoi** (not ***atsui** 厚い) **ito (yubi, eda**, etc.)
   太い糸 (指、枝, etc.)
   thick thread (fingers, branch, etc.)

   Atsui 厚い "thick" has a different accent from **atsui** 熱い "hot." Whereas the latter is accented on the second syllable, the former is accentless. Thus examples (3) and (4), when spoken, may be differentiated only by accent.

EXAMPLES:

(3)   **a⌐tsui hottokē⌐ki**
   厚いホットケーキ
   thick pancakes

(4) a⌐tsu⌐i hottokēki
    熱いホットケーキ
    hot pancakes

A⌐tsu⌐i 熱い、暑い *hot*

In Japanese there are two words for "hot," both pronounced **atsui**. For the sake of convenience, I shall distinguish them here by calling one **atsui₁** and the other **atsui₂**. They are represented by different kanji and are used with reference to different types of objects.

Atsui₁, written 熱い, is used in reference to gases, fluids, and solids.

EXAMPLES:
(1) **atsui₁ kaze**
    熱い風
    a hot wind
(2) **atsui₁ ofuro**
    熱いお風呂
    a hot bath
(3) **atsui₁ tabemono**
    熱い食べ物
    hot food

Atsui₂, written 暑い, on the other hand, is used mainly in reference to weather, as in

EXAMPLES:
(4) **Kyō wa atsui₂.**
    今日は暑い。
    It's hot today.
(5) **Ichiban atsui₂ tsuki wa shichi-gatsu ka hachi-gatsu da.**
    一番暑い月は七月か八月だ。
    The hottest month is either July or August.

The difference between **atsui₁** 熱い when it is used in reference to gases, as in example (1) above, and **atsui₂** 暑い parallels the difference between **tsumetai** 冷たい and **samui** 寒い, both of which mean "cold." **Atsui₁** refers to a sensation of heat affecting a limited part or parts of the body, such as the face and the hands, whereas **atsui₂** is used for a sensation of heat affecting the whole body. According to Kunihiro (p. 22), **atsui₁** belongs to one series of temperature words: **tsumetai** "cold," **nurui** ぬるい "lukewarm," **atatakai** 暖かい "warm," and **atsui₁**, while **atsui₂** is part of the other series: **samui** "cold," **suzushii** 涼しい "cool," **atatakai** "warm," and **atsui₂**. (All these adjectives of temperature are explained in their respective entries.)

A⌐u 会う *to see, to meet [someone]; to come across*

In English, one says "see someone" or "meet someone," with "someone" as the direct object of "see" or "meet." In Japanese, on the other hand, **au** 会う is an intransitive verb and takes the particle **ni** に rather than **o** を.

EXAMPLES:

(1)   **Tanaka-san wa mainichi gārufurendo ni atte-iru rashii.**
田中さんは毎日ガールフレンドに会っているらしい。
Mr. Tanaka seems to be seeing his girlfriend every day.

(2)   **Yamashita-san ni hajimete atta no wa go-nen-gurai mae datta.**
山田さんに初めて会ったのは五年ぐらい前だった。
It was about five years ago that I met Mr. Yamashita for the first time.

Au 会う can refer to seeing or meeting someone either by accident or on purpose. For example, in (3) below, **au** together with **battari** ばったり "unexpectedly" refers to an accidental encounter (in this case, **au** is synonymous with **deau** 出会う "to meet by chance"), whereas in (4) **au** obviously signals meeting someone for some purpose.

EXAMPLES:

(3)   **Kinō densha no naka de Yoshida-san ni battari atta.**
きのう電車の中で吉田さんにばったり会った。
Yesterday I met Mr. Yoshida on the train by chance.

(4)   **Kyō no gogo Satō-san ni au yotei da.**
きょうの午後佐藤さんに会う予定だ。
I plan to meet Mr. Sato this afternoon (e.g., to discuss some matter).

Seeing a doctor for medical reasons is not **au** 会う but **mitemorau** みてもらう "to have oneself seen."

EXAMPLE:

(5)   **Kubi ga itai kara, ashita isha ni mite-morau** (not **au* 会う) **tsumori desu.**
首が痛いから、あした医者にみてもらうつもりです。
Because I have a neck ache, I'm going to see my doctor tomorrow.

Meeting someone who is arriving at an airport, a station, etc., is not **au** 会う but **mukae ni iku** 迎えに行く "to go to welcome" or **mukae ni kuru** 迎えに来る "to come to welcome."

EXAMPLE:

(6)   **Ato de chichi ga Narita ni tsuku no o mukae ni iku koto ni natte-iru.**
あとで父が成田に着くのを迎えに行くことになっている。
I am supposed to meet my father later when he arrives at Narita.

"Meet" sometimes means "to be introduced to." **Au** 会う normally doesn't mean that. One must say something more specific to express that idea, as in

EXAMPLE:

(7)   **Kobayashi-san o goshōkai-shimasu.**
小林さんをご紹介します。
I'd like you to meet Mr. Kobayashi. (lit., I'm going to introduce Mr. Kobayashi.)

Au 会う corresponds to English "see [someone]" in the sense of "to meet up with and talk to" but usually not in the sense of "to catch sight of" or "to look at" (Jorden, 1, p. 171). For the latter, use **miru** 見る "to look at" (see MIRU) or **mikakeru** 見かける "to catch sight of" instead.

Au 会う is never used to refer to a class period, as in (8).

EXAMPLE:

(8) *Nihongo no kurasu wa shū ni go-kai aimasu.

　　*日本語のクラスは週に五回あいます。

　　The Japanese class meets five times a week.

To convey that meaning, one has to say the following:

EXAMPLE:

(9) **Nihongo no kurasu wa shū ni go-kai arimasu/desu.**

　　日本語のクラスは週に五回あります/です。

Sentence (10) below, which is often directed to me by my American students, sounds strange (apart from the non-use of **keigo** 敬語) and should be restated as sentence (11):

EXAMPLES:

(10) *Kyō sensei ni ai ni kenkyūshitsu e itte mo ii desu ka.

　　*今日先生に会いに研究室へ行ってもいいですか。

　　May I come to your office to see you today?

(11) **Kyō wa sensei ni gosōdan-shitai koto ga aru node, kenkyūshitsu e ukagatte mo yoroshii deshō ka.**

　　きょうは先生にご相談したい事があるので、研究室へ伺ってもよろしいでしょうか。

　　Lit., Today I have something I'd like to consult you about. May I come to your office?

In other words, when one goes to see one's teacher to ask him a favor or a question, or when one goes to see one's doctor, **ai ni iku** 会いに行く should be avoided.

Ban 晩 *evening, night*

Unlike **yoru** 夜 "night," **ban** 晩 is an anthropocentric term, i.e., a word closely tied to man's daily life. It roughly refers to the time span from dinner time until bedtime, and thus covers a slightly narrower range of time than does **yoru** (although there are some exceptions to this rule, most notably **hito-ban-jū** 一晩中 "all night long," which is synonymous with **yoru-jū** 夜中). Nine P.M., for example, could be called either **ban** or **yoru**, but 2 A.M. is more likely called **yoru** than **ban**. When one talks solely about the natural phenomenon of night with no reference to human life, **yoru** is the only choice (Tokugawa and Miyajima, pp. 409–10), as in

EXAMPLE:

Tsuki wa yoru ga samui.

月は夜が寒い。

Night on the moon is frigid.

B⌈an-go⌉han 晩ご飯、晩御飯 *evening meal*

Although there are other variants meaning the same thing, **ban-gohan** 晩ご飯 is probably the most common word in speech for "evening meal." In America, the evening meal is the biggest meal and is called dinner, but dinner is not always served in the evening; on Sundays, for instance, some families serve dinner at lunchtime. In Japan, too, the evening meal is the main meal, but if, on some special occasion, the biggest meal of the day happens to be served at lunchtime, it has to be called **ohiru-gohan** お昼ご飯 "lunch" (lit., "noon meal") and not **ban-gohan**, since **ban-gohan** literally means "evening meal." In other words, whereas dinner may be served at noon, in the afternoon, or in the evening, **ban-gohan** is always served in the evening, usually at 6 P.M. or thereabouts.

Other variants are **ban-meshi** 晩飯 (used by men only, informal speech), **yūhan** 夕飯 (used by both men and women; probably not as common as **ban-gohan**), and **yūshoku** 夕食 (used in writing or in formal speech).

B⌈enjo⌉ 便所 *toilet*

English has many expressions for "toilet," such as "bathroom," "washroom," "rest room," "men's room," "ladies' room," and "john." Likewise, Japanese has a variety of expressions for "toilet," of which **benjo** 便所 is one. The word should be avoided, however, in polite conversation. Use **tearai** 手洗い (lit., "hand-washing [place]"), or **otearai** お手洗い to be even more polite. **Toire** トイレ, derived from English "toilet," is also quite acceptable.

Using the word **benjo** is all right if it occurs as part of compounds such as **suisen-benjo** 水洗便所 "flush toilet" and **kōshū-benjo** 公衆便所 "public toilet."

Benkyō 勉強 *study*

Benkyō 勉強 most often means "study."

EXAMPLE:
(1) **Uchi no musuko wa ima juken-benkyō-chuu desu.**
うちの息子はいま受験勉強中です。
Our son is in the midst of studying for entrance examinations.

The noun **benkyō** 勉強, with the addition of the verb **suru** する "to do," becomes the compound verb **benkyō-suru** 勉強する "to study" (see BENKYŌ-SURU).

EXAMPLE:
(2) **Itsu Nihongo o benkyō-shita n desu ka.**
いつ日本語を勉強したんですか。
When did you study Japanese?

Having a learning experience is also **benkyō** 勉強, especially in the expression **benkyō ni naru** 勉強になる.

EXAMPLE:
(3) **Sensei no ohanashi o ukagatte, taihen ii benkyō ni narimashita.**
先生のお話を伺って、たいへん良い勉強になりました。
I learned a lot listening to your (lit., teacher's) talk.

After hearing a talk, Americans commonly say to the speakers, "I really enjoyed your talk." Japanese, on the other hand, would normally focus on what they learned from the talk, as in (3) above.

Benkyō-suru 勉強する *to study*

With the compound verb **benkyō-suru** 勉強する, do not use the object marker **o** twice, as in sentence (1), to mean "I am studying Japanese."

EXAMPLE:
(1) ***Nihongo o benkyō o shite-imasu.**
*日本語を勉強をしています。

Instead, use either (2a) or (2b).

EXAMPLES:

(2a) **Nihongo o benkyō-shite-imasu.**
日本語を勉強しています。

(2b) **Nihongo no benkyō o shite-imasu.**
日本語の勉強をしています。

This rule of not repeating **o** を is also applicable to other compound verbs such as **renshū-suru** 練習する "to practice," **ryokō-suru** 旅行する "to travel," and **shūri-suru** 修理する "to repair" (see RYOKŌ-SURU).

B⌈ikku⌉ri-suru びっくりする *to be surprised*

Bikkuri-suru びっくりする, like **odoroku** おどろく, means "to be surprised," the only difference being that **bikkuri-suru** is probably more subjective and colloquial than **odoroku**.

In English, a number of verbs relating to one's emotions are used in the passive, as in "I was surprised/amazed/astonished/touched/moved/pleased/overjoyed." The Japanese counterparts, however, all occur in the active, as in

EXAMPLES:

(1a) **Bikkuri-shita/Odoroita.**
びっくりした/驚いた。
I was surprised/amazed/astonished.

(1a) **Kandō-shita.**
感動した。
I was touched/moved.

Although these Japanese verbs may be used in the causative-passive, as in "**Bikkuri-saserareta/Odorokasareta/Kan-dō-saserareta** びっくりさせられた/おどろかされた/感動させられた, etc.," they are wordier that way, sound more translation-like, and occur much less frequently.

Bi⌉nbō 貧乏 *poor, needy*

Whereas English *poor* has several meanings, **binbō** 貧乏 has only one. It is the opposite of **kanemochi** 金持ち "wealthy" and is a **na**-adjective

EXAMPLE:

(1) **Kuni no keizai ga akka-suru to, binbō na hito ga fueru.**
国の経済が悪化すると、貧乏な人が増える。
When the national economy deteriorates, the number of poor (people) increases.

Unlike "poor," **binbō** 貧乏 cannot be used figuratively to describe things such as talent, ability, and knowledge. For that, one must use another word, e.g., **mazushii** 貧しい "poor" or **toboshii** 乏しい "lacking."

EXAMPLE:

(2) **mazushii** (or **toboshii**) **sainō**
貧しい(乏しい)才能
poor talent

Whereas "poor" is often used to express compassion, **binbō** 貧乏 must be replaced by another word such as **kawaisō** かわいそう.

EXAMPLE:

(3) **Tanaka-san jidōshajiko de kega-shita n datte, kawaisō ni.**
田中さん自動車事故で怪我したんだって、かわいそうに。
Mr. Tanaka got hurt in a car accident, poor man.

Unlike **kanemochi** 金持ち, which can mean both "wealthy" and "wealthy person," **binbō** 貧乏 can mean only "poor" and not "poor person." For the latter, one must say **binbōnin** 貧乏人.

EXAMPLE:

(4) **Binbōnin** (not *binbō 貧乏) **wa kanemochi yori kokoro ga kiyoi ka mo shirenai.**
貧乏人は金持ちより心が清いかもしれない。
The poor might be more pure-hearted than the rich.

Bo⌐ku 僕 *I, me*

Boku 僕 meaning "I" is used only by males, and most often by boys and young men. Although young boys use **boku** on all occasions, adult men use it, or are supposed to use it, only on informal occasions. (On formal occasions, they normally switch to **watashi** 私 or **watakushi** 私.)

The strangest use of **boku** 僕 occurs when, in some families, family members of a little boy who calls himself **boku** start calling him **boku** as well. This occurs, however, only when the little boy is the only, or the youngest, son in the family. **Boku** in this case is used, as it were, like the boy's given name. (In fact, the diminutive suffix **-chan** ちゃん, which is normally attached to a child's name, as in **Yoshiko-chan** よし子ちゃん, is sometimes added to **boku** 僕, forming **boku-chan** 僕ちゃん.)

EXAMPLE:

Boku[-chan], hayaku irasshai.
僕［ちゃん］、早くいらっしゃい。
lit., Me, come here quickly.

This "fictive" use of **boku** 僕 is explained by Suzuki (p. 124) thus: "When she [i.e., a mother calling her son **boku**] speaks in this way, she is thinking of the boy as he would be called viewed from the position of the youngest member of the family, in this case the boy himself. The boy would naturally call himself **boku**. Therefore, by identifying with him, adults in the family can call him **boku** as well."

Bukka 物価 *prices*

Bukka 物価 means "general commodity prices."

EXAMPLE:

(1) **Konogoro wa bukka ga takakute komarinasu nē.**
このごろは物価が高くて困りますねえ。
Isn't it terrible that prices are so high these days!

Bukka 物価 does not refer to the price of a specific object. For that, one has to use nedan 値段 "price" instead. In example (2), therefore, nedan must be used.

EXAMPLE:

(2) **Gasorin no nedan (not *bukka 物価) ga mata agatta.**
ガソリンの値段がまた上がった。
The price of gasoline has gone up again.

Byōki 病気 *sick, sickness*

Byōki 病気 can be translated into English as either "sick" or "sickness," or "ill," "illness," or "disease," depending on the context.

EXAMPLES:

(1) **Tanaka-san wa byōki desu.**
田中さんは病気です。
Mr. Tanaka is sick.

(2) **Gan wa iya na byōki da.**
がんはいやな病気だ。
Cancer is a nasty disease.

Unlike "sick," however, **byōki** 病気 cannot refer to a temporary state of being nauseous. To express that state, other expressions must be used.

EXAMPLES:

(3) **Kuruma ni yotte-shimatta.**
車に酔ってしまった。
I became carsick.

(4) **Chi o mite kimochi (or mune) ga waruku-natta.**
血を見て気持ち(胸)が悪くなった。
I became sick at the sight of blood.

Unlike "sick," **byōki** 病気 does not refer to boredom or disgust. To express the idea of "I'm sick of parties," for example, one would have to say something like (5) or (6).

EXAMPLES:

(5) **Pātī ga iya ni natta.**
パーティーがいやになった。
Lit., Parties have started boring me.

(6) **Pātī wa mō takusan da.**
パーティーはもうたくさんだ。
Lit., I can't take any more parties.

Whereas **genki** 元気 "healthy, well, vigorous," the opposite of **byōki** 病気, is a na-noun, **byōki** is a genuine noun and therefore requires **no** の instead of **na** な when used in prenoun position. Note the difference between (7) and (8).

EXAMPLES:

(7) **genki na (not *genki no 元気の) kodomo**
元気な子供
a healthy (or vigorous, lively) child

(8) **byōki no** (not *__byōki na__ 病気な) **kodomo**
病気の子供
a sick child

In English, it is perfectly all right to say "I am very sick," using "very" as an intensifier. Since "very" is **totemo** とても, **taihen** たいへん, **hi-jōni** 非常に, etc., in Japanese, American students of Japanese have a tendency to say:

EXAMPLE:
(9) *__Kinō wa totemo (taihen, hijōni) byōki deshita.__
*きのうはとても(たいへん、非常に)病気でした。
I was very sick yesterday.

This is wrong, however, because, unlike English "sick," **byōki** 病気 is not an adjective, but a noun. It therefore cannot be modified by an adverb such as **totemo** とても, **taihen** たいへん, and **hi-jōni** 非常に. Compare this with **genki** 元気, a **na**-adjective, which may be modified by adverbs.

EXAMPLE:
(10) **Merī wa konogoro totemo (taihen, hijōni) genki da.**
メリーはこのごろとても(たいへん、非常に)元気だ。
Mary has been very well recently.

To intensify **byōki** 病気, adjectives must be used instead.

EXAMPLE:
(11) **Kinō wa hidoi byōki de ichinichijū nete ita.**
きのうはひどい病気で一日中寝ていた。
Yesterday I was in bed all day because of a terrible illness.

In other words, **byōki** 病気 functions like nouns for specific illnesses such as **kaze** 風邪 "a cold" and **zutsū** 頭痛 "a headache."

EXAMPLE:
(12) **Kinō wa hidoi kaze/zutsū de ichinichijū nete ita.**
きのうはひどい風邪/頭痛で一日中寝ていた。
Yesterday I was in bed all day because of a terrible cold/headache.

Chi⌈chi⌉ 父 *father*

When an adult talks to an outsider (i.e., a non-family member) about his own father, **chichi** 父 is the correct term to be used.

EXAMPLE:
Chichi wa mō hachijū ni narimashita.
父はもう八十になりました。
My father has turned 80 already.

When an adult talks to a member of his family (e.g., his mother and siblings) about his father, he usually uses **otōsan** お父さん. (Inside-the-family terms for *father* vary from family to family, e.g., **otō-sama** お父様 and **papa**, but **otō-san** お父さん is probably the most common.)

When an adult male is engaged in an informal conversation with close associates or friends, he is likely to refer to his father as **oyaji** 親父 "my old man." The use of **oyaji** is far more common in Japanese than that of "my old man" in English, but it is restricted to men only.

When an adult talks to an outsider about the latter's or someone else's father, **otō-san** お父さん is probably the most common term.

The above rules apply to adults only. Children, whether boys or girls, most often use the term **otō-san** in almost all situations.

When referring to both parents, one must put **chichi** 父 before **haha** 母 unlike in English, where "mother and father" or "Mom and Dad" is quite acceptable. In Japanese, however, whether one says **otōsan to okāsan** お父さんとお母さん or **chichi to haha** 父と母 to mean "Dad and Mom" or "father and mother," the word order is set and should not be changed, just as one would never say in English "pepper and salt" instead of "salt and pepper."

Chigau 違う *to be different, to be incorrect*

Chigau 違う has roughly two meanings: "to be different" and "to be incorrect."

EXAMPLES:

(1) **Nihonjin wa Chungoknjin to zuibun chigau.**
日本人は中国人とずいぶん違う。
The Japanese are quite different from the Chinese.

(2) **Kono kotae wa chigaimasu yo.**
この答えは違いますよ。
This answer is incorrect, you know.

These two meanings may seem unrelated at first, but they are actually not as far apart as one may think. After all, an *incorrect* answer is an answer that is *different* from the correct one.

Iie, chigaimasu いいえ、違います is often used in lieu of **Iie, sō ja arimasen** いいえ、そうじゃありません to mean "No, that's not so." **Iie** いいえ is frequently left out. The direct English translation of **Iie, chigaimasu** would be "No, it's incorrect"; English speakers might therefore feel that this Japanese expression is probably a strong denial. It is, however, not as strong as the English translation might suggest and is at least as commonly used as **Iie, sō ja arimasen**.

As is the case with **Sō ja arimasen** そうじゃありません, **Chigaimasu** 違います is most often used to contradict a question ending with a noun + **desu ka** ですか.

EXAMPLE:

(3) A: **Are wa Tanaka-san desu ka.**
あれは田中さんですか。
Is that Mr. Tanaka?

B: **Chigaimasu. Suzuki-san desu.**
ちがいます。鈴木さんです。
No, that's Mr. Suzuki.

The use of **Chigaimasu** 違います is not appropriate as a response to a question ending with an adjective + **desu ka** ですか, or a verb + **ka** か (see SŌ DESU).

In American English, "different" is used with "from," as in "Japanese is quite different from Chinese." In Japanese, however, the particle used is **to** と, not **kara** から.

EXAMPLE:

(4) **Nihongo wa Chūgokugo to zuibun chigau.**
日本語は中国語とずいぶん違う。
Japanese is quite different from Chinese.

In American English, one usually says "A is quite/a lot/very different from B." However, the Japanese counterparts of "very," such as **totemo/taihen** とても/たいへん, don't go well with **chigau** 違う. Other adverbs, such as **zuibun** ずいぶん and **kanari** かなり, are preferred instead, as in

EXAMPLE:

(5) **Ōsaka wa Tōkyō to zuibun/kanari chigau.**
大阪は東京とずいぶん/かなり違う。
Osaka is a lot/quite different from Tokyo.

Chokin 貯金 *savings*

Chokin 貯金 can mean either "saving money" or "saved money."

EXAMPLES:

(1a) **Tarō wa otoshidama o zenbu chokin-shita.**
太郎はお年玉を全部貯金した。
Taro put all his New Year's cash gifts into his savings.

(1b) **Tarō wa amari chokin o hikidasanai.**
太郎はあまり貯金を引き出さない。
Taro does not withdraw money from his savings very often.

In Japan, savings one can keep at the post office are called **chokin** 貯金, whereas bank savings are referred to as **yokin** 預金. For some reason, therefore, nobody says ***yūbin-yokin** 郵便預金 or ***ginkō-chokin** 銀行貯金. Actually, **chokin** is a much more common word, while **yokin** sounds more professional. If you put a coin in a piggy bank, therefore, call it **chokin**, not **yokin**!

Ch⌈ōse⌉n 朝鮮 *Korea*

Most Japanese unfortunately have been rather prejudiced against the Koreans for no apparent reason. Especially during the time when Korea was under Japanese rule (1910–45), the word **Chōsenjin** 朝鮮人 "Korean[s]" was almost always uttered with contempt. It was for this reason that the name **Chōsen** 朝鮮 was almost completely discarded when Japan lost World War II. Since then, the Japanese have adopted the names **Hokusen** 北鮮 for "North Korea" and **Kankoku** 韓国 for "South Korea." What is really inconvenient, however, is the lack of an appropriate prejudice-free name for Korea as a whole. Linguists, for example, still have to refer to the Korean language as **Chōsengo** 朝鮮語, since the language is one and the same in North Korea and in South Korea. The word **Kankokugo** 韓国語 (lit., "South Korean language"), which some people use, is not really an accurate label for the language.

Cho┐sha 著者 *the author*

Chosha 著者 means "person who has written a specific (usually nonfiction) book."

EXAMPLE:
Kono hon no chosha wa Tanaka Ichirō to iu hito desu.
この本の著者は田中一郎という人です。
The author of this book is called Ichiro Tanaka.

English "author" is broader in meaning. It can mean "person who has written a specific book" (as in "He is the author of this book") or "person who writes books" (as in "He is an author"). **Chosha** 著者 can never be used in the latter sense. (See also SAKKA and SHŌSETSUKA.)

Cho┐tto ちょっと *a little*

Chotto ちょっと is very much like **sukoshi** 少し.

EXAMPLES:
(1) **Kyō wa chotto (or sukoshi) samui.**
今日はちょっと(少し)寒い。
It's a bit cold today.
(2) **Onaka ga suite-inai kara, chotto (or sukoshi) shika taberarenakatta.**
おなかが空いていないから、ちょっと(少し)しか食べられなかった。
Since I wasn't hungry, I could eat only a little.

The only difference between **chotto** ちょっと and **sukoshi** 少し in the above examples is that **chotto** is perhaps slightly more conversational than **sukoshi**.

Chotto ちょっと, however, is used on many other occasions where **sukoshi** 少し would be inappropriate. This occurs especially when one wishes to soften a request, as in (3) below, or express reluctance in a polite way, as in (4).

EXAMPLE:
(3) **Chotto misete-kudasai.**
ちょっと見せて下さい。
Would you please show it to me?

Chotto ちょっと in this sentence does not mean "a little." Rather it expresses the idea that the request being made is not a significant one. It is almost like saying "May I ask a small favor?" The use of **chotto** in requests is very common; in fact, in stores and restaurants some customers use **Chotto!** by itself when they wish to catch the attention of a salesclerk or waitress.

EXAMPLE:
(4) A: **Ashita kite-itadakemasu ka.**
あした来ていただけますか。
Could you come tomorrow?
B: **Ashita wa chotto.**
あしたはちょっと。
I'm afraid I can't.

The answer in (4) literally means "Tomorrow is a little [inconvenient]." Japanese speakers don't normally reject requests, suggestions, and invitations flatly with **Iie** いいえ "No" since that would make them sound too direct and discourteous; they prefer to use **chotto** ちょっと, which sounds less direct and more tactful.

-Chū 中 *during*

EXAMPLE:
(1) **Kyō wa gozen-chū totemo isogashikatta.**
今日は午前中とても忙しかった。
Today I was very busy in the morning.

If you use **ni** に after **chū** 中, the combination means "by the end of," as in:

EXAMPLE:
(2) **Konshū-chū ni kore o yatte kudasai.**
今週中にこれをやって下さい。
Please do this by the end of this week.

There is another suffix, **-jū** 中, which is often written 中 also, but is used a little differently. (See -JŪ.)

Chūi 注意 *attention, caution, advice*

Chūi-suru 注意する often means "to pay attention" or "to be careful," as in (1) and (2).

EXAMPLES:
(1) **Yuki no hi wa korobanai yō ni chūi-shite kudasai.**
雪の日は転ばないように注意して下さい。
On a snowy day, please be careful not to slip and fall.
(2) **Natsu wa kenkō ni chūi-su beki da.**
夏は健康に注意すべきだ。
In the summer one should pay attention to one's health.

Sentence (3) below, however, is wrong, and has to be rephrased as in sentence (4).

EXAMPLES:
(3) *****Nemui to sensei no kōgi ni chūi dekinai.**
*眠いと先生の講義に注意できない。
When sleepy, one cannot pay attention to the professor's lecture.
(4) **Nemui to sensei no kōgi ni chūi ga shūchū dekinai.**
眠いと先生の講義に注意が集中できない。
When sleepy, one cannot concentrate on the professor's lecture.

Chūi-suru 注意する also means "to caution," "to warn," or "to advise," as in

EXAMPLE:
(5) **Shiken de amari warui ten o totta no de, sensei ni chūi-sareta.**
試験であまり悪い点を取ったので、先生に注意された。
Since I received a bad grade on the exam, I was cautioned by the teacher.

Because of this, **chūi-jinbutsu** 注意人物 (lit., caution person) means "someone we must treat with suspicion," i.e., a black-listed person.

Daigaku 大学 *college, university*

"College" and "university" are both **daigaku** 大学 in Japanese. Although one can use **tanka-daigaku** 単科大学 (lit., "single-subject **daigaku**") for "college" and **sōgō-daigaku** 総合大学 (lit., "comprehensive **daigaku**") for "university," these terms are more or less for dictionaries only and are never attached to college or university names, nor are they much used in speech.

Most Japanese are unaware of the usage difference between "college" and "university" in the United States and simplistically believe that "university" is a more prestigious term than "college." The official English translations of the names of Japanese colleges and universities are, consequently, always something like "The University of So-and-so." It is for this reason that the names of some Japanese institutions of higher learning sound very strange in English, e.g., "The X University of Science" or "The Y University of Economics."

Da⌈ijō⌉bu 大丈夫 *all right*

Daijōbu 大丈夫 is, to a certain extent, like "all right." For example, if you see someone fall, you run up to him and ask **Daijōbu desu ka** 大丈夫ですか, meaning "Are you all right?" But there are some situations where **daijōbu** cannot be used to mean "all right." For example, in English, if someone asks, "How are you?" you might answer, "All right," meaning "Fine." **Daijōbu** could not be used in a comparable situation in Japanese unless you happened to have been ill. In English, you can also say, "All right!" when something turns out the way you were hoping it would, e.g., your favorite baseball team scores a run in a crucial inning. In Japanese, **Ii zo!** いいぞ (lit., "Great!") would be used in that case instead of **daijōbu**. Likewise, **daijōbu** may not be used in accepting a suggestion. In English, if someone suggests "Let's go to a movie," you can indicate your willingness by answering "All right," but in Japanese you would have to say **Ee, ikimashō** ええ、行きましょう "Yes, let's go."

To summarize, **daijōbu** 大丈夫 is most appropriate when there is a good reason for concern. The function of **daijōbu** is to dispel that concern. In other words, it is an expression of reassurance. Study the following examples:

EXAMPLES:
(1) A: **Abunai!**
    あぶない。
    Look out!
   B: **Daijōbu desu yo.**
    大丈夫ですよ。
    I'm all right.
(2) A: **Tanaka-san ni anna shigoto ga dekiru deshō ka.**
    田中さんにあんな仕事ができるでしょうか。
    Do you think Mr. Tanaka can handle that kind of job?
   B: **Daijōbu desu yo.**
    大丈夫ですよ。
    He'll be all right.

In both examples above, **Daijōbu desu yo** 大丈夫ですよ can be paraphrased as "Although you may have a good reason to worry, you don't really have to."

Da⌈ke⌉ だけ *only*

Although **dake** だけ often corresponds to English "only," as in sentences (1) and (2) below, it does not carry a negative overtone, as "only" does.

EXAMPLES:

(1) **Tanaka-san dake kite, hoka no hito wa konakatta.**
田中さんだけ来て、他の人は来なかった。
Only Mr. Tanaka came; nobody else did.

(2) Housewife (to maid): **Kaimono ni iku nara, gyūnyū dake katte-kite-moraeba ii wa.**
買い物に行くなら、牛乳だけ買って来てもらえばいいわ。
If you're going shopping, the only thing I'd like you to buy is milk.

The positive overtone in **dake** だけ becomes clear when **dake** is contrasted with **shika . . . nai** しか . . . ない, which always carries a negative connotation.

EXAMPLES:

(3) **Tanaka-san dake kita.**
田中さんだけ来た。
Only Mr. Tanaka came. (i.e., Mr. Tanaka alone came.)

(4) **Tanaka-san shika konakatta.**
田中さんしか来なかった。
Only Mr. Tanaka came. (i.e., No one but Mr. Tanaka came.)

In (3), the speaker's focus is on the fact that Mr. Tanaka came (though he was the only one who came). On the other hand, in (4), the speaker's focus is on the fact that nobody else came. It is because of this difference between **dake** and **shika . . . nai** しか . . . ない that we can use only **dake** in (5), and only **shika . . . nai** in (6).

EXAMPLES:

(5) **Hoka no hito wa konakatta keredo, Tanaka-san**   (a)   **dake wa kita.**
他の人は来なかったけれど、田中さん   だけは来た。
                                            (b)   *****shika konakatta.**
                                                 しか来なかった。

Nobody else came, but Mr. Tanaka, though he was the only one, did come.

(6) **Okane ga ni-doru**   (a)   *****dake atta.**
お金が2ドル   だけあった。

                          (b)   **shika nakatta.**   **kara, eiga e ikarenakatta.**
                                  しかなかった。   から、映画へ行かれなかった。

Since I had only (i.e., no more than) two dollars, I couldn't go to the movies.

Da⌈re⌉ 誰 *who?*

In English, "who" may refer to other things than just persons, e.g.:

EXAMPLES:

(1) In World War II, whom did Japan fight against?

(2) Who beat the Yankees yesterday?

In Japanese, **dare** 誰 may not be used in the above circumstances. One would use **doko** どこ (lit., "what place") instead, as in

EXAMPLES:

(3) **Dainijitaisen no toki, Nihon wa doko to tatakatta n desu ka.**
第二次大戦の時、日本はどこと戦ったんですか。
lit., At the time of World War II, what places (i.e., what countries) did Japan fight against?

(4) **Kinō wa doko ga Yankīzu ni katta n desu ka.**
きのうはどこがヤンキーズ勝ったんですか。
lit., Yesterday, what place (i.e., what team) beat the Yankees?

Dekakeru 出かける *to go out*

Dekakeru 出かける is usually translated into English as "to go out" and is therefore often confused by American students of Japanese with **deru** 出る, which is also matched up with "to go out." **Dekakeru**, however, is quite different from **deru** in that it is used only in reference to human beings. For example, in sentence (1), either **dekakeru** 出かける or **deru** may be used, but in sentence (2), only **deru** would be correct.

EXAMPLES:

(1) **Chichi wa kyō dekakete-imasu (or dete-imasu).**
父は今日出かけています（出ています）。
My father is out today.

(2) **Konban wa ku-ji-goro tsuki ga deru** (not *dekakeru 出かける) **hazu da.**
今晩は九時頃月が出るはずだ。
The moon is expected to be out about nine tonight.

Dekakeru 出かける also differs from **deru** 出る in that it specifically refers to leaving one's abode, whereas **deru** may refer to going out of any place. "To go out of a room" would therefore be **heya o deru** 部屋を出る (not *dekakeru 出かける).

Furthermore, **dekakeru** is different from **deru** in that it implies some sort of outing covering a distance, be it a walk, a visit, or a trip. **Deru**, on the other hand, is noncommital as to distance or reason. In sentence (3), therefore, only (a) is correct.

EXAMPLE:

(3) **Tonari no denwa o kari ni**
隣の電話を借りに

    (a) **uchi o deta.**
    家を出た。

    (b) *dekaketa.**
    *出かけた。

I left the house to ask the next-door neighbor to let me use the phone.

Dekakeru 出かける meaning "to go out" is accentless. This word should not be confused with **de-kakeru** "to be about to go out," which is accented. This latter is a compound verb formed by the **-te** form of **deru** 出る followed by **kakeru** かける "to be about to do such-and-such," and is used as follows:

EXAMPLE:

(4) **Tsuki ga de-kakete** (not *dekakete 出かけて) **mata kumo ni kakureta.**
月が出かけてまた雲に隠れた。
The moon was about to come out but hid again behind the clouds.

De⌐ki⌐ru できる、出来る *to come about, to be able to*

Roughly speaking, **dekiru** できる has two meanings: (a) "to come about, to be born, to be produced, to be built, to be completed," as in sentences (1) and (2) below, and (b) "to be possible, to be able to, can do," as in (3) and (4).

EXAMPLES:

(1) **Sūpu ga dekita.**
　　スープができた。
　　The soup is ready. (lit., The soup has come about.)

(2) **Asoko ni atarashii depāto ga dekita.**
　　あそこに新しいデパートができた。
　　A new department store has been built over there. (lit., A new department store has come about over there.)

(3) **Watanabe-san wa eigo ga yoku dekiru.**
　　渡辺さんは英語が良く出来る。
　　Mr. Watanabe is very good in English. (lit., Mr. Watanabe can do English well.)

(4) **Ano hito wa gorufu ga dekiru.**
　　あの人はゴルフが出来る。
　　He knows how to play golf. (lit., He can do golf.)

At first glance, these two meanings do not seem to have much in common; but, on second thought, they are related, for if you know how to do something, it does "come about" for you.

Since the original meaning of **dekiru** 出来る is "to come about" (Morita, p. 309), the subject marker **ga** が rather than the object marker **o** を is used with it even when it means "can do."

EXAMPLE:

(5) **Watanabe-san wa eigo ga** (not *o を) **dekiru.**
　　渡辺さんは英語が出来る。
　　Mr. Watanabe is good in English.

Dekiru 出来る in the sense of "can do" is used much less often in Japanese than "can" is in English. The reason is that in Japanese many verbs have their own potential forms. For example, **taberu** 食べる "to eat" has the potential form, **taberareru** 食べられる "can eat," and **yomu** 読む "to read" has **yomeru** 読める "can read." Although it is also grammatically correct to say **taberu koto ga dekiru** 食べる事が出来る "one can eat" or **yomu koto ga dekiru** 読む事が出来る "one can read," these forms are lengthier and are therefore not used as often. In fact, **dekiru** 出来る is basically used only as the potential form of **suru** する "to do." It cannot even be used in place of the potential forms of other verbs. In English, it is perfectly correct to say, "Yes, I can" in response to "Can you read this?" for example. In Japanese, on the other hand, the answer in (6) below would be incorrect.

EXAMPLE:

(6) A: **Kore ga yomemasu ka.**
　　　これが読めますか。
　　　Can you read this?

　　B: **Hai, *dekimasu.**
　　　*はい、出来ます。
　　　Yes, I can.

Dekimasu 出来ます in this case must be replaced by **yomemasu** 読めます, the same potential verb meaning "can read" that appears in the question.

De¹mo でも *but*

Demo でも meaning "but" is used at the beginning of a sentence, as in

EXAMPLE:

(1)   **Shiken wa muzukashikatta desu. Demo ganbatta kara, ii ten o moraimashita.**
試験は難しかったです。でもがんばったから、いい点をもらいました。
The exam was difficult, but I tried hard and got a good grade.

Do not, however, connect the two sentences above, as in (2) below. That would create an ungrammatical sentence.

EXAMPLE:

(2)   *****Shiken wa muzukashikatta demo, ganbatta kara, ii ten o moraimashita.**
*試験は難しかったでも、がんばったから、いい点をもらいました。

To make this grammatical, one would have to use either **ga** が or **keredo** けれど as in (3).

EXAMPLES:

(3a)   **Shiken wa muzukashikatta desu ga, ganbatta kara, ii ten o moraimashita.**
試験は難しかったですが、がんばったから、いい点をもらいました。

(3b)   **Shiken wa muzukashikatta (desu) keredo, ganbatta kara, ii ten o moraimashita.**
試験は難しかった(です)けれど、がんばったから、いい点をもらいました。

Please note that in (3a) **desu** です is obligatory, whereas in (3b) **desu** is optional.
Demo でも meaning "even, even though" may not follow a verb or an adjective, but may follow a noun, as in (4).

EXAMPLE:

(4)   **Muzukashii shiken demo, ganbareba pasu dekimasu yo.**
難しい試験でも、がんばればパスできますよ。
Even though the exam might be difficult, you can pass if you try hard.

Denwa 電話 *telephone*

Denwa 電話 is a noun meaning "telephone."

EXAMPLE:

(1)   **Kono hen ni denwa wa arimasen ka.**
この辺に電話はありませんか。
Is there a telephone around here?

One difference between **denwa** and "telephone" is that **denwa** 電話 is often used to mean "telephone call" whereas "telephone" is not.

EXAMPLE:

(2)   **Kinō Tanaka-san kara denwa ga arimashita.**
きのう田中さんから電話がありました。
There was a telephone call (lit., There was a telephone) from Mr. Tanaka yesterday.

In English, "telephone" is also used as a verb; in Japanese, on the other hand, **suru** する has to be added to change **denwa** 電話 into a verb, that is, **denwa-suru** 電話する "to telephone [someone]."

EXAMPLE:

(3) **Yoshida-san ni denwa-shite kudasai.**
吉田さんに電話してください。
Please call Mr. Yoshida.

De⌐nwa o kake¬ru 電話をかける *to phone, make a phone call*

Denwa o kakeru 電話をかける "to make a phone call" and **denwa o ireru** 電話を入れる, a fairly new coinage meaning "to give [someone] a call," may be used in place of **denwa-suru** 電話する, as in

EXAMPLE:

(1) **Yoshida-san ni denwa o kakete (or irete) kudasai.**
吉田さんに電話をかけて（入れて）ください。
Please give Mr. Yoshida a call.

When the person to whom the phone call is made is not mentioned or even implied, only **denwa o kakeru** 電話をかける is acceptable. In (2), therefore, only (a) would be correct.

EXAMPLES:

(2) **Uchi no ko wa**   (a) **denwa o kakeru**   **no ga suki de komarimasu.**
うちの子は   電話をかける   のが好きで困ります。
              (b) ***denwa o ireru**
                 *電話を入れる
              (c) ***denwa-suru**
                 *電話する

Our child likes making phone calls too much.

Morita (1985) calls the following sentence not quite correct.

EXAMPLE:

(3) ***Denwa o kake yō to shita ga, kakaranakatta.**
*電話をかけようとしたが、かからなかった。
I tried to reach him by phone, but could not get through.

To convey the meaning above, Morita suggests using (4) below.

EXAMPLE:

(4) **Denwa o kaketa ga, ohanashi-chū datta.**
電話をかけたが、お話し中だった。
I tried to call him, but the line was busy.

In other words, **denwa o kakeru** 電話をかける may be used whether or not the call goes through, whereas in English "to phone" may not.

According to Morita, **denwa o kake yō to suru** 電話をかけようとする describes the stage before one picks up the receiver, puts in a coin, or inserts a telephone card. The following sentence would, therefore, be acceptable, unlike (3) above.

EXAMPLE:

(5) **Denwa o kake yō to shita ga, denwachō ga miatara-nakatta.**
電話をかけようとしたが、電話帳が見当たらなかった。
I tried to make a phone call but could not find a phone book.

De⌐ru 出る *to go out, to leave, to graduate, to attend*

Deru 出る most often means "to go out, to come out, to get out."

EXAMPLES:

(1) **Amari atsui kara, niwa ni demashō.**
あまり暑いから、庭に出ましょう。
It's so hot; let's go out into the yard.

(2) **Nihon o deta no wa nijū-nen mae datta.**
日本を出たのは二十年前だった。
It was 20 years ago that I left Japan.

With reference to school, **deru** 出る is used as a synonym for **sotsugyō-suru** 卒業する "to graduate."

EXAMPLE:

(3) **Daigaku o dete (or sotsugyō-shite) kara nani o suru tsumori desu ka.**
大学を出て（卒業して）から何をするつもりですか。
What do you plan to do after graduating from college?

Don't equate **deru** 出る meaning "to graduate" with English "leave," since "to leave school" might mean "to leave school without graduating."
This latter meaning would be expressed in Japanese by another verb: **chūtai-suru** 中退する "to drop out of school."

EXAMPLE:

(4) **Ano hito wa daigaku o chūtai-shite haiyū ni natta sō desu.**
あの人は大学を中退して俳優になったそうです。
I hear he dropped out of college and became an actor.

One should beware of the difference between **ni deru** に出る and **o deru** を出る. The former means "to attend," while the latter means "to go out of" or "to leave." For example,

EXAMPLES:

(5) **kurasu ni deru**
クラスに出る
to attend class

(6) **kurasu o deru**
クラスを出る
to leave class

(See also DEKAKERU.)

Dō¹ [Do¹o] itashimashite どう致しまして *Not at all, You are welcome*

Dō itashimashite どう致しまして, with or without a preceding **Iie** いいえ, serves as a response to someone's expression of gratitude. In (1) below, therefore, all of speaker B's answers are correct.

EXAMPLE:

(1) A: **Dōmo arigatō gozaimashita.**
      どうもありがとうございます。
      Thank you very much for what you did for me.
     B: (a) **Iie.**
           いいえ。
        (b) **Dō itashimashite.**
           どう致しまして。
        (c) **Iie, dō itashimashite.**
           いいえ、どう致しまして。
           Not at all.

It is safer not to equate **Dō itashimashite** どう致しまして with English "You are welcome," because **Dō itashimashite** may also be used as a response to apologies.

EXAMPLE:

(2) A: **Dōmo gomeiwaku o okake-shimashita.**
      どうもご迷惑をおかけしました。
      I'm very sorry for causing so much trouble.
     B: **Dō itashimashite.**
      どう致しまして。
      Not at all.

   In some cases, **Dō itashimashite** どう致しまして may also be used in response to compliments (Jorden, 1, p. 3), but that particular use is very limited. It is much safer, therefore, to say just **Iie**, which is always a correct response to compliments. (See also ARIGATŌ GOZAIMASU and IIE.)

Dō¹mo [Do¹omo] どうも *Thanks, Sorry*

Dōmo どうも is most often an abbreviation of **Dōmo arigatō gozaimasu** (or **gozaimashita**) どうもありがとうございます（ございました）"Thank you very much" or **Dōmo shitsurei-shi-mashita** どうも失礼しました "I am very sorry for what I have done." Lately, **Dōmo** seems to have started developing a wider and wider range of meaning, however. Thus it is begin-ning to function as a salutation in a tremendous number of situations. Some people use it in lieu of other more established greetings such as **Konnichi wa** こんにちは "Good day!" and **Sayonara** さようなら "Good-by!" and, according to Maruya (p. 153), even **Moshi-moshi** もしもし (a greeting on the phone, meaning "Hello!"). Its usage has become so broad that Maruya suggests (p. 154), though tongue in cheek, that it may someday even acquire the meaning of "I love you"!

Do⌉nna どんな *what kind [of]*

Whereas, in English, "what kind" can be used alone without "of" + noun, Japanese **donna** どんな has to be followed by a noun.

EXAMPLE:

(1) **Kore wa donna shōsetsu desu ka.**
これはどんな小説ですか。
What kind of novel is this?

In questions like this, **dōiu** どういう can also be used to mean "what kind."

EXAMPLE:

(2) **Kore wa dōiu shōsetsu desu ka.**
これはどういう小説ですか。
(same meaning as (1) above)

When **donna** どんな and **dōiu** どういう are used in **te mo** ても (or **de mo** でも) clauses meaning "no matter . . . , " however, there is a difference between the two (Tokugawa and Miyajima, p. 294). **Dōiu** in such clauses can signal only "[no matter] what kind," whereas **donna** can be used to mean either "[no matter] what kind" or "[no matter] to what degree." Compare the following:

EXAMPLES:

(3) **Donna (or Dōiu) koto ni natte mo kamaimasen.**
どんな（どういう）事になってもかまいません。
I don't care what happens. (lit., No matter what kind of result ensues, I don't care.)

(4) **Donna (not *Dōiu どういう) samui toki de mo jogingu o shimasu.**
どんな寒い時でもジョギングをします。
I jog no matter how cold it is.

In (3), either **donna** どんな or **dōiu** どういう may be used because "what kind" is the issue; in (4), however, only **donna** is correct because **dōiu** どういう cannot mean "how" in the sense of "to what degree."

Donna hito どんな人 *What kind of person?*

Although **donna hito** どんな人 and **dōiu hito** どういう人 are both translated into English as "what kind of person," they are not really synonymous. For example, although (1a) and (1b) both mean "What kind of man did Ms. Tanaka marry?," the answers will probably be different.

EXAMPLES:

(1a) **Tanaka-san donna hito to kekkon-shita no.**
田中さんどんな人と結婚したの。

(1b) **Tanaka-san dōiu hito to kekkon-shita no.**
田中さんどういう人と結婚したの。

Question (1a) is asking about the man's looks, personality, etc.; the answer will be something like (2a) and (2b).

EXAMPLES:

(2a) **Sugoku hansamu na hito yo.**

すごくハンサムな人よ。

A really handsome man.

(2b) **Hansamu ja nai kedo, yūmoa ga atte omoshiroi hito yo.**

ハンサムじゃないけど、ユーモアがあっておもしろい人よ。

He's not handsome, but he's a fun guy with a sense of humor.

Question (1b) is asking about the man's background; the answer will most likely be like (3a) or (3b).

EXAMPLES:

(3a) **Tōdai dete, Gaimushō ni tsutomete-iru n desutte.**

東大出て、外務省に勤めているんですって。

I hear he's a University of Tokyo graduate and works for the Foreign Office.

(3b) **Kanojo no kōkō-jidai kara no tomodachi na no yo.**

彼女の高校時代からの友達なのよ。

He's a friend of hers from her high school days.

Dō⌐zo [Do⌐ozo] どうぞ *please*

Dōzo どうぞ by itself is most often used when one invites someone to do something, e.g., when a host or a hostess invites a guest to come in, or when one offers someone something such as food, a beverage, or a cigarette. (Offering something to someone is really like inviting that person to have and enjoy the item offered.)

Dōzo どうぞ by itself rarely functions as a request. It may, however, be attached to a request.

EXAMPLES:

(1) **Dōzo onegai-shimasu.**

どうぞお願いします。

Please do me this favor.

(2) **Dōzo okamai naku.**

どうぞおかまいなく。

Please don't bother.

English-speaking students of Japanese often make the error of assuming that **dōzo** どうぞ makes requests more polite, as does "please" in English. Adding **dōzo** to a request, does not make it any more polite—it just intensifies it. For example, in (1) above, the politeness lies not in the word **Dōzo**, but in the verb **onegai-shimasu** お願いします (lit., "I humbly request"), which is the polite-humble form of **negau** 願う "to request." In fact, Japanese polite requests are uttered more often without **dōzo** than English polite requests are made without "please."

E⌐ 絵 *picture*

E 絵 means "picture," but only in reference to a drawn or painted picture. Unlike English "picture" it cannot refer to a movie or a photograph. A movie is an **eiga** 映画, and a photograph is a **shashin** 写真. **E** may mean "photograph" only in the compound **e-hagaki** 絵はがき "picture postcard."

E¹e ええ *yes*

Ee ええ is a more conversational version of **hai** はい. Use it, however, only as a response to a question.

EXAMPLE:

A: **Are wa Ueda-san deshō ka.**
あれは上田さんでしょうか。
Might that be Mr. Ueda?

B: **Ee, sō desu yo.**
ええ、そうですよ。
Yes, it is.

Do not use **ee** ええ as a response to a knock on the door or the calling of your name. For that purpose, only **hai** はい is appropriate.

Eiga 映画 *movie*

English has several words meaning "motion picture," but Japanese has only one, **eiga** 映画. A movie theater is **eigakan** 映画館. "To go to a movie" is **eiga e** (or **ni**) **iku** 映画へ（に）行く, but not *eigakan e (or ni) iku 映画館へ（に）行く. Until the 1930s or so, movies were called **katsudō-shashin** 活動写真 (or **katsudō** 活動 for short), which literally means "motion picture." It was a very common word until it was gradually replaced by **eiga** 映画, which is now the only term for "movie."

Enpitsu 鉛筆 *pencil*

In English, not only a regular pencil but also a mechanical pencil may be called a pencil. In Japanese, however, **enpitsu** 鉛筆 refers to a regular pencil only. A mechanical pencil is called **shāpu-penshiru** シャープペンシル, or simply **shāpen** シャーペン, which is traceable to "Eversharp," the brand name of the first U.S.-made mechanical pencil.

E¹ra¹i 偉い *great; celebrated; praiseworthy; admirable*

In his *Zoku Nihonjin no Eigo* (1990), Mark Petersen describes **erai** 偉い as one of those common Japanese words that are extremely hard to translate into English. First, **erai** means "great."

EXAMPLE:

(1) **Ryōshin o hontō ni erai to omotte irareru kodomo wa shiawase da.**
両親を本当に偉いと思っていられる子供は幸せだ。
Children who can think their parents are truly great are fortunate.

Sometimes, **erai** 偉い means "of higher rank."

EXAMPLE:

(2) A: **Boku-tachi koko ni suwatte mo ii?**
僕たちここに座ってもいい？
May we sit here?

B: **Soko wa erai hito-tachi no seki da kara dame.**
そこは偉い人たちの席だからだめ。
No, you can't. Those seats are reserved for VIPs.

Such translations as "praiseworthy" and "admirable" make it sound as though **erai** 偉い is indeed a big word reserved for special occasions, but it is not so at all. In fact, it is used all the time on ordinary occasions. For example, if a child brings home a good report card from school, his or her mother might say,

EXAMPLE:

(3) **Erakatta ne!**
偉かったね！
Good for you! (lit., That was great!)

If a little child falls and skins his or her knee but tries not to cry, his or her mother will definitely say,

EXAMPLE:

(4) **Erai, erai!**
偉い、偉い！
Good boy/girl!

Fudan ふだん *usual*

Fudan ふだん means "usual" in the sense of "occurring at normal times or in everyday situations." Sentence (1) is, therefore, correct, but sentence (2) is not.

EXAMPLES:

(1) **Fudan kara benkyō-shite oku to, shiken ni natte mo komaranai.**
ふだんから勉強しておくと、試験になっても困らない。
If you keep studying (normally), you won't have trouble with exams.
(2) ***Kenji wa fudan no seinen da.**
*健二はふだんの青年だ。
Kenji is an average young man.

In (2) above, **fudan** ふだん should be replaced by **futsū** ふつう, as in (3).

EXAMPLE:

(3) **Kenji wa futsū no seinen da.**
健二はふつうの青年だ。
Kenji is an average young man.

Fujin 婦人 *A woman*

Fujin 婦人, meaning "woman," sounds quite old-fashioned as compared with **josei** 女性. Until a few decades ago, women's restrooms in public places were designated as **fujin-yō** 婦人用 (lit., "for women's use"). Nowadays, however, such restrooms probably just have a red logo shaped like a woman on the doors or are designated as **josei** instead. I am certain no enlightened Japanese women of today would like to be referred to as **fujin** or even **go-fujin** ご婦人 with the addition of an honorific prefix.

Fu⌈ku⌉ 服 *clothes; clothing*

Fuku 服, unlike "clothes" or "clothing," does not include underwear. **Kinō fuku o aratta** きのう服を洗った (lit., "I washed clothes yesterday") sounds as though you washed washable dresses or suits.

Fuku usually refers to Western-style clothes such as dresses and suits, and not to kimonos. However, if one really wants to make a clear distinction between kimonos and Western-style clothes, one should use **wafuku** 和服 or **kimono** 着物 for the former and **yōfuku** 洋服 for the latter, as in

EXAMPLE:

Konogoro no wakamono wa yōfuku bakari de, wafuku wa motte-iru hito mo sukunai darō.
このごろの若者は洋服ばかりで、和服は持っている人も少ないだろう。
Young men these days wear only Western clothes, and there are probably very few who own kimonos.

Fu⌈ru⌉i 古い *old*

Furui 古い meaning "old" is used, as a rule, in reference to inanimate things.

EXAMPLES:

(1) **Anna furui ie wa kawanai hō ga ii desu yo.**
あんな古い家は買わない方がいいですよ。
You shouldn't buy an old house like that.

(2) **Kono ōbā mo zuibun furuku-natta.**
このオーバーもずいずん古くなった。
This overcoat has gotten quite old.

With reference to persons, other words such as **toshi o totta** 年をとった "old, aged," **toshiyori** 年寄り "old person," and **rōjin** 老人 "old person" have to be used.

EXAMPLES:

(3) **Murata-san mo toshi o totta nē.**
村田さんも年をとったねえ。
Hasn't Mr. Murata grown old!

(4) **Asoko ni toshiyori no obāsan ga suwatte-iru deshō.**
あそこに年寄りのおばあさんが座っているでしょう。
Do you see that old lady sitting there?

(5) **Ano rōjin-tachi ni seki o yuzurō.**
あの老人達に席をゆずろう。
Let's give our seats to those old people.

When **furui** 古い is used with reference to persons, it can carry different meanings.

EXAMPLES:

(6) **Kono kaisha de ichiban furui no wa Yamada-san da.**
この会社で一番古いのは山田さんだ。
The person with the most seniority in this firm is Mr. Yamada.

(7) **Ano hito wa mō furui.**
あの人はもう古い。
He is passé (or behind the times)

Furui 古い is sometimes shortened to **furu** 古 and added to other words to form compounds.

EXAMPLE:

(8) **furu-hon, furu-gi, furu-shinbun**
古本、古着、古新聞
used books, used clothes, old newspapers

Fu⌐ru⌐sato ふるさと *birthplace; home village, hometown*

If you asked Japanese people what words sound the best to them, I have a feeling they might choose **furusato** ふるさと as one of them. **Furusato** (lit., "old home village") is indeed a poetic-sounding, nostalgia-soaked word. It is probably not very frequently used in ordinary conversation but more commonly in literary works such as poems. The same is true with **kokyō** 故郷, which also means "old home village." The most common expression in daily conversation is **kuni** 国 (lit. "country"), as in

EXAMPLE:

Obon ni wa, chotto kuni no ryōshin no tokoro e ikō to omotte-imasu.
お盆には、ちょっと国の両親の所へ行こう思っています。
I'm thinking of going home to visit my parents in the country for the Bon Festival.

Fu⌐to⌐ru 太る *to become fat; to gain weight*

"To gain weight" is **futoru** 太る, and not **futoku naru** 太くなる "to become thick."

EXAMPLE:

(1) **Yoshida-san wa mukashi zuibun yasete ita keredo, kekkon-shite sukoshi futotta yō da.**
吉田さんは昔ずいぶんやせていたけれど、結婚して少し太ったようだ。
Mr. Yoshida used to be very thin, but he seems to have gained some weight since he got married.

Futoku naru 太くなる may refer to a person's arms and legs, as in sentence (2), but not his/her whole body.

EXAMPLE:

(2) **Ano rikishi wa kono goro futotte, ude mo ashi mo futoku-natta.**
あの力士はこのごろ太って、腕も足も太くなった。
Recently that sumo wrestler has gained weight; both his arms and his legs have become bigger.

Since **futoru** 太る by itself means "to become fat" or "to gain weight," it is totally unnecessary to add **naru** なる to express the sense of "to become." It is therefore wrong to use (3) below to mean "I have gained weight."

EXAMPLE:

(3) *****Watashi wa futotte ni natta.**
＊私は太ってになった。

Gaijin 外人 *foreigner*

Gaijin 外人, in a broad sense, means "foreigner." In a narrower sense, however, it refers only to Caucasians, especially those staying in Japan.

Gaikokujin 外国人 (lit., "foreign-country person"), another word for "foreigner," on the other hand, is more general and simply means "alien (from any country and of any color)."

Gakkō 学校 *school*

In English, "school" not only refers to nursery school through high school, but sometimes may refer to a college, university, or part thereof, as in

EXAMPLES:
(1) Harvard is a famous school.
(2) That university has a law school, a medical school, an engineering school, etc.

Gakkō 学校, on the other hand, normally refers to schools from the elementary-school level through the high-school level only. Sentence (1) and (2) above, therefore, would be translated into Japanese without the use of **gakkō**.

EXAMPLES:
(3) **Hābādo wa yūmei na daigaku** (not ***gakkō** 学校) **desu.**
ハーバードは有名な大学です。
Harvard is a famous university.
(4) **Ano daigaku ni wa hō-gakubu, i-gakubu, kō-gabuku** (not ***hō-gakkō** 法学校,
***i-gakkō** 医学校, ***kō-gakkō** 工学校) **nado ga arimasu.**
*あの大学には法学部、医学部、工学部などがあります。
That university has a law school, a medical school, an engineering school, etc.

Gakusei 学生 *student*

Students in a formal educational system, i.e., nursery school through college, are called **seito** 生徒 or **gakusei** 学生, depending on the level. **Gakusei** refers to older students, especially college students. Students of high-school age or younger are usually referred to as **seito**, although high school students may sometimes be called **gakusei** also (see SEITO).

Gaᒣnbaᒣru がんばる *to try one's best; to stick it out*

Ganbaru がんばる is a very frequently used expression, especially in its imperative form, **ganbare** がんばれ or **ganbatte** がんばって. It is often used to encourage people who are about to take an exam, play an important game, etc., as in (1) and (2).

EXAMPLES:
(1) A: **Kyō wa rekishi no shiken ga aru n da.**
今日は歴史の試験があるんだ。
Today I have a history exam.
B: **Sō ka. Ja, ganbare yo.**
そうか。じゃ、がんばれよ。
Do you? Good luck then.

(2) A: **Ashita tenisu no shiai ga aru n desu yo.**
あしたテニスの試合があるんですよ。
Tomorrow I have a big tennis match coming up.

B: **Sore ja, ganbatte kudasai.**
それじゃ、がんばってください。
Good luck then.

Although **ganbare** がんばれ or **ganbatte** がんばって is thus used when English speakers would say "Good luck!", this usage is limited to situations where making effort is involved. If you find out a friend is going into a hospital with a serious illness, therefore, **Ganbatte!** がんばって! might sound a little out of place. In such a case, **Odaiji ni!** おだいじに! ("Take care of yourself!") would sound more considerate.

Gekijō 劇場 *theater*

Gekijō 劇場 means "theater" in the sense of "building or place where there is regularly a theatrical performance on the stage." Although some movie theaters may have names such as **X-gekijō**, they are not **gekijō** in the real sense of the word. Movie theaters are normally referred to as **eigakan** 映画館 instead.

Unlike English "theater," **gekijō** can never mean "drama" or "theater arts." (See also SHIBAI.)

Ge˥nki 元気 *healthy, well; in good spirits*

In English, "healthy" can mean either "in good health," as in "a healthy person," or "good for the health," as in "a healthy drink." **Genki** 元気, on the other hand, means "in good health" but can never mean "good for the health." Sentence (1) is, therefore, right, but sentence (2) is not.

EXAMPLES:
(1) **Ogenki desu ka.**
お元気ですか。
Are you well?
(2) *****Sushi wa genki na tabemono to iwarete-iru.**
*寿司は元気な食べ物と言われている。
Sushi is said to be healthy food.

Instead of **genki na tabemono** 元気な食べ物, one should say **karada ni yoi tabemono** 体によい食べ物 "food that is good for the body" or **kenkōteki na tabemono** 健康的な食べ物 "healthful food."

Genki 元気 is thus most often used as the opposite of **byōki** 病気 "sick."

EXAMPLE:
(3) **Nagai aida byōki deshita ga, mō genki ni narimashita.**
長い間病気でしたが、もう元気になりました。
I was sick for a long time, but I'm fine now.

Genki 元気 also means "vigor, energy, good spirits" or their corresponding adjectives, i.e., "vigorous, energetic, in good spirits," as in

EXAMPLES:

(4) **Uchi no musuko wa Tōdai no nyūgakushiken ni ochite genki ga nai. Hayaku genki ni natte** (or **genki o dashite**) **kureru to ii n da ga.**

うちの息子は東大の入学試験に落ちて元気がない。早く元気になって（元気を出して）くれるといいんだが。

My son is in low spirits, having failed the entrance exam to the University of Tokyo. I hope he will cheer up soon.

(5) **Yamada-san wa okusan o nakushite genki ga nakatta ga, konogoro mata genki ni natte-kita.**

山田さんは奥さんを亡くして元気がなかったが、このごろまた元気になってきた。

Mr. Yamada was in low spirits after he lost his wife, but lately he's been cheerful (or *in better spirits*) *again.*

(See also BYŌKI and OGENKI DESU KA.)

Gimon 疑問 *a question; doubt*

Although **gimon** 疑問 is often translated as "question," it can mean that only in the sense of a question one has in one's mind. When that question is uttered, it becomes a **shitsumon** 質問.

EXAMPLE:

Chotto gimon ni omotta node, shitsumon-shite mita.

ちょっと疑問に思ったので、質問してみた。

I had a question in mind, so I asked him.

Because of this difference, although one can say **shitsumon-suru** 質問する "to ask a question," one cannot say ***gimon-suru** 疑問する.

Go˺go 午後 *afternoon,* P.M.

Gogo 午後 means "afternoon," as in

EXAMPLE:

(1) **Ashita no gogo mata kite-kudasai.**

あしたの午後また来てください。

Please come again tomorrow afternoon.

Gogo 午後 also means "P.M.," but unlike "P.M.," which follows the time (i.e., "2 P.M.," "3 P.M.," etc.), it precedes the time.

EXAMPLE:

(2) **gogo ni-ji**

午後二時

2 P.M.

(See also GOZEN.)

Go⌐han ご飯, 御飯 *cooked rice, meal*

In a narrow sense, **gohan** ご飯 means "cooked rice."

EXAMPLE:

(1) **Gohan o mō ip-pai kudasai.**
ご飯をもう一杯ください。
Please give me one more bowl of rice.

In a broader sense, **gohan** ご飯 means "meal."

EXAMPLE:

(2) **Mō sorosoro ohiru da kara, gohan ni shimashō.**
もうそろそろお昼だから、ご飯にしましょう。
Since it's almost noon, let's have lunch.

The fact that the same word may mean both "cooked rice" and "meal" points to the important role cooked rice used to play in the traditional Japanese meal. The names of the three daily meals are, most commonly, **asa-gohan** 朝ご飯 "breakfast," **hiru-** (or **ohiru-**) **gohan** 昼 (お昼)ご飯 "lunch," and **ban-gohan** 晩ご飯 "dinner."

Men sometimes use the word **meshi** 飯 instead of **gohan** ご飯, especially in informal situations. **Meshi**, like **gohan**, means both "cooked rice" and "meal." There is another word meaning "cooked rice," i.e., **raisu** ライス from English "rice." This word, however, has a very limited range of meaning, referring only to cooked rice served on a plate in a Western-style restaurant (Miura, p. 128). It never means "meal."

Go⌐ku⌐rō-sama ご苦労様 *Thank you for your work*

Gokurō-sama ご苦労様 is an expression of thanks for service rendered such as delivering things or running an errand, and "is most often said to newspaper boys, porters, bellboys, delivery men and the like ... as a verbal tip" (Mizutani and Mizutani, 1, p. 117). It should not be used when someone "has done something for you out of sheer kindness" (ibid.), or when someone does something for his own good (e.g., someone who is studying hard for an examination or jogging for his own health and pleasure).

This greeting may sometimes be directed to a person of higher status. Since it is difficult to predict its appropriateness in a given situation, however, it might be safer to avoid the expression when addressing a person of higher status.

Go⌐men-kudasa⌐i ごめんください *Is anybody home?*

When visiting a Japanese home, you first ring the bell and wait for someone to answer. But what should you do if the bell is not working or if there is no bell at the front door? In that case, the best thing would be to shout out **Gomenkudasai** ごめんください, which literally means "Please excuse me" but is used in the sense of "Is anybody home?" If the door is not locked, you can even open the door (this is accepted behavior in Japan though totally unacceptable in the U.S.) and shout out **Gomenkudasai!** (see GOMEN-NASAI.)

Go⌐men-nasa⌐i ごめんなさい *Sorry!*

Gomen-nasai ごめんなさい "Sorry!" is an apology used mostly at home between family members, especially by children apologizing to parents (Mizutani and Mizutani, pp. 14–15). Outside the home, too, **Gomen-nasai** is used mostly by children. An adult may say it, in informal situations, to someone lower in status. In formal situations, adults use **Shitsurei-shimasu** 失礼します or **Shitsurei-shimashita** 失礼しました (see SHITSUREI-SHIMASU).

-Go⌐ro ごろ *about, approximately*

-Goro ごろ is a variant of **koro** ころ "about, approximately" and is used exclusively as a suffix attached to nouns indicating points in time.

EXAMPLES:
(1) **go-ji-goro**
五時ごろ
about 5 o'clock
(2) **san-gatsu-goro**
三月ごろ
about March

Because of the Japanese speaker's reluctance to be precise or exact, **-goro** ごろ is used more frequently in Japanese than "about" is used in English in reference to points in time. For example, instead of using **Nanji desu ka** 何時ですか to mean "What time is it?" many Japanese speakers ask **Nanji-goro desu ka** 何時ごろですか "About what time is it?" In English, however, "About what time is it?" is much rarer than "What time is it?"

Some speakers use **koro** ころ instead of **-goro** ごろ to mean the same thing.

EXAMPLE:
(3) **san-gatsu koro**
三月ころ
about March

When not preceded by a noun, **koro** ころ, not **-goro** ごろ, is the correct word. In the following sentence, therefore, **-goro** cannot be used.

EXAMPLE:
(4) **Wakai koro** (not *****-goro** ごろ) **wa yokatta!**
若いころは良かった！
Ah, those good old days when I was still young!

(See also KONOGORO and KORO.)

Go⌐zen 午前 A.M.

Gozen 午前 is the opposite of **gogo** 午後 meaning "P.M." (see GOGO).

EXAMPLE:
(1) **Gozen san-ji desu ka, gogo san-ji desu ka.**
午前三時ですか、午後三時ですか？
Do you mean 3 A.M. or 3 P.M. ?

Whereas **gogo** 午後 is often used adverbially, **gozen** 午前 is not. For example, while sentence (2) below is perfectly normal, (3) is a little unnatural.

EXAMPLES:

(2) **Ashita no gogo kite-kudasai.**
あしたの午後来てください。
Please come tomorrow afternoon.

(3) **?Ashita no gozen kite-kudasai.**
あしたの午前来て下さい。
Please come tomorrow morning.

When used adverbially **gozen** 午前 usually takes the suffix **-chū** 中 "during."

EXAMPLE:

(4) **Ashita no gozen-chū kite-kudasai.**
あしたの午前中来て下さい。
Please come tomorrow morning.

Sentence (4) is not synonymous with **Ashita no asa kitekudasai** あしたの朝来て下さい since **gozen-chū** 午前中 covers a longer time span (i.e., up to noon) than **asa** does (see ASA).

-Gu⌐rai ぐらい *about, approximately*

-Gurai ぐらい, as well as its variant **-kurai** くらい, indicates an approximate amount of anything.

EXAMPLES:

(1) **Ano hon wa ikura ka shirimasen ga, tabun nisen-en-gurai deshō.**
あの本はいくらか知りませんが、たぶん二千円ぐらいでしょう。
I'm not sure how much that book is, but it's probably about two thousand yen.

(2) **Ano hito wa gojū-gurai deshō.**
あの人は五十ぐらいでしょう。
He is probably about fifty.

Although **-gurai** ぐらい is quite similar in meaning to its English counterparts such as "about" and "approximately," it is probably used more often in Japanese than "about" or "approximately" are in English because of the Japanese speaker's reluctance to be too precise, definite, or specific. Japanese speakers often say to a salesclerk **Mittsu-gurai kudasai** 三つぐらいください (lit., "Give me about three"), for example, even when they want exactly three of something. This is the same psychology that leads them to say **nan-ji-goro** 何時ごろ "about what time" instead of **nan-ji** 何時 "what time."

 -Gurai ぐらい is different from **-goro** ごろ (see -GORO) in that the latter is specifically for *points* in time (e.g., **san-ji-goro** 3時ごろ "about 3 o'clock" and **roku-gatsu-goro** 6時ごろ "about June") while the former is for *amounts* of anything. Some native speakers of Japanese do occasionally use **-gurai** with a word indicating a point in time, e.g., **ni-ji-gurai** 2時ぐらい instead of **ni-ji-goro** 2時ごろ for about 2 o'clock." This particular use of **-gurai** ぐらい, however, is not really advisable.

Gyaku 逆 *opposite; reverse*

Gyaku 逆 and **hantai** 反対 are both translated as "opposite" and are often used interchangeably. For example, in sentence (1), either may be used.

EXAMPLE:

(1) **Kyū ni gyaku/hantai no hōkō kara kare ga arawareta node bikkuri-shita.**
急に逆/反対の方向から彼が現れたのでびっくりした。
I was surprised to see him suddenly appear from the opposite direction.

However, there is a slight difference in connotation. **Gyaku** 逆 connotes "the opposite of what's normal or correct," whereas **hantai** 反対 has no such connotation. For example,

EXAMPLE:

(2) **Ichi kara jū made gyaku ni itte mite kudasai.**
一から十まで逆に言ってみてください。
Please try saying 1 through 10 backwards.

When one recites 1 through 10, one usually does it in normal order, i.e., **ichi** 一, **ni** 二, **san** 三, . . . Saying the numbers backwards, i.e., **jū** 十, **kyū** 九, **hachi** 八, . . . would be contrary to the norm. In sentence (2), therefore, **hantai ni** 反対に would sound a little strange. Even in sentence (1) above, that difference is still there. The expression **gyaku no hōkō** 逆 の方向 connotes "direction contrary to my expectation," whereas **hantai no hōkō** 反対の 方向 simply means "opposite direction."

Ha⌈bu⌉ku 省く *to leave out*

Habuku 省く basically means "to leave out" or "to omit," as in

EXAMPLE:

(1) **Nihongo de wa bun no shugo o habuku koto ga ōi.**
日本語では文の主語を省くことが多い。
In Japan, the subject of a sentence is often left out.

In this sense, **habuku** 省く is very much like **ryakusu** 略す, which also can mean "to omit." **Ryakusu** 略す, therefore, can be used instead of **habuku** 省く in sentence (1). **Ryakusu**, however, is different in the sense it also means "to abbreviate," as in

EXAMPLE:

(2) **"Terebi" wa "terebijon" o ryakushita mono da.**
「テレビ」は「テレビジョン」を略したものだ。
Terebi is an abbreviation of terebijon.

Habuku 省く has no such meaning.

Hadaka 裸 *naked*

To be described as **hadaka** 裸, one does not have to be completely naked. A Japanese fisherman with nothing but a loincloth on may be described as **hadaka**. If a boy is lying down with nothing covering his upper body, his mother might say **Hadaka de nete-iru to kaze o hikimasu yo** 裸で寝ていると風邪をひきますよ "You'll catch a cold if you lie down half-naked." In a pickup basketball game in America, if one of the teams is shirtless, its members are called the Skins. Their Japanese counterparts would be referred to as **Hadaka**.

To convey the meaning "completely naked," one would have to say **mappadaka** 真っ裸 (lit., "truly naked").

Ha⌈gema⌉su 励ます *to encourage*

Once an American student wrote sentence (1) in a composition.

EXAMPLE:

(1) *****Amerika no sensei wa gakusei ga shitsumon o kiku koto o hagemasu.**
*アメリカの先生は学生が質問を聞くことを励ます。
American teachers encourage their students to ask questions.

Aside from the fact that **shitsumon o kiku** 質問を聞く should be replaced by **shitsumon o suru** 質問する to mean "to ask questions," the above sentence is wrong in that **hagemasu** 励ます is not used correctly. **Hagemasu** basically means "to encourage someone who is down-hearted," as in

EXAMPLE:

(2) **Nyūgakushiken ni ochita tomodachi o hagemashita.**
入学試験に落ちた友達を励ました。
I encouraged a friend who flunked an entrance exam.

Sentence (1) should probably be rephrased as below.

EXAMPLE:

(3) **Amerika no sensei wa gakusei kara no shitsumon o kangei-suru.**
アメリカの先生は学生からの質問を歓迎する。
American teachers welcome questions from their students.

Ha⌈geshi⌉i 激しい *violent*

Hageshii 激しい in the sense of "violent" may be used to describe weather-related things such as **kaze** 風 "wind," **ame** 雨 "rain," **arashi** 嵐 "storm," and **yuki** 雪 "snow." It may also serve an adjective for **kotoba** 言葉 "words," **kanjō** 感情 "feelings," etc., as in:

EXAMPLE:

(1) **Hageshii kotoba o butsuke-atta.**
激しい言葉をぶつけ合った。
They hurled fiery words at each other.

Hageshii 激しい, however, is inappropriate for describing such things as societies and movies. For example, sentences (2a) and (2b) are both strange.

EXAMPLES:

(2a) *****Konogoro shakai ga hageshiku natte-kita.**
*このごろ社会が激しくなってきた。
Recently society has become violent.

(2b) *****Watashi wa hageshii eiga wa suki ja nai.**
*私は激しい映画は好きじゃない。
I don't like violent movies.

To make these sentences appropriate, use **bōryoku** 暴力 "violence" or its derivatives.

EXAMPLES:

(3a) **Konogoro shakai ga bōryoku-teki ni natte-kita** (or **bōryoku-ka shite-kita**).
このごろ社会が暴力的になってきた。(暴力化してきた。)

(3b) **Watashi wa bōryoku-eiga wa suki ja nai.**
私は暴力映画は好きじゃない。

Ha'ha 母 *mother*

Words for "mother" function in parallel to those for "father." The basic rules are: **haha** 母 corresponds to **chichi** 父, **okā-san** お母さん to **otō-san** お父さん, and **ofukuro** お袋 to **oyaji** 親父 (see CHICHI).

Ha'i はい *yes*

Hai はい is used in response to questions (also requests, demands, and suggestions) to signal agreement or assent. Although **hai** is often equated with "yes," it is not the same as "yes"; it is more like "That's right." In fact, it corresponds to "yes" only when used as a response to affirmative questions. In response to negative questions, it corresponds to "no."

EXAMPLES:

(1) A: **Wakarimasu ka.** (affirmative question)
分かりますか。
Do you understand?

   B: **Hai, wakarimasu.**
はい、分かります。
Yes, I do. (lit., That's right. I understand.)

(2) A: **Wakarimasen ka.** (negative question)
分かりませんか。
Don't you understand?

   B: **Hai, wakarimasen.**
はい、分かりません。
No, I don't. (lit., That's right. I don't understand.)

From the above examples, the following becomes clear. In English, what determines the choice between "yes" and "no" is what follows; i.e., if what follows is in the affirmative (e.g., "I do"), you use "yes," whereas if what follows is in the negative (e.g., "I don't"), you use "no." In Japanese, on the other hand, what determines the choice of **hai** はい or **iie** いいえ (see IIE) is whether you wish to indicate agreement or disagreement with the question. If you agree, you use **hai** はい, and if you disagree, you use **iie** いいえ; whether what follows is in the affirmative (e.g., **wakarimasu** 分かります) or in the negative (e.g., **wakarimasen** 分かりません) is immaterial.

   Hai はい, when used in response to negative questions, usually corresponds to "no," as explained above. There are some cases, however, where **hai** はい used as a response to negative questions corresponds to "yes" instead.

EXAMPLE:

(3) A: **Genki-sō ni natta ja arimasen ka.**
元気そうになったじゃありませんか。
Aren't you looking perfectly well!

B: **Hai, okage-sama de, kono goro wa sukkari genki ni narimashita.**
はい、おかげさまで、このごろはすっかり元気になりました。
Yes, I'm perfectly well now, thank you.

The above question, though negative in form, is actually affirmative in spirit. What the question really means is "You're looking perfectly well, and that's great!" Speaker B therefore says **hai** はい to show agreement with the spirit of the question. Consider two more examples.

EXAMPLES:
(4) A: **Ashita mo kite-kuremasen ka.**
あしたも来てくれませんか。
Will you come again tomorrow? (lit., Won't you come again tomorrow?)

  B: **Hai, ukagaimasu.**
はい、伺います。
Yes, I'll be glad to.

(5) A: **Tenki ga ii kara, yakyū de mo shimasen ka.**
天気がいいから、野球でもしませんか。
Since the weather is so nice, how about playing baseball or something (lit., shall we not play baseball or something)?

  B: **Hai (or Ee), shimashō.**
はい（ええ）、しましょう。
Yes, let's!

Although the A sentences above are negative in form, (4A) is actually a request with the meaning of "Please come again tomorrow," and (5A) is a suggestion meaning "How about doing such-and-such?" This use of **hai** はい is, therefore, not really an exception; it still follows the basic rule: If you are in agreement, use **hai.**

Hai はい is a formal expression. In less formal speech, **hai** is often replaced by **ee** ええ. In even more informal speech (especially by men, youngsters, and little children), **un** うん, or simply **n** ん, is used.

In addition to the main use explained above, **hai** はい has other functions, some of which are described below. With the exception of (6), neither **ee** ええ nor **un** うん can be used in place of **hai** in these examples.

Hai sometimes indicates "I'm listening" instead of "That's right."

EXAMPLE:
(6) Boss: **Kinō hanami ni ittara ne.**
きのう花見に行ったらね。
Yesterday we went to see the cherry blossoms.

  Employee: **Hai.**
はい。
Yes?

  Boss: **Yuki ga futte-ki-chatta n da yo.**
雪が降ってきちゃったんだよ。
It started snowing, of all things.

Hai はい, when used in response to the calling of one's name, signals "Here!" or "Present!" In (7) below, a teacher is taking attendance in class.

EXAMPLE:

(7) Teacher: **Tanaka-san.**
田中さん。
Miss Tanaka!

    Miss Tanaka: **Hai.**
はい。
Here!

    Hai はい serves to draw the addressee's attention, for example, when one hands something to someone (e.g., when a salesclerk gives change back to a customer), as in (8), or when a student raises his hand to draw the teacher's attention, as in sentence (9).

EXAMPLES:

(8) Salesclerk: **Hai. Go-hyaku-en no otsuri desu.**
はい。五百円のおつりです。
Here you are. Five hundred yen.

(9) Student: **Hai!** (raising his hand)
はい!
Sir?

    Teacher: **Nan desu ka.**
なんですか。
What is it?

    Student: **Chotto shitsumon ga aru n desu ga.**
ちょっと質問があるんですか。
May I ask you a question?

Ha⌐iru 入る *to enter; join*

Hairu 入る has several meanings. The most common one is "to enter," as in

EXAMPLES:

(1a) **Musuko ga kondo daigaku ni hairimashita.**
息子が今度大学に入りました。
My son just entered college.

(1b) **Yūbe dorobō ni hairareta.**
ゆうべ泥棒に入られた。
Last night a thief entered (i.e., broke into) my house.

    Hairu 入る can also mean "to join" (such things as clubs).

EXAMPLE:

(2) **Tarō wa kōkō de tenisubu ni haitta.**
太郎は高校でテニス部に入った。
Taro joined the tennis club in high school.

    It should be noted that English "enter" does not necessarily correspond to **hairu** 入る.

EXAMPLE:

(3) **Tōnamento ni deru** (not *hairu 入る) **tsumori desu.**
トーナメントに出るつもりです。
I'm planning on entering the tournament.

Hajime はじめ *beginning*

Hajime はじめ "beginning" and **hajimete** "for the first time" sound very much alike and are therefore often mistakenly used. Sentences (1a) and (2a) are wrong, while (1b) and (2b) are correct.

EXAMPLES:

(1a) ***Nihon de wa, shinnen no hajimete no mikkakan yoku omochi o taberu.**
*日本では、新年のはじめての三日間よくおもちを食べる。
lit., In Japan, they eat a lot of mochi for three days that occur for the first time in the new year.

(1b) **Nihon de wa, shinnen no hajime no mikkakan yoku omochi o taberu.**
日本では、新年のはじめの三日間よくおもちを食べる。
In Japan, they eat a lot of mochi during the first three days of the new year.

(2a) ***Hajimete Nihongo ga heta deshita.**
*はじめて日本語が下手でした。
lit., For the first time, I was bad at Japanese.

(2b) **Hajime wa Nihongo ga heta deshita.**
はじめは日本語が下手でした。
In the beginning, I was bad at Japanese.

Hajimeru 始める *to begin something*

At the beginning of something such as a meeting or a class, one may say "Let's begin!" in English. English speakers, transferring this sentence to Japanese, often make the error of saying **Hajimarimashō** 始まりましょう. One must use the transitive counterpart as in sentence (1).

EXAMPLE:

(1) **Hajimemashō.**
始めましょう。
Let's begin.

Hajimaru 始める is intransitive and means "something begins." It cannot mean "someone begins something." For the latter, the transitive **hajimeru** 始める is required. Although, in sentence (1) above, the object of the verb is not stated, it is clearly implied in that one wants to begin something such as a meeting or a class, hence the use of the transitive verb.

Likewise, the following sentence is also incorrect.

EXAMPLE:

(2) ***Fuyu ni naru to, yuki ga furi-hajimaru.**
*冬になると、雪が降り始まる。
When winter comes, it starts snowing.

In this case, although there is no noun that serves as the object, the verb **furi-** 降り is the object. The intransitive verb **hajimaru** 始まる, therefore, has to be changed to the transitive **hajimeru** 始める, as in

EXAMPLE:

(3) **Fuyu ni naru to, yuki ga furi-hajimeru.**
冬になると、雪が降り始める。

Ha⌈ji⌉mete 初めて *for the first time;* Hajimete 始めて *beginning something*

There are two kinds of **hajimete**. One means "for the first time" and is written 初めて, as in

EXAMPLE:

(1) **Hajimete Kankokugo o kiita toki, zuibun Nihongo to chigau na to omotta.**
初めて韓国語を聞いたとき、ずいぶん日本語と違うなと思った。
When I heard Korean for the first time, I thought it was really different from Japanese.

The other **hajimete** is the **te**-form of **hajimeru** 始める and is written 始めて, as in

EXAMPLE:

(2) **Kyō wa kono shigoto o hajimete mikka-me da.**
きょうはこの仕事を始めて三日目だ。
Today is the third day since I started this work.

These two words are not only written differently, but are pronounced differently. **Hajimete** 初めて has an accent on the second syllable, whereas **hajimete** 始めて is accentless.

Haku はく *to put on, to wear*

Haku はく is reserved for wearing hosiery (e.g., **kutsushita** 靴下 "socks" and **sutokkingu** ストッキング "stockings"), footwear (e.g., **kutsu** 靴 "shoes" and **būtsu** ブーツ "boots"), and other items that are worn on the lower part of the body by putting one's legs through them (e.g., **sukāto** スカート "skirt" and **zubon** ズボン "trousers").

EXAMPLES:

(1) **Nihon no josei wa itsu-goro kara sukāto o haku yō ni natta n deshō ka.**
日本の女性はいつごろからスカートをはくようになったんでしょうか。
I wonder when Japanese women started wearing skirts.

(2) **Kono-goro no onna-no-hito wa tenki ga yokute mo būtsu o haite-iru.**
このごろ女の人は天気がよくてもブーツをはいている。
Women these days wear boots even when the weather is good.

As a rule, the act of putting on certain items is **haku** はく while the state of wearing them is **haite-iru** はいている. In (3), for example, where the act of putting shoes on is the issue, only **haku** can be used whereas in (4), where the state of wearing a skirt is the issue, **haite-iru** is correct.

EXAMPLES:

(3) **Nihonjin wa uchi o deru mae ni kutsu o haku** (not *****haite-iru** はいている).
日本人は家を出る前に靴をはく。
Japanese put on their shoes before leaving the house.

(4) **Asoko ni pinku no sukāto o haite-iru** (not *****haku** はく) **onnano-hito ga iru deshō.**
あそこにピンクのスカートをはいている女の人がいるでしょう。
Do you see that woman who is wearing a pink skirt?

(See also HAMERU, KABURU, and KIRU.)

Ha˺ku 吐く *to vomit; to eject out of the mouth*

Ejecting something out of the mouth is **haku** 吐く, whatever it is that comes out, e.g.,

EXAMPLES:

(1a) **tsuba o haku**
つばを吐く
to spit

(1b) **Samui hi ni wa, haku iki ga shiroku mieru.**
寒い日には、吐く息が白く見える。
On cold days our breath looks white.

(1c) **Nihon no yopparai wa yoku haku.**
日本の酔っ払いはよく吐く。
Drunks in Japan often vomit.

Haku 吐く in the sense of "vomit" is an acceptable expression, but **modosu** もどす might be a little more genteel. **Gero o haku** げろを吐く is very much like English "puke" and should be avoided in polite company.

Hameru はめる *to put on, to wear*

Things that one puts on by putting a hand or fingers through them require the verb **hameru** はめる.

EXAMPLE:

(1)   **yubiwa (udewa, udedokei, tebukuro, gurōbu, etc.) o hameru**
指輪（腕輪、腕時計、手袋、グローブ）をはめる
to put on a ring (a bracelet, a wristwatch, gloves, a baseball glove, etc.)

Hameru はめる is often replaced by **suru** する.

EXAMPLE:

(2)   **Samui hi ni wa tebukuro o hameta (or shita) hō ga ii.**
寒い日は手袋をはめた（した）方がいい。
It's better to wear gloves on cold days.

Ha˺na˺su 話す *to tell; to speak*

Hanasu 話す, unlike **iu** 言う, is not used for uttering just a word or a sentence, i.e., it is used with reference to a whole conversation or a whole talk, or when such is implied.

EXAMPLES:

(1)   **Yūbe wa tomodachi to nagai aida hanashite** (not **itte* 言って) **tanoshikatta.**
ゆうべは友達と長い間話して楽しかった。
Last night I had a good time talking with a friend.

(2)   **Kare wa "Ja mata" to itte** (not **hanashite* 話して) **kaette-itta.**
彼は「じゃ、また」と言って帰っていった。
He left, saying, "See you!"

When the object is a language, **hanasu** 話す, not **iu** 言う, is used.

EXAMPLE:

(3) **Konogoro wa jōzu ni Nihongo o hanasu** (not *****iu** 言う) **gaikokujin ga fuete-kita.**
このごろは上手に日本語を話す外国人が増えてきた。
These days, foreigners who speak Japanese well have increased in number.

When the particle is not **o** を but **de** で, either **hanasu** 話す or **iu** 言う may be used, as in the following example. However, there is a slight difference in meaning between (4a) and (4b), which, I hope, is clear from the translations given.

EXAMPLES:

(4a) **Eigo de hanashite mo ii desu ka.**
英語で話してもいいですか。
May I speak/talk in English?

(4b) **Eigo de itte mo ii desu ka.**
英語で言ってもいいですか。
May I say it in English?

Another difference between **hanasu** 話す and **iu** 言う is that, while **hanasu** 話す does not need an object, **iu** 言う does.

EXAMPLE:

(5) **Asoko de hanashite-iru** (not *****itte-iru** 言っている) **no wa Suzuki-san darō.**
あそこで話しているのは鈴木さんだろう。
The person talking over there must be Mr. Suzuki.

Hane 羽 *feather; wing*

Hane 羽 means both "feather" and "wing," but the context usually makes the meaning clear, as in

EXAMPLES:

(1) **Hane no tsuita bōshi o kabutte-iru.**
羽のついた帽子をかぶっている。
She is wearing a hat with a feather.

(2) **Hane ga areba sugu tonde-ikimasu yo.**
羽があればすぐとんでいきますよ。
If I had wings, I would fly over right away.

Hantai-suru 反対する *to oppose*

Hantai-suru 反対する means "to oppose," as in

EXAMPLE:

(1) **Heiwa ni hantai-suru hito ga iru darō ka.**
平和に反対する人がいるだろうか。
I wonder if there is anybody who opposes peace.

Hansuru 反する, on the other hand, means "to violate." The difference between **hantai-suru** 反対する and **hansuru** should be clear from the following example.

EXAMPLES:

(2a) **Sono hōritsu ni hantai-suru hito ga ōi.**
その法律に反対する人が多い。
There are many people who oppose the law.

(2b) **Hōritsu ni hansuru kōi wa yokunai.**
法律に反する行為はよくない。
Illegal acts (lit., acts that violate the law) are not good.

Hataraku 働く *to work*

Hataraku 働く means "to work" as in

EXAMPLES:

(1) **Tonari no otetsudai-san wa itsumo daidokoro de hataraite-iru.**
となりのお手伝いさんはいつも台所で働いている。
The maid next door is always working in the kitchen.

(2) **Ano kōba no kōin-tachi wa yoku hataraku.**
あの工場の工員たちはよく働く。
The workers at that factory work very hard.

Although **hataraku** 働く and **shigoto o suru** 仕事をする "to do a job" are similar in meaning, the latter is probably more appropriate for desk work.

EXAMPLE:

(3) **Ano sakka wa hiruma ni nete, yoru shigoto o suru sō da.**
あの作家は昼間に寝て、夜仕事をするそうだ。
I hear that novelist sleeps during the day and works at night.

English "work" is sometimes almost synonymous with "study," e.g.,

EXAMPLE:

(4) He is working for his doctorate.

In Japanese, however, **hataraku** 働く cannot be used in that sense. Studying is referred to as **benkyō-suru** 勉強する (see BENKYŌ-SURU).

EXAMPLE:

(5) **Kare wa hakushigō o toru tame ni benkyō-shite-iru.**
彼は博士号を取るために勉強している。
He is studying for a doctorate.

Unlike "work," **hataraku** 働く cannot be used in reference to pastimes and hobbies. Therefore, to express the idea of "work" as expressed in (6) below, some word other than **hataraku** 働く would have to be used, as in (7).

EXAMPLES:

(6) He is working hard to organize his stamp collection in his spare time.

(7) **Kare wa hima na toki, kitte no korekushon o isshōkenmei seïri-shite-iru.**
彼はひまな時、切手のコレクションを一生懸命整理している。
lit., He is assiduously organizing his stamp collection in his spare time.

In English, if you are an employee of General Motors, you "work for" General Motors. **Hataraku** 働く cannot be used in this sense. **Tsutomete-iru** 勤めている (see TSUTOMERU) is the correct word.

EXAMPLE:

(8) **Kare wa Sonī ni tsutomete-iru.**
彼はソニーに勤めている。
He works for Sony. (lit., He is employed at Sony.)

Ha⌐ya⌐i 速い *fast;* 早い *early*

Hayai means both "fast," as in sentence (1), and "early," as in (2).

EXAMPLES:

(1) **Jidōsha wa jitensha yori hayai.**
自動車は自転車より速い。
Automobiles are faster than bicycles.

(2) **Hayakawa-san wa okiru no ga hayai.**
早川さんは起きるのが早い。
Mr. Hayakawa gets up early.

These two meanings of **hayai**, however, require two different kanji. In the sense of "fast, quick, speedy," **hayai** is usually written 速い **hayai**, while in the sense of "early," it is always written 早い **hayai**.

Although context usually makes the meaning quite clear, the word could be ambiguous in some cases, as in

EXAMPLE:

(3) **hayai basu**
早いバス
a fast (or early) bus

This ambiguity can be avoided, however, by the use of other expressions.

EXAMPLES:

(4) **supīdo ga hayai basu**
スピードが速いバス
a fast bus (lit., a bus whose speed is fast)

(5) **asa hayai basu**
朝早いバス
an early morning bus

Ha⌐ya⌐ru はやる *to become fashionable; to become popular*

Hayaru はやる is most normally used with reference to fads and fashions, as in

EXAMPLES:

(1a) **Konogoro Nihon de wa donna heasutairu ga hayatte-imasu ka.**
このごろ日本ではどんなヘアスタイルがはやっていますか。
What hairstyle is fashionable in Japan these days?

(1b) **Furafūpu ga hayatta no wa nanjū-nen mo mae no koto datta.**
フラフープがはやったのは何十年も前のことだった。
It was decades ago that hula hoops were the rage.

Hayaru はやる could be used about infectious diseases, too.

EXAMPLE:

(2) **Fuyu ni naru to, itsumo iya na kaze ga hayaru.**
冬になると、いつもいやな風邪がはやる。
Every winter nasty colds become rampant.

Hayaru はやる also means "to become popular," as in

EXAMPLE:

(3) **Ano mise wa hayatte-iru rashii.**
あの店ははやっているらしい。
That store seems popular.

You can talk about a kind of art, such as a type of music and a particular literary genre, as being **hayatte-iru** はやっている, but you cannot talk about a particular person being **hayatte-iru** はやっている. For a person being popular, **ninki ga aru** 人気がある is used instead.

EXAMPLES:

(4a) **Bītoruzu no ongaku wa rokujū-nendai ni zuibun hayatte-ita** (or **ninki ga atta**).
ビートルズの音楽は六十年代にずいぶんはやっていた（人気があった）。
The Beatles' music was very popular in the 60s.

(4b) **Ronarudo Rēgan wa nakanaka ninki no aru** (not *hayatte-iru はやっている) **daitōryō datta.**
ロナルド・レーガンはなかなか人気のある大統領だった。
Ronald Reagan was a pretty popular president.

Although both **hayatte-ita** はやっていた and **ninki ga atta** 人気があった are acceptable in (4a) above, there is a difference in connotation. **Hayatte-ita** はやっていた connotes that the Beatles' music was prevalent, i.e., everywhere you went, you heard it, whereas **ninki ga atta** 人気があった simply means their music was popular, i.e., it was well-liked by a large number of people.

Hayaru はやる also connotes "fashionable, prevalent, or popular over a limited length of time." In the following sentence, therefore, **hayatte-iru** はやっている is inappropriate and should be replaced by **ninki ga aru** 人気がある because the sentence is about an almost timeless situation.

EXAMPLE:

(5) **Amerika-eiga wa Nihon de Nihon-eiga yori ninki ga aru** (not *hayatte-iru はやってい る).
アメリカ映画は日本で日本映画より人気がある。
American films are more popular than Japanese ones in Japan.

If you used **hayatte-iru** はやっている in this case, it would indicate that the phenomenon is just a temporary fad, which certainly is far from the fact. (See also NINKI and SAKAN.)

Ha⌈zukashi⌉i はずかしい *ashamed, shameful, shy, embarrassed, embarrassing*

The Japanese sense of morality is shame oriented while the Western counterpart is sin oriented, so say a number of scholars including Ruth Benedict, author of *The Chrysanthemum and the Sword*. It is probably true. Japanese speakers certainly use the word **hazukashii** は ずかしい very frequently.

EXAMPLES:

(1) **Musuko ga hen na koto o shite hazukashii.**
息子が変な事をしてはずかしい。
I am ashamed that my son behaved so strangely.

(2) **Aitsu wa hazukashii yatsu da.**
あいつは、はずかしいやつだ。
He is a shameful scoundrel.

(3) **Ano ko wa hazukashii rashikute koko e ki-tagaranai.**
あの子は、はずかしいらしくてここへ来たがらない。
That child apparently feels shy; he doesn't want to come out here.

"Ashamed" and "shy" are two entirely different adjectives in English, but in Japanese **hazukashii** はずかしい takes care of both. Obviously, in the Japanese speaker's mind, being ashamed and being shy have something in common. A person who feels ashamed does not wish to face others. The same holds true with a shy person.

Hē? へえ *Really?*

Hē? へえ expresses mild suprise and disbelief in response to someone's remark, as in the following dialogue.

EXAMPLE:

(1) A: **Tanaka no yatsu Tōdai ni ukatta n datte sa.**
田中のやつ東大に受かったんだってさ。
Did you hear Tanaka was accepted by the University of Tokyo?

B: **Hē? Tanaka ga?**
へえ？田中が？
Really? Tanaka was?

Hē? へえ sounds informal and perhaps should be replaced in polite speech by **E?** え, which may be used in both informal and polite speech.

EXAMPLE:

(2) Male teacher: **Tanaka Tōdai ni ukatta sō da yo.**
田中東大に受かったそうだよ。
Did you hear Tanaka was accepted by the University of Tokyo?

Male student: **E? Tanaka ga?**
え？田中が？
What? Tanaka was?

The difference between **Hē?** へえ and **E?** え, however, is that the latter expresses only surprise (probably less mildly than **Hē?** へえ) and not disbelief.

There is another interjection, **Hō?** ほう, which may be used in either informal or polite speech and indicates mild surprise like **Hē?** へえ, but without the connotation of disbelief.

EXAMPLE:

(3) A: **Uchi no musuko ga okagesama de Tōdai ni ukarimashita.**
うちの息子がおかげさまで東大に受かりました。
My son was fortunately accepted by the University of Tokyo.

B: **Hō? Sore wa subarashii desu ne.**
ほう？それはすばらしいですね。
By God! How wonderful!

Hō? ほう is usually used by middle-aged or old people. As seen in (3) above, it often carries a sense of admiration.

Finally, **Hē?** へえ and **Hō?** ほう are both pronounced with a mild rising intonation at the end, while **E?** え is pronounced with a jerky rising intonation.

He⌐nji¬ 返事 *answer*

Henji 返事 is a noun meaning "answer, reply." Most often it refers to the act of saying **Hai** はい when one's name is called, as in sentence (1), or the act of writing a reply to a letter, as in (2).

EXAMPLES:

(1) **"Tanaka-san!" to yonda no ni henji ga nakatta.**
「田中さん」と呼んだのに返事がなかった。
I called out, "Mr. Tanaka!" but there was no answer.

(2) **Tegami o morattara sugu henji o dasu koto ni shite-iru.**
手紙をもらったらすぐ返事を出すことにしている。
I make it a rule to write a reply as soon as I receive a letter.

In sentence (1) above, **henji** 返事 is synonymous with **kotae** 答え, which also means "answer," but in sentence (2), **henji** 返事 cannot be replaced by **kotae** 答え.

As a variation of sentence (1) above, **henji** 返事 might refer to the act of responding to a knock on the door or to a doorbell by saying **Hai!** はい!

EXAMPLE:

(3) **Nokku o shitara (or Yobirin o narashitara) "Hai!" to henji ga atta.**
ノックしたら（呼び鈴を鳴らしたら）「はい」と返事があった。
When I knocked on the door (or rang the doorbell), someone answered, "Coming!"

Henji 返事 cannot be used to mean "answering the telephone." The verb **deru** 出る would have to be used.

EXAMPLE:

(4) **Denwa ga natte-iru no ni, dare mo denakatta (not *henji o shinakatta 返事をしなかった).**
電話が鳴っているのに、誰も出なかった。
Although the phone was ringing, nobody answered.

Hi 日 *day, sun*

Hi 日 means "day," as in

EXAMPLES:

(1) **Sono hi wa samukatta.**
その日は寒かった。
It was cold that day.

(2) **Haru ni wa hi ga nagaku naru.**
春には日が長くなる。
The days become longer in the spring.

Hi 日 also means "sun."

EXAMPLES:
(3) **Ashita wa nanji-goro hi ga noboru darō.**
あしたは何時ごろ日が昇るだろう。
I wonder what time the sun will rise tomorrow.
(4) **Kono heya wa hi ga yoku ataru kara attakai.**
この部屋は日が良く当たるから暖かい。
This room is warm because it's very sunny (lit., because it's well exposed to the sun).

There is another word meaning "sun," **taiyō** 太陽. There is, however, a definite difference between **hi** 日 meaning "sun" and **taiyō** in that the latter refers to the sun as the central body of the solar system, while **hi** is conceived of as a heavenly body that, like **tsuki** 月 "moon," rises and sets around us humans. In other words, **hi** is an anthropocentric term while **taiyō** is scientific, objective, and detached. Therefore, when one talks about sunspots, the solar system, solar observation, the diameter of the sun, etc., **taiyō** rather than **hi** has to be used.

EXAMPLES:
(5) **taiyō** (not *****hi** 日) **no kokuten**
太陽の黒点
sunspots
(6) **taiyō** (not *****hi** 日) **no chokkei**
太陽の直径
the diameter of the sun

Hi 日 is accentless when it is used in the sense of "sun," but it becomes accented when it is used in the sense of "day" and has a modifier, as in (1) and (7).

EXAMPLE:
(7) **Samui ⌈hi⌉ ni wa dare mo kimasen deshita.**
寒い日には誰も来ませんでした。
On cold days nobody came.

Hi⌈atari ga i⌉i 日当りがいい *having good exposure to the sun*

When you look up "sunny" in an English-Japanese dictionary, you find among some choices **hiatari ga ii** 日当りがいい. However, it cannot be used as in (1) below.

EXAMPLE:
(1) ***Kyō wa hiatari ga ii tenki desu.**
*きょうは日当りがいい天気です。
The weather is sunny today.

Hiatari ga ii is used only in reference to a sunny place, as in

EXAMPLE:
(2) **Fuyu wa hiatari no ii ie ga arigatai.**
冬は日当りのいい家がありがたい。
In winter, it is nice to live in a house exposed to a lot of sunshine.

Just to mean "It's sunny today," say one of the following:

EXAMPLES:
(3a) **Kyō wa hi ga yoku tette-iru.**
きょうは日がよく照っている。
lit., The sun is shining well today.
(3b) **Kyō wa harete-iru.**
きょうは晴れている。
It's sunny today.

Hige ひげ *beard, mustache, whiskers*

Although English has different words for facial hair, depending on where it grows, Japanese has just one word **hige** ひげ. If one wishes to make distinctions, however, it is possible to say the following.

EXAMPLES:
(1a) **kuchihige**
口ひげ
*mustache (lit., mouth **hige**)*
(1b) **agohige**
あごひげ
*beard (lit., chin **hige**)*
(1c) **hohohige/hōhige**
頬ひげ
*whiskers (lit., cheek **hige**)*

We used to use three different kanji for these three types of **hige**: 髭 for "mustache," 鬚 for "beard," and 髯 for "whiskers," but nowadays we simply write ひげ **hige** in hiragana for all of them.

Hi⌈kko⌉su 引っ越す *to move from one residence to another*

In American English, "move" may be used to mean "to change domiciles." Japanese **ugoku** 動く ("to move" in the sense of "to change position") cannot be used in that way. In the following example, only (1b) is correct.

EXAMPLES:
(1a) *****Ashita atarashii manshon ni ugoku koto ni narimashita.**
*あした新しいマンションに動くことになりました。
We are moving to a new apartment tomorrow.
(1b) **Ashita atarashii manshon ni hikkosu koto ni narimashita.**
あした新しいマンションに引っ越すことになりました。

For some reason, **hikkosu** 引っ越す is not used when the moving is to a different country. For example, the following does not quite sound right:

EXAMPLE:
(2) *****Teinentaishoku-shite kara gaikoku ni hikkosu hito mo iru yō da.**
*定年退職してから外国に引っ越す人もいるようだ。
It seems that there are some people who move to another country after retirement.

In that case, it is better to say **ijū-suru** 移住する, as in

EXAMPLE:

(3) **Teinentaishoku-shite kara gaikoku ni ijū-suru hito mo iru yō da.**
定年退職してから外国に移住する人もいるようだ。

Hi⌈ku⌉i 低い *low*

Hikui 低い "low" is the opposite of **takai** 高い meaning "high" (not **takai** meaning "expensive").

EXAMPLE:

(1) **hikui yama (tana, kumo**, etc.)
低い山(棚、雲 etc.)
low mountain (shelf, cloud, etc.)

Hikui 低い corresponds to English "short" when a person's height is the issue.

EXAMPLE:

(2) **se ga hikui hito**
背が低い人
short person (lit., person whose height is low)

In this case, however, **hikui** 低い has to be preceded by **se ga** 背が and cannot by itself mean "short."

The opposite of **takai** 高い meaning "expensive" is not **hikui** 低い but **yasui** 安い "cheap, inexpensive" (see YASUI). However, **hikui** as well as **yasui** 安い may be used in connection with nouns such as **nedan** 値段 "price," **bukka** 物価 "commodity prices," and **chingin** 賃金 "wage."

EXAMPLE:

(3) **hikui** (or **yasui**) **nedan (bukka, chingin**, etc.)
低い(安い)値段(物価、賃金 etc.)
low (or cheap) price (commodity prices, wage, etc.)

Hi⌈ro⌉i 広い *wide, broad, spacious*

Hiroi 広い can be either one-dimensional as in (1) or two dimensional as in (2).

EXAMPLES:

(1) **hiroi michi (katahaba, rōka**, etc.)
広い道(肩幅、廊下 etc.)
wide road (shoulders, corridor, etc.)
(2) **hiroi heya (niwa, kuni**, etc.)
広い部屋(庭、国 etc.)
spacious room (yard, country, etc.)

When used two-dimensionally, **hiroi** 広い is similar in meaning to **ōkii** 大きい "large." But while **ōkii** 大きい refers objectively to large size, **hiroi** implies subjective awareness of spaciousness for a particular purpose. As Morita states (p. 260), even an **ōkii torikago** 大きい鳥かご "large birdcage" isn't **hiroi** "spacious" if an ostrich is placed in it. (See also SEMAI, the opposite of **hiroi**.)

Hi⌈ru⌉ 昼 *noon, daytime*

Hiru 昼 has two basic meanings: "noon" and "daytime." In the following examples **hiru** 昼 means "noon" in (1) and "daytime" in (2).

EXAMPLES:

(1) **Doyō wa hiru made kurasu ga aru.**
土曜は昼までクラスがある。
On Saturdays, there are classes until noon.

(2) **Hiru wa atsui ga, yoru wa suzushiku naru.**
昼は暑いが、夜は涼しくなる。
In the daytime it is hot, but at night it gets cooler.

Hiru 昼 is sometimes used as an abbreviation of **hiru-gohan** 昼ご飯 "lunch" (lit., "noon meal"), as in

EXAMPLE:

(3) **Mō hiru(-gohan) wa tabemashita ka.**
Have you had lunch yet?

For some strange reason, the honorific prefix **o-** may precede **hiru** 昼 in the sense of "noon" but not **hiru** 昼 meaning "daytime." **Ohiru** お昼 therefore can mean only "noon," but not "daytime." **Hiru** in the sense of "daytime" may be construed to be an abbreviation of **hiruma** 昼間 "daytime," which never takes the prefix **o-** either. **Hiruma**, unlike **hiru**, can never mean "noon."

Hi⌉ssha 筆者 *the writer of a particular piece of writing*

A **hissha** 筆者 is the writer of a particular piece of writing such as an essay or an article, especially one that expresses his/her opinion. It could be any length and is usually non-fiction. It could even be a letter to the editor of a newspaper, magazine, etc., as in

EXAMPLE:

Nihon no shinbun no tōsho ni wa, kanarazu hissha no nenrei ga kaite aru.
日本の新聞の投書には、かならず筆者の年齢が書いてある。
In Japanese newspapers, a letter to the editor always includes the writer's age.

Compare this word with **chosha** 著者, which has to be the author of a particular, usually non-fiction, book, **sakusha** 作者, which means "the writer of a particular piece of fiction," and **sakka** 作家, which refers to a professional fiction writer. (See also CHOSHA, SAKKA and SAKUSHA.)

Hito 人 *person*

Hito 人 means "person."

EXAMPLE:

(1) **Kimura-san wa ii hito desu ne.**
木村さんはいい人ですね。
Mr. Kimura is a nice person, isn't he!

In very polite speech, use **kata** 方 instead of **hito** 人 when talking about someone to whom you wish to show respect.

EXAMPLE:

(2) **Ano kata** (not *__hito__ 人) **wa otaku no goshujin deshō ka.**
あの方はおたくのご主人でしょうか。
Might that person be your husband?

Do not use **hito** to refer to yourself. Example (3) is wrong.

EXAMPLE:

(3) *__Miura to iu hito desu.__ (man introducing himself)
*三浦という人です。
lit., I'm a person called Miura.

In such a case, either use **mono** 者, the humble equivalent of **hito** 人, as in (4), or try a different construction, as in (5) or (6).

EXAMPLES:

(4) **Miura to iu mono desu.**
三浦という者です。
lit., I'm a person called Miura.

(5) **Miura desu.**
三浦です。
I'm Miura.

(6) **Miura to iimasu** (or **mōshimasu**).
三浦といいます（申します）。
My name is Miura. (lit., I'm called Miura.)

Hō¹ ga ii 方がいい *one should do such and such*

Although **hō ga ii** 方がいい is often equated with English "had better," its tone is not as strong. It should probably be translated as "should."

EXAMPLE:

(1) **Nihongo ga jōzu ni naritakattara, narubeku hayaku hajimeta hō ga ii.**
日本語が上手になりたかったら、なるべく早く始めた方がいい。
If you want to become good at Japanese, you should start studying it as soon as possible.

Basically, **hō ga ii** 方がいい is used when you are comparing two alternatives, one of which you are recommending. In sentence (1) above, the speaker is comparing the option of starting early with the other option of not starting early. Thus, **hō** 方 fits in well. The following sentence, however, sounds strange.

EXAMPLE:

(2) *__Gaikogugo o naraitai nara, Nihongo o naratta hō ga ichiban ii.__
*外国語を習いたいなら、日本語を習った方が一番いい。
lit., If you want to study a foreign language, the alternative of studying Japanese will be the best.

In sentence (2), the word **ichiban** "best, most" implies that there are more than two options. In such a case, use **no ga ii** のがいい instead, as in

EXAMPLE:

(3) **Gaikokugo o naraitai nara, Nihongo o narau no ga ichiban ii.**

外国語を習いたいなら、日本語を習うのが一番いい。

If you want to study a foreign language, studying Japanese will be the best.

Hontō ni 本当に *really, truly*

Hontō ni 本当に (lit., "in truth") has three basic uses. First of all, it indicates that something actually happens.

EXAMPLE:

(1) **Sonna koto ga hontō ni aru darō ka.**

そんな事が本当にあるだろうか。

Do you think such a thing is actually possible?

Second, it is used as an intensifier indicating a high degree of some quality.

EXAMPLE:

(2) **Yoshida-san wa hontō ni shinsetsu da.**

吉田さんは本当に親切だ。

Mr. Yoshida is really kind.

In this sense, **hontō ni** 本当に is similar in meaning to **totemo** とても "very" or **taihen** たいへん "very."

Third, it indicates the speaker's genuine sentiment.

EXAMPLE:

(3) **Hontō ni arigatō gozaimashita.**

本当にありがとうございました。

Thank you very much for what you did for me.

Although **jitsu ni** じつに also means "in truth" or "really," it can be used only in the second sense above (Tokugawa and Miyajima, p. 364). In other words, although **jitsu ni** can replace **hontō ni** 本当に in sentence (2), it cannot in sentence (1) or (3). **Hontō ni** is also more conversational in tone than **jitsu ni**, which is mainly used in writing.

In informal speech, **hontō ni** 本当に is very often shortened to **honto ni** ほんとに.

Hontō wa 本当は *actually*

Hontō wa 本当は is different from **hontō ni** 本当に. **Hontō ni** is used like "really," whereas **hontō wa** is used like "actually," "the fact is," or "to tell you the truth."

EXAMPLES:

(1) **Tōkyō no rasshuawā no komikata wa hontō ni sugoi.**

東京のラッシュアワーの込み方は本当にすごい。

The rush hour crowds in Tokyo are really something else.

(2) **Tōkyō no jinkō wa kyūhyakuman nante kaite aru kedo, hontō wa issenman ijō no hazu da.**

東京の人口は九百万なんて書いてあるけど、本当は一千万以上のはずだ。

It says here that the population of Tokyo is nine million, but actually it should be over ten million.

Hʳoshiʹi 欲しい *to want (something)*

Hoshii 欲しい is an adjective used with nouns and the particle **ga** が.

EXAMPLES:

(1) **Okane ga hoshii.**
お金が欲しい。
I want (or wish I had) money.

(2) **Atarashii kamera ga hoshii n desu ga, okane ga nakute kaemasen.**
新しいカメラが欲しいんですが、お金がなくて買えません。
I'd like a new camera, but I don't have enough money to buy one.

With **hoshii** 欲しい, the subject is generally first person, as in (1) and (2) above. In questions, however, the subject is usually second person.

EXAMPLE:

(3) **Kore hoshii?**
これ欲しい?
Do you want this?

With a third-person subject, **hoshigaru** 欲がる "to want (something)" is used instead. **Hoshigaru** is a verb that takes the particle **o**.

EXAMPLE:

(4) **Uchi no musuko wa atarashii sukī o hoshigatte-iru.**
うちの息子は新しいスキーを欲しがっている。
Our son wants new skis.

Hoshigaru 欲しがる implies that the person who wants something expresses that desire verbally or otherwise.

Hoshii 欲しい should not be used in polite requests. For example, if you happen to be visiting someone's house and would like to drink some water, don't say

EXAMPLE:

(5) **Mizu ga hoshii n desu ga.**
水が欲しいんですが。
I want some water.

Say one of the following:

EXAMPLES:

(6a) **Omizu o itadaki-tai n desu ga.**
お水をいただきたいんですが。
I'd like some water.

(6b) **Omizu o itadakemasen ka.**
お水をいただけませんか。
Could I (lit., Couldn't I) have some water?

(6c) **Omizu o onegai-shimasu.**
お水をお願いします。
May I have some water? (lit., I humbly request some water.)

Hoshii 欲しい should not be used to ask someone of higher status whether he would like something. It is not a polite enough expression. If you want to ask someone higher in status than you whether he would like, for example, some coffee, you shouldn't say

EXAMPLE:

(7) **Kōhī ga hoshii desu ka.**
コーヒーが欲しいですか。

The following question would be much more polite.

EXAMPLE:

(8) **Kōhī de mo ikaga desu ka.**
コーヒーでもいかがですか。
Would you like some coffee? (lit., How about coffee or something?)

Unlike English "want," **hoshii** 欲しい is not used with the dictionary form of a verb.

EXAMPLE:

(9) ***Kore o kau koto ga hoshii.**
*これを買うことが欲しい。
I want to buy this.

With verbs, **-tai** たい is used instead of **hoshii** 欲しい.

EXAMPLE:

(10) **Kore ga kai-tai.**
これが買いたい。
I want to buy this.

However, **hoshii** 欲しい may be used with the **-te** form of a verb if the doer of the action expressed by the verb is not the speaker.

EXAMPLE:

(11) **Kore o katte hoshii.**
これを買って欲しい。
I want you to buy this.

When used this way, **hoshii** 欲しい is synonymous with **morai-tai** もらいたい, as in

EXAMPLE:

(12) **Kore o katte-morai-tai.**
これを買ってもらいたい。
I want you to buy this.

Neither (11) or (12), however, is a polite enough sentence if you are talking to someone higher in status than you. In that case, say "**Kore o katte-itadaki-tai n desu ga**" これを買っていただきたいんですが "I'd like you to buy this."

Hotto-suru ほっとする *to feel relieved*

Hotto-suru ほっとする is not exactly the same as **anshin-suru** 安心する, its synonym. **Hotto-suru** describes a brief mental response, as in

EXAMPLE:

(1) **Kodomo no netsu ga hiite hotto-shita.**
子供の熱が引いてほっとした。
I was relieved to see my child's fever go down.

Anshin-suru 安心する, on the other hand, may be used in reference to either a brief or a long-lasting state. For example, in (2) below, only **anshin-suru** would be appropriate.

EXAMPLE:

(2) **Ima kenkō da to itte, anshin** (not ***hotto** ほっと) **bakari-shite wa irarenai.**
いま健康だと言って、安心ばかりしてはいけない。
Although I am healthy now, that does not mean I can remain relaxed forever.

I⌈chi⌉ 一 *one*

Ichi 一 meaning "one" can stand alone only when used in mathematics. For example,

EXAMPLE:

(1) **Ichi wa ni no hanbun da.**
一は二の半分だ。
One is one half of two.

Ichi 一 cannot stand alone in other cases, such as

EXAMPLE:

(2) *****Nihon to iu kuni wa ichi shika nai.**
*日本という国は一しかない。
There is only one country called Japan.

To express this idea, one must say **hitotsu** 一つ instead, as in

EXAMPLE:

(3) **Ninon to iu kuni wa hitotsu shika nai.**
日本という国は一つしかない。

Even **hitotsu** 一つ is not used very often since all sorts of "counters" must be used with numerals, depending on the noun referred to. Some of these are introduced at the beginning level, e.g.

EXAMPLES:

(4a) **Koko ni enpitsu ga ip-pon (ni-hon, san-bon, etc.) arimasu.**
ここに鉛筆が一本（二本、三本…）あります。
There is/are one, two, three ... pencil(s) here.

(4b) **Zasshi o is-satsu (ni-satsu, san-satsu, etc.) kaimashita.**
雑誌を一冊（二冊、三冊…）買いました。
I bought one, two, three ... magazine(s).

What is often not emphasized is the fact that the accompanying particle, e.g., **ga** が, **o** を, etc., does not follow the numeral plus counter; rather it precedes them. The following sentences, therefore, sound very strange. They almost sound like the direct translations of the English equivalents.

EXAMPLES:

(5a) *****Koko ni enpitsu san-bon ga arimasu.**
*ここに鉛筆三本があります。

(5b) *****Zasshi ni-satsu o kaimashita.**
*雑誌二冊を買いました。

Ichiban 一番 *the most*

Ichiban 一番, meaning "the most" or "the –est," is accentless.

EXAMPLES:

(1) **Ichiban ōkii kuni wa Roshia desu.**
一番大きい国はロシアです。
The largest country is Russia.

(2) **Watashi no uchi de wa otōto ga ichiban hayaku nemasu.**
私のうちでは弟が一番早く寝ます。
In my family, my younger brother goes to bed the earliest.

This should be differentiated from ⌈ichi⌉-ban 一番, meaning "No. 1," which is accented.

EXAMPLE:

(3) **Boku no kurasu de wa Ueda ga itsumo ichi-ban da.**
僕のクラスでは上田がいつも一番だ。
In my class, Ueda is always the best student.

Ichininmae 一人前 *one serving; self-supporting, full-fledged*

Ichininmae 一人前 has two meanings. First, it means "one serving" (of food), as in

EXAMPLE:

(1) **Wakai dansei wa sushi ichininmae de wa tarinai darō.**
若い男性は寿司一人前では足りないだろう。
Young men probably need more than one serving of sushi.

Although 一人 usually reads **hitori**, in this case **ichinin** is the only possible reading, i.e., "**hitorimae**" is nonexistent. Servings for two, three, four, etc., are **nininmae** 二人前, **sanninmae** 三人前, **yoninmae** 四人前, etc.

Ichininmae 一人前 also means "full-fledged" or "self-supporting," as in

EXAMPLE:

(2) **Daigaku o sotsugyō-shite mo shūshoku-shinakereba, ichininmae ni natta to wa ie-nai.**
大学を卒業しても就職しなければ、一人前になったとは言えない。
Even if you graduate from college, you are not a full-fledged adult until you are employed.

This latter kind of **ichininmae** 一人前 is a fixed expression, i.e., **ichi** 一 and **ninmae** 人前 are inseparable. Even in reference to more than one person, the same word must be used.

EXAMPLE:

(3) **Tarō mo Hanako mo kodomo no kuse ni kuchi dake wa ichininmae da.**
太郎も花子も子供のくせに、口だけは一人前だ。
Although Taro and Hanako are still only kids, when they talk, they sound like grown-ups.

I⌐e⌐ 家 *house, home*

Ie 家 is very much like **uchi** うち(内/家) "home, house" in meaning, but there are some differences in usage. According to Matsuo et al. (p. 36), **ie** is more appropriate when one is discussing the home as an abstract concept or as the basic unit within the traditional family system. **Ie** is also preferred in legal references to a house as property.

According to Tokugawa and Miyajima (p. 35), there is a geographical difference between the words **ie** and **uchi**. Generally speaking, **uchi** is more common in the Kanto region (where Tokyo is located) and the Chubu region (where Nagoya is located); in the remaining regions, **ie** is the preferred form.

I⌐i いい *good*

Ii いい normally means "good, excellent," as in

EXAMPLES:
(1) **Ano eiga wa ii desu nē.**
   あの映画はいいですねえ。
   That's a good movie, isn't it?
(2) **Mori-san wa ii hito da.**
   森さんはいい人だ。
   Ms. Mori is a nice person.

What is confusing is that **ii** いい may sometimes mean "No, thank you" or "You don't have to," when used in the expression **Ii desuyo** いいですよ. Suppose you ask someone **Shimashō ka** しましょうか, meaning "Shall I do it [for you]?" If he answers **Ii desu yo** いいですよ, the sentence must mean "You don't have to" or "No, thank you." **Ii desu yo** いいですよ in this sense is always pronounced with a falling intonation and is thereby distinguishable from **Ii desu yo** いいですよ meaning "It's good, you know," which is usually pronounced with a rising intonation.

EXAMPLE:
(3) A: **Ano eiga wa dō desu ka.**
   あの映画はどうですか。
   How is that movie?
   B: **Ii desu yo.**
   いいですよ。
   (rising) It's good.

I⌐ie⌐ いいえ *no*

Iie いいえ is most often used in response to a question to signal contradiction. In response to affirmative questions, therefore, **iie** corresponds to English "no," as in (1) below, but in response to negative questions it corresponds to "yes," as in example (2).

EXAMPLES:
(1) A: **Wakarimasu ka.** (affirmative question)
   分かりますか。
   Do you understand?

B: **Iie, wakarimasen.**
いいえ、分かりません。
No, I don't.

(2) A: **Wakarimasen ka** (negative question)
分かりませんか。
Don't you understand?

B: **Iie, wakarimasu.**
いいえ、分かります。
Yes, I do. (lit., That's wrong. I understand.)

English speakers, if they equate **iie** with English "no," will have difficulty when **iie** corresponds to "yes." There are two possible solutions to this problem. First, stop equating **iie** with "no"; instead take **iie** to mean "That's wrong." Second (if the first method doesn't work), drop **iie** and just say the rest. For example, in the case of (2) above, **Wakarimasu** 分かります "I understand" alone would suffice as B's answer.

Iie is a formal word and is rarely used in informal speech (except sometimes by women). **Iya** いや, a less formal variant used by men, may occur in informal, as well as formal, speech. **Uun** ううん, another variant, is very informal and occurs only between relatives or very close friends.

As shown in example (2) above, **iie** used as a response to a negative question usually corresponds to "yes." There are some cases, however, where **iie** used as a response to a negative question corresponds to English "no."

EXAMPLE:

(3) A: **Genki-sō ni natta ja arimasen ka.**
元気そうになったじゃありませんか。
You're looking much better, aren't you!

B: **Iie, mada dame na n desu.**
いいえ、まだだめなんです。
No, I'm not well yet.

The above question, though negative in form, is actually affirmative in spirit. What the question really means is "You're looking much better, and that's great!" Speaker B therefore says **iie** いいえ to show disagreement.

Iie いいえ may also be used as a response to a compliment, an apology, or an expression of appreciation.

EXAMPLES:

(4) A: **Zuibun rippa na otaku desu nē.** (compliment)
ずいぶん立派なお宅ですねえ。
What a nice house you have!

B: **Iie [, tonde mo arimasen].**
いいえ［、とんでもありません］。
lit., No, not at all.

(5) A: **Shitsurei-shimashita.** (apology)
失礼しました。
Sorry [for what I've done].

B: **Iie.**
いいえ。
Never mind.

(6) A: **Senjitsuwa dōmo arigatō gozaimashita.** (appreciation)
先日はどうもありがとうございました。
Thank you for what you did for me the other day.

B: **Iie [, dō itashimashite].**
いいえ［、どういたしまして］。
Not at all.

There are many situations where "no" might be used in English but **iie** いいえ cannot be in Japanese. The following are some of these cases.

(1) **Iie** いいえ may not be used to signal prohibition. For example, if you notice that your little child is about to touch something dangerous, don't yell **Iie!** いいえ! to stop him. Say **Dame!** だめ! "You mustn't!" instead.

(2) At a meeting, if you want to express verbally your disagreement with a speech being made, don't yell out **Iie!** but say **Hantai!** 反対! "I disagree!" instead.

(3) Don't use **Iie** to express surprise. In English, upon hearing bad or incredible news, you may react by saying "No!" or "Oh, no!" In Japanese, say **Hontō desu ka** 本当ですか? "Is that true?" or, on more informal occasions, **E?** え? "What did you say?" If you discover something really alarming (for example, if you suddenly realize that your wallet is gone), don't use **Iie!** Say **Taihen da!** 大変だ! "Good heavens!" instead.

(4) When playing tennis and your opponent's shot goes too long or too wide, don't say **Iie!** Say **Auto!** アウト! "Out!"

I'jō 以上 *more than*

Ijō 以上 means "more than" and usually follows a noun that includes a number, as in sentence (1), but may sometimes be attached to a non-number, as in sentence (2).

EXAMPLES:

(1) **Watashi no shōgakkō de wa, hito-kurasu ni nanajūnin ijō mo seito ga ita.**
私の小学校では、1クラスに70人以上も生徒がいた。
At my elementary school, there were more than seventy students per class.

(2) **Sore ijō no koto wa ienai.**
それ以上のことは言えない。
I cannot say more than that.

The following sentence seems to be used increasingly often these days, especially at the end of an oral report.

EXAMPLE:

(3) **Ijō desu.**
以上です。
That's all.

I「ka」ga desu ka いかがですか *How are you? How about such-and-such?*

This is the Japanese question that comes closest to "How are you?" in meaning and is therefore used very often by Americans in Japan. But the fact is that Japanese speakers rarely use it in that sense. Although they ask this question when they visit a sick person or when they see someone who they know has been ill, they don't say it to someone they see all the time whom they assume to be well.

Ikaga desu ka いかがですか, in fact, is probably used more often to mean "How about such-and-such?" For example, in situations where an American would say "Would you like some ice cream?" to a visitor, a Japanese would either ask **Aisu-kurīmu de mo ikaga desu ka** アイスクリームでもいかがですか "How about ice cream or something?" or bring in some ice cream without asking any question at all. (See also OGENKI DESU KA.)

I⌐ken 意見 *opinion*

In English, the expression "in my opinion" is used quite commonly, but the direct translation of this in Japanese, **watashi no iken de wa** 私の意見では, sounds quite stilted.

EXAMPLE:
(1) **?Watashi no iken de wa, Nihonjin wa hito no iu koto o ki ni shisugiru.**
?私の意見では、日本人は人の言うことを気にしすぎる。
In my opinion, the Japanese worry too much about what others say about them.

Try other ways of expressing the above, for example,

EXAMPLES:
(2a) **Nihonjin wa hito no iu koto o ki ni shisugiru to omou.**
日本人は人の言うことを気にしすぎると思う。
I think the Japanese worry too much about what others say about them.
(2b) **Nihonjin wa hito no iu koto o ki ni shisugiru n ja nai darō ka.**
日本人は人の言うことを気にしすぎるんじゃないだろうか。
The Japanese worry too much about what others say about them, don't they?

I⌐ki⌐ru 生きる *to live*

The English verb "to live" means (a) "to be alive," (b) "to reside," and (c) "to make a living; to lead a life." In Japanese, however, each of these requires a different verb, i.e., **ikiru** 生きる, **sumu** 住む, and **kurasu** 暮らす, respectively.

EXAMPLES:
(1) **Hyaku made ikiraretara sugoi.**
百まで生きられたらすごい。
It is fantastic to be able to live to be one hundred.
(2) **Ichido Furanku Roido Raito no sekkai-shita ie ni sunde mitai.**
一度フランク・ロイド・ライトの設計した家に住んでみたい。
I wish I could live in a Frank Lloyd Wright–designed house once.
(3) **Konogoro isogashiku kurashite-iru.**
このごろ忙しく暮らしている。
I am living a busy life these days.

Iku 行く *to go*

Iku 行く refers to movement away from where the speaker is at the moment of speech. If you are at home while talking about attending school every day, you use **iku** 行く, as in (1); if you are at school while talking about the same activity, you must use **kuru** 来る instead, as in (2) below (see KURU).

EXAMPLES:
(1) **Mainichi gakkō e ikimasu.** (speaker not at school)
   毎日学校へ行きます。
   I go to school every day.
(2) **Mainichi gakkō e kimasu.** (speaker at school)
   毎日学校へ来ます。
   I come to school every day.

The speaker's movement toward the addressee also requires **iku** 行く, although in English the verb "come" would be used in that case.

EXAMPLE:
(3) A: **Hayaku kite kudasai.**
      早く来て下さい。
      Please come right away.
   B: **Ima ikimasu** (not *kimasu 来ます) **yo.**
      いま行きますよ。
      I'm coming! (lit., I'm going!)

Like other verbs of motion, **iku** 行く takes the particle **o** when the preceding noun indicates the place along which the motion takes place.

EXAMPLE:
(4) **Kono michi o ikimashō.**
   この道を行きましょう。
   Let's take this road (lit., Let's go along this road.)

I˥ma いま, 今 *now*

The most common way of asking the time is

EXAMPLE:
(1) **Ima nan-ji desu ka.**
   いま何時ですか。
   What time is it now?

Whereas, in English, "now" is usually left out, in Japanese, **ima** いま is more often used than not.

The prenoun use of "now" meaning "trendy" has lately been introduced into Japanese as **nau na**, and most recently **nau-i (!)**.

EXAMPLE:
(2) **nau na fasshon**
   ナウなファッション
   the now fashion

The expression **nau na** seems to carry a new up-to-date quality that **ima** does not possess.

I⌈mōto⌉ 妹 *younger sister*

The use of **imōto** 妹 "younger sister" parallels that of **otōto** "younger brother" (see OTŌTO). In other words, what can be said about **otōto** 弟 on the male side can also be said about **imōto** on the female side. The female counterpart of **otōto-san** 弟さん is, predictably, **imōto-san** 妹さん.

I⌈nochi⌉ 命 *life*

In English, "life" means, among other things, (a) "that which resides within a living thing and keeps it alive," (b) "the state of living," and (3) "a time span from birth to death." In Japanese, (a) is **inochi** 命, (b) is **seikatsu** 生活, and (c) is **isshō** 一生.

EXAMPLES:
(1) **Inochi dake wa tasukete kudasai.**
命だけは助けてください。
Please spare my life.
(2) **Nihon no daigakusei no seikatsu wa Amerika no daigakusei no seikatsu to kuraberu to nonbiri shite-iru.**
日本の大学生の生活はアメリカの大学生の生活とくらべるとのんびりしている。
The life of a college student in Japan is more relaxed than that of a college student in America.
(3) **Isshō o Tōkyō de sugosu hito wa mezurashiku nai.**
一生を東京で過ごす人は珍しくない。
People who spend their entire lives in Tokyo are not rarities.

(See also SEIKATSU.)

I⌈ppai⌉ 一杯 *one cup;* Ippai いっぱい *a lot*

Ippai has different meanings, depending on the accent. When it is pronounced **ippai** 一杯, with an accent on the first syllable, it means "one cup/glass," as in

EXAMPLE:
(1) **"Geko" to iu no wa bīru ippai de mo yopparatte shimau hito no koto da.**
「下戸」というのはビール一杯でも酔っぱらってしまう人のことだ。
"Geko" refers to someone who gets drunk with only one glass of beer.

On the other hand, when **ippai** いっぱい is accentless, it means "a lot" or "full."

EXAMPLES:
(2) **Kyō wa dōzo bīru o ippai nonde kudasai.**
今日はどうぞビールをいっぱい飲んでください。
Please drink a lot of beer today.
(3) **Itsuka sushi o onaka ippai tabete mitai nā!**
いつか寿司をおなかいっぱい食べてみたいなあ！
I hope I can eat my fill of sushi someday!

Ippai in the sense of "one cup/glass" may be written in kanji, i.e., 一杯, but **ippai** in the sense of "a lot" or "one's fill," is almost always in hiragana.

I⌈ppō⌉ [I⌈ppo⌉o] de wa 一方では *on the one hand; on the other hand*

Ippō de wa 一方では is a tricky phrase in that it changes its meaning, depending on whether it is used alone or with **tahō de wa** 他方では "on the other hand." Observe the following examples.

EXAMPLES:

(1) **Nihon de wa kankyōshugisha ga fuete kite-iru. Shikashi ippō de wa shigen no muda-zukai mo aikawarazu medatsu.**
日本では環境主義者が増えてきている。しかし一方では資源の無駄使いも相変わらず目立つ。
In Japan, the number of environmentalists is increasing; on the other hand, however, the wasting of natural resources is as conspicuous as ever.

(2) **Nihon de wa, ippō de wa kankyōshugisha ga fuete kite-iru ga, tahō de wa shigen no mudazukai mo aikawarazu medatsu.**
日本では、一方で環境主義者が増えてきているが、他方では資源の無駄使いも相変わらず目立つ。
In Japan, on the one hand, the number of environmentalists is increasing; on the other hand, however, the wasting of natural resources is as conspicuous as ever.

Ippō de wa 一方では used in the sense of "on the other hand," as in sentence (1) above, may be preceded by **sono** その, i.e., one can say **sono ippō de wa shigen no mudazukai mo** その一方では資源の無駄遣いも···. When **ippō de wa** is used in the sense of "on the one hand," as in sentence (2), however, it can never be preceded by **sono** その. Also, whereas **ippō de wa**, meaning "on the other hand," may be used in speech, the pair **ippō dewa. . . tahō de wa** 一方では···他方では is bookish and does not appear in spoken language.

Irasshai いらっしゃい *Welcome [to our place]!*

Irasshai いらっしゃい (or its more formal version, **Irasshaimase** いらっしゃいませ) is a greeting for welcoming a customer to one's establishment (e.g., a store, restaurant, inn, etc.) or for welcoming a guest to one's home. As you walk into a department store in Japan and reach the foot of the elevator on the main floor, you are destined to be greeted by the **erebētā-gāru** (lit., "elevator girl") with a polite **Irasshaimase** and a bow.

Iroiro いろいろ *various*

Iroiro いろいろ and **samazama** 様々 are often synonymous, as in

EXAMPLE:

(1) **Sushi to itte mo, jitsu wa iroiro na/samazama na shurui ga aru.**
寿司といっても、実はいろいろな/様々な種類がある。
The name sushi actually covers all kinds.

Iroiro いろいろ and **samazama** 様々, however, are not quite the same. For one thing, **iroiro** いろいろ is a very common word that can be used by anyone in all kinds of situations whereas **samazama** 様々 sounds more bookish and is very unlikely to be used by children. For another, **iroiro** いろいろ often connotes "a lot," as in

EXAMPLE:

(2) **Iroiro na hito ni kiite mita keredo, wakaranakatta.**

いろいろな人に聞いてみたけれど、分からなかった。

I asked lots of people (lit., all kinds of people), but nobody knew.

In situations such as (2), **samazama** 様々 would be out of place.

Also, **iroiro** いろいろ by itself (i.e., without **na** な or **ni** に) is often used adverbially, but **samazama** 様々 is not.

EXAMPLE:

(3) **Iroiro** (not *samazama 様々) **tasukete itadaite arigatō gozaimashita.**

いろいろ助けていただいてありがとうございました。

Thank you for helping me in all kinds of ways.

Iru いる, 居る *to be, to exist*

Iru いる, 居る meaning "[someone] exists" takes an animate being (excluding plants) as its subject.

EXAMPLES:

(1) **Tanaka-san ga asoko ni imasu.**

田中さんがあそこにいます。

Mr. Tanaka is over there.

(2) **Akai tori ga ano ki no eda ni iru.**

赤い鳥があの木の枝にいる。

There is a red bird on that branch.

Iru いる, 居る contrasts with **aru** ある "[something] exists," in that the latter takes an inanimate subject (see ARU).

The only exception to the rule is when the subject is a vehicle (e.g., **kuruma** 車 "car" and **takushī** タクシー "taxi") with a driver inside. **Iru** is used then instead of **aru**.

EXAMPLE:

(3) **Asoko ni takushī ga iru kara, notte ikimashō.**

あそこにタクシーがいるから、乗って行きましょう。

There's a taxi over there. Let's catch it.

Iru いる, 要る *to need*

Iru いる, 要る meaning "to need" takes the particle **ga** が.

EXAMPLE:

(1) **Motto kami ga iru n desu ga.**

もっと紙がいるんですが。

I need more paper. (In some contexts, "I'd like some more paper" might be a better translation.)

Iru いる, 要る, though similar in meaning to the English transitive verb "need," does not take **o**. The following sentence is therefore ungrammatical.

EXAMPLE:

(2) ****Motto kami o iru n desu ga.**
　*もっと紙をいるんですが。

For some reason, **iru** いる, 要る is rarely used in the past tense.

EXAMPLE:

(3) **?Okane ga ichiman-en irimashita.**
　?お金が一万円いりました。
　I needed 10,000 yen.

Most speakers would express this idea otherwise, as in the following:

EXAMPLE:

(4) **Okane ga ichiman-en hitsuyō deshita** (or **hitsuyō ni narimashita**).
　お金が一万円必要でした (必要になりました)。
　I needed 10,000 yen.

I「sogashi」i 忙しい *busy*

As a rule, only persons, not things, can be **isogashii**.

EXAMPLES:

(1) **Konogoro isogashikute komatte-iru.**
　このごろ忙しくて困っている。
　I'm so busy these days, it's awful.
(2) **Sumisu-san wa mainichi isogashi-sō desu.**
　スミスさんは毎日忙しそうです。
　Mr. Smith looks busy every day.

The following are therefore wrong.

EXAMPLES:

(3) ***Denwa ga isogashii desu.**
　*電話が忙しいです。
　The line is busy.
(4) ***isogashii tōri**
　*忙しい通り
　a busy street

Instead of (3) and (4), one would have to use (5) and (6), respectively.

EXAMPLES:

(5) **Ohanashi-chū desu.**
　お話中です。
　The line is busy. (lit., [My party] is talking.)
(6) **nigiyaka na tōri**
　賑やかな通り
　a busy (lit., lively) street

Issho 一緒 *together*

Issho 一緒, a noun, is most often used adverbially with a following **ni** に.

EXAMPLE:

(1) **Issho ni utaimashō.**
一緒に歌いましょう。
Let's sing together.

When the person together with whom someone does something is mentioned, the particle **to** と is required, as in the following example:

EXAMPLE:

(2) **Kyō wa Suzuki-san to issho ni shokuji o shimashita.**
今日は鈴木さんと一緒に食事をしました。
Today I ate [together] with Mr. Suzuki.

Thus (3) and (4) have different meanings.

EXAMPLES:

(3) **Minna issho ni utaimashita.**
みんな一緒に歌いました。
Everybody sang together.
(4) **Minna to issho ni utaimashita.**
みんなと一緒に歌いました。
I sang [together] with everybody.

Since **issho** 一緒 is a noun, if it is used adjectivally as a prenoun modifier, **no** の (not *na な) must be inserted.

EXAMPLE:

(5) **Kobayashi-san to issho no hito wa dare deshō.**
小林さんと一緒の人は誰でしょう。
I wonder who that person is who is with Miss Kobayashi.

To issho ni と一緒に is sometimes used in place of **to** alone, with **issho ni** 一緒に adding the meaning of "together." Thus sentence (6) refers to the same event with or without the word **issho ni**.

EXAMPLE:

(6) **Tomodachi to (issho ni) shukudai o shita.**
友達と(一緒に)宿題をした。
I did homework (together) with a friend.

There are some verbs that regularly take **to** と, such as **kekkon-suru** 結婚する ("to marry"), **dēto-suru** デートする ("to date"), and **tatakau** 戦う ("to fight"). With these verbs, **to** と used by itself and **to issho ni** would represent different meanings. For example,

EXAMPLES:

(7a) **Tarō wa Hanako to kekkon-shita.**
太郎は花子と結婚した。
Taro married Hanako.

(7b) **Tarō wa Hanako to issho ni kekkon-shita.**
太郎は花子と一緒に結婚した。
Taro got married together with Hanako (i.e., they had a joint wedding).

(8a) **Tarō wa Hanako to dēto-shita.**
太郎は花子とデートした。
Taro dated Hanako.

(8b) **Tarō wa Hanako to issho ni dēto-shita.**
太郎は花子と一緒にデートした。
Taro dated together with Hanako (i.e., Taro dated someone, Hanako dated someone else, and they all went out together).

(9a) **Dainijitaisen de Nihon wa Amerika to tatakatta.**
第二次大戦で日本はアメリカと戦った。
In World War II, Japan fought America (i.e., Japan was Amerca's enemy).

(9b) **Dainijitaisen de Eikoku wa Amerika to issho ni tatakatta.**
第二次大戦で英国はアメリカと一緒に戦った。
In World War II, Great Britain fought together with America (i.e., Great Britain was America's ally).

To issho ni と一緒に is used when the two nouns that are juxtaposed with each other are compatible. That is not the case with sentence (10).

EXAMPLE:

(10) ***Dorobō wa okane to issho ni nigeta.**
*泥棒はお金と一緒に逃げた。
The thief ran away with money.

The sentence above is wrong because **dorobō** 泥棒 "thief," which is juxtaposed with **okane** お金, is an animate noun and is therefore incompatible with **okane** お金, which is inanimate. To make this sentence correct, one would have to say

EXAMPLE:

(11) **Dorobō wa okane o motte nigeta.**
泥棒はお金を持って逃げた。

The following sentence, however, is correct because **okane** is juxtaposed with **hōseki** "jewels," not with **dorobō**.

EXAMPLE:

(12) **Dorobō wa okane to issho ni hōseki mo motte nigeta.**
泥棒はお金と一緒に宝石も持って逃げた。
The thief ran away with money and also jewels.

American students sometimes compose a sentence like the following:

EXAMPLE:

(13) ***Kongakki wa Buraun-sensei to issho ni kojinkenkyū o shite-imasu.**
*今学期はブラウン先生と一緒に個人研究をしています。
This semester I'm doing independent study with Professor Brown.

In example (13), the English sentence is of course correct, but the Japanese is not quite appropriate because **to issho ni** sounds as though the student and the professor were studying together at the same level, which is not really the case. In Japanese, it would be better to phrase it as follows:

EXAMPLE:
(14) **Kongakki wa Buraun-sensei ni kojinkenkyū no shidō o shite itadaite-imasu.**
今学期はブラウン先生に個人研究の指導をしていただいています。
This semester I'm doing independent study under the guidance of Professor Brown.

I⌐tadakima⌐su いただきます *I humbly accept*

Itadakimasu いただきます (lit., "I humbly accept") is a greeting regularly used at the beginning of a meal. It is an expression of gratitude for the food one is about to eat. To start a meal without this salutation is bad manners at home and unforgivable when visiting someone else's house.

Although at one's own home **Itadakimasu** is only used to start a meal, it may be used by a person visiting someone else's house to acknowledge some food or drink that does not necessarily constitute a meal. A polite visitor, for example, may say **Itadakimasu** just for a cup of tea.

Since **Itadakimasu** literally means "I humbly accept," it may also be used when accepting a present from a non-family member of higher status.

I⌐ta⌐i 痛い *painful*

Although **itai** 痛い is an adjective, it does not always correspond to English adjectives such as "painful" and "sore." Instead, it often corresponds to a verb (e.g., "[something] hurts") or a verb + noun (e.g., "have an ache").

EXAMPLES:
(1) **Nodo ga itai.**
のどが痛い。
I have a sore throat.
(2) **Sore wa itai.**
それは痛い。
That hurts.
(3) **Atama ga itai.**
頭が痛い。
I have a headache.

Itai is also used as an exclamation.

EXAMPLE:
(4) **Itai!**
痛い！
Ouch!

A variant of **itai** 痛い used only as an exclamation is **Aita!** あいた！ "Ouch!"

I'tsu いつ *When?*

Ordinarily, to answer a question containing an interrogative word (e.g., **dare** 誰, **doko** どこ, **nani** 何, etc.), you have to listen for the particle that follows the interrogative so that you can use the same particle in the answer.

EXAMPLES:

(1) A: **Dare ga kita n desu ka.**
      誰が来たんですか。
      Who came?

   B: **Takagi-san ga kita n desu.**
      高木さんが来たんです。
      Mr. Takagi came.

(2) A: **Doko e iku n desu ka.**
      どこへ行くんですか。
      Where are you going?

   B: **Yūbinkyoku e iku n desu.**
      郵便局へ行くんです。
      I'm going to the post office.

(3) A: **Nani o tabete-iru n desu ka.**
      何を食べているんですか。
      What are you eating?

   B: **Hanbāgā o tabete-iru n desu.**
      ハンバーガーを食べているんです。
      I'm eating a hamburger.

Itsu いつ, on the other hand, often appears without a particle.

EXAMPLE:

(4) **Itsu** (not *__Itsu ni__ いつに) **kita n desu ka.**
   いつ来たんですか。
   When did you come?

   In the answer to question (4), **ni** に may or may not be used, depending on the preceding noun. Compare (5) and (6) below. Without **ni** に:

EXAMPLE:

(5) **Kinō** (**Ototoi, Senshū, Sengetsu**, etc.) **kita n desu.**
   きのう(おととい, 先週, 先月, etc.)来たんです。
   I came yesterday (the day before yesterday, last week, last month, etc.).

With **ni** に:

EXAMPLE:

(6) **Ni-kagetsu-mae** (**Ni-gatsu, Tō-ka**, etc.) **ni kita n desu.**
   二ヶ月前(二月, 十日, etc.)に来たんです。
   I came two months ago (in February, on the 10th, etc.).

I「tte-irassha」i いっていらっしゃい *Hurry home!*

Itte-irasshai いっていらっしゃい, which literally means "Please go and come back," is a farewell most often used by someone seeing off a member of his own household. **Sayonara** さよなら "Good-by" should not be used in this case. The closest English equivalent would be *Hurry home!* but **Itte-irasshai** is used much more frequently; it is a well-established formula for everyday use.

Itte-irasshai may also be said to a person leaving his office or community on a trip. Don't use it unless you know the person is sooner or later returning to the same place. In rapid, less careful speech, **Itte-irasshai** いっていらっしゃい is regularly reduced to **Itte-rasshai** いってらっしゃい.

I「tte-mairima」su 行ってまいります *I'm leaving*

Itte-mairimasu 行ってまいります (lit., "I'm going and coming back") is an expression of leave-taking used by someone departing from his own home (or his office, town, country, etc.) on an errand or trip from which he expects to return sooner or later. **Sayonara** さよなら "Good-by" cannot be used in this case.

Whether **Itte-mairimasu** 行ってまいります precedes or follows **Itte-irasshai** いってい らっしゃい (see ITTE-IRASSHAI) is immaterial. It does not really matter whether the person leaving home speaks first and says **Itte-mairimasu** to someone staying at home, who then responds with **Itte-irasshai**, or the person staying at home speaks first and says **Itte-irasshai** to someone leaving, who then answers with **Itte-mairimasu**. Either way is acceptable.

A more informal version, **Itte-kimasu** 行ってきます, has lately become very widely used, especially among young people. It may not be too long before **Itte-mairimasu** becomes completely obsolete.

Iu 言う *to say*

As a rule, **iu** 言う takes only animate objects although the English verb "say" is often used with inanimate subjects, as in

EXAMPLES:
(1a) My watch says ten-thirty.
(1b) Today's paper says there was a terrible earthquake in Japan yesterday.

The Japanese counterparts of (1a) and (1b) would not use the verb **iu**, but rather some other phrase to express the same meanings, as in

EXAMPLES:
(2a) **Watashi no tokei de wa jūji-han desu.**
私の時計では十時半です。
It's ten-thirty by my watch.
(2b) **Kyō no shinbun ni yoru to, kinō Nihon de ōkii jishin ga atta sō da.**
今日の新聞によると、きのう日本で大きい地震があったそうだ。
According to today's paper, there was a terrible earthquake in Japan yesterday.

I⌐wa˥ 岩 *rock*

In American English, "rock" can be used to refer to even a small stone or pebble, as in "throw a rock." **Iwa** 岩, on the other hand, refers to only large pieces. Whoever can throw an **iwa** must be at least as strong as Samson! Ordinary people could throw only an **ishi** 石.

EXAMPLE:
Ishi (not *****iwa** 岩) **o nageau kenka wa abunai.**
石を投げ合うけんかは危ない。
Rock-throwing fights are dangerous.

I⌐ya˥ いや *unpleasant, awful, detestable, nasty*

Iya いや means "unpleasant, awful," etc.

EXAMPLE:
(1) **Konna tenki wa iya desu nē.**
こんな天気はいやですねえ。
This kind of weather is awful, isn't it!

Iya いや takes **na** な before a noun.

EXAMPLE:
(2) **Iya na hito desu nē.**
いやな人ですねえ。
Isn't he a nasty man!

Iya いや is sometimes used to mean **kirai** きらい "dislike."

EXAMPLE:
(3) **Kimi wa anna nekutai ga suki ka mo shirenai keredo, boku wa iya** (or **kirai**) **da na.**
君はあんなネクタイが好きかもしれなけれど、ぼくはいや（きらい）だな。
Maybe you like a necktie like that, but I don't like it.

Children and women might use **iya** いや by itself as an informal interjection to show annoyance when bothered by someone (a tickler, for instance).

EXAMPLE:
(4) **Iya!**
いや!
Don't!

This **iya** いや must be clearly distinguished from the **iya** used by men as a variant (perhaps a slightly less polite variant) of **iie** "no." I⌐ya˥ いや meaning "unpleasant" is accented on the second syllable, whereas I⌐ya いや meaning "no" is accented on the first.

EXAMPLE:
(5) A: **Kyō wa ame ga furu deshō ka.**
今日は雨が降るでしょうか。
Do you think it'll rain today?
B: **I⌐ya, furanai deshō.**
いや？降らないでしょう。
No, I don't think it will.

-Ji 時 *o'clock*

-Ji 時 is attached to a numeral to indicate "o'clock," as in **ichi-ji** 一時 "1 o'clock" and **ni-ji** 二時 "2 o'clock." Whereas English "o'clock" is often left out (e.g., "It's two now"), **-ji** 時 is never left out. The same is true of **-fun** 分 "minute." In the following example, therefore, only (a) is correct for the meaning given.

EXAMPLES:
(a) **Ima ichi-ji go-fun desu.**
    いま一時五分です。
(b) ***Ima ichi-go desu.**
    *いま一五です。
    It's 1:05 now.

Ji⌈biki⌉ 字引 *dictionary*

Jibiki 字引 used to be the only word meaning "dictionary" in spoken Japanese. **Jisho** 辞書, a more formal version, used to occur mainly in written Japanese. Nowadays, however, **jibiki** seems to be in the process of being replaced by **jisho** even in spoken Japanese. **Jiten** 辞典, an even more formal version, is mainly used to indicate a particular type of dictionary, as in (1), or as part of the title of a dictionary, as in (2).

EXAMPLES:
(1) **wa-ei jiten, ei-wa jiten, gairaigo-jiten, akusento-jiten**
    和英辞典、英和辞典、外来語辞典、アクセント辞典
    a Japanese-English dictionary, English-Japanese dictionary, loanword dictionary, accent dictionary
(2) **Kenkyūsha Shin Wa-Ei Daijiten**
    研究社新和英辞典
    Kenkyusha's New Japanese-English Dictionary

Jibun 自分 *self*

Jibun 自分 is used only in reference to a human being or an animal.

EXAMPLES:
(1) **Watashi wa jibun ga iya ni natta.**
    私は自分がいやになった。
    I've come to hate myself.
(2) **Jibun no koto wa jibun de shinasai.**
    自分のことは自分でしなさい。
    Take care of your own (lit., self's) affairs yourself.

Unlike English "self," which can be attached to pronouns (e.g., "myself," "yourself," "himself"), **jibun** 自分 is never attached to "pronouns" such as **watakushi** わたくし, **anata** あなた, and **kare** かれ. One either uses **jibun** by itself, as in (1) and (2) above (which is usually the case in speech), or attaches the word **jishin** 自身 to a "pronoun" (e.g., **watakushi-jishin** わたくし自身 "myself," **anata-jishin** あなた自身 "yourself"). The use of **jishin**, however, occurs almost exclusively in writing.

Jibun de 自分で meaning "of one's own accord, for oneself, in person, by one's own ability" is not exactly the same as **hitori de** 一人で meaning "by oneself" (i.e., "unaccompanied"). Although, in some contexts, either **jibun de** or **hitori de** may be used, their meanings are slightly different, as in (3) and also (4).

EXAMPLES:

(3) **Jibun de iki-nasai.**
自分で行きなさい。
Go yourself, (i.e., Don't ask anyone to go in your place.)

(4) **Hitori de iki-nasai.**
一人で行きなさい。
Go alone.

Sometimes only one of them can be used. In (5), for example, only **hitori de** can be used.

EXAMPLE:

(5) **Hitori de** (not ***Jibun de** 自分で) **sunde-imasu.**
一人で住んでいます。
I'm living alone.

Jikan 時間 *hour, time*

Jikan 時間, when attached to a numeral, means "hour[s]," as in **ichi-jikan** 一時間 "one hour," **ni-jikan** 二時間 "two hours," **san-jikan** 三時間 "three hours," etc. In this case, **jikan** 時間 is accented on the first syllable, i.e., **-ji˥kan** 時間.

When **jikan** is used without an attached numeral, it means "time."

EXAMPLE:

(1) **Jikan ga amari arimasen.**
時間があまりありません。
I don't have much time.

In this case, it is accentless.

According to Tokugawa and Miyajima (p. 238), **jikan** 時間 meaning "time" is different from its near synonym **toki** 時 "time" in at least four senses. First, although both words may be used in the sense of "duration of time," **jikan** refers to a shorter length of time than **toki**. Compare the following sentences, both of which mean "time certainly passes by fast."

EXAMPLES:

(2) **Jikan no tatsu no wa hayai mono da.**
時間の経つのは早いものだ。

(3) **Toki no tatsu no wa hayai mono da.**
時の経つのは早いものだ。

In (2), a time span of just a certain number of hours within one day is the issue, whereas (3) is concerned with a much longer period of time, such as days, months, or years.

Second, **toki** 時 may just refer to opportunities or occasions, but **jikan** 時間 never does. Compare the following:

EXAMPLES:

(4) **Isogashikute ochitsuite shokuji o suru toki ga nai.**
忙しくて落ち着いて食事をする時がない。
I am so busy that on no occasion do I have a leisurely meal.

(5) **Isogashikute ochitsuite shokuji o suru jikan ga nai.**
忙しくて落ち着いて食事をする時間がない。
I am so busy that I don't have time for a leisurely meal.

Third, a particular or definite point in time, as indicated by a clock, is **jikan** 時間 and not **toki** 時. In (6), therefore, **jikan** is correct, but **toki** is not.

EXAMPLE:

(6) **Asa okita jikan** (not ****toki** 時) **o kiroku shinasai.**
朝起きた時間を記録しなさい。
Please record the time you get up in the morning.

Fourth, **toki** 時 is regularly used to form clauses meaning "when such-and-such happens," but **jikan** 時間 is not. In the following example, therefore, only **toki** can be used.

EXAMPLE:

(7) **Watashi ga soto e deta toki** (not ****jikan** 時間)**, chōdo takushī ga tōri-kakatta.**
私が外へ出た時、ちょうどタクシーが通りかかった。
A taxi just happened to pass by when I went outside.

Ji⌐ken 事件 *happening*

Once an American student wrote to me in Japanese:

EXAMPLE:

(1) ****Nani ka Nihonjin ga atsumaru jiken ga attara oshirase kudasaimasen ka.**
*何か日本人が集まる事件があったらお知らせくださいませんか。
Will you please tell me if there is an event for Japanese people?

My suspicion is he looked up the word "event" in an English-Japanese dictionary, found **jiken** 事件 as the Japanese "equivalent," and used it. **Jiken** 事件, however, carries a negative connotation, usually referring to the kind of event welcomed by the mass media such as murder, adultery, and bribery Since the writer of sentence (1) above meant events such as parties, picnics, and lectures, he should have used **gyōji** 行事 instead. As a matter of fact, nowadays, the loanword **ibento** イベント might be even more appropriate, as in

EXAMPLE:

(2) **Nani ka Nihonjin ga atsumaru ibento ga attara oshirase kudasaimasen ka.**
なにか日本人が集まるイベントがあったらお知らせくださいませんか。

Ji⌐koku 時刻 *point in time*

Jikan 時間 can mean either "amount/length of time," as in (1a), or "point in time," as in (1b).

EXAMPLES:

(1a) **Mō jikan ga nai.**
もう時間がない。
We have no more time.

(1b) **Mō okiru jikan da.**
もう起きる時間だ。
It's already time for me to get up.

Jikoku 時刻, on the other hand, refers only to a "point in time."

EXAMPLE:

(3) **Jikoku o oshirase-shimasu.**
時刻をお知らせします。
We'll let you know what time it is (lit., the present point in time).

   Jikoku 時刻, however, sounds formal and is rarely used in speech except in the word **jikokuhyō** 時刻表 "time table" (for buses, trains, airplanes, etc.).

Ji˥mu˥sho 事務所 *office*

When American students of Japanese learn the word **jimusho** 事務所, they often start using it in Japanese whenever they would use "office" in English. For example, they might ask their teacher

EXAMPLE:

*Sensei no jimusho wa nan-gai desu ka.
*先生の事務所は何階ですか。

to convey the meaning "What floor is your office on?" A professor's office, however, is not **jimusho** but **kenkyūshitsu** 研究室 (lit., "research room").
   In fact, the use of **jimusho** 事務所 is limited to a small number of occupations. Lawyers, accountants, and architects generally call their offices **jimusho**, but doctors do not. A student of Japanese should therefore check with a native speaker before using **jimusho** with reference to a specific type of office.

(See also KAISHA.)

Jinkō 人口 *population*

Jinkō 人口 refers to the number of people within a certain geographical area. Since one of the Chinese characters representing **jinkō** is 人, meaning "person," this word can refer only to humans, although English "population" may sometimes be used in reference to animals.
   In English, one usually talks about a certain population being large or small, as in

EXAMPLE:

(1) The population of New York City is the largest in the United States.

   In Japanese, on the other hand, one talks about **jinkō** 人口 being **ōi/sukunai** 多い/少ない "many/few" rather than **ōkii/chiisai** 大きい/小さい "large/small," e.g.,

EXAMPLE:

(2) **Tōkyō no jinkō wa ō-sugiru** (not ***ōki-sugiru** 大きすぎる).
東京の人口は多すぎる。
The population of Tokyo is too large (lit., too many).

Ji˥tsu˥ wa 実は *to tell you the truth*

The most common use of **jitsu wa** 実は is when one has to start talking about something one feels reluctant to bring up, e.g., something one feels shy about, ashamed of, etc., as in

EXAMPLE:

(1) A. **Kyō wa nan no yō?**
今日は何の用？
What do you want to see me about today?

B. **Jitsu wa chotto komatta koto ga arimashite.**
実はちょっと困った事がありまして。
The truth is (or I hate to bother you with my problem but) there's something that's troubling me.

Jitsu wa 実は is quite different in usage from **jitsu ni** 実に ("truly"), which is used to emphasize the degree of some quality. For example,

EXAMPLE:

(2) **Arasuka no fuyu wa jitsu ni** (not *jitsu wa 実は) **samui.**
アラスカの冬は実に寒い。
Winters in Alaska are truly cold.

In this context, **jitsu wa** 実は could be used only if it were commonly believed that winters in Alaska are not cold, which is of course untrue.

Jōbu 丈夫 *healthy, robust, strong*

Jōbu 丈夫 may be used in reference to either persons (or animals) or limited kinds of objects. In reference to persons, it means "healthy, robust, strong."

EXAMPLE:

(1) **Ano hito wa jōbu de, metta ni byōki ni naranai.**
あの人は丈夫で、めったに病気にならない。
He is very healthy and rarely becomes ill.

Jōbu 丈夫 cannot be used, however, to indicate good health over a very short period of time, e.g., one day, one week, or even one month. Just as it is wrong to say "*He is robust today" in English, we do not use ***Kyō wa jōbu desu** *今日は丈夫です in Japanese to mean "I am well today." In such situations, we use **genki** 元気 (see GENKI).

EXAMPLE:

(2) **Kinō wa byōki deshita ga, kyō wa mō genki ni narimashita.**
きのうは病気でしたが、今日はもう元気になりました。
I was ill yesterday, but I'm already fine today.

Jōbu 丈夫, in other words, is concerned with one's physical makeup rather than with one's temporary physical state.

When used in reference to objects, **jōbu** 丈夫 may describe only a limited number of things, including leather, fabrics, and products made of such materials.

EXAMPLE:

(3) **jōbu na kawa** (or **kutsu**)
丈夫な皮（靴）
strong leather (or shoes)
jōbu na kiji (or **fuku**)
丈夫な生地（服）
strong fabric (or clothes)

Josei 女性 *woman*

Josei 女性 used to be a written expression, but nowadays it is used more and more in conversation as well, although it still sounds somewhat formal and is unlikely to be used by children.

EXAMPLE:

Nihon no josei wa mada dansei to byōdō ni atsukawarete-inai.
日本の女性はまだ男性と平等にあつかわれていない。
Women in Japan are not yet treated the same as men.

Whereas **onna** 女 sometimes carries a derogatory tone, **josei** 女性 never does.

Jo¹shi 女子 *woman*

Although 女 means "female" and 子 means "child," the combination of the two kanji 女子, pronounced **joshi**, does not mean "girl" but rather "human female." It is not used in reference to one female person, but rather to girls/women in general. For example,

EXAMPLE:

(1) **Ano daigaku ni wa joshiryō to danshiryō ga aru.**
あの大学には女子寮と男子寮がある。
That university has women's dormitories and men's dormitories.

To mean "a girl," one has to use **onna-no-ko** 女の子 instead of **joshi** 女子.

EXAMPLE:

(2) **Asoko ni iru onna-no-ko wa kawaii ne.**
あそこにいる女の子はかわいいね。
That girl over there is cute, isn't she?

-Jū 中 *throughout*

-jū 中 is a suffix attached to a time word or a place word to mean "throughout," as in

EXAMPLES:

(1a) **Yoru-jū nenai de mājan o sureba, karada o kowasu ni kimatte-iru.**
夜中寝ないで麻雀をすれば、体をこわすに決まっている。
It's only natural that you ruin your health if you stay up all night, playing mahjong.

(1b) **Haru ni wa Nihon-jū de ohanami ga dekiru.**
春には日本中でお花見が出来る。
In the spring, one can go cherry-blossom viewing throughout Japan.

-chū is also written 中 in kanji, but the meaning is "among," "during," or "in the course of," as in

EXAMPLES:

(2a) **Kyōdai-chū daigaku e itta no wa kare hitori datta.**
兄弟中大学へ行ったのは彼ひとりだった。
Of the siblings, he was the only one who went to college,

(2b) **Rusu-chū dorobō ni hairareta.**
留守中泥棒に入られた。
I was burglarized during my absence.

(2c) **Natsu no kurasu wa gozen-chū dake da.**
夏のクラスは午前中だけだ。
Summer classes are held only in the morning.

What is really confusing is that this **-chū** is pronounced **-jū** when attached to some time words, especially **kyō** 今日 ("today") and **ashita** あした ("tomorrow"). For example,

EXAMPLE:
(3) **Kono shukudai wa kyō-jū ni shinakereba naranai.**
この宿題は今日中にしなければならない。
I must do this homework before today is over.

Ju˥gyō 授業 *class*

Jugyō 授業 means "class" in the sense of "the teaching given in a class," not "a group of people learning together and taught by the same teacher." It may therefore be used in sentence (1), but not in sentence (2).

EXAMPLES:
(1) **Aren Sensei no jugyō wa tame ni natta.**
アレン先生の授業はためになった。
Mr. Allen's class was instructive.
(2) **Shōgakkō no toki no kurasu** (not *****jugyō** 授業) **wa ōkikatta.**
小学校の時のクラスは大きかった。
My class in elementary school was large.

The loanword **kurasu** クラス (from English "class"), on the other hand, is broader in meaning and can be used in example (1) above as well as in (2).

Ju˥ku 塾 *after-school school*

A **juku** 塾 is an after-school school for younger students, i.e., elementary through high school students. All kinds of subjects could be taught there, but there may be some **juku** that specialize in one particular skill, such as **sorobanjuku** そろばん塾 ("abacus **juku**") and **shodōjuku** 書道塾 ("caligraphy **juku**"). **Juku** connotes a school attended by students from regular schools for extra work usually to improve in subjects where they are weak or to prepare themselves for entrance exams at various levels.

A **yobikō** 予備校 ("cram school") is very much like a **juku** in that it is not a regular school. There is some difference, however. First of all, a **yobikō** is basically for **rōnin** 浪人, i.e., students who have finished high school but have flunked college entrance examinations, although students who are still in high school may also attend **yobikō** after regular school hours to better prepare for the coming entrance exam. Second, a **yobikō** teaches only subjects required for college entrance exams; a **yobikō** specializing only in one subject or offering non-required subjects such as abacus and calligraphy would thus be unthinkable. Third, a **yobikō** is usually a large-sized school whereas a **juku** could be of any size. Fourth, at a **yobikō**, students are often there all day since they have no other school to go to whereas, at a **juku**, students usually come in in the late afternoon after attending their regular school.

Ka⌐bu⌐ru かぶる *to put on, to wear*

Kaburu かぶる is limited in its use in that it is reserved for wearing things to cover the head.

EXAMPLE:

(1) **bōshi (berē, herumetto, etc.) o kaburu**
帽子(ベレー, ヘルメット, ...)をかぶる
put on a hat (beret, helmet, etc.)

Occasionally, the item that covers the head may also cover the body.

EXAMPLE:

(2) **Tarō wa futon o kabutte nete-iru.**
太郎はふとんをかぶって寝ている。
Taro is sleeping, pulling a blanket over the head.

Ka⌐do 角 *corner*

Corners such as street corners are **kado** 角.

EXAMPLE:

(1) **Ano kado o magatte kudasai.**
あの角を曲がってください。
Please turn at that corner.

In referring to boxes, bureaus, dressers, desks, and other angular things, Japanese makes a distinction between outside corners and inside corners. Outside corners are **kado** 角, but inside ones are called **sumi** 隅. One therefore says:

EXAMPLES:

(2) **Tsukue no kado ni atama o butsuketa.** (outside corner)
机の角に頭をぶつけた。
I hit my head against the corner of the desk.

(3) **Tsukue no sumi ni haizara o oita.** (inside corner)
机の隅に灰皿を置いた。
I put the ashtray on the corner of the desk.

Ka⌐eru 帰る *to return*

Kaeru 帰る means "to go (or come) back to the place where one belongs" (Mizutani and Mizutani, 1977, p. 38). Going back to one's house is one typical instance of such an action. To mean "to go home," the Japanese speaker therefore says **uchi e kaeru** うちへ帰る (lit., "to return to one's home"), rather than **uchi e *iku** うちへ*行く (lit., "to go home").

EXAMPLE:

(1) **Koyama-san wa mō uchi e kaerimashita** (not *ikimashita 行きました).
小山さんはもううちへ帰りました。
Mr. Koyama has already gone home.

Although **kaeru** 帰る is often translated into English as "to return," it is different from "return" in that **kaeru** is a much more commonly used word than "return." While "return," at least intransitively, is not all that frequent a conversational expression, **kaeru** is a very common term in both speech and writing.

Since **kaeru** 帰る may mean either "to go back" or "to come back," the compound verbs **kaette-iku** 帰って行く "to go back" (lit., "to go returning") and **kaette-kuru** 帰って来る "to come back" (lit., "to come returning") are frequently used to specify the direction of motion.

EXAMPLES:

(2) **Ueno-san wa go-ji-goro kaette-itta.**
上野さんは五時頃帰って行った。
Miss Ueno left [to go home] about 5 o'clock.

(3) **Musuko wa yūbe zuibun osoku kaette-kita.**
息子はゆうべ随分遅く帰って来た。
My son came home very late last night.

Since the basic meaning of **kaeru** 帰る is "to return to the place where one belongs," a foreigner saying **Nihon e kaeri-tai** 日本へ帰りたい sounds very strange. If a foreign student, for example, goes to Japan for a year's study, enjoys his/her stay there, and wishes to go back there, he or she should say **Nihon e mata ikitaidesu** 日本へまた行きたいです instead (See also MODORU.)

Ka˩gaku 化学 *science;* 科学 *chemistry*

Kagaku, written 科学 in kanji, means "science," usually "natural science." **Kagakusha**, written 科学者, means "scientist," most likely "scholar whose field is natural science."

There is another word, **kagaku** 化学 "chemistry," which is pronounced exactly the same as **kagaku** 科学. In written Japanese, there is no problem because of the difference in kanji, i.e., 化 versus 学. To distinguish them clearly in speech, however, 化学 "chemistry" is often called **bakegaku** 化学, using the **kun**-reading of 化, as in

EXAMPLE:

Suzuki-san wa kōkō de bakegaku o oshiete-imasu.
鈴木さんは高校で化学を教えています。
Mr. Suzuki teaches chemistry in high school.

Kaimono 買い物 *shopping*

Although **kaimono** 買い物 is usually equated with "shopping," these two are not the same. The difference becomes clear when one examines the dictionary definitions of these two terms. "Shopping" is defined as "the act of visiting shops and stores for purchasing or examining goods" whereas **kaimono** is defined as **mono o kau koto** 物を買う事, i.e., "the act of buying something." In other words, shopping does not necessarily end in a purchase, while **kaimono**, especially in **kaimono o suru** 買い物をする, involves a purchase. For example, sentence (1) below is correct, but (2) is not.

EXAMPLES:

(1) I was out shopping all morning but came home without buying anything.

(2) *****Gozen-chū zutto kaimono o shita keredo, nani mo kawanai de uchi e kaetta.**
*午前中ずっと買い物をしたけれど、何も買わないでうちへ帰った。
lit., I did the shopping all morning, but came home without buying anything.

Sentence (2) would become correct only if one used **kaimono ni iku** 買い物に行く "to go shopping" instead.

EXAMPLE:

(3) **Gozen-chū kaimono ni itta keredo, nani mo kawanai de uchi e kaetta.**
午前中買い物に行ったけれど、何も買わないでうちへ帰った。
I went shopping in the morning, but came home without buying anything.

Kaisha 会社 *business company*

Kaisha 会社 meaning "business company, firm" is used quite frequently in Japanese, in fact more frequently than its English counterparts. The reason is that it is often used in Japanese in situations where "office" or "work" would be used in English. In America, for example, a company employee who goes to work every day would not say "*I go to the company every day" but rather "I go to work (or the office) every day." In Japanese, however, **kaisha e iku** 会社へ行く (lit., "to go to the company") is the most common expression to use in such a case. The Japanese equivalent of "He is at work (or the office)" is also **Ima kaisha desu** いま会社です (lit., "I'm at the company") if the person in question works for a business company.

The Japanese word for "company employee" is **kaishain** 会社員 (lit., "company member").

EXAMPLE:

(1) **Ano hito wa kaishain desu.**
あの人は会社員です。
He is a company employee.

However, within or in reference to a specific company, its employees are called **shain** 社員 instead of **kaishain** 会社員. In (2) below, a company president is talking about an employee.

EXAMPLE:

(2) **Ano shain wa nan to iu namae ka ne.**
あの社員はなんと言う名前かね。
What's the name of that [company] employee?

In other words, while **kaishain** 会社員 represents an occupation and stands in contrast with other occupations such as **ginkōin** 銀行員 "bank employee" and **kōmuin** 公務員 "government employee, civil servant," **shain** 社員 indicates a position and stands in contrast with other positions such as **shachō** 社長 "company president" and **kachō** 課長 "section chief."

Ka⌐ka⌐ru かかる *[it] takes, costs*

Kakaru かかる meaning "[it] takes, costs" is most typically used in reference to money or time. The preceding particle is **ga** が.

EXAMPLES:

(1) **Kono shigoto wa jikan ga kakaru.**
この仕事は時間がかかる。
This job takes time.

(2) **Kodomo no kyōiku wa okane ga kakaru.**
子供の教育はお金がかかる。
Children's education costs money.

However, when lengths of time or amounts of money are the issue, **ga** が must be dropped.

EXAMPLES:

(3) **Kono hon o yomu no ni tō-ka** (not *****tō-ka ga** 十日が) **kakatta.**
この本を読むのに十日かかった。
It took me ten days to read this book.

(4) **Kuruma o naoshite-morau no ni dono-gurai** (not *****donogurai ga** どのぐらいが) **kaka-rimashita ka.**
車を直してもらうのにどのぐらいかかりましたか。
How much did it cost to have the car repaired?

Actually, **tō-ka kakatta** 十日かかった "it took ten days" in (3) is short for **jikan ga tō-ka kakatta** が十日かかった "timewise it took ten days," and **dono-gurai kakarimashita ka** どのぐらいかかりましたか "how much did it cost?" in (4) is an abbreviation of **okane ga dono-gurai kakarimashita ka** お金がどのぐらいかかりましたか "how much did it cost moneywise?" When **jikan** 時間 and **okane** お金 are deleted, **ga** が naturally goes with them—hence no **ga** in (3) or (4).

Ka⌈keru かける *to sit down*

Kakeru かける has many meanings, but one of them is "to sit down." **Kakeru** used in this sense could be written かける and is short for **koshi o kakeru** 腰をかける or simply **koshikakeru** 腰かける, both of which literally mean "to hang one's bottom." Unlike **suwaru** 座る, which can refer to any mode of sitting down, however, **kakeru** can only represent sitting down on such things as a chair, bench, and sofa. Please study the following examples:

EXAMPLES:

(1) **Amerika no daigakusei wa, pātī de mo yuka ni suwatte** (not *****kakete** 掛けて) **shimau koto ga aru.**
アメリカの大学生は、パーティーでも床に座ってしまうことがある。
American college students sometimes sit on the floor even at a party.

(2) **Dōzo sofā ni okake/osuwari kudasai.**
どうぞソファーにお掛け/お座りください。
Please sit on the sofa.

(See also SUWARU.)

Ka⌉ku 書く, かく, 掻く *to write, to draw, to scratch*

In Japanese, "writing," "drawing (a picture)," and "scratching" all require the same verb, **kaku**, as in

EXAMPLES:

(1a) **Tegami o kaku no ga kirai na hito ga fuete-iru.**
手紙を書くのがきらいな人が増えている。
People who hate to write letters are on the increase.

(1b) **Nihongo-kyōshi wa e o kaku no ga jōzu na hō ga benri da.**

日本語教師は絵をかくのが上手な方が便利だ。

For Japanese language teachers, the ability to draw pictures well comes in handy.

(1c) **Toshi o toru to, senaka o kaku no ga dandan muzukashiku naru.**

年を取ると、背中を掻くのがだんだん難しくなる。

As one grows older, it becomes more and more difficult to scratch one's back.

Note that, although **kaku** could be written in three different ways (i.e., 書く, かく and 掻く), it is basically the same verb in that it is pronounced the same and could be written in the same hiragana (i.e., かく). The best way to remember that **kaku** could represent these three different activities would be that writing and drawing are also kinds of scratching, although the tools used might be different!

In English, the verb "write" by itself can mean "to correspond in writing," as in "Please write me more often." Japanese **kaku** does not function like this; one must use **tegami o kaku** 手紙を書く instead. Sentence (2) below is wrong.

EXAMPLE:

(2) *__Hima ga areba, dōzo kaite kudasai.__

*ひまがあれば、どうぞ書いてください。

Please write when you have time.

To make this sentence correct, one must say the following:

EXAMPLE:

(3) **Ohima na toki ni otegami o kudasai.**

おひまな時にお手紙をください。

Note that, when **kaku** means "to draw," it is written in hiragana alone (i.e., かく); the kanji 書 is normally reserved for **kaku** meaning "to write" (i.e., 書く).

Ka⌐maise⌐n ka　かまいませんか　*Do you mind?*

In English, to ask someone if you may do something, you say "Do you mind if I do such-and-such?" or "Would you mind if I did such-and-such?" In either case, the question is in the affirmative. The Japanese counterpart, however, is in the negative, i.e., **Kamaimasen ka** かまいませんか, which comes from **kamau** かまう "to care, to mind."

EXAMPLE:

(1) **Mado o akete mo kamaimasen** (not ***kamaimasu** かまいます) **ka.**

窓を開けてもかまいませんか。

Do you mind (lit., Don't you mind) if I open the window?

The addressee then answers **Kamaimasen yo** かまいませんよ "That's all right" or "I don't mind" if it is all right, and **Sumimasen ga akenai de kudasai** すみませんが開けないでください "I'm sorry, but please don't open it" or some such thing if it is not (but never ***Kamaimasu** かまいます).

Kamaimasen ka かまいませんか is another version of **Ii desu ka** いいですか (or, more formally, **Yoroshii desu ka** よろしいですか) "Would that be all right?" Sentence (1) above, therefore, can be restated as

EXAMPLE:

(2) **Mado o akete mo ii** (or **yoroshii**) **desu ka.**
窓を開けてもいい(よろしい)ですか。
May I open the window? (lit., Will it be all right if I open the window?)

In this case, of course, the question is in the affirmative (although the meaning remains the same).

Kaminari 雷 *lightning, thunder*

Although in English "lightning" and "thunder" are clearly distinguished, in Japanese both are often taken care of by one word, **kaminari** 雷.

EXAMPLES:

(1) **Tōku de kaminari ga pikapika shite-iru.**
遠くで雷がピカピカしている。
There are flashes of lightning in the distance.

(2) **Kyō no kaminari wa zuibun yakamashii.**
今日の雷はずいぶんやかましい。
The thunder is really loud today.

There are also, however, such words as **inabikari** 稲光 and **inazuma** 稲妻, both meaning "lightning." They can be used when the speaker wishes to refer to lightning specifically.

Ka¹nai 家内 *my wife*

Kanai 家内 "wife" most typically refers to one's own wife. Though one could use **uchi no kanai** うちの家内 or **watashi no kanai** 私の家内 to mean "my wife," **uchi no** (or **watashi no**) is usually left out.

EXAMPLE:

Kanai ga byōki na node komatte-iru n desu.
家内が病気なので困っているんです。
I am being inconvenienced because my wife is sick.

Nowadays, however, some youngsters seem to prefer **waifu** ワイフ (from English "wife").
   There are other expressions that also mean "my wife," such as **nyōbō** 女房 and **tsuma** 妻. **Nyōbō**, an informal expression, is getting rather unpopular; **tsuma** is formal and somewhat bookish (see TSUMA).

Kanarazu 必ず *without fail*

Kanarazu 必ず is used when the probability of something happening is, or should be, one hundred percent.

EXAMPLE:

(1) A. **Ashita no asa made ni kanarazu shukudai o dashite kudasai yo.**
あしたの朝までに必ず宿題を出してください。
Please hand in your homework by tomorrow morning without fail.

   B. **Hai, kanarazu dashimasu.**
はい、必ず出します。
Yes, without fail.

Kitto きっと "certainly; I am certain" is similar to **kanarazu** 必ず in that the probability of something happening is high, but the difference is that the probability **kitto** implies is not quite as high. For something that always happens without any exception whatsoever, **kitto** therefore is not as appropriate as **kanarazu**, as in

EXAMPLE:

(2) **Ningen wa dare de mo kanarazu** (not *kitto きっと) **shinu.**
人間は誰でも必ず死ぬ。
All human beings die without exception.

Whereas **kanarazu** 必ず may be used to describe a past event, **kitto** cannot.

EXAMPLE:

(3) **Tanaka-san wa, pātī ga aru to kanarazu** (not *kitto きっと) **kita.**
田中さんは、パーティーがあると必ず来た。
Mr. Tanaka never missed a party.

Kitto きっと, however, may be used for a present conjecture about a past event.

EXAMPLE:

(4) **Tanaka-san wa pātī ni yonde agetara kitto kita darō.**
田中さんはパーティーに呼んであげたらきっと来たでしょう。
I'm sure Mr. Tanaka would have come if we had invited him.

Kanarazu 必ず is normally not used with a negative, but **kitto** きっと may be so used.

EXAMPLE:

(5) **Tsuyu ni wa mainichi kanarazu** (not *kitto きっと) **ame ga furu to wa kagiranai.**
梅雨には毎日必ず雨が降るとはかぎらない。
During the Japanese rainy season, it doesn't necessarily rain every day.

(See also KITTO.)

Kanemochi 金持ち *wealthy (person)*

Kanemochi 金持ち is often translated into English as "rich."

EXAMPLE:

(1) **Amerika ni wa kanemochi no seijika ga ōi.**
アメリカには金持ちの政治家が多い。
In America, there are lots of rich politicians.

Kanemochi 金持ち, however, as can be seen from the kanji used, literally means "having money," and is basically a noun meaning "wealthy person," as in

EXAMPLE:

(2) **Nyūyōku ni wa kanemochi ga takusan sunde iru.**
ニューヨークには金持ちが沢山住んでいる。
There are lots of rich people living in New York.

Unlike "rich," which can be used figuratively in reference to things like talent, knowledge, experience, etc., **kanemochi** 金持ち cannot. For those items, use **yutaka** 豊か. For example,

EXAMPLE:

(3) **yutaka na** (not *__kanemochi no__ 金持ちの) **sainō/chishiki/keiken**
豊かな才能/知識/経験
rich in talent/knowledge/experience

-Kane¹ru かねる *to be in no position to*

-kaneru かねる is attached to the stem of another verb to indicate that the speaker feels hesitant, or too shy, to do something. It is most often used when the speaker wishes to negate or decline something politely.

EXAMPLES:

(1a) **Mōshiwake arimasen ga, chotto itadaki-kanemasu.**
申し訳ありませんが、ちょっと頂きかねます。
I'm sorry, but I'm in no position to accept this.

(1b) **Chotto wakari-kanemasu ga.**
ちょっと分かりかねますが。
This is beyond my comprehension.

Since **-kaneru** かねる is affirmative in form, though negative in meaning, it sounds much less brusque than negative expressions such as **wakarimasen** 分かりません when conveying essentially the same message, i.e., "I don't understand."

The negative form **-kanenai** かねない, on the other hand, is used when someone will not hesitate to do something daring or out of the ordinary.

EXAMPLE:

(2) **Kare wa sensei ni taishite shitsurei na koto o ii-kanenai otoko da.**
かれは先生に対して失礼な事を言いかねない男だ。
He is the kind of man who will not hesitate to say something rude to his teacher.

Ka¹nga¹eru 考える *to think, to consider*

The semantic range of **kangaeru** 考える and that of **omou** 思う "to think" (see OMOU) overlap to a considerable degree, as in (1) through (3).

EXAMPLES:

(1) **Shiyō to kangaeta** (or **omotta**) **koto wa sugu shita hō ga ii.**
しようと考えた（思った）事はすぐした方がいい。
It is better to do immediately what one thinks of doing.

(2) **Kimi wa sono koto o dō kangaeru** (or **omou**)**?**
君はそのことをどう考える（思う）？
What do you think of that?

(3) **Watashi mo sō kangaeta** (or **omotta**) **n desu.**
私もそう考えた（思った）んです。
I thought so too.

However, there are at least two differences between **kangaeru** 考える and **omou** 思う. First, **kangaeru** is more analytical. It is for this reason that forms of **kangaeru** must be used in (4) and (5) below.

EXAMPLES:

(4) **Dō yattara ii ka kangaete** (not *omotte- 思って) **kudasai.**
どうやったらいいか考えてください。
Please think about how to do it.

(5) **Sono mondai wa muzukashikute zuibun kangaeta** (not *omotta 思った) **ga wakara-nakatta.**
その問題は難しくてずいぶん考えたが分からなかった。
The problem was so difficult I couldn't figure it out though I really thought hard.

Second, **kangaeru** 考える does not need an object, whereas **omou** 思う does need one, whether explicit or implicit. In (6), therefore, only **kangaeru** can be used.

EXAMPLE:

(6) **Ningen wa kangaeru** (not *omou 思う) **dōbutsu da.**
人間は考える動物だ。
Man is an animal that thinks.

Ka⌐nojo 彼女 *she*

Kanojo 彼女 came into use during the Meiji era (1868–1912) under the influence of Western languages and literature, as the Japanese counterpart of "she," just as **kare** 彼 (see KARE) was adopted as the "equivalent" of "he." The difference between **kare** and **kanojo** is that while **kare** had existed in classical Japanese with the meaning of "that person" or "that thing," **kanojo** was a new coinage made up of **kano** 彼 "that" and **jo** 女 (another reading of the *kanji* for **onna** 女 "woman").

Kanojo 彼女 was first used in written Japanese only, especially in Japanese translations of Western literary works. Gradually, it came to appear in original literary works as well. Nowadays, it is sometimes used in speech, too, although its use is still quite limited. Sandness (pp. 85–86) points out some interesting characteristics of **kanojo** as used in contemporary magazine articles: (a) a foreign woman is more likely to be referred to as **kanojo** than is a Japanese woman; (b) a woman is more likely to be called **kanojo** than is a man to be called **kare** 彼; (c) articles translated from Western languages use **kanojo** more often than nontranslations; (d) women who warrant deference, such as Queen Elizabeth and Empress Michiko, are never referred to as **kanojo**.

While **kanojo** 彼女 basically means "she," it is also often used to mean "girlfriend," as in

EXAMPLE:

(1) **Tanaka no kanojo ni wa mada shōkai-sarete-inai.**
田中の彼女にはまだ紹介されていない。
I haven't been introduced to Tanaka's girlfriend yet.

Strangely, the most recent use of **kanojo** 彼女 is as a second-person "pronoun" in addressing a woman of equal or lower status, as in

EXAMPLE:

(2) **Kanojo, kore shite kurenai?**
彼女、これしてくれない？
Won't you do this for me?

Although this usage does strike us as odd at first, it ceases to sound strange when we consider the fact that even **anata** originally meant "over there." Japanese speakers do like to communicate indirectly!

The rule of thumb for a student learning Japanese, in my opinion, is to avoid using **kanojo** 彼女 in speech. When you do, never use it in reference to a person whose social status (on the Japanese scale, of course) is higher than yours.

Kanshin 感心 *admirable, praiseworthy;* Kanshin-suru 感心する *to be impressed*

Kanshin 感心, with the addition of **suru** する, becomes the compound verb **kanshin-suru** 感心する, which is usually translated into English as "to admire," "to be deeply impressed by," and such. To be precise, however, **kanshin** and **kanshin-suru** tend not to be used in reference to persons higher in status than the speaker. Sentence (1) is therefore correct, but sentence (2) is not quite proper.

EXAMPLES:

(1) **Ano ko no shūji ga amari rippa na no ni wa kanshin-shimashita.**
あの子の習字があまりりっぱなのには感心しました。
I was deeply impressed by that child's superior calligraphy.

(2) **?Yoshida-sensei ga shūmatsu mo kenkyūshitsu de kenkyū-shite-irassharu no ni wa kanshin-shimasu.**
?吉田先生が週末も研究室で研究していらっしゃるのには感心します。
I am deeply impressed by Professor Yoshida's studying in his office even on weekends.

This tendency is even clearer when **kanshin** 感心 is directed toward the addressee.

EXAMPLES:

(3) Son:　　**Mō shukudai yatchatta yo.**
　　　　　もう宿題やっちゃったよ。
　　　　　I've already done my homework.

　　Father: **Kanshin da nē!**
　　　　　感心だねえ！
　　　　　Good for you!

(4) Section chief: **Ano shigoto wa yūbe tetsuya de yatte shimatta yo.**
　　　　　　　あの仕事はゆうべ徹夜でやってしまったよ。
　　　　　　　I stayed up working all night last night and finished that job.

　　Secretary:　　***Kanshin desu nē!**
　　　　　　　感心ですねえ！

In (3), the father's saying **kanshin** 感心 is correct because he is talking to his son, who is lower in status. In (4), however, **kanshin** is unacceptable because the secretary is talking to her superior. She should say

EXAMPLE:

(5) **Taihen deshita nē!**
大変でしたねえ！
That must have been very tiring!

Since **kanshin-suru** 感心する conveys positive evaluation, in the following examples (6a) is correct, but (6b) is not.

EXAMPLES:

(6a) **Kare no ie no ōkisa ni kanshin-shita.**
彼の家の大きさに感心した。
I was (favorably) impressed by the huge size of his house.

(6b) ***Kare no ie no kitanasa ni kanshin-shita.**
*彼の家の汚さに感心した。
I was (unfavorably) impressed by the filthiness of his house.

In the case of (6b), **kanshin-shita** 感心した must be replaced by another verb, as in

EXAMPLE:

(7) **Kare no ie no kitanasa ni akireta.**
彼の家の汚さに呆れた。
I was disgusted by the filthiness of his house.

Kantoku 監督 *director; manager; supervisor*

In terms of movies, **kantoku** 監督 is "director," as in **Kurosawa-kantoku** 黒澤監督 "Director Kurosawa." In terms of sports, it means "manager," as in **yakyū-kantoku** 野球監督 "baseball manager." In terms of construction work, it means "supervisor," as in **genba-kantokbu** 現場監督 "construction site supervisor."

Kanzen 完全 *perfect*

English speakers often use the adjective "perfect" to mean "excellent," as in

EXAMPLE:

(1) A: Did you have a good weekend?
B: Yes, I had a perfect weekend.

The Japanese counterpart, **kanzen (na)** 完全(な), however, is not used that way. Use other adjectives such as **subarashii** すばらしい, **totemo yoi** とても良い, etc.

EXAMPLE:

(2) **Kono shūmatsu wa subarashikatta** (not ***kanzen datta** 完全だった).
この週末はすばらしかった。
This weekend was just marvelous.

Kara から *from*

English "Where are you from?" should not be translated directly into Japanese. So, for example, (1b) and (1c) would be better than (1a).

EXAMPLES:

(1a) **?Dochira kara desu ka.**
?どちらからですか。
lit., Where are you from?

(1b) **Okuni wa dochira desu ka.**
お国はどちらですか。
lit., Where is your hometown?

(1c) **Dochira no goshusshin desu ka.**
どちらのご出身ですか。
lit., Where do you originate from?

Karada 体 *body*

While the English speaker says "good (or bad) for the health," the Japanese speaker usually says **karada ni ii** (or **warui**) 体に良い（悪い）, which literally means "good (or bad) for the body." **Kenkō ni ii** (or **warui**) 健康に良い（悪い）, which literally means "good (or bad) for the health," may be used sometimes, but it is not as common an expression.

Ka⌉re 彼 *he*

Kare 彼, which used to mean "that person" or "that thing" in classical Japanese, was adopted by writers during the early years of the Meiji era to represent the idea of English "he." First it was used only as a written form. Recently, however, some people have started using it in speech as well, as in

EXAMPLE:

(1) **Kare wa kyō byōki rashii.**
彼は今日病気らしい。
He seems to be sick today.

Kare 彼 in Japanese is far more restricted in use than "he" in English. There are at least two reasons for this. First of all, most sentences in Japanese have no explicit subject. Second, **kare** is used mainly by young people in informal speech. It is never used in speaking to a person of higher status in reference to another person of high status. A student talking to a teacher about another teacher, for example, should not use **kare**; he should either say **ano sensei** あの先生 "that teacher" or name the teacher (e.g., **Yamashita-sensei** 山下先生).

EXAMPLE:

(2) Teacher: **Kimi no eigo no sensei wa dare.**
君の英語の先生は誰。
Who's your English teacher?
Student: **Yamashita-sensei desu. Ano sensei** (or **Yamashita-sensei**) **no kurasu wa muzukashii desu.**
山下先生です。あの先生（山下先生）のクラスは難しいです。
Mr. Yamashita. His (lit., that teacher's or Mr. Yamashita's) class is tough.

Kare 彼 and **kareshi** 彼氏, in addition to meaning "he; that person," are often used to mean "boyfriend," as in

EXAMPLE:

(3) **Are Mari no kare** (or **kareshi**)?
あれマリの彼（彼氏）？
Is that Mary's boyfriend?

Kareshi 彼氏 is sometimes used informally as a second-person "pronoun" when addressing a man of equal or lower status, as in

EXAMPLE:

(4) **Kareshi, kore yatte kurenai?**
彼氏、これやってくれない？
Do you mind doing this for me?

(See KANOJO.)

Kariru 借りる *to borrow, to rent [from someone]*

Kariru 借りる often corresponds to English "borrow."

EXAMPLE:

(1) **Saifu o wasureta kara, Ishii-san ni sen-en karita.**
財布を忘れたから、石井さんに千円借りた。
Since I forgot my wallet, I borrowed 1,000 yen from Mr. Ishii.

Sometimes **kariru** 借りる corresponds to other English verbs.

EXAMPLES:

(2) **Ano hito no karite-iru apāto wa zuibun ōkii desu nē.**
あの人の借りているアパートはずいぶん大きいですねえ。
Isn't the apartment he's renting huge!

(3) **Uchi no denwa ga koshō da kara, tonari no denwa o karite denwa-gaisha ni kaketa.**
うちの電話が故障だから、となりの電話を借りて電話会社に掛けた。
Since our phone was out of order, I used the neighbor's phone to call the phone company.

(4) **Toshokan ni hon o kari ni iku tokoro desu.**
図書館に本を借りに行くところです。
I'm on my way to the library to take out a book.

Concerning example (2) above, English speakers should remember that **kariru** 借りる does not mean "to rent [to someone]." The word for this is **kasu** 貸す (see KASU). Example (3) demonstrates why Japanese speakers often make the error of saying in English "*May I borrow your telephone?*"

Although **kariru** 借りる corresponds to a different English verb in each of the four examples above, it maintains the same basic meaning: "to use something that belongs to someone else."

Kasu 貸す *to lend, to rent [to someone]*

Kasu 貸す is the opposite of **kariru** 借りる (see KARIRU) and, as such, corresponds to various English verbs.

EXAMPLES:

(1) **Terada-san ni gosen-en kashite ageta.**
寺田さんに五千円貸してあげた。
I lent Mr. Terada 5,000 yen.

(2) **Ooya wa kono ie wa nijū-man-en-ika de wa kasenai to itte-iru.**
大家はこの家は二十万円以下では貸せないと言っている。
The landlord says he can't rent this house [to anyone] for less than 200,000 yen.

(3) **Chotto denwa o kashite kudasai.**
ちょっと電話を貸してください。
Please let me use your phone.

(4) **Ano toshokan de wa firumu mo kasu sō desu.**
あの図書館ではフィルムも貸すそうです。
I hear that library lets you take out movies too.

Although **kasu** 貸す is represented by a different English verb in each sentence above, its basic meaning remains the same in all: "to let [someone] use [something]."

Katei 家庭 *home*

Katei 家庭 means "home," as in

EXAMPLE:

(1) **Atatakai katei ni sodatta kodomo wa yasashii ningen ni naru.**
あたたかい家庭に育った子供は優しい人間になる。
Children who grow up in warm homes become loving people.

Although in English "home" may refer to a physical structure, as in "We finally bought a home last year," the word **katei** 家庭 can never be used that way. For that, one has to use **ie** or **uchi** うち. **Kazoku** 家族, meaning "family," is sometimes used almost synonymously with **katei**, as in

EXAMPLE:

(2) **Shōnen no furyōka wa kazoku/katei no sekinin da.**
少年の不良化は家族/家庭の責任だ。
Juvenile delinquency is the fault of the family/home.

The difference between **kazoku** 家族 and **katei** 家庭, however, is that whereas **kazoku** refers to "members of a family," **katei** means "home," i.e., a place inhabited by the family. **Katei** also appears in a number of compounds such as

EXAMPLES:

(3a) **katei-ryōri**
家庭料理
home cooking

(3b) **katei-kyōshi**
家庭教師
tutor (lit., home teacher)

(3c) **kateika**
家庭科
home economics

In these compounds, **katei** 家庭 cannot be replaced by **kazoku** 家族.

Ka⌐tsu 勝つ *to win*

Katsu 勝つ behaves very much like English "win" in such phrases as below:

EXAMPLE:

(1) **shiai/gēmu/senkyo ni katsu**
試合/ゲーム/選挙に勝つ
to win a match/a game/an election

In the following phrases, however, **katsu** 勝つ must be replaced by other verbs.

EXAMPLES:

(2a) **Takarakuji ni ataru** (not *katsu 勝つ)
宝くじに当たる
to win a lottery

(2b) **Akademīshō o toru** (not *katsu 勝つ)
アカデミー賞をとる。
to win an Oscar

Ka⌐wa⌐ 川 *river*

"River" is defined as "a natural stream of water of fairly large size." **Kawa** 川, on the other hand, may refer to a stream of almost any size, wide or narrow. As Ogasawara (p. 129) points out, therefore, while "jump over a river" (instead of "stream") sounds strange in English, **kawa o tobikoeru** 川を飛び越える "to jump over a **kawa**" is perfectly acceptable in Japanese.

Kawari 代わり *instead of; in compensation for*

Kawari (ni) 代わり（に）usually means "instead of."

EXAMPLE:

(1) **Wakai Nihonjin wa, ocha no kawari ni kōhī o nomu yō ni natte kita.**
若い日本人は、お茶の代わりにコーヒーを飲むようになってきた。
Young Japanese have started drinking coffee instead of tea.

It is, however, sometimes used to mean "in compensation for" or "to make up for," as in

EXAMPLES:

(2a) **Kono shigoto wa kitsui kawari ni kyūryō ga ii.**
この仕事はきつい代わりに給料がいい。
This job is demanding, but (to make up for that) it pays well.

(2b) **Fujisan ni noboru no wa taihen da ga, sono kawari chōjō kara no nagame ga subarashii.**
富士山に登るのは大変だが、その代わり頂上からの眺めがすばらしい。
Although it's tough to climb Mt. Fuji, (to compensate for that) the view from the top is gorgeous.

Ka⌐zoku 家族 *family*

Kazoku 家族 means "family," as in

EXAMPLE:
(1) **Ninon no kazoku wa chiisaku natte-kite-iru.**
日本の家族は小さくなってきている。
Japanese families have been getting smaller.

Kazoku 家族 can also mean "family member."

EXAMPLE:
(2) **Watashi ni wa kazoku ga go-nin aru.**
私には家族が五人ある。
I have five family members (i.e., There are five in my family [excluding myself]).

Example (2) should be clearly distinguished from **Uchi wa go-nin kazoku desu** うちは五人家族です "Ours is a five-member family [including myself]." Example (2) also shows why some Japanese make the mistake of using "*I have five families" in English to mean "I have five family members."

Ka⌐zu 数 *number*

Kazu 数 meaning "number" is used only when the amount is the issue.

EXAMPLE:
(1) **Jidōsha no kazu ga hidoku fuete-kita.**
自動車の数がひどく増えてきた。
The number of automobiles has increased tremendously.

Phone numbers and such serial numbers as license numbers are **bangō** 番号, not **kazu** 数.

EXAMPLE:
(2) **Denwa-bangō o oshiete kudasai.**
電話番号を教えてください。
Please give me your phone number.

To ask "what number," however, say **nan-ban** 何番, not *****nan-bangō** 何番号.

EXAMPLE:
(3) **Otaku no denwa-bangō wa nan-ban desu ka.**
お宅の電話番号は何番ですか。
What (lit., What number) is your phone number?

Ke⌐ga⌐ けが, 怪我 *injury*

In English, to describe someone sustaining an injury, one most likely uses the passive, as in

EXAMPLE:
(1) I was hurt/injured in a car accident.

In Japanese, on the other hand, the active is the norm, as in

EXAMPLE:

(2) **Jidōshajiko de kega o shita.**
自動車事故で怪我をした。
I was hurt/injured in a car accident.

One could use the passive-causative form **kega o saserareta** 怪我をさせられた only when one is hurt willfully.

EXAMPLE:

(3) **Aitsu to no kenka de, hidoi kega o saserareta.**
あいつとのけんかで、ひどい怪我をさせられた。
When I had a fight with him, I was seriously injured.

Keizaiteki 経済的 *economic; economical*

Keizaiteki 経済的 means both "economic" and "economical," as in

EXAMPLES:

(1a) **Nihon wa tojōkoku ni jūbun na keizaiteki-enjo o ataete-iru darō ka.**
日本は途上国に十分な経済援助を与えているだろうか。
Is Japan giving enough economic aid to developing nations?

(1b) **Kuruma no enjin o fukashi-tsuzukeru no wa keizaiteki de wa nai.**
車のエンジンをふかしつづけるのは経済的ではない。
Leaving a car engine idling for a long time is not economical.

This is exactly the reason Japanese speakers of English have a hard time distinguishing *economic* from *economical*.

Ke¹kkō けっこう *quite*

Kekkō けっこう means "quite" and usually modifies adjectives and verbs with positive meanings.

EXAMPLES:

(1a) **Kekkō oishii ne.**
けっこうおいしいね。
This tastes quite good (or better than expected), doesn't it?

(1b) **Kare kekkō yaru ne.**
彼、けっこうやるね。
He does pretty well (or better than expected), doesn't he?

Kekkō けっこう is somewhat similar to **zuibun** ずいぶん and **nakanaka** なかなか.

EXAMPLES:

(2) **Kimi no gāru-furendo**
君のガールレンド

    (2a) **zuibun**
        ずいぶん

    (2b) **nakanaka**
        なかなか

    (2c) **kekkō kirei dane.**
        けっこうきれいだね。

(2a), (2b), (2c) all state that the woman in question is quite beautiful. (2a), however, is the highest compliment, signaling that the speaker is highly impressed. (2b) signals that the speaker is somewhat surprised because the addressee's girlfriend is much more beautiful than expected. There is a sense of admiration implied, albeit less than in the case of (2a). (2c) is a somewhat risky statement. It certainly is not as strong a compliment as the other two. In fact, it might be taken to mean that the speaker had low expectations. The implication is like "She isn't bad at all, is she?"

Ke˺kkō desu 結構です *That's fine*

Kekkō desu 結構です is a politer and more humble variant of **Ii desu** いいです. It is used, for example, as a response to a request.

EXAMPLE:
(1)　A: **Ashita ukagatte mo yoroshii deshō ka.**
　　　あした伺ってもよろしいでしょうか。
　　　May I visit you tomorrow?
　　B: **Kekkō desu yo.**
　　　結構ですよ。
　　　By all means. (lit., That would be fine.)

　　Kekkō desu 結構です usually occurs in affirmative statements. In (1), for example, if speaker B does not want speaker A to come tomorrow, he should not say ***Kekkō ja arimasen** 結構じゃありません (lit., "That wouldn't be good") but something else, such as

EXAMPLE:
(2)　**Ashita wa chotto komarimasu ga.**
　　あしたはちょっと困りますが。
　　Tomorrow would be a bit inconvenient.

　　Kekkō desu 結構です is also a polite way of declining a suggestion or an invitation.

EXAMPLE:
(3)　A: **Kōhī de mo nomimashō ka.**
　　　コーヒーでも飲みませんか。
　　　Shall we have coffee or something?
　　B: **Kekkō desu.**
　　　結構です。
　　　No, thank you.

Although most Japanese would take **Kekkō desu** 結構です in this case to mean "No, thank you," some might interpret it as "That would be fine." To avoid ambiguity, say **Iie, kekkō desu** いいえ、結構です for "No, thank you," and **Kekkō desu nē** 結構ですねえ for "That would be fine."

Kekkon-suru 結婚する *to marry (someone); get married*

In English, "to marry" is a transitive verb and takes a direct object, as in "He married a beautiful woman," whereas Japanese **kekkon-suru** 結婚する is an intransitive verb and takes the particle **to** と instead of **o** を, as in **Kare wa bijin to kekkon-shita** 彼は美人と結婚した. There are other Japanese verbs that take **to** whose English counterparts are transitive verbs. Some examples follow.

EXAMPLES:

(1a) **Kare wa bijin no okusan to sugu rikon-shite-shimatta.**

彼は美人の奥さんとすぐ離婚してしまった。

He divorced his beautiful wife immediately.

(1b) **Dainijitaisen de, Nihon wa Amerika to tatakatta.**

第二次大戦で、日本はアメリカと戦った。

In World War II, Japan fought America.

Students of Japanese whose native language is English often confuse **kekkon-suru** 結婚する "to get married" and **kekkon-shite-iru** 結婚している "to be in the state of having gotten married." The reason for this confusion is that, in English, "be married" not only means "be in the state of marriage" but is often used in the sense of "get married," as in "He was (or got) married yesterday." In Japanese, the distinction between **kekkon-suru** and **kekkon-shite-iru** is clearly observed.

EXAMPLES:

(2) **Ano hito wa raigetsu kekkon-suru** (not *****kekkon-shitei-ru** 結婚している) **sō desu.**

あの人は来月 結婚するそうです。

I hear he will be getting married next month.

(3) **Ano hito wa dokushin ja arimasen. Mō kekkon-shite-imasu** (not *****kekkon-shimasu** 結婚します) **yo.**

あの人は独身じゃありません。もう 結婚していますよ。

He isn't single. He's already married.

Like **kekkon-suru** 結婚する, **kekkon-shite-iru** 結婚している takes the particle **to** と.

EXAMPLE:

(4) **Sumisu-san wa Nihonjin to** (not *****o** を or *****ni** に) **kekkon shimashita** (or **kekkon-shite-imasu**).

スミスさんは日本人と結婚しました(結婚しています)。

Mr. Smith married (or is married to) a Japanese.

Kenbutsu 見物 *sightseeing*

Kenbutsu 見物 is often confused with **kankō** 観光, which also means "sightseeing." There are some differences between these two, however. First, **kankō** is, more likely than not, used as part of compound nouns, such as **kankōryokō** 観光旅行 "sightseeing trip," **kankōkyaku** 観光客 "sightseer; tourist," and **kankōbasu** 観光バス "sightseeing bus." Second, **kenbutsu** 見物 is generally used as a verb with the addition of **-suru** する. See the example below.

EXAMPLE:

(1) **Kyōto e kankōryokō** (not *****kenbutsuryokō** 見物旅行) **ni itte, takusan no jinja ya otera o kenbutsu-shite** (not *****kankō-shite** 観光して) **aruita.**

京都へ観光旅行へ行って、たくさんの神社やお寺を見物して歩いた。

I went on a sightseeing trip to Kyoto and toured around, visiting a lot of shrines and temples.

Third, **kankō** 観光 implies a trip over some distance, i.e., it is very unlikely that the word is used for a little trip to a local event, while **kenbutsu** 見物 would be acceptable for that occasion as well.

EXAMPLE:

(2) **Kyō wa machi de Kurisumasu no parēdo ga aru kara kenbutsu** (not **kankō 観光) **ni itte koyō.**

今日は町でクリスマスのパレードがあるから見物に行ってこよう。

There's a Christmas parade downtown today; I think I'll go see it.

Ke˥redomo けれども *but*

Keredomo けれども is most often used to connect two clauses whose meanings oppose or contradict each other. In such a case, the most appropriate English equivalent would be "but."

EXAMPLE:

(1) **Nihonjin wa minna gakkō de eigo o narau keredomo, hontō ni jōzu na hito wa sukunai.**

日本人はみんな学校で英語を習うけれども、本当に上手な人は少ない。

All Japanese study English in school, but very few are really good at it.

Keredomo けれども is often used, however, just to prepare a setting for the statement that follows.

EXAMPLE:

(2) **Samuku natte kimashita keredomo, mado o shimemashō ka.**

寒くなってきましたけれども、窓を閉めましょうか。

It has become chilly. Shall I close the window?

As example (2) shows, **keredomo けれども** used this way should be left unsaid in English. **Keredomo けれども** used to identify oneself at the beginning of a telephone conversation functions basically the same way.

EXAMPLE:

(3) **Miura desu keredomo, Suzuki-san irasshaimasu ka.**

三浦ですけれども、鈴木さんいらっしゃいますか。

This is Miura. Is Mr. Suzuki there, please?

Keredomo けれども may also appear in sentence-final position. Since the Japanese speaker has a tendency to leave things unsaid but rather to imply or suggest things instead, this expression is a favorite device for that purpose, as in

EXAMPLE:

(4) **Sensei, chotto onegai-shitai koto ga aru n desu keredomo...**

先生、ちょっとお願いしたい事があるんですけれども...。

Sir, I have a favor I'd like to ask you (but may I do so?).

Keredomo けれども has two other versions: **keredo けれど** and **kedo けど**. These three forms all mean the same, but the shorter the form, the more casual and colloquial it is. In writing, therefore, **kedo** should be avoided except in informal letters.

Keredomo けれども and **ga が** are just about the same in both meaning and function. For instance, **keredomo** in the four example sentences above may all be replaced by **ga**. There are, however, some slight differences. First, **ga** is probably a little more suited to writing than **keredomo**. Second, **ga** is not used at the beginning of a new sentence, while **keredomo** may be so used, as in

EXAMPLE:

(5) **Hokkaidō no fuyu wa totemo samui desu. Keredomo** (not *ga が), **natsu wa kaiteki desu.**
北海道の冬はとても寒いです。けれども、夏は快適です。
Winters in Hokkaido are frigid. Summers, however, are pleasant.

Third, when two clauses are connected with **ga** が, both clauses should be in the same style, i.e., if the second clause is in the formal **desu-masu** style, the first one should be in the same style; if the first clause is in the plain **da** or **dearu** style, the second clause should follow suit. With **keredomo** けれども, this rule need not be observed as strictly. For example,

EXAMPLE:

(6) **Hokkaidō no fuyu wa totemo samui keredo (?ga** が) **natsu wa kaiteki desu.**
北海道の冬はとても寒いけれども、夏は快適です。
Winters in Hokkaido are frigid, but summers are pleasant.

Kesshite 決して *by no means*

Kesshite 決して is used in a negative sentence to mean "by no means." Although it can occur by itself as a statement, it usually combines with a negative word to convey a strong negation. Using **kesshite** is like saying "I swear to you that such-and-such cannot happen."

EXAMPLES:

(1) **Sonna koto wa kesshite arimasen.**
そんなことは決してありません。
That is by no means possible.

(2) **Kare wa kesshite baka de wa nai.**
彼は決して馬鹿ではない。
He is by no means stupid.

Equating **kesshite** 決して with "never" is dangerous, for this equation can hold only as long as "never" is used in the sense of "absolutely not." **Kesshite** should not be equated with "never" meaning "at no time."

EXAMPLES:

(3) **Sonna koto wa kesshite yurusenai.**
そんな事は決して許せない。
I shall never allow such a thing.

(4) **Hawai de wa yuki ga faru koto ga nai.**
ハワイでは雪が降る事がない。
It never snows in Hawaii.

In example (3), "never" corresponds to **kesshite** 決して because "never" is used in the sense of "absolutely not." In (4), however, "never" means "at no time"; the corresponding Japanese version, therefore, does not use **kesshite**.

Kesshite 決して is mostly used in writing. In speech, it sounds formal; in informal conversation, use **zettai ni** 絶対に "absolutely."

EXAMPLE:

(5) **Sonna koto wa zettai ni nai yo.**
そんな事は絶対にないよ。
That's absolutely impossible.

K⌐ika⌐i 機会 *opportunity; chance*

Kikai 機会 basically means "a suitable time to do something." Since the loanword **chansu** チャンス means about the same, they are often used interchangeably, as in

EXAMPLE:

(1) **Jugyō-chū wa sensei ni shitsumon-suru kikai/chansu ga nai.**
授業中は先生に質問する 機会/チャンス がない。
In class, I don't have a chance to ask the teacher a question.

There are a few differences between the two words. First, unlike **chansu** チャンス, **kikai** 機会 is sometimes used almost interchangeably with **toki** 時, as in

EXAMPLE:

(2) **Ōsaka e itta kikai** (not **chansu* チャンス) **ni Ōsakajō o mite-kita.**
大阪へ行った機会に大阪城を見て来た。
When I went to Osaka, I visited (lit., took the opportunity to visit) Osaka Castle.

Second, **chansu** チャンス is often used specifically in such sports as baseball to mean "chance to score," as in

EXAMPLE:

(3) **Nanakai-ura chansu ga yatte-kimashita.**
(sportscaster broadcasting): 7回裏チャンスがやって来ました。
Here in the bottom of the seventh inning, the team has a chance to score.

Third, since loanword equivalents appeal more to younger people than to older people, the former are more likely than the latter to use **chansu** チャンス when either will do.

Kiku 聞く *to listen, to hear, to ask [a question]*

Kiku 聞く means "to listen, to hear," as in (1) and (2).

EXAMPLES:

(1) **Maiasa rajio no nyūsu o kiku.**
毎朝ラジオのニュースを聞く。
Every morning I listen to the news on the radio.

(2) **Tanabe-san ga byōki ni natta to kiite bikkuri-shita.**
田辺さんが病気になったと聞いてびっくりした。
I was surprised to hear that Mr. Tanabe had gotten ill.

Note that while English "listen" is an intransitive verb and takes "to," as in "listen to the news," **kiku** 聞く is a transitive verb and takes **o**; e.g., **nyūsu** (**rajio**, **ongaku**, etc.) **o kiku** ニュース(ラジオ, 音楽, ...)を聞く "listen to the news (the radio, music, etc.)." **Kiku** preceded by a sentence + **to** と, as in (2), means "to hear."

Kiku 聞く also means "to ask [a question]." The noun signifying the person to whom the question is directed is followed by the particle **ni** に.

EXAMPLE:

(3) **Sensei ni kikimashō.**
先生に聞きましょう。
Let's ask the teacher [the question].

Sometimes **dare-dare** 誰々 (i.e., "someone") **ni** に (as in **sensei ni**) is followed by **nani-nani** 何々 (i.e., "something") **o** を.

EXAMPLE:

(4) **Junsa ni michi o kikimashita.**
巡査に道を聞きました。
I asked a policeman the way [to a place].

When the word **shitsumon** 質問 "question" is used, **kiku** 聞く must be avoided. *Shitsumon o kiku** 質問を聞く would be just as wrong in Japanese as "*inquire a question" would be in English. Use **shitsumon-suru** 質問する instead.

EXAMPLE:

(5) **Sensei ni shitsumon-shimashō** (not *shitsumon o kikimashō** 質問を聞きましょう).
先生に質問しましょう。
Let's ask the teacher some questions.

Kiku 聞く meaning "to ask" also occurs in the structure "question + **to kiku** と聞く."

EXAMPLE:

(6) **Nan-ji desu ka to kikimashita.**
何時ですかと聞きました。
I asked what time it was.

Kimi 君 *you*

Kimi 君 is more restricted in use than **anata** あなた, which also means "you" (see ANA-TA). It is used only by men when talking either to a close friend or to someone of lower status (e.g., a teacher talking to a student). Although it is most often used in addressing males, females may sometimes be addressed as **kimi** (e.g., an executive talking to a female clerk, or a young man addressing his wife).

Kimono 着物 *kimono, clothing*

Kimono 着物 has two meanings. First, in a narrow sense, it refers to **kimono**, i.e., traditional Japanese-style clothing. When it is used in this sense, as in (1) below, it is synonymous with **wafuku** 和服 "Japanese clothing," the only difference being that **kimono** is a more colloquial term than the latter.

EXAMPLE:

(1) **Kyō wa yōfuku o kinai de kimono o kiyō.**
今日は洋服をを着ないで着物を着よう。
I think I'll wear a kimono today instead of Western clothing.

More broadly, however, **kimono** 着物 may refer to clothing in general.

EXAMPLE:

(2) **Ofuro no ato de sugu kimono o kinai to kaze o hikimasu yo.**
お風呂の後ですぐ着物を着ないと風邪をひきますよ。
If you don't put on your clothes right after a/the bath, you'll catch a cold.

My hunch is that this second use is on the decline, and that **kimono** 着物 in the sense of "clothing in general" is gradually being replaced by other words such as **fuku** 服 "clothes." This is no doubt due to the fact that more and more Japanese wear Western clothes rather than **kimono**.

Ki¹njo 近所 *neighborhood*

Kinjo 近所 means "neighborhood" in the sense of "vicinity."

EXAMPLE:

(1) **Uchi no kinjo ni wa posuto ga nai.**
うちの近所にはポストがない。
In my neighborhood there aren't any mailboxes.

Kinjo 近所 does not mean "neighborhood" in the sense of "locality." The use of **kinjo** in (2) is therefore wrong.

EXAMPLE:

(2) *__Koko wa modan na kinjo desu nē.__
*ここはモダンな近所ですねえ。
This is a modern neighborhood, isn't it!

To convey the idea of the English sentence above, one would have to replace **kinjo** by another word, such as **jūtakuchi** 住宅地 "residential district."

EXAMPLE:

(3) **Koko wa modan na jūtakuchi desu nē.**
ここはモダンな住宅地ですねえ。
This is a modern residential district, isn't it!

Although, in English, "in the neighborhood of" may mean "about," as in *The population of Tokyo is in the neighborhood of ten million*, **kinjo** 近所 is never used in that sense. Use **-gurai** ぐらい (see GURAI) instead.

Kirei きれい *pretty, beautiful, clean*

Kirei きれい has two basic meanings. First, it means "pretty, beautiful, lovely."

EXAMPLES:

(1) **Kirei desu nē.**
きれいですねえ。
Isn't she pretty!

(2) **Kirei na hana o arigatō.**
きれいな花をありがとう。
Thanks for the beautiful flowers.

Second, **kirei** きれい means "clean, neat."

EXAMPLES:
(3) **Te o kirei ni arai-nasai.**
手をきれいに洗いなさい。
Wash your hands till they're clean.
(4) **Motto kirei ni kaite kudasai.**
もっときれいに書いてください。
Please write more neatly.

It is extremely interesting that the ideas of cleanliness and beauty are expressed by one and the same word in Japanese. This is, however, not surprising when one thinks of the high regard Shintoists hold for cleanliness. (See also UTSUKUSHII.)

Kiru 着る *to put on, to wear*

Kiru 着る means "to put on (or wear), on the body," usually by putting one's arms through sleeves (Soga, p. 281). The head and the limbs may be involved, but the trunk must be the main portion to be covered. Nouns that may be used as the object of **kiru** are, for example, **kimono** 着物, **yōfuku** 洋服 "Western clothes," **wafuku** 和服 "Japanese clothes" (i.e., ki-mono), **uwagi** 上着 "jacket," **ōbā** オーバー "overcoat," **sētā** セーター "sweater," **shatsu** シャツ "undershirt," **waishatsu** ワイシャツ "dress shirt," **rēnkōto** レインコート "raincoat," **burausu** ブラウス "blouse," **yukata** 浴衣 "informal summer **kimono**," **pajama** パジャマ, "pajamas," and **sebiro** 背広 "men's suit."

EXAMPLES:
(1) **Nihonjin wa konogoro taitei yōfuku o kite-iru.**
日本人はこのごろたいてい洋服を着ている。
Nowadays the Japanese are wearing Western clothes most of the time.
(2) **Ono-san wa wafuku o kiru to suteki desu nē.**
小野さんは和服を着るとすてきですねえ。
Ms. Ono looks terrific in a kimono, doesn't she!

Clothing and other wearable items not intended for the trunk of the body require other verbs, such as **haku** はく, **kaburu** かぶる, and **hameru** はめる, depending on where and how they are put on. (See the entries for these verbs for more detail.)

As is the case with other verbs meaning "to put on," **kiru** refers to the act of putting on clothes, whereas the **te**-form + **iru** いる refers to the state of having put something on. Compare the following:

EXAMPLES:
(3) **Soto wa samui kara, ie o deru mae ni ōbā o kiru** (not *****kite-iru** 着ている) **hō ga ii.**
外は寒いから、家を出る前にオーバーを着る方が良い。
Since it's cold, you should put on your overcoat before you go out of the house.
(4) **Ano shiroi sebiro o kite-iru** (not *****kiru** 着る) **hito wa dare desu ka.**
あの白い背広を着ている人は誰ですか。
Who's that man in a white suit?

Ki⌐setsu 季節 *season*

If you ask native English speakers to name the four seasons, some may start with "winter" while others may begin with "spring," i.e., there is no absolutely set order. In Japanese, however, the order is always set: invariably, it is **haru-natsu-aki-fuyu** 春夏秋冬 ("spring, summer, fall, winter"). Even when the **on** readings are used, there is no difference: it still is **shun-ka-shū-tō** 春夏秋冬. The fact that the school year in Japan begins in the spring may have something to do with this, i.e., as far as the Japanese are concerned, everything starts in the spring, when cherry blossoms bloom.

Kitai-suru 期待する *to expect*

Once a student of mine said about a classmate who was ill:

EXAMPLE:

(1) ***Kare wa kinō byōki datta kara, kyō wa yasumu koto o kitai-shimasu.**
    *彼はきのう病気だったから、今日は休む事を期待します。

He meant "He was ill yesterday, so I expect him to be absent today," which would be perfectly all right in English. He did not realize, however, that **kitai-suru** 期待する, unlike "expect," is used only with reference to desirable occurrences, such as

EXAMPLE:

(2) **Tanaka-san kara no enjo o kitai-shite-iru.**
    田中さんからの援助を期待している。
    I am expecting help from Mr. Tanaka.

Sentence (1) above should be restated as follows:

EXAMPLE:

(3) **Kare wa kinō byōki datta kara, kyō wa yasumu darō to omoimasu.**
    彼はきのう病気だったから、今日は休むだろうと思います。
    He was ill yesterday, so I think he'll be absent today.

Kitto きっと *I am sure (such and such) is the case.*

Kitto きっと usually means the speaker is quite sure something is the case, or something will definitely happen, as in

EXAMPLE:

(1) **Tanaka-san wa kitto kuru yo.**
    田中さんはきっと来るよ。
    I'm sure Mr. Tanaka will come.

Kanarazu 必ず, too, is used similarly, but it is more like "without fail," i.e., something happens without any exception, as in

EXAMPLE:

(2) **Tanaka-san wa natsu ni naru to kanarazu Karuizawa e iku.**
    田中さんは夏になると必ず軽井沢へ行く。
    Every summer Mr. Tanaka never fails to go to Karuizawa.

Although **kitto** きっと and **kanarazu** 必ず are quite similar, they are not exactly the same. **Kitto** has to do with one's conjecture, whereas **kanarazu** is used to express more objective certainties. For conjectures, therefore, use **kitto**, as in

EXAMPLE:

(3) **Tarō wa kinō kurasu o yasunda kara, kitto** (not *__kanarazu__ 必ず) **byōki datta no darō.**
太郎はきのうクラスを休んだから、きっと病気だったのだろう。
Taro was absent from school yesterday; he must have been sick.

For something for which no exception can be granted, use **kanarazu** 必ず rather than **kitto** きっと, as in

EXAMPLE:

(4) **Kono gakkō de wa mainichi kanarazu** (not *__kitto__ きっと) **seifuku de tōkō-suru koto ga yōkyū-sareru.**
この学校では毎日必ず制服で登校する事が要求される。
At this school, it is required that every day the students come to school in uniforms without fail.

Kitto may be used with negatives, whereas **kanarazu** 必ず is unlikely to be so used.

EXAMPLE:

(5) **Tanaka-san wa kitto** (not *__kanarazu__ 必ず) **konai yo.**
田中さんはきっと来ないよ。
I am sure Mr. Tanaka won't come.

(See also KANARAZU.)

Ki⌈wa⌉mete きわめて *extremely*

Kiwamete きわめて means "extremely" and is used as in

EXAMPLE:

(1) **Tanaka wa kiwamete yūshū na gakusei de aru.**
田中はきわめて優秀な学生である。
Tanaka is an extremely fine student.

Kiwamete きわめて is a written expression and is rarely used in ordinary speech. In conversation, one would say something like (2).

EXAMPLE:

(2) **Tanaka wa sugoku dekiru gakusei da.**
田中はすごく出来る学生である。
Tanaka is an excellent student.

Ko 子 *child*

Ko 子, like **kodomo** 子供 (see KODOMO), means "child," but, unlike **kodomo**, it is rarely used without a modifier, especially in conversation. In sentences (1) and (2) below, for example, **kodomo** is correct but **ko** is not quite acceptable.

EXAMPLES:
(1) **Kodomo** (not *Ko 子) **wa kawaii.**
子供はかわいい。
Children are cute.
(2) **Asoko ni kodomo** (not *ko 子) **ga iru.**
あそこに子供がいる。
There is a child over there.

When there is a modifier, however, **ko** 子 is just as acceptable as **kodomo** 子供.

EXAMPLE:
(3) **ano** (**uchi no, ōkii, genki na,** etc.) **ko** (or **kodomo**)
あの(うちの, 大きい, 元気な, ...)子(子供)
that (my, big, vigorous, etc.) child

Kōba 工場 *factory*

Kōba 工場 is synonymous with **kōjō** 工場. In fact, they are two different readings of the same characters. They are, however, not exactly interchangeable. **Kōba** sounds more informal than **kōjō**. In proper names referring to factories, **kōjō** is the norm. While **kōba** calls to mind a smaller, less than modern factory, **kōjō** conjures up the image of a larger, modern, well-equipped factory (Tokugawa and Miyajima, p. 159).

Kodomo 子供 *child*

Kodomo 子供 is similar to English "child" in meaning in that it means both "child" as the antonym of "adult," as in (1), and "child" as the antonym of "parent," as in (2).

EXAMPLES:
(1) **Nihon no kodomo wa konogoro ōkiku-natta.**
日本の子供はこのごろ大きくなった。
Japanese children have grown larger these days.
(2) **Watashi no ichiban ue no kodomo wa mō nijū-go desu.**
私の一番上の子供はもう二十五です。
My oldest child is already 25.

(See also KO.)

Kōen 公園 *park*

In English, the word "park" brings to mind a spacious grassy area surrounded by trees. **Kōen** 公園 may refer to that kind of place, too, but it may also refer to a tiny public playground with swings and seesaws but without any greenery.

"Park" has a wider range of meaning than **kōen**. For example, whereas the former appears in such compounds as "ballpark" and "amusement park," **kōen** cannot. "[Base] ball park" is **yakyūjō** 野球場 (lit., "baseball place"), and "amusement park" is **yūenchi** 遊園地 (lit., "play-garden area").

Kōfuku 幸福 *happy/happiness*

Kōfuku 幸福 is a noun meaning "happiness" but is also used as a **na**-adjective. **Kōfuku** usually refers to a person's happy state over a long period of time. For example, sentence (1) below is correct but (2) sounds a little odd because the sentence is about happiness for a short period of time. In this sense, **kōfuku** is different from English "happy," which may be used in either way.

EXAMPLES:

(1) **Jōji wa kōfuku na isshō o okutta.**
ジョージは幸福な一生を送った。
George lived a happy life.

(2) **?Jōji wa kinō kōfuku na ichinichi o okutta.**
?ジョージはきのう幸福な一日を送った。
George had a happy day yesterday.

Tanoshii 楽しい, too, is often equated with "happy," as in (3) below.

EXAMPLE:

(3) **Jōji wa tanoshii isshō o okutta.**
ジョージは楽しい一生を送った。
George lived a happy life.

There is a difference in connotation between (1) and (3). **Kōfuku** 幸福 refers to a mentally or spiritually satisfied state, whereas **tanoshii** 楽しい connotes "having fun" or "enjoying oneself." In sentence (1), therefore, George was likely to be blessed with a nice family, trustworthy friends, a good job, etc., which gave him inner contentment; sentence (3), on the other hand, focuses on George having had a great time all through his life— enjoying his hobbies, for example.

Sentence (2) above becomes totally legitimate if **kōfuku na** 幸福な is replaced by **tanoshii**.

EXAMPLE:

(4) **Jōji wa kinō tanoshii ichinichi o okutta.**
ジョージはきのう楽しい一生を送った。
George had a happy (i.e., fun-filled) day yesterday.

(See also TANOSHII.)

Kʰōgi¹ [Koʰogi¹] 講義 *lecture*

Academic lectures given as a course at a college or a university are **kōgi** 講義.

EXAMPLE:

(1) **Mainichi Ogura-sensei no kōgi ni dete-iru.**
毎日小倉先生の講義に出ている。
I attend Professor Ogura's lecture every day.

Public lectures on nonacademic topics are not **kōgi** 講義 but **kōen** 講演. **Kōen** can be on academic topics, but there are at least two differences between **kōgi** and **kōen**: a **kōen** is (a) usually directed to a wider audience, and (b) generally a one-shot affair.

EXAMPLE:

(2) **Kinō wa kōkaidō de sekiyu-kiki ni tsuite yūmei na keizai-hyōronka no tokubetsu-kōen ga atta.**

きのうは公会堂で石油危機について有名な経済評論家の特別講演があった。

Yesterday at the public hall there was a special lecture on the oil crisis by a well-known economic critic.

Kōhai 後輩 *one's junior*

If a person enters, and graduates from, the same school or college that you do but behind you in time, he is not a **tomodachi** 友達 "friend" (see TOMODACHI) to you no matter how close the relationship. He is your **kōhai** 後輩 (lit., "junior") instead, and you are his **senpai** 先輩 (lit., "senior"). In Japanese society, which views human relationships in terms of higher and lower status, even one year's difference in time makes a crucial difference in terminology. Furthermore, a **kōhai** must speak to a **senpai** more politely than vice versa (see SENPAI).

Koibito 恋人 *sweetheart*

Someone of the opposite sex whom one loves is a **koibito** 恋人. The term is reserved for a premarital sweetheart only, however.

EXAMPLE:

(1) **Koibito to kekkon dekiru to iu no wa shiawase da.**

恋人と結婚できるというのは幸せだ。

It is fortunate to be able to marry someone one loves.

Nowadays, other more up-to-date expressions such as **bōifurendo** ボーイフレンド "boyfriend" and **gārufurendo** ガールフレンド "girlfriend" are much more commonly used, especially in speech. The difference is that **koibito** 恋人 could also be someone one secretly longs for, whereas **bōifurendo/gārufurendo** must be friends in real life.

Aijin 愛人 also means someone of the opposite sex whom one loves, but its implications are negative, i.e., "someone with whom one has a physical relationship other than one's spouse."

EXAMPLE:

(2) **Jibun no tsuma no hoka ni aijin o motsu no wa, Meiji no koro no seijika ni wa kanari futsū no koto datta no de wa nai darō ka.**

自分の妻の他に愛人を持つのは、明治の頃の政治家にはかなり普通の事だったのではないだろうか。

Wasn't it fairly common for a Meiji politician to have a mistress-like woman in addition to a wife?

Kō˧kai [Ko˧okai] 後悔 *regret*

Kōkai 後悔 literally means "after regret," which explains why it can refer only to a sense of remorse, guilt, or self-reproach concerning a previous act.

EXAMPLE:

(1) **Wakai koro sake o nomi-sugita koto o kōkai-shite-imasu.**

若い頃酒を飲み過ぎた事を後悔しています。

I regret having drunk too much when I was younger.

Regret about something that has not taken place requires **zannen** 残念 rather than **kōkai** 後悔. In example (2) below, therefore, only (b) is correct.

EXAMPLE:

(2) **Byōki de ashita no pikunikku ni ikarenai**
病気であしたのピクニックに行かれない

  (a) ***koto o kōkai-shite-imasu.**
    *事を後悔しています。

  (b) **no ga zannen desu.**
    のが残念です。

I regret not being able to go to tomorrow's picnic because of my illness.

One can feel a sense of **kōkai** 後悔 only about one's own acts and not about someone else's. In the latter case, **zannen** 残念 must be used. In example (3), therefore, only (b) is correct.

EXAMPLE:

(3) **Musuko ga kōtsūjiko o okoshita koto o**
息子が交通事故を起こした事を

  (a) ***kōkai-shite-imasu.**
    *後悔しています。

  (b) **zannen ni omoimasu.**
    残念に思います。

I regret that my son caused a traffic accident.

If, however, the speaker feels directly responsible for his son's accident, **kōkai** 後悔 is the correct word.

EXAMPLE:

(4) **Musuko ni kōtsūjiko o okosasete-shimatte kōkaishite-imasu.**
息子に交通事故を起こさせてしまって後悔しています。
I regret having caused my son's traffic accident.

Likewise, if "my son" is the person who feels guilty about his own deed, **kōkai** 後悔 is the word to be used.

EXAMPLE:

(5) **Musuko wa kōtsūjiko o okoshita koto o kōkai-shite-imasu.**
息子は交通事故を起こした事を後悔しています。
My son regrets having caused a traffic accident.

Incidentally, note the use of **wa** は in (5), as compared with **ga** が in (3), and the difference in meaning between the two sentences. (See also ZANNEN.)

Ko˥kyō 故郷 *hometown, birthplace*

Kokyō 故郷 "birthplace" is mainly used in writing, as in

EXAMPLE:

Tōkyō wa amari ōkisugite kokyō to iu kanji ga shinai.
東京はあまり大きすぎて故郷という感じがしない。
Tokyo is so large that it does not have the aura of a hometown.

(See also FURUSATO.)

K⌈oma⌉ru 困る *to be at a loss*

Komaru 困る may be translated as a great variety of English words, such as "be at a loss," "be troubled," "be distressed," "be embarrassed," "be in difficulty," to name a few. It basically refers to the unsure state of a person who has met a situation which he does not know how to handle.

EXAMPLES:

(1) **Megane o nakushite komatte-iru n desu.**
眼鏡をなくして困っているんです。
I'm at a loss without my glasses. (lit., Having lost my glasses, I'm being inconvenienced.)

(2) **Ano hito wa konogoro kane ni komatte-iru rashii.**
あの人はこのごろ金に困っているらしい。
It seems that he's hard up these days. (lit., It seems that he is in need of money these days.)

The informal past form **komatta** 困った is often used adjectivally in prenoun position.

EXAMPLE:

(3) **komatta mondai**
困った問題
an embarrassing (or *perplexing, deplorable, distressing) problem*

Komatta 困った in this case means that the problem is of such a nature that it troubles (embarrasses, distresses, etc.) the speaker or whoever is involved. Likewise, **komatta hito** 困った人 most often means not "a person who became troubled" (although this is indeed possible), but "someone who troubles me" (Mizutani and Mizutani, 2, p. 73).

EXAMPLE:

(4) **Uchi no shachō mo komatta hito desu nē.**
うちの社長も困った人ですねえ。
Doesn't our [company] president give us a big headache?

Ko⌈me⌉ 米 *uncooked rice*

Kome 米 is what you buy at a rice shop, i.e., uncooked rice. Once it is cooked, it becomes **gohan** (see GOHAN) or **meshi** 飯 (see MESHI). In women's speech and men's polite speech, **kome** usually becomes **okome** お米.

Ko⌉mu 込む *to become crowded/congested*

Komu 込む/混む is a punctual verb, i.e., a verb indicating a momentary action, in this case "to become crowded," as in

EXAMPLE:

(1) **Kyūjitsu wa dōro ga komu.**
休日は道路が込む。
Roads become congested on holidays.

To indicate "something is crowded," **konde-iru** 込んでいる is normally used.

EXAMPLE:

(2) **Kono densha konde-masu ne.**

この電車込んでますねえ。

This train is crowded, isn't it?

In a prenoun position, **konde-iru** 込んでいる is often replaced by **konda** 込んだ.

EXAMPLE:

(3) **Konda densha ni noru to tsukareru.**

込んだ電車に乗ると疲れる。

It is tiring to ride a crowded train.

In English, it is perfectly all right to say "Japan is a crowded country" or "Tokyo is a crowded city." In Japanese, however, the direct translations of these English sentences sound odd.

EXAMPLES:

(4a) **?Nihon wa konda/konde iru kuni da.**

?日本は 込んだ/込んでいる 国だ。

Japan is a crowded country.

(4b) **?Tōkyō wa konda/konde iru machi da.**

?東京は 込んだ/込んでいる 町だ。

Tokyo is a crowded city.

Apparently such places as Japan and Tokyo are too large to be described as **konda/konde iru** 込んだ/込んでいる. If one narrows one's focus, these sentences become acceptable.

EXAMPLE:

(5) **Nihon/Tōkyō wa doko e itte mo konde iru.**

日本/東京は どこへ行っても込んでいる。

No matter where one goes within Japan/Tokyo, it's crowded.

Ko¹ndo no 今度の *next, this coming*

"Next Sunday" meaning "this coming Sunday" is normally **kondo no nichi-yōbi** 今度の日曜日, rather than **tsugi no nichi-yōbi** 次の日曜日.

EXAMPLE:

(1) **Kondo no nichi-yōbi ni pikunikku ni ikimasu kara, issho ni irasshaimasen ka.**

今度の日曜日にピクニックに行きますから、一緒にいらっしゃいませんか。

We are going on a picnic next (or this coming) Sunday. Would you like to join us?

Tsugi no nichi-yōbi 次の日曜日 would mean "the following Sunday" or "a week from Sunday."

EXAMPLE:

(2) **Kondo no nichi-yōbi wa tsugō ga warui kara, tsugi no nichi-yōbi ni shimashō ka.**

今度の日曜日は都合が悪いから、次の日曜日にしましょうか。

Since next (or this coming) Sunday is inconvenient, shall we make it the following Sunday (or a week from Sunday)?

Ko⌈nnichi wa⌉ こんにちは *Good day!*

Konnichi wa こんにちは is usually equated with "Good afternoon!" but they are not identical. Although **Konnichi wa** is most often used in the afternoon, it is also used in the morning, and sometimes even in the evening.

Konnichi wa こんにちは is not the same as "Hello!" either. Unlike "Hello!" **Konnichi wa** may not be said more than once to the same person on the same day. For example, if you have met someone in the morning and have exchanged **Ohayō gozaimasu** おはようございます with him, don't say **Konnichi wa** to him when you meet him again elsewhere in the afternoon of that same day. Just exchange a bow or say something like **Mata oaishimashita ne** またお会いしましたね "Here we meet again."

Unlike **Ohayō gozaimasu**, which can be said to anyone, **Konnichi wa** may be said only to outsiders, i.e., people who do not belong to one's own group (Mizutani and Mizutani, 1, p. 17). One does not therefore say **Konnichi wa** to a member of one's own household; nor is **Konnichi wa** normally exchanged between persons working in the same office.

Konnichi wa is a less formal greeting than **Ohayō gozaimasu**. It is not proper, therefore, to use it to a person of higher status. On such occasions, use a substitute, such as talking about the weather (ibid.), e.g., **Oatsū gozaimasu** お暑うございます "What a hot day!" (see OHAYŌ GOZAIMASU).

In rapid, casual speech, **Konnichi wa** こんにちは is often shortened to **Konchiwa** こんちは.

Kono-aida この間 *the other day, recently*

Kono-aida この間 should not be confused with **konogoro** このごろ "these days" (see KONOGORO). In sentence (1), only **kono-aida** is correct, whereas in (2), only **konogoro** is correct.

EXAMPLES:
(1) **Kono-aida** (not ****konogoro** このごろ) **Yoshida-san ni aimashita.**
   この間吉田さんに会いました。
   I saw Mr. Yoshida the other day.
(2) **Konogoro** (not ****kono-aida** この間) **yoku Yoshida-san ni aimasu.**
   このごろよく吉田さんに会います。
   I often see Mr. Yoshida these days.

Kono-aida この間 and **senjitsu** 先日 are more or less synonymous, but the latter is more formal. Some speakers of Japanese may also feel that **kono-aida** can refer to a slightly more distant past than **senjitsu**. **Senjitsu** can be anywhere between "two or three days ago" and "a week or two ago," whereas **kono-aida** may range from "two or three days ago" to even "a month or two ago."

Kono-aida この間 becomes **konaida** こないだ in rapid familiar speech.

EXAMPLE:
(3) **Ano eiga wa mō konaida michatta yo.**
   あの映画はもうこないだ見ちゃったよ。
   I already saw that movie just the other day.

Konogoro このごろ *these days*

Konogoro このごろ means "these days."

EXAMPLE:

(1) **Yamashita-san wa konogoro futotte-kimashita ne.**
山下さんはこのごろ太ってきましたね。
Mr. Yamashita has gotten a little heavier these days, hasn't he!

Konogoro このごろ (accentless) is different in meaning from ko⌐no ko⌐ro この頃 (accented on the next to last syllable) "about this time," which refers to a specific past time (see KORO).

EXAMPLE:

(2) **Watakushi wa sen-kyūhyaku-yonjū-go-nen ni umaremashita ga, chichi ga byōki ni natta no wa kono koro desu.** (example from **Bunka-cho**, p. 370)
私は1945年に生まれましたが、父が病気になったのはこの頃です。
I was born in 1945, and it was about this time that my father fell ill.

Strangely enough, we do not have such words as ***sonogoro** そのごろ or ***anogoro** あのごろ, but only **sono koro** その頃 and **ano koro** あの頃, both meaning "about that time" or "in those days." (For the semantic difference between **sono** その and **ano** あの, see ARE.)

Kore これ *this*

Kore これ is used for referring to something near the speaker.

EXAMPLE:

(1) **Kore wa kyō no shinbun desu.** (speaker touching a newspaper)
これは今日の新聞です。
This is today's paper.

In English, "this" is used in telephone conversations to refer to oneself or to the person at the other end of the line.

EXAMPLE:

(2) A: Who is this?
B: This is John Doe.

In Japanese, on the other hand, **kore** これ cannot refer to the speaker or the hearer. (In polite telephone conversations, **kochira** こちら "this side" is used to refer to the speaker, and **sochira** そちら "that side" to the hearer.)

Kore これ, as a rule, cannot refer to a person directly. In English, one can introduce A to B by saying "This is Mr. A." In Japanese, however, ***Kore wa A-san desu** これはAさんです would be inappropriate (unless the speaker is pointing to a picture of A). **Kore** これ should be replaced by **kochira** こちら.

EXAMPLE:

(3) **Kochira wa Suzuki-san desu.**
こちらは鈴木さんです。
This is Mr. Suzuki.

The only exception would be when you are introducing a member of your family (or someone of lower social status).

EXAMPLE:

(4) **Kore wa uchi no musuko desu. Yoroshiku onegaishimasu.**
これはうちの息子です。よろしくお願いします。
This is my son. I'd like you to meet him (lit., Please treat him favorably).

Ko˺ro　ころ　*approximate time*

Koro ころ means "about the time when," and refers not to a specific point in time but rather to a less clearly defined length of time. Compare the following:

EXAMPLES:

(1) **Haha ga byōki ni natta no wa watashi ga kekkon-shita koro datta.**
母が病気になったのは私が結婚したころだった。
It was about the time I got married that my mother became ill.

(2) **Haha ga byōki ni natta no wa watashi ga kekkon-shita toki datta.**
母が病気になったのは私が結婚した時だった。
It was when I got married that my mother became ill.

In (1), **koro** ころ signals that "my mother" may have become ill either before or after the wedding, but in (2), because **toki** 時 is used instead of **koro**, it is clear that she became ill immediately after the wedding.

When **koro** ころ is used as a suffix to a noun that indicates a point in time, it usually becomes **-goro** ごろ, as in **san-ji-goro** 3時ごろ "about 3 o'clock." (See also -GORO, KONOGORO, and TOKI.)

Koshi　腰　*waist; lower back*

When a gym teacher calls out the following, **koshi** 腰 means "waist":

EXAMPLE:

(1) **Te o koshi ni!**
手を腰に！
Put your hands on your waist!

In terms of size or style, especially with reference to Western-style clothing, however, **uesuto** ウエスト, a loanword from English "waist," is used instead of **koshi** 腰. For example,

EXAMPLES:

(2a) **Uesuto** (not ****koshi** 腰) **wa nan-senchi desu ka.**
ウエストは何センチですか。
How many centimeters is your waist?

(2b) **Ano moderu no uesuto** (?**koshi**) **zuibun hosoi ne.**
あのモデルのウエスト（腰）ずいぶん細いね。
That fashion model's waist is extremely slim, isn't it?

If someone makes the following complaint, however, **koshi** 腰 refers to the lower back.

EXAMPLE:

(3) **Koshi ga itai n desu.**
腰が痛いんです。
My lower back hurts.

Before World War II, there were a large number of **koshi no magatta rōjin** 腰の曲がった老人, "old people with a bent lower back," in Japan, but thanks to an improved lifestyle including better nutrition, old Japanese people nowadays seem to have better posture.

An interesting **koshi**-related idiom is **koshi ga hikui** 腰が低い "humble, modest" (lit., someone's back is low). A humble/modest Japanese bows frequently (sometimes even excessively), an act that keeps his/her lower back rather low. Hence the expression. Needless to say, the opposite is **koshi ga takai** 腰が高い, meaning "haughty."

Ko⌐tae⌐ru 答える *to answer*

Kotaeru 答える has two basic meanings (although there are some other minor uses as well): to answer a question, as in (1), and to answer by saying **Hai!** はい when one's name is called, as in (2).

EXAMPLES:

(1) **Shitsumon ni kotaete-kudasai.**
質問に答えてください。
Please answer my questions.

(2) **Namae o yobarete "Hai!" to kotaeta.**
名前を呼ばれて「はい！」と答えた。
I answered, "Here!" when my name was called.

Answering a door, the telephone, or a letter cannot be **kotaeru** 答える. In each of the following examples, (b) is correct, but (a) is not.

EXAMPLES:

(3) **Dare ka ga nokku-shita no de, genkan ni**
誰かがノックしたので、玄関に

   (a) *****kotaeta.**
      *答えた。

   (b) **deta** (from **deru** 出る).
      出た。

I answered the door because someone knocked.

(4) **Denwa ga natte-iru no ni dare mo**
電話が鳴っているのに誰も

   (a) *****kotaenakatta.**
      *答えなかった。

   (b) **denakatta** (from **deru** 出る).
      出なかった。

Although the telephone was ringing, nobody answered.

(5) **Tegami o moratte sugu**
手紙をもらってすぐ

   (a) *****kotaeta.**
      *答えた。

   (b) **henji o dashita.**
      返事を出した。

I answered (lit., sent a reply) immediately after receiving the letter.

(See also HENJI.)

Ko⌐to⌐ こと, 事 *thing, matter, fact*

Koto 事, like **mono** 物, is often translated into English as "thing." **Koto**, however, refers only to an intangible thing (i.e., an event, a fact, or an act) and thus contrasts with **mono**, which basically refers to a tangible thing.

EXAMPLES:

(1) **Hen na koto ga atta.**
変な事があった。
A strange thing (i.e., event or act) happened.

(2) **Hen na mono ga atta.**
変な物があった。
There was a strange thing (i.e., object).

It is for the same reason that, in example (3), only **koto** 事 is correct, while in (4), only **mono** 物 can be used.

EXAMPLES:

(3) **Omoshiroi koto** (not *mono 物) **o shitta.**
面白い事を知った。
I learned something interesting (e.g., interesting news).

(4) **Depāto de takai mono** (not *koto 事) **o katta.**
デパートで高い物を買った。
I bought something expensive at the department store.

Koto ga aru ことがある *to have had the experience of doing (such and such)*

Koto ga aru ことがある, when preceded by a V-**ta** form, is often translated as "have done (such and such)," as in

EXAMPLE:

(1) **Watashi wa Fujisan ni ichido nobotta koto ga aru.**
私は富士山に一度登ったことがある。
I have climbed Mt. Fuji once.

This does not always mean, however, that English "have done (such and such)" may always be translated as **-ta koto ga aru**. For example,

EXAMPLE:

(2) A: Have you done your homework yet?
B: Yes, I've already done it.

In (2) above, "have done" is correct in English because "have done" can express not only past experience but completion as well. When you translate (2) into Japanese, however, don't use **-ta koto ga aru** たことがある, which can express only past experience, not completion. See (3) below.

EXAMPLE:

(3) A: **Mō shukudai yarimashita ka** (not *yatta koto ga ari-masu ka やったことがありますか).
もう宿題やりましたか。
Have you done your homework yet?

B: **Ee, mō yarimashita** (not *yatta koto ga arimasu やったことがあります).
ええ、もうやりました。
Yes, I've already done it.

A question using **-ta koto ga arimasu ka** たことがありますか is best translated as "Have you ever done (such and such)?"

EXAMPLE:
(4) A: **Fujisan ni nobotta koto ga arimasu ka.**
富士山に登ったことがありますか。
Have you ever climbed Mt. Fuji?
　　B: **Ee, arimasu yo. Kyonen nobotta n desu.**
ええ、ありますよ。去年登ったんです。
Yes, I have. I climbed it last year.

Kōyō 紅葉 *fall colors (lit., red leaves)*

Kōyō means "fall colors." Since the two characters 紅葉 stand for "red," and "leaves," respectively, they literally mean "red leaves" and, strictly speaking, should not refer to "yellow leaves," which are written 黄葉 and also pronounced **kōyō**. 紅葉, however, is normally used broadly to include yellow leaves as well, as in

EXAMPLE:
(1) **Nikkō e kōyō o mi ni ikimashō ka.**
日光へ紅葉を見に行きましょうか。
Shall we go to Nikko to see the fall colors?

　　Momiji, written either in hiragana もみじ or with the same combination as **Kōyō** 紅葉. also may refer to fall colors. **Momiji**, however, has another meaning, i.e., "maple."

EXAMPLE:
(2) **Uchi no niwa ni momiji no ki o ueta.**
うちの庭にもみじの木を植えた。
We planted a maple tree in our yard.

　　In this particular use, **momiji** もみじ is synonymous with **kaede** 楓 "maple." **kōyō** 紅葉, on the other hand, can never mean "maple."
　　There is an interesting word **momijigari** もみじ狩り "excursion for viewing fall colors" (lit. "hunting for fall colors").

EXAMPLE:
(3) **Nikkō e momijigari ni ikimashō ka.**
日光へもみじ狩りに行きましょうか。
Shall we go to Nikko to view the fall colors?

　　Kōyō 紅葉 can never be used with **-gari** 狩り; i.e., the word *kōyōgari 紅葉狩り simply does not exist.

Kubi 首 *neck, head*

Kubi 首 usually means "neck," as in

EXAMPLE:

(1) **Kubi ga nagai/mijikai/futoi/hosoi.**
首が長い/短い/太い/細い。
(Someone) has a long/short/thick/slender neck.

Sometimes, however, **kubi** 首 is interchangeable with **atama** 頭 "head," as in

EXAMPLE:

(2) **Kubi** (or **Atama**) **o furu.**
首（頭）を振る。
(Someone) shakes his/her head.

Although in (2) above, either **kubi** 首 or **atama** 頭 may be used, **kubi** is probably more common. The difference between English and Japanese here is that, in English, "shake one's head" always means "move one's head sideways," and never "move one's head vertically," whereas, in Japanese, **kubi/atama o furu** 首/頭を振る, especially if accompanied by **tate ni** 縦に, "vertically," could mean "nod one's head," as in

EXAMPLE:

(3) **Kubi** (or **Atama**) **o tate ni furu.**
首（頭）を縦に振る。
(Someone) nods his/her head.

If one therefore wishes to make it absolutely clear that sideways motion is meant, one should include **yoko ni** 横に "sideways," as in

EXAMPLE:

(4) **Kubi** (or **Atama**) **o yoko ni furu.**
首（頭）を横に振る。
(Someone) shakes his/her head.

Although **kubi** 首 and **atama** 頭 are interchangeable in (2) through (4) above, they are usually totally separate in use. For example, in (5a) and (5b) below, they refer to different parts of the body.

EXAMPLES:

(5a) **Atama ga itai.**
頭が痛い。
My head hurts.

(5b) **Kubi ga itai.**
首が痛い。
My neck hurts.

Kubi 首, even when it means "head," cannot, at least in one case, be replaced by **atama** 頭. Sentence (6) below, an order that might have been given by a samurai general to a retainer, is an example of that.

EXAMPLE:

(6) **Teki no taishō no kubi** (not *atama 頭) **o totte koi!**
敵の大将の首を取ってこい！
Go get the enemy general's head!

-Kun 君 *(suffix attached to a name)*

-Kun 君, like **-san** さん, is attached to someone's family, given, or full name. This suffix is mostly used by a male in speaking to or about another male, usually a friend or someone of lower status. A male college professor, for example, names a male student of his in this manner (e.g., **Sakamoto-kun** 坂本君).

As a result of coeducation, however, female students have started using **-kun** 君 in reference to male students, especially in informal conversations. This is but one of the many areas where the traditional male-female distinction is breaking down.

Unlike **-san** さん, **-kun** 君 is normally not attached to occupation names (see -SAN).

Ku¹ru 来る *to come*

Kuru 来る basically refers to movement toward the speaker.

EXAMPLE:

(1) **Ashita mata kite-kudasai.**
あしたまた来てください。
Please come [here] again tomorrow.

Unlike English "come," **kuru** 来る cannot refer to the speaker's movement toward the addressee unless the speaker is with the addressee at the moment of speech, as in (2).

EXAMPLE:

(2) **Ashita mata kimashō ka.**
あしたまた来ましょうか。
Shall I come [here] again tomorrow?

If, for example, A is outside B's house and asks B to come out, B must respond by using the verb **iku** 行く instead of **kuru** 来る. He must call out (3b) instead of (3a) to indicate "I'm coming."

EXAMPLES:

(3a) *****Ima kimasu yo.**
*いま来ますよ。
(3b) **Ima ikimasu yo.**
いま行きますよ。

Kuru 来る, however, may refer to someone else's movement toward the addressee if the speaker identifies with the latter as in

EXAMPLE:

(4) **Ueda-san ga otaku e kitara, yoroshiku itte-kudasai.**
植田さんがお宅へ来たら、よろしく言ってください。
If Mr. Ueda comes to your house, please remember me to him.

If there is no such identification with the addressee, **iku** 行く is used instead.

EXAMPLE:
(5) **Ueda-san ga otaku e ittara, yoroshiku itte-kudasai.**
植田さんがお宅へ行ったら、よろしく言ってください。
If Mr. Ueda goes to your house, please remember me to him.

Ku⌈sa⌉ 草 *grass, weed*

"Grass" in English usually refers either to the kind of plant that is grown in a lawn or to the kinds of plants that are cut and dried as hay. The latter are **kusa** 草 in Japanese, but the former is called either **shiba** 芝 or **shibakusa** 芝草, and never simply **kusa**. **Kusa** also refers to weeds, but when one wants to focus on the useless or troublesome aspect of weeds, **zassō** is more appropriate. Study the following examples:

EXAMPLES:
(1) **Kinō wa ichi-nichi-jū niwa no kusa-tori o shimashita.**
きのうは一日中庭の草取りをしました。
Yesterday I did the weeding in the yard all day long.
(2) **Kyō wa shiba o karanakereba naranai n desu.**
今日は芝を刈らなければならないんです。
Today I must mow the grass (or lawn).
(3) **Kotoshi wa zassō ga ōkute komarimasu.**
今年は雑草が多くて困ります。
Weeds are rampant this year, much to my annoyance.

Kusuri 薬 *medicine*

In English, "medicine" most commonly refers to a medical substance taken orally. **Kusuri** 薬 has a much broader range of meaning. It refers not only to orally taken medicine but also to ointments, antiseptics, suppositories, eye drops, restoratives, and the like. Although **kusuri** most often refers to a substance that is good for the health, in a broader sense it may refer to any chemical. Even insecticides, for example, can be called **kusuri**. Kurokawa (p. 71) cites **gokiburi no kusuri** ゴキブリの薬 "roach killer" (lit., "roach medicine") as an example.

Ku⌈tsu⌉shita 靴下 *socks*

Kutsushita 靴下 in a broad sense refers to all kinds of socks. Some speakers, however, seem to differentiate between **kutsushita** and **sokkusu** ソックス (from English "socks"). Women's socks are often called **sokkusu** instead of **kutsushita**, while men's socks are generally **kutsushita**. Sports socks, either all white or white with colored stripes, are frequently called **sokkusu** whether they are worn by men or women.

Ku⌉u 食う *to eat*

Kuu 食う is vulgar for **taberu** 食べる and is, as a rule, used only by men. Therefore, to mean "I've already eaten dinner," (1a) below can be used by both men and women, while (1b) is most likely used by men only.

EXAMPLES:

(1a) **Bangohan wa mō tabeta.**
晩ご飯はもう食べた。

(1b) **Banmeshi wa mō kutta yo.**
晩ご飯はもう食ったよ。

Women as well as men regularly use **kuu** 食う to refer to eating done by little bugs and the like or as a part of such idioms as **gasorin o kuu** ガソリンを食う "eat up gas."

EXAMPLES:

(2a) **Mukashi wa yoku nomi ni kuwareta mono desu.**
昔はよくノミに食われたものです。
Long ago, we used to be bitten by fleas quite often.

(2b) **Ōki na kuruma wa gasorin o kuu kara dame desu.**
大きな車はガソリンを食うからだめです。
Big cars are no good because they eat up gas.

Ku⌐yashi⌐i くやしい *?mortifying*

Kuyashii くやしい is a very common colloquial expression used all the time, even by children. Yet, when one looks up the word in a Japanese-English dictionary, one finds difficult words such as "vexing," "vexatious," and "mortifying" that are hardly ever used in English conversation. The reason is simple. It is because there is no corresponding colloquial English equivalent. Mark Petersen explains **kuyashii** as "a certain mixture of anger and frustration and bitter resentment (over a perceived injustice to oneself)."

I believe one reason for the lack of appropriate equivalents is that, in English, one would often just curse in situations where **kuyashii** would be called for in Japanese. Suppose you are insulted in front of others, for example. When an English speaker recalls the incident later, he will perhaps mumble to himself things like "Damn, he was so insulting, that s.o.b.!" whereas a Japanese speaker would say **Kuyashikatta na!** くやしかったな! When an English speaker loses a close tennis match, he will keep repeating "Damn! Damn! Damn!" in his mind while a Japanese speaker would inwardly feel **Kuyashii**!

Kyaku 客 *visitor, guest, customer*

Kyaku 客 refers to a person who goes to someone else's place (e.g., house, store, office, hotel, theater) for a visit, for business, for shopping, etc. **Kyaku** is usually a written form; in conversation, especially in women's speech, the more polite **okyaku-san** お客さん is the norm.

EXAMPLE:

(1) Housewife (to maid): **Okyaku-san ga kuru kara, kudamono de mo katte-kite-chōdai.**
お客さんが来るから、くだものでも買って来てちょうだい。
Since I'm expecting a visitor, will you go out and buy some fruit?

At stores known for their elegance, the staff speaks even more politely by saying **okyaku-sama** お客さま. At such places, you may hear this over the PA system:

EXAMPLE:

(2) **Okyaku-sama ni mōshi-agemasu.**
お客様に申し上げます。
Attention, please. (lit., I humbly announce to you customers.)

A passenger is also an **okyaku-san** お客さん from the standpoint of the person (or persons) providing the transportation. After all, a passenger is in a sense a visitor, too. A cab driver, for example, will often address a passenger in his taxi as **okyaku-san**. There is another word meaning "passenger," **jōkyaku** 乗客, which is a written form. Sometimes **jōkyaku no minasama** 乗客の皆様 is used to address passengers on an airplane.

Kyō⌐ [Kyo⌐o] 今日 *today*

Kyō 今日 means "today" in the sense of "this present day."

EXAMPLE:

(1) **Kyō wa ii otenki desu nē.**
今日はいいお天気ですねえ。
Isn't the weather beautiful today!

Although, in English, "this" is sometimes substituted for "today," as in "This is Sunday," in Japanese, **kore** これ (or **kono** この) "this" does not replace **kyō** 今日. "This is Sunday" is therefore

EXAMPLE:

(2) **Kyō** (not *****Kore** これ) **wa nichi-yōbi desu.**
今日は日曜日です。

Likewise, "this afternoon" is **kyō no gogo** 今日の午後, not *****kono gogo** この午後.

Unlike "today," **kyō** 今日 normally does not mean "this present time (or age)" although a more formal version, **konnichi** 今日, often does express this meaning in written Japanese, as in **konnichi no Nihon** 今日の日本 "today's Japan."

Kyō⌐dai [Kyo⌐odai] 兄弟 *brother, sibling*

Kyōdai 兄弟 has two meanings. In a narrow sense, it contrasts with **shimai** "sister," and refers to brothers only, as in **kyōdai-shimai** 兄弟姉妹 "brothers and sisters." This use, however, occurs exclusively in written Japanese. More commonly, **kyōdai** means "sibling," regardless of sex.

EXAMPLE:

(1) **A to B wa kyōdai da.**
AとBは兄弟だ。
A and B are siblings.

In (1), A and B might be both males, both females, or one male and one female.

EXAMPLE:

(2) **Boku wa kyōdai ga san-nin aru.**
僕は兄弟が三人ある。
I have three siblings.

In (2) also, the speaker might have any combination of brothers and sisters. The following example might be particularly puzzling to English speakers.

EXAMPLE:

(3) **Boku no uchi wa san-nin-kyōdai da.**
僕のうちは三人兄弟だ。

The above literally means "My family is three siblings." What it actually means is, however, that the speaker is one of the three children in the family. In other words, he has two siblings, not three.

If one wishes to specify the sexes of one's **kyōdai** 兄弟, the best thing is to say **otoko no kyōdai** 男の兄弟 (lit., "male siblings") for brothers and **onna no kyōdai** 女の兄弟 (lit., "female siblings") for sisters.

EXAMPLE:

(4) **Boku wa otoko no kyōdai ga futari to onna no kyōdai ga san-nin aru.**
僕は男の兄弟が二人と女の兄弟が三人ある。
I have two brothers and three sisters.

There is one big difference between "sibling" and **kyōdai** 兄弟. While "sibling" is not a colloquial expression, **kyōdai** is an everyday term used by anyone.

Kyōju 教授 *professor; instruction*

Kyōju 教授 means "professor."

EXAMPLE:

(1) **Ano hito wa Tōdai no kyōju da sō da.**
あの人は東大の教授だそうだ。
I hear he is a Tokyo University professor.

Kyōju 教授 can also be used as a title (e.g., **Kimura-kyōju** 木村教授 "Professor Kimura"), but its use is different from the use of "professor" as a title in English. In English, someone called Professor Brown, for example, could be a full, associate, or assistant professor. In Japanese, on the other hand, to be called **Kimura-kyōju**, for example, the person has to be a full professor. If he is an associate professor, he is called **Kimura-junkyōju** 准教授 (lit., "Associate Professor Kimura") instead. This difference demonstrates how fussy the Japanese are about ranks and social standing.

The word **kyōju** 教授 sounds quite formal, and its use is usually restricted to written Japanese. In conversation, professors, like teachers, are all addressed or referred to as **sensei** 先生.

EXAMPLE:

(2) **Kyō no Nomura-sensei no kōgi wa omoshirokatta ne.**
今日の野村先生の講義は面白かったね。
Professor Nomura's lecture today was interesting, wasn't it!

Kyōju 教授 may also mean "instruction" but is rarely used in this sense in conversation except at a very formal level, as in

EXAMPLE:

(3) **Sensei ni sadō no gokyōju o tamawaritai no desu ga.**
先生に茶道のご教授を賜りたいのですが。
Would you be so kind as to give me lessons in the tea ceremony?

In more normal speech, one would say something like

EXAMPLE:

(4) **Sensei ni sadō o oshiete itadakitai no desu ga.**
先生に茶道を教えていただきたいのですが。
Would you please teach me the tea ceremony?

When **kyōju** 教授 is used to mean "instruction," it is normally combined with other words, as in **kojinkyōju** 個人教授 "individual instruction" and **kyōjuhō** 教授法 "teaching method," as in

EXAMPLES:

(5a) **Ane wa 80-ijō ni naru noni, mada piano no kojinkyōju o shite-iru.**
姉は80以上になるのに、まだピアノの個人教授をしている。
Although my sister is over 80, she still gives private piano lessons.

(5b) **Konogoro wa Nihongo no kyōjuhō o benkyō-suru hito ga fuete-iru.**
このごろは日本語の教授法を勉強する人が増えている。
Lately an increasing number of people are studying how to teach Japanese.

In the following sentence, therefore, use **jugyō** 授業 "teaching classes," not **kyōju** 教授.

EXAMPLE:

(6) **Sensei wa konogoro jugyō** (not *kyōju 教授) **de oisogashii deshō.**
先生はこのごろ授業でお忙しいでしょう。
These days you must be busy teaching.

(See also JUGYŌ.)

Kyō˥mi [Kyo˥omi] 興味 *interest*

Kyōmi 興味 meaning "interest" is most typically used in the phrase **ni kyōmi ga aru** に興味がある "to be interested in something," as in

EXAMPLE:

(1) **Watashi wa kodomo no koro kara Eigo ni kyōmi ga atta.**
私は子供の頃から英語に興味があった。
I have been interested in English since I was little.

There is another word, **kanshin** 関心, which is similar in meaning to **kyōmi** 興味. According to *Ruigo Reikai Jiten*, pp.302–03, **kyōmi** is emotive while **kanshin** is more intellectual. That is probably why **kanshin** sounds better in (2) than **kyōmi**.

EXAMPLE:

(2) **Amerikajin no Nichibeibōeki ni taisuru kanshin** (not *kyōmi 興味) **wa mae hodo tsuyoku nai yō da.**
アメリカ人の日米貿易に対する関心は前ほど強くないようだ。
Americans do not seem to be as strongly interested in (or concerned about) U.S.-Japan trade as before.

There is an expression **kyōmibukai** 興味深い "of deep/great interest." In this word, **kyōmi** 興味 may not be replaced by **kanshin** 関心.

EXAMPLE:

(3) **Chūgaku no koro Sōseki no "Kokoro" o kyōmi** (not *kanshin 関心) **bukaku yonda.**
中学の頃漱石の「こころ」を興味深く読んだ。
When I was in middle school, I read Soseki's Kokoro *with great interest.*

-Ma 間 *(counter for rooms)*

Rooms in houses are counted as follows: **hito-ma** 広間 "one room," **futa-ma** 二間 "two rooms," **mi-ma** 三間 "three rooms," **yo-ma** 四間 "four rooms," **itsu-ma** 五間 "five rooms," **mu-ma** 六間 "six rooms," **nana-ma** 七間 "seven rooms," and **iku-ma** 幾間 "how many rooms." What is intriguing is the fact that **-ma** 間 cannot be added to numbers over seven. This is probably due to the fact that Japanese houses rarely have more than seven rooms. For eight rooms or more, use **yattsu** 八つ, **kokonotsu** 九つ, **tō** 十, **jūichi** 十一, **jūni** 十二, etc., without **-ma** 間.

Rooms in inns and hotels may be counted in the same manner as rooms in houses (i.e., by using **-ma** 間), but **-ma** 間 is never used to count rooms in office or school buildings.

Ma┐da まだ *still, not yet*

Basically, **mada** まだ indicates that no change has taken place, as in

EXAMPLES:

(1a) **Mada samui desu.**
まだ寒いです。
It's still cold. (i.e., It was cold before, and the situation hasn't changed.)

(1b) **Mada attakaku naranai.**
まだ暖かくならないです。
It hasn't become warm yet. (i.e., It was not warm before, and the situation hasn't changed.)

Mada まだ is often mistakenly used with **deshita** でした rather than **desu** です by English speakers in situations such as the following:

EXAMPLE:

(2) Teacher: **Mō shukudai shimashita ka.**
もう宿題しましたか。
Have you done the homework yet?

    Student: ****Iie, mada shimasen deshita.**
*いいえ、まだしませんでした。
No, I haven't done it yet.

Iie, mada shite-imasen いいえ、まだしていません is the correct answer in this case. Since the question is in the past tense, students feel tempted to answer in the past tense, too. The **-ta** form, however, is not really a past tense form, but rather a perfective. Since the act of doing the homework has not taken place, **-ta** is not used in the answer. A much simpler form **Iie, mada desu** いいえ、まだです is used quite often, too.

Ma˥do 窓 *window*

Mado 窓 means "window," as in

EXAMPLE:

(1) **Kono mado kara Fujisan ga miemasu ka.**
この窓から富士山が見えますか。
Can you see Mt. Fuji from this window?

A store window used specifically for a display is not **mado** 窓, but **shōwindō** ショーウ
ィンドー "show window" or simply **windō** ウィンドー, as in

EXAMPLE:

(2) **Kurisumasu no koro no depāto no (shō)windō** (not *****mado** 窓) **wa kirei da.**
クリスマスの頃のデパートの（ショー）ウィンドーはきれいだ。
Department store show windows at Christmas time are pretty.

Windows for customers at such places as banks, post offices, and railroad stations are
called **madoguchi** 窓口 rather than **mado** 窓.

EXAMPLE:

(3) **Kitte wa ichiban no madoguchi** (not *****mado** 窓) **de utte-imasu.**
切手は一番の窓口で売っています。
Postage stamps are sold at Window #1.

Incidentally, there is a humorous euphemism using **mado** 窓, i.e.,

EXAMPLE:

(4) **Shakai no mado ga aite-imasu yo.**
社会の窓が開いていますよ。
Your fly is open. (lit., Your window to the world is open.)

The person cautioned this way may not feel as embarassed as he could be.

Ma˥e 前 *before, ago, front*

Mae 前, when used as a time expression, means either "before," as in (1), or "ago," as in
(2).

EXAMPLES:

(1) **Ima shichi-ji go-fun mae desu.**
いま7時5分前です。
It's five minutes before 7 o'clock.

(2) **Go-nen mae ni kekkon-shimashita.**
5年前に結婚しました。
I got married five years ago.

When used in reference to space, **mae** 前 means "front."

EXAMPLE:

(3) **Posuto no mae ni tatte-iru no wa dare desu ka.**
ポストの前に立っているのは誰ですか。
Who is that person standing in front of the mailbox?

Mae 前, however, may tolerate a greater space between the two objects involved than does "in front of." For example, it is perfectly all right to say in Japanese

EXAMPLE:

(4) **Maru-biru wa Tōkyō eki no sugu mae ni aru.**

丸ビルは東京駅のすぐ前にある。

lit., The Marunouchi Building is right in front of Tokyo Station.

even though there is a large plaza between the building and the station. In English, however, one would more likely say

EXAMPLE:

(5) The Marunouchi Building is right across from Tokyo Station.

Mai- 毎 *every*

Mai- is a prefix attached to certain words indicating units of time, e.g., **mainichi** 毎日 "every day," **maiasa** 毎朝 "every morning," **maiban** 毎晩 "every night," **maishū** 毎週 "every week," **maitsuki** 毎月 "every month," and **maitoshi** 毎年 "every year."

EXAMPLE:

(1) **Nihonjin wa mainichi sankai shokuji o suru no ga futsū da.**

日本人は毎日三回食事をするのが普通だ。

Japanese people normally eat three meals every day.

毎月 and 毎年 have two readings each. 毎月 can be either **maitsuki** or **maigetsu**; 毎年 may be pronounced either **maitoshi** or **mainen**.

Words attached to **mai-** 毎 are usually one-character words, as seen above. One may sometimes hear such combinations as **mainichiyōbi** 毎日曜日 "every Sunday" and **maigakunen** 毎学年 "every school year," but they are rather rare. It is more normal to use **gotoni** ごとに in such cases, e.g.,

EXAMPLE:

(2) **Merī wa nichiyōbi gotoni kyōkai e iku.**

メリーは日曜日ごとに教会へ行く。

Mary goes to church every Sunday.

Do not use **mai-** 毎 with non-time words. For example, don't say ***maikoku** *毎国 to mean "every country" or ***mainihonjin** *毎日本人 to mean "every Japanese." In such cases, use other expressions such as

EXAMPLES:

(3a) **Doko no kuni ni mo kokki ga aru.**

どこの国にも国会がある。

Every country has a national flag.

(3b) **Nihonjin wa dare demo** (or **minna**) **Fujisan ga daisuki da.**

日本人は誰でも（みんな）富士山が大好きだ。

Every Japanese person loves Mt. Fuji.

Majime まじめ *serious*

Majime まじめ means "serious."

EXAMPLES:
(1) **majime na kao**
     まじめな顔
     a serious (or solemn) look
(2) **majime na gakusei**
     まじめな学生
     a serious-minded student

   Majime まじめ, however, is different from "serious" in that it cannot mean "important" or "giving cause for apprehension." One therefore cannot say

EXAMPLE:
(3) *****Infurēshon wa Amerika de ichiban majime na mondai desu.**
     *インフレーションはアメリカで一番まじめな問題です。

This sentence was written by a student of mine who was trying to convey the idea "Inflation is the most serious problem in America." He should of course have used **shinkoku** 深刻 "grave" or **jūyō** 重要 "important" as follows:

EXAMPLE:
(4) **Infurēshon wa Amerika de ichiban shinkoku na** (or **jūyō na**) **mondai desu.**
     インフレーションはアメリカで一番深刻な(重要な)問題です。

Ma⌈mo⌉ru 守る *to keep, observe, protect*

Mamoru 守る means "to keep," but only in the sense of "to observe," i.e., "not to break."

EXAMPLE:
(1) **Yakusoku wa mamoranakereba naranai.**
     約束は守らなければならない。
     Promises must be kept.

   Mamoru 守る cannot be used in the following sentence, because "keep" in the following case means "to retain," not "to observe."

EXAMPLE:
(2) *****Toshokan no hon o mamotte wa ikenai.**
     *図書館の本を守ってはいけない。
     One must not keep library books.

   Most normally, this idea would be expressed instead as in (3) below.

EXAMPLE:
(3) **Toshokan no hon wa kaesanakereba ikenai.**
     図書館の本は返さなければいけない。
     One must return library books.

Mamoru 守る may be correctly used as follows:

EXAMPLES:

(4a) **Hōritsu wa mamoru beki mono da.**

法律は守るべきものだ。

Laws are to be observed/followed.

(4b) **Kurisuchan wa Kirisuto no oshie o mamoru hazu da.**

クリスチャンはキリストの教えを守るはずだ。

Christians should observe/obey Christ's teachings.

Mamoru 守る also means "to protect/defend."

EXAMPLE:

(5) **Sensō wa jibun no kuni o mamoru tame dake to wa kagiranai.**

戦争は自分の国を守るためだけとは限らない。

Wars are not just for defending one's country.

Mamoru used in this sense may be written 護る, as well.

Marude まるで *just like; completely*

Marude まるで has two basic meanings: (a) "just like" and (b) "completely." When it is used in the first sense, it is often, though not always, accompanied by **yō** よう or **mitai** みたい, both meaning "like." See (1a) and (1b) below.

EXAMPLES:

(1a) **Sumisu-san wa Nihongo ga jōzu de, marude Nihonjin (no yō) da.**

スミスさんは日本語が上手で、まるで日本人（のよう）だ。

Mr. Smith's Japanese is so good he is just like a Japanese person.

(1b) **Ano rōjin wa marude akanbō (mitai) da.**

あの老人はまるで赤ん坊（みたい）だ。

That old man is just like a baby.

Marude まるで in the sense of "completely" is used with negative forms, as in (2a), or with words with negative meanings, as in (2b).

EXAMPLES:

(2a) **Kyō no shiken wa marude wakaranakatta.**

今日の試験はまるで分からなかった。

I didn't understand today's exam at all.

(2b) **Kyō no shiken wa marude dame datta.**

今日の試験はまるでだめだった。

Today's exam was totally beyond me.

Marude まるで in this sense is synonymous with **mattaku** まったく and **zenzen** ぜんぜん but is not exactly the same. First, **marude** implies the speaker's negative judgment, whereas the other two do not. For example, in (3a) all three variants would be acceptable, but in (3b) **marude** sounds a little strange.

EXAMPLES:

(3a) **Furansu e itta toki, Furansugo ga marude/mattaku/zenzen wakaranakute komatta.**

フランスへ行ったとき、フランス語が まるで/まったく/全然 分からなくて困った。

When I went to France, I had a hard time because I didn't understand French at all.

(3b) **Heta na Furansugo o hanasu kurai nara, mattaku/zenzen/?marude hanasenai hō ga ii to Furansujin wa iu.**

下手なフランス語を話すくらいなら、/まったく/全然/?まるで話さない方がいいとフランス人は言う。

The French say that not being able to speak any French at all is better than speaking bad French.

Marude まるで is different from **mattaku** まったく in that the former has to be used with negative forms or with words of negative orientation, while **mattaku** can be used in affirmative sentences as well. In (4) below, **mattaku** may not be replaced by **marude**.

EXAMPLE:

(4) **Fujisan no nagame wa mattaku (not *marude まるで) subarashikatta.**

富士山の眺めはまったくすばらしかった。

The view of Mt. Fuji was totally fantastic.

Mashi まし *the better of two poor options*

If one looks up **mashi** まし in a small Japanese-English dictionary, all one can find is the definition "better." That is misleading. **Mashi** is used only when there are two poor options, of which one is better than the other, e.g.,

EXAMPLE:

(1) **Anna mono o taberu kurai nara, nani mo tabenai hō ga mashi da.**

あんな物を食べるくらいなら、何も食べない方がました。

I'd rather not eat anything than eat terrible food like that.

To compare two good options, use **hō ga ii** 方がいい, as in

EXAMPLE:

(2) **Kono resutoran de wa sushi mo tenpura mo oishii keredo, dochira ka to iu to, sushi no hō ga ii to omou.**

このレストランでは寿司も天ぷらもおいしいけれど、どちらかと言うと、寿司の方がいいと思う。

At this restaurant, both the sushi and the tempura are good, but if one had to choose, I would say the sushi is better.

In order to use **mashi** まし in sentence (2), the first half of it would have to be changed, as follows:

EXAMPLE:

(3) **Kono resutoran de wa sushi mo tenpura mo mazui keredo, dochira ka to iu to sushi no hō ga mashi da to omou.**

このレストランでは寿司も天ぷらもまずいけれど、どちらかと言うと、寿司の方がましだと思う。

At this restaurant, both the sushi and the tempura are bad, but if one had to choose, I'd say the sushi is the more tolerable of the two.

Mattaku まったく、全く *entirely, totally, truly*

Mattaku まったく is quite similar to **zenzen** 全然 when used with negative forms or with words of negative orientation, as in

EXAMPLES:
(1a) **Watashi wa Roshiago ga mattaku/zenzen dekinai.**
私はロシア語が まったく/全然 できない。
I don't know any Russian at all.
(1b) **Watashi wa Roshiago ga mattaku/zenzen dame da.**
私はロシア語が まったく/全然 だめです。
I am truly hopeless at Russian.

One big difference between these two expressions, however, is that **mattaku** まった く can be used affirmatively whereas **zenzen** 全然, as a rule, cannot, except in fun (see ZENZEN).

EXAMPLE:
(2) **Fujisan no chōjō kara no nagame wa mattaku** (not **zenzen* 全然) **subarashikatta.**
富士山の頂上からの眺めはまったくすばらしかった。
The view from the top of Mt. Fuji was simply fantastic.

Mawari 周り *around*

English-speaking students of Japanese tend to equate **mawari** 周り with English "around" and make sentences such as

EXAMPLE:
(1) **Nihonjin no tomodachi ni kyanpasu no mawari o misete agemashita.**
日本人の友達にキャンパスの周りを見せてあげました。

to mean "I showed a Japanese friend around campus." Sentence (1) is grammatically correct, but the problem is **kyanpasu no mawari** キャンパスの周り means "the surroundings of the campus," which, by definition, excludes the campus itself, whereas "around campus" is similar to "all over campus" and definitely refers to the campus itself. The Japanese equivalent of "I showed a Japanese friend around campus" is

EXAMPLE:
(2) **Nihonjin no tomodachi ni kyanpasu o annai-shite agemashita.**
日本人の友達にキャンパスを案内してあげました。

Sentence (3), which was once made by a student of mine, contains the same kind of problem as sentence (1).

EXAMPLE:
(3) **Kaji to iu no wa, ie no mawari no shigoto desu.**
家事というのは、家の周りの仕事です。

With this sentence, the student meant "Household chores are chores around the house." Since **ie no mawari** 家の周り means "the surroundings of the house," however, **ie no mawari no shigoto** 家の周りの仕事 can only indicate chores such as gardening and sweeping just outside the house, and not chores such as cooking, house cleaning, and washing clothes. The student should have said, **ie no shigoto** 家の仕事 rather than **ie no mawari no shigoto**.

    Mawari 周り can be translated as "around" in such sentences as follows:

EXAMPLES:

(4a) **Chikyū no mawari o mawatte-iru jinkōeisei no kazu wa taihen na mono da sō da.**
地球の周りを回っている人工衛星の数はたいへんなものだそうだ。
I understand that the number of man-made satellites flying around the earth is astounding.

(4b) **Bashō wa ike no mawari o aruki nagara haiku o tsukutta koto ga aru.**
芭蕉は池の周りを歩きながら俳句を作った事がある。
Basho once composed a haiku walking around a pond.

Ma˩zu まず *first of all*

Mazu まず usually means "first of all," as in

EXAMPLE:

(1) **Watashi wa asa okiru to mazu kao o arau.**
私は朝起きるとまず顔を洗う。
After I get up in the morning, I wash my face first of all.

    When used in this sense, **mazu** まず is synonymous with **daiichi ni** 第一に, **saisho ni** 最初に, or **hajime ni** はじめに. **Mazu** may be used either by itself or in combination with these words, as in

EXAMPLE:

(2) **Watashi wa asa okiru to mazu daiichi ni/saisho ni/hajime ni kao o arau.**
私は朝起きるとまず 第一に/最初に/はじめに 顔を洗う。

    Mazu まず has another meaning, which is similar to **daitai** だいたい or **tabun** たぶん, as in

EXAMPLE:

(3) **Tanaka wa Tōdai ni hairitagatte-iru ga, mazu dame darō.**
田中は東大に入りたがっているが、まずだめだろう。
Tanaka wants to get into the University of Tokyo, but he probably won't make it.

    This second meaning is an extended one from the primary meaning of "first." The implication in sentence (3) is: "When I think about Tanaka's wish to get into the University of Tokyo, my first guess would be that he won't make it."

Ma˩zu˩i まずい *bad-tasting; unwise, awkward*

Mazui まずい most frequently is the opposite of **oishii** おいしい "tasty."

EXAMPLE:

(1) **Gakuseishokudō no karē wa mazui kara, soto e tabe ni ikō.**
学生食堂のカレーはまずいから、外へ食べに行こう。
The curry in the college cafeteria tastes bad; let's go out to eat somewhere else.

Figuratively, **mazui** まずい can describe non-food items. For example,

EXAMPLE:

(2) **Shukudai o wasureta no wa mazukatta.**
宿題を忘れたのはまずかった。
It was unwise/awkward to forget my homework.

Ma⌐zushi⌐i 貧しい *needy, poor, meager*

Mazushii 貧しい can be used in two ways. First, it works as a synonym for **binbō** 貧乏.

EXAMPLE:

(1) **Mazushii** (or **Binbō na**) **ie ni umareta hito wa kawaisō da.**
貧しい（貧乏な）家に生まれた人はかわいそうだ。
I feel sorry for those who are born into poor families.

In this usage, **mazushii** 貧しい sounds more formal than **binbō** 貧乏.
Second, **mazushii** can be used figuratively to refer to nonmoney matters.

EXAMPLES:

(2a) **Mazushii sainō**
貧しい才能
eager talent

(2b) **Mazushii keiken**
貧しい経験
meager experience

Mazushii 貧しい used in this sense cannot be replaced by **binbō** 貧乏. (See also BINBŌ.)

Me⌐ndō⌐ [Me⌐ndo⌐o] 面倒 *troublesome, bothersome; care*

Mendō 面倒 is usually a **na**-adjective.

EXAMPLE:

(1) **Tsūkan no tame ni wa, itsumo mendō na tetsuzuki ga hitsuyō da.**
通関の為には、いつも面倒な手続きが必要だ。
For customs clearance, a troublesome procedure must always be followed.

Mendō 面倒 may also be used as a noun meaning "care."

EXAMPLE:

(2) **Konogoro no Nihon no wakamono wa oya no mendō o mitagaranai sō da.**
このごろの日本の若者は親の面倒を見たがらないそうだ。
Young Japanese today do not want to take care of their parents, I hear.

In this second meaning, however, **mendō** 面倒 is always used with **miru** 見る and never by itself. In (3) below, one must use **mendō o miru** 面倒を見る or **sewa** 世話, but not **mendō** by itself.

EXAMPLE:

(3) **Kazuko wa hahaoya no sewa de** (or **mendō o miru koto de**) **tsukarete-iru.**
和子は母親の世話で（面倒を見ることで）疲れている。
Kazuko is tired from taking care of her mother.

Me⌐shi⌐ 飯 *cooked rice, meal*

Meshi 飯, like **gohan** ご飯, has two meanings: "cooked rice" and "meal." The difference between **meshi** and **gohan** is purely stylistic, the former being used only by men in informal situations. According to Tokugawa and Miyajima (p. 387), the verb for "eat" would most likely be **taberu** 食べる for **gohan**, and **kuu** 食う for **meshi**.

EXAMPLES:

(1) **Gohan o tabemashita.**
ご飯を食べました。
I ate some rice (or a meal).

(2) **Meshi o kutta.**
飯を食った。
(same meaning as above)

(See also GOHAN.)

Mi⌐dori 緑 *green*

Green is normally **midori** 緑, although **ao** may be used in reference to certain items (see AOI). **Midori** seems to be gaining ground these days, so that the range of meaning of **ao** 青 is becoming increasingly restricted to "blue." Youngsters in particular use **ao** less and less to mean "green," and say **midori** or even **gurīn** グリーン (from English "green") instead. The latter is probably preferred in reference to Western-type things such as cars and Western clothing.

In English, "green" often connotes envy, as the expression "green with envy" indicates. Japanese **midori** (or even **gurīn**) has no such connotation.

Mi⌐e⌐ru 見える *to be visible*

Although **mieru** 見える is sometimes translated as "can see," as in (1) below, it is not the same as **mirareru** 見られる "can see," which is the potential form of **miru** 見る.

EXAMPLE:

A, mukō ni mizu'umi ga mieru!
あ、向こうに湖が見える!
Look, I can see a lake over there!

Mieru 見える means "something is visible regardless of one's intention," whereas **mirareru** implies one's wish/effort to see something. In sentence (1) above, where a lake just naturally came into view, **mirareru** 見られる would sound odd. (See also MIRARERU.)

Mi⌐jika⌐i 短い *short*

Mijikai 短い means "short," both temporally and spatially.

EXAMPLES:

(1) **Fuyu wa hi ga mijikai.**
冬は日が短い。
Days are short in the winter.

(2) **Enpitsu ga mijikaku-natta kara, atarashii no o kaimashita.**
鉛筆が短くなったから、新しいのを買いました。
Since my pencil became short, I bought a new one.

Mijikai 短い is different from "short," however, in that it cannot mean "short in height." To express the idea of "He is short," use (3a), not (3b).

EXAMPLES:
(3a) **Ano hito wa se ga hikui.**
あの人は背が低い。
(lit., His height is low.)
(3b) *Ano hito wa mijikai.
*あの人は背が短い。

(See also HIKUI.)

Mi⌈na⌉-san みなさん, 皆さん *everyone, all of you*

Mina-san 皆さん (lit., "everyone") is often used as the plural "you" and is more polite than **anata-tachi** あなた達 "you (plural)."

EXAMPLES:
(1) **Kondo mina-san o omaneki-shi-tai to omotte-iru n desu.**
今度皆さんをお招きしたいと思っているんです。
I'd like to invite you folks one of these days.
(2) **Mina-san ogenki desu ka.**
皆さんお元気ですか。
Is everyone [at your house] well?

When you refer to your family, delete **-san** さん and use **mina** みな.

EXAMPLE:
(3) **Okage-sama de mina genki desu.**
おかげさまでみな元気です。
We are all well, thank you.

Mina みな can be replaced by **minna** 皆, a more conversational variant. **Minna**, however, never takes **-san** さん. *Minna-san みんなさん is therefore a nonexistent word.

EXAMPLE:
(4) **Mina-san** (not *Minna-san みんなさん) **ni yoroshiku.**
皆さんによろしく。
Please say hello to everyone [in your family].

Mi⌈nna⌉ みんな *everyone, all*

Minna みんな, like its less colloquial version **mina** みな, is normally not followed by **wa** は, though sometimes preceded by it. (1a) is therefore correct, but (1b) is not.

EXAMPLES:
(1a) **Kazoku wa minna** (or **mina**) **genki desu.**
家族はみんな（みな）元気です。
(The members of) my family are all well.

(1b) *家族みんな(みな)は元気です。

Minna/mina みんな/みな may be used in conjunction with inanimate objects, too.

EXAMPLE:

(2) **Mochi wa mō minna** (or **mina**) **tabete shimatta.**
餅はもうみんな(みな)食べてしまった。
We've already eaten all the mochi.

Mi⌐rare⌐ru 見られる *can be seen*

Mirareru 見られる is the potential form of **miru** 見る.

EXAMPLE:

(1) **Tōkyō de wa iroiro na kuni no eiga ga mirareru.**
東京ではいろいろな国の映画が見られる。
In Tokyo, one can see movies from lots of countries.

Mirareru 見られる is also the passive form of **miru** 見る.

EXAMPLE:

(2) **Warui koto o shite-iru tokoro o hito ni mirareru no wa komaru.**
悪い事をしている所を人に見られるのは困る。
It's embarrassing to have been seen by others while doing something bad.

Because of this double function of **mirareru** 見られる, a large number of young people (and sometimes not so young people, as well) have started using **mireru** 見れる instead of **mirareru** for the potential form. Instead of (1) above, they would say:

EXAMPLE:

(3) **Tōkyō de wa iroiro na kuni no eiga ga mireru.**
東京ではいろいろな国の映画が見れる。

This phenomenon of **-reru** れる used in place of **-rareru** られる is not limited to the verb **miru** 見る alone. In fact, it is becoming so common that it is labeled as **ranuki-kotoba** ら抜き言葉 "ra-less words." **Ranuki-kotoba** seems to affect other fairly short, commonly used verbs such as **taberu** 食べる and **kuru** 来る.

EXAMPLES:

(4a) **Ashita hachiji ni koreru** (or **korareru**)?
あした八時に来れる(来られる)
Can you come at 8 tomorrow?

(4b) **Konna mono tabere** (or **taberare**) **nai yo.**
こんなもの食べれ(食べられ)ないよ。
I can't eat things like this.

Teachers of Japanese invariably frown upon this phenomenon, and most Japanese textbooks for foreigners do not include these forms despite their prevalence. The reason **mireru** 見れる, **tabereru** 食べれる, etc., are often used in place of **mirareru** 見られる, **taberareru** 食べられる, etc., is because the potential forms and the passive forms being exactly the same could sometimes cause confusion. I am sure those who use **ranuki-kotoba** ら抜き言葉 are instinctively avoiding that. Also, **-reru** れる versions being shorter and simpler than their **-rareru** られる counterparts may be contributing to the popularity of **ranuki-kotoba**. My suggestion would be: "Don't hesitate to use **ranuki-kotoba** in the company of young people on informal occasions but, on formal occasions, and especially in the presence of older Japanese or Japanese language teachers, try to avoid the shorter versions. Although I myself avoid their use, **ranuki-kotoba** will probably win out in the long run despite the purists' disapproval.

Mi˥ru 見る *to see, to look, to watch*

Miru 見る is like "look" and "watch" in that it is intentional and not passive (Hattori, p. 198).

EXAMPLES:
(1) **Kono hana o mite kudasai.**
    この花を見てください。
    Please look at these flowers.
(2) **Terebi o mite-imasu.**
    テレビを見ています。
    I'm watching TV.

Miru 見る is like "see" in that the object may or may not be stationary.

EXAMPLES:
(3) **Kinō wa Kōrakuen e yakyū o mi ni ikimashita.**
    昨日は後楽園へ野球を見に行きました。
    Yesterday I went to Korakuen Stadium to see some baseball.
(4) **Fujisan o mita koto ga arimasu ka.**
    富士山を見たことがありますか。
    Have you ever seen Mt. Fuji?

Unlike "see," however, **miru** 見る cannot be used in the sense of "to meet and converse with." **Au** 会う is the verb for that purpose (see AU). In (5), therefore, only (a) is correct.

EXAMPLES:
(5a) **Ato de Sumisu-san ni au tsumori desu.**
     あとでスミスさんに会うつもりです。
(5b) **Ato de Sumisu-san o miru tsumori desu.*
     *あとでスミスさんを見るつもりです。
     I plan to see Mr. Smith later.

Unlike "see," **miru** 見る cannot mean "to visit and consult." Sentence (6) is therefore incorrect.

EXAMPLE:
(6) **Isha o mimashita.*
    *医者を見ました。
    I saw my doctor.

To indicate "visit the doctor for a consultation" in Japanese, you say **mite-morau** 見てもらう "to have the doctor look at [me]."

EXAMPLE:

(7) **Isha ni mite-moraimashita.**
医者に見てもらう。
I saw my doctor. (lit., I had my doctor look at me.)

Mi⌈se⌉ 店 *store*

Mise 店 has a broader range of meaning than English "store." **Mise** 店 can refer not only to stores but also to such places as restaurants, teahouses, coffee shops, and even gas stations.

EXAMPLES:

(1) A: **Kono kissaten wa konde-imasu nē.**
この喫茶店は込んでいますねえ。
This coffee shop is crowded, isn't it!

   B: **Sō desu nē. Motto suite-iru mise o sagashimashō.**
そうですねえ。もっと空いている店を探しましょう。
It is, isn't it! Let's look for a less crowded one.

(2) A: **Ano resutoran wa tsubureta sō desu yo.**
あのレストランはつぶれたそうですよ。
That restaurant has gone bankrupt, I hear.

   B: **Sō desu ka. Sekkaku ii mise datta no ni nē.**
そうですか。せっかくいい店だったのにねえ。
Has it? Too bad; it was such a nice place.

Mi⌈soshi⌉ru 味噌汁 *miso soup*

Very often, words denoting items of food vary, depending on whether they are used at home or at restaurants. Miso soup, for example, is usually called **omiotsuke** おみおつけ domestically, but **(o)misoshiru** (お)味噌汁 at restaurants. Likewise, Japanese pickles are most normally called **okōko** おこうこ or **(o)tsukemono** 漬け物 at home, but **oshinko** お新香 at restaurants. Some expressions such as **murasaki** むらさき (for **shōyu** しょうゆ) "soy sauce" and **agari** あがり (for **ocha** お茶) "tea" sound so professional that lay people should refrain from using them.

Mi⌉tai みたい *like (such and such)*

Mitai みたい is an informal, colloquial equivalent of **yō** よう and can be used wherever the latter is used in the sense of "like." For example,

EXAMPLES:

(1a) **Kondo no shiken wa muzukashii mitai (or yō) da.**
今度の試験は難しいみたい(よう)だ。
The exam that's coming up sounds like a difficult one.

(1b) **Konban wa yuki ga furu mitai (or yō) da.**
今晩は雪が降るみたい(よう)だ。
It looks like it's going to snow this evening.

One difference in usage between **mitai** みたい and **yō** よう, however, is that, after a noun, **yō** must be preceded by **no** の, whereas **mitai** can be attached to a noun directly.

EXAMPLE:

(2) **Asoko ni Tanaka-san mitai (or no yō) na hito ga iru.**
あそこに田中さんみたい（のよう）な人がいる。
There's a man over there who looks like Mr. Tanaka.

Needless to say, **mitai** みたい cannot be replaced by **yō** よう where the latter does not mean "like."

EXAMPLE:

(3) **Sensei ni sugu repōto o kaku yō ni** (not *mitai ni みたいに) **iwareta.**
先生にすぐレポートを書くように言われた。
I was told by the teacher to write a report immediately.

Mitai みたい sounds like another **mitai** 見たい, which is the stem of **miru** 見る (i.e., **-mi** 見) plus **tai** たい, and means "want to see."

EXAMPLE:

(4) **Sakura ga/o mitai.**
桜が/を見たい。
I want to see cherry blossoms.

Since, in informal conversation, particles such as **ga** が and **o** を are consistently dropped, (4) above without **ga** or **o** would sound and look very much like (5) below.

EXAMPLE:

(5) **sakura mitai**
桜みたい
like cherry blossoms

There are two important differences, however. First, **mitai** meaning "want to see" is usually written 見たい, whereas **mitai** meaning "like" always appears in hiragana, i.e., みたい Second, the accent is different. 見たい is accented on **ta**, i.e., mi**tai**, while みたい is accented on **mi**, i.e., **mi**tai. Therefore, **Sakura mitai** would mean "I want to see cherry blossoms," but **Sakura mitai** would mean "That's like cherry blossoms."

Mitsukaru 見つかる *to be found*

Japanese has a large number of intransitive/transitive verb pairs such as **shimaru** 閉まる ("something closes"); **shimeru** 閉める ("to close something"); **aku** 開く ("something opens"); **akeru** 開ける ("to open something"), etc. **Mitsukaru** 見つかる ("something is found") **-mitsukeru** 見つける ("to find something") is one of those pairs. What one should note about **mitsukaru** is: there is no single-word English counterpart, and the idea of **mitsukaru** must be expressed in a passive construction. For example,

EXAMPLE:

(1) **Kakurete ita no da ga, sugu mitsukatte shimatta.**
隠れていたのだが、すぐ見つかってしまった。
I was hiding but was discovered right away.

In this situation, one could also express the same English sentence with the passive form of the transitive counterpart **mitsukeru** 見つける, as in

EXAMPLE:

(2) **Kakurete ita no da ga, sugu mitsukerarete shimatta.**
隠れていたのだが、すぐ見つけられてしまった。

Although the two sentences basically mean the same, most Japanese speakers would probably use (1) rather than (2), preferring to describe the situation as something that happened spontaneously rather than as an action taken by someone.

Another example that might be even more revealing follows:

EXAMPLE:

(3) **Shigoto ga mitsukaranakute** (rather than **mitsukerare-nakute**) **komatte-iru n desu.**
仕事が見つからなくて(見つけられなくて)困っているんです。
I'm in trouble, not being able to find a job.

This example makes it even clearer that English prefers to describe a situation from the standpoint of someone doing something whereas Japanese prefers to do the same from the standpoint of something happening.

Mitsukeru 見つける *to find (out)*

Mitsukeru 見つける is, as a rule, used with reference to a concrete object, as in

EXAMPLE:

(1) **Nakushita pen o mitsuketa.**
なくしたペンを見つけた。
I found a pen I had lost.

Mitsukeru 見つける is sometimes used about an action, too.

EXAMPLE:

(2) **Gakusei ga kanningu shite-iru no o mitsuketa.**
学生がカンニングしているのを見つけた。
I found a student cheating.

This verb, however, is not used about a fact. For example, suppose you were an admirer of President John F. Kennedy. One day you learn that he was quite a womanizer and feel crushed. Use **shiru** 知る rather than **mitsukeru** 見つける in that case.

EXAMPLE:

(3) **Kenedī Daitōryō ga onnazuki datta koto o shitte** (not *****mitsukete 見つけて**) **gakkari shita.**
ケネディ大統領が女好きだったことを知ってがっかりした。
I was disappointed to find out that President Kennedy was a womanizer.

Miyage みやげ *gift, present*

The generic expression for "gift" is **okurimono** 贈り物 lit., "a thing to present someone with."

EXAMPLE:

(1) **Dare datte okurimono o morau no wa ureshii.**
誰だって贈り物をもらうのはうれしい。
Everyone is happy to receive a gift.

Miyage みやげ, or **omiyage** おみやげ, is a kind of **okurimono** 贈り物, but its use is limited to two specific occasions. First, it is a gift you buy on a trip to take home to your family or friends.

EXAMPLE:

(2) **Hawai kara omiyage ni makadamia nattsu o katte kuru.**
ハワイからおみやげにマカダミア・ナッツを買って来る。
I'll buy you guys a gift of macadamia nuts in Hawaii.

Second, **(o)miyage** (お)みやげ refers to a gift one takes along when one visits someone.

EXAMPLE:

(3) **Tanaka-san no uchi e iku toki, chīzu no omiyage o motte ikō.**
田中さんのうちへ行く時、チーズのおみやげを持って行こう。
I think I'll take a gift of cheese when I visit the Tanakas.

In this second sense, **temiyage** 手みやげ (lit., hand-**miyage**) may also be used just to focus on the fact that the gift is being carried by hand.

Because of these restrictions, **(o)miyage** (お)みやげ cannot be used for things like Christmas presents.

EXAMPLE:

(4) **Pātī e ittari purezento** (or **okurimono**, but not **miyage** みやげ) **o kōkan-shitari suru dake ga Nihon no Kurisumasu desu.**
パーティーへ行ったりプレゼント(贈り物)を交換したりするだけが日本のクリスマスです。
Japanese Christmas is just going to parties and exchanging gifts.

Mizu 水 *[cold] water*

Mizu 水 is different from "water" in that it does not refer to hot water. In Japanese, hot water is referred to by an entirely different word, **yu** 湯, or more commonly, **oyu** お湯 (see OYU). Example (1) below is therefore correct, but sentence (2) is incorrect.

EXAMPLES:

(1) **Nodo ga kawaita kara, mizu o nonda.**
のどが渇いたから、水を飲んだ。
I drank some [cold] water because I was thirsty.

(2) *****atsui mizu**
*熱い水
lit., hot water

To refer to really cold water, one may say

EXAMPLE:

(3) **tsumetai mizu**
冷たい水
very cold water

which is not redundant.

Drinking water may be referred to not only as **mizu** 水 but also, when served very cold, as **ohiya** お冷や or **aisu-wōtā** アイス・ウォーター (from English "ice water"). (This last variant, however, is used only at Western-style restaurants and coffee shops.) Nondrinking cold water can be called only **mizu** 水.

Mō⌐ [Mo⌐o] もう *already*

Mō もう is the opposite of **mada** まだ and is used when a state of being changes, whether it is used in an affirmative or negative sentence.

EXAMPLES:

(1a) **Mō onaka ga ippai da.**
もうおなかがいっぱいだ。
I'm already full.

(1b) **Mō nani mo taberarenai.**
もう何も食べられない。
I can't eat any more.

Although the English translation of **mō** もう comes out quite differently in a negative sentence such as (1b) above, its basic meaning remains the same, i.e., "I'm already in the state where I can't eat anything."

Mō もう is colloquially used quite often when a speaker finds himself in a helpless situation or has just seen or heard something highly unpleasant or unbearable. For example, when a mother goes into her child's room and finds it in a total mess, she might mumble to herself:

EXAMPLE:

(2) **Mattaku mō!**
まったくもう！

This literally means "Totally already," i.e., "I'm already aggravated enough. Don't try to shock me any further!" It is similar to the English phrase "Enough already!"

Mō もう meaning "already" looks the same as another **mō** meaning "more" used with numerals.

EXAMPLE:

(3) **Kōhī o mō ippai nonda.**
コーヒーをもう一杯飲んだ。
I drank one more cup of coffee.

This **mō** もう is accentless, whereas **mō** meaning "already" is accented on the first syllable, as in (4) below.

EXAMPLE:

(4) **Kōhī o <u>mō</u> ippai nonda.**
コーヒーをもう一杯飲んだ。
I already drank a cup of coffee.

Mo⌐chi⌐iru 用いる *to use, utilize*

Mochiiru 用いる is quite similar in meaning to **tsukau** 用う, which also means "to use." In conversation, the latter is the standard form since the former is basically a written expression. Compare (1) and (2).

EXAMPLES:

(1) **Surangu ga wakaranai toki wa, atarashii jisho o tsukawanakya.**
スラングが分からない時は、新しい辞書を使わなきゃ。
You've got to use a new dictionary when you don't understand a slang word.

(2) **Surangu ga rikai dekinai toki wa, atarashii jisho o mochiiru hitsuyō ga aru.**
スラングが理解できない時は、新しい辞書を用いる必要がある。
You need to make use of a new dictionary when you fail to comprehend a slang expression.

Mo⌐chi⌐ron もちろん *of course*

Mochiron もちろん means "of course," as in

EXAMPLE:

(1) **Nihonjin wa mochiron Ajiajin da.**
日本人はもちろんアジア人だ。
A Japanese is of course an Asian.

There is an extended use of **mochiron** もちろん, which could be translated into English as "let alone," in the sense of "not only."

EXAMPLE:

(2) **Nihongo no gakusei wa, kana wa mochiron kanji mo benkyō-shinakereba naranai.**
日本語の学生は、仮名はもちろん漢字も勉強しなければならない。
Students of Japanese must study kanji, not to mention kana.

Although this extended use may look a little different, it comes from the idea of "of course they must study kana but, in addition, they must also study kanji." The basic idea for (1) and (2) is therefore virtually the same.

Mo⌐do⌐ru 戻る *to return, to go back, to come back, to turn back*

Modoru 戻る is often synonymous with **kaeru** 帰る (see KAERU).

EXAMPLE:

(1) **Roku-ji-goro modorimasu.**
六時ごろ戻ります。
He'll be back about six.

In sentence (1), **modorimasu** 戻ります may be replaced by **kaerimasu** 帰ります. There are, however, at least three important differences between **modoru** 戻る and **kaeru** 帰る. First, **modoru** is sometimes used as an antonym of **susumu** 進む "to go forward," but **kaeru** 帰る is not used in this way.

EXAMPLE:

(2) **Michi ga konde-ite saki e susumenai kara, ushiro e modorimashō** (not ***kaerimashō** 帰りましょう**).**
道が込んでいて先へ進めないから、後ろへ戻りましょう。
Since the street is so crowded, we can't go forward; let's go back.

Second, sometimes **kaeru** 帰る focuses on "leaving" rather than "getting back," while **modoru** 戻る focuses on "getting back." For example, if you call Mr. Watanabe's office and are told **Mō kaerimashita** もう帰りました, it simply means "He has already left here to go home."

Third, **kaeru** 帰る implies "going back to where one belongs (e.g., one's country or home)," whereas **modoru** 戻る implies "going back to and arriving where one was before" (Shibata et al., pp. 142–43). In example (3), therefore, only **modoru** would be correct.

EXAMPLE:

(3) **kōsaten ni modoru** (not *kaeru 帰る)
交差点に戻る。
to return to the intersection

In this case, **kaeru** 帰る is wrong because an intersection is not where a pedestrian (or a driver) belongs.

Mo┐nku 文句 *word, phrase; complaint, objection*

Monku 文句 is sometimes used to simply mean "word" or "phrase."

EXAMPLES:

(1a) **Sotsugyō-arubamu ni nani ka kaku yō ni tanomareta ga, ii monku o omoitsuka-nakatta.**
卒業アルバムになにか書くように頼まれたが、いい文句を思いつかなかった。
I was asked to write something in the graduation album, but I couldn't think of anything worthwhile to say.

(1b) **Nihongo wa kimarimonku no ōi kokugo da to omou.**
日本語は決まり文句の多い国語だと思う。
I think Japanese is a language with a large number of set phrases.

More commonly, however, **monku** 文句 means "complaint," especially in the phrase **monku o iu** 文句を言う "to make a complaint."

EXAMPLE:

(2) **Monku bakari itte-iru hito wa kirawareru.**
文句ばかり言っている人は嫌われる。
A person who complains all the time will be disliked.

Morau もらう *to receive*

Although **morau** もらう is usually translated as "to receive," there are many cases where **morau** would be inappropriate. In each of the examples below, the first sentence is wrong and should be replaced by the second.

EXAMPLES:

(1a) *Watashi wa Hanako no ai o moratta.**
*わたしは花子の愛をもらった。
I received Hanako's love.

(1b) **Watashi wa Hanako no ai o uketa.**
わたしは花子の愛を受けた。

(2a) *Chichi wa gan no shujutsu o moratta.**
*父はガンの手術をもらった。
My father had a cancer operation.

(2b) **Chichi wa gan no shujutsu o uketa.**
父はガンの手術を受けた。

(3a) *Kodomo-tachi wa terebi kara ōki na eikyō o morau.*
*子供たちはテレビから大きな影響をもらう。
lit., Children receive a huge influence from TV.

(3b) **Kodomo-tachi wa terebi kara ōki na eikyō o ukeru.**
子供たちはテレビから大きな影響を受ける。

The above examples simply show that with some nouns such as **ai** 愛 "love," **shujutsu** 手術 "operation," and **eikyō** 影響 "influence," **morau** もらう cannot be used.

Mo⌐shimoshi もしもし *Hello*

Moshimoshi もしもし is the Japanese equivalent of "Hello" used at the beginning of a telephone conversation. In Japanese, however, as Jorden (1, p. 194) explains, "it is the person who places the call who says **Moshimoshi** first; he speaks when he hears a click at the other end of the line."

EXAMPLE:

Moshimoshi, kochira wa Suzuki desu ga, Takahashi-san wa irasshaimasu ka.
もしもし、こちらは鈴木ですが、高橋さんはいらっしゃいますか。
Hello, this is Suzuki. Is Mr. Takahashi there, please?

Moshimoshi もしもし may also be used to attract a stranger's attention. For example, if you see a stranger drop something, you call out **Moshimoshi!** to catch his attention. However, if used at a restaurant or a store to get service, it will probably sound too formal. In that case, say **Onegai-shimasu** お願いします or **Chotto!** ちょっと instead (see CHOTTO and ONEGAI-SHIMASU).

Mo⌐ttaina⌐i もったいない *wasteful*

Mottainai もったいない is often used as follows:

EXAMPLE:

(1) **Gohan o tabenai de suteru no wa mottainai.**
御飯を食べないで捨てるなのはもったいない。
It's wasteful to throw away uneaten rice.

Mottainai もったいない implies that the object wasted is something valuable that should be utilized to the fullest. It often carries a reproachful tone.

Mottainai もったいない describes an act or an action, never a person, whereas English "wasteful" could mean "wasting" and may modify a person, as in "He is a wasteful man." To express the same idea in Japanese, however, one would have to say the following instead:

EXAMPLE:

(2) **Kare wa rōhiteki na** (not *mottainai もったいない) **otoko da.**
彼は浪費的な男だ。
He is a wasteful man.

Mo⌐tto もっと *more*

Motto もっと may be used with a transitive verb, as in (1), or may modify an adjective or an adverb, as in (2) or (3).

EXAMPLES:
(1) **Motto kudasai.**
もっとください。
Please give me more.
(2) **Motto yasui no wa arimasen ka.**
もっと安いのはありませんか。
Aren't there cheaper ones?
(3) **Motto hayaku arukimashō.**
もっと早く歩きましょう。
Let's walk faster.

Motto もっと may not be used with a numeral. Use **mō** もう instead in that case, as in

EXAMPLE:
(4) **Mō** (not *motto もっと) **hitotsu kudasai.**
もう一つください。
Please give me one more.

Motto もっと may not be used negatively, as in (5). Use **mō** もう instead.

EXAMPLE:
(5) **Mō** (not *motto もっと) **tabetakunai.**
もう食べたくない。
I don't want to eat any more.

Mo⌐tto⌐mo もっとも *the most*

Mottomo 最も is used for superlatives just as **ichiban** いちばん is. For example,

EXAMPLE:
(1) **Fujisan wa Nihon de mottomo** (or **ichiban**) **takai yama da.**
富士山は日本で最も(いちばん)高い山です。
Mt. Fuji is the highest mountain in Japan.

The difference between **mottomo** 最も and **ichiban** いちばん is that the former is a written form and is not suitable for conversation while the latter may be used in most cases. **Mottomo** therefore would sound strange if used with a highly colloquial expression, as in

EXAMPLE:
(2) **Ichiban** (not *mottomo 最も) **tamageta no wa dare?**
いちばんたまげたのは誰?
Who was the one that was the most flabbergasted?

Ichiban いちばん is sometimes followed by **da** だ to mean "(such and such) is the best thing," but **mottomo** 最も may not be so used, as in

EXAMPLE:

(3) **Atsui hi ni wa tsumetai bīru ga ichiban da** (not *****mottomo da** 最もだ).
暑い日には冷たいビールがいちばんだ。
On a hot day, nothing surpasses cold beer.

Mu¹ri 無理 *unreasonable*

Once a student of mine who was exasperated about Japanese wrote in a composition, **Nihongo wa muri da** 日本語は無理だ to mean "Japanese is impossible." The sentence should have been either (1a) or (1b).

EXAMPLES:

(1a) **Nihongo wa watashi ni wa muri da.**
日本語は私には無理だ。
It is unreasonable to expect me to learn Japanese, (i.e., Japanese is impossible for me to learn.)

(1b) **Nihongo o ichi-ninen de masutā-suru no wa muri da.**
日本語を一、二年でマスターするのは無理だ。
It's unreasonable to expect to master Japanese in a year or two.

　Muri 無理 is often used in the phrase **muri o suru** 無理をする "to do something to an unreasonable extent, e.g., to work too hard."

EXAMPLE:

(2) **Muri o suru to byōki ni narimasu yo.**
無理をすると病気になりますよ。
If you work unreasonably hard, you'll get sick.

Na¹do など *and so on, and the like*

Nado など is often the equivalent of "and so on."

EXAMPLE:

(1) **Watashi wa ringo, orenji, momo nado ga suki desu.**
私はリンゴ、オレンジ、モモなどが好きです。
I like apples, oranges, peaches, and so on.

Nado など may be used in conjunction with **ya** や, which is inserted between the items cited.

EXAMPLE:

(2) **Watashi wa ringo ya, orenji ya, momo nado ga suki desu.**
私はリンゴや、オレンジや、モモなどが好きです。

In (1) and (2), **nado** など may be replaced by **nanka** なんか (which also means "and so on"), as in (3) and (4), the only difference being that **nanka** makes the sentences more conversational.

EXAMPLES:

(3) **Watashi wa ringo, orenji, momo nanka ga suki desu.**
私はリンゴ、オレンジ、モモなんかが好きです。

(4) **Watashi wa ringo ya, orenji ya, momo nanka ga suki desu.**
私はリンゴや、オレンジや、モモなんかが好きです。

Actually, since **ya** や by itself implies "and things like that," neither **nado** など nor **nanka** なんか is really necessary in this case.

EXAMPLE:
(5) **Watashi wa ringo ya, orenji ya, momo ga suki desu.**
私はリンゴや、オレンジや、モモが好きです。

Another use of **nado** など (and **nanka** なんか) is to provide an illustration to substantiate what precedes.

EXAMPLES:
(6) **Konogoro wa nan de mo takaku-natta. Gasorin nado** (or **nanka**) **toku ni takai.**
このごろはなんでも高くなった。ガソリンなど（なんか）特に高い。
These days everything has gotten expensive. Gasoline, for example, is particularly expensive.
(7) **Kyō wa isogashikute tegami nado** (or **nanka**) **kaku hima wa nai.**
今日は忙しくて手紙など（なんか）書くひまはない。
I'm so busy today I have no time to write things like letters.

It is of course possible to be more direct and specific by using **o** instead of **nado** など.

EXAMPLE:
(8) **Kyō wa isogashikute tegami o kakn hima wa nai.**
今日は忙しくて手紙を書くひまはない。
I'm so busy today I have no time to write letters.

In Japanese, however, one often prefers to be less direct and specific. Although (8) is of course correct, many speakers would prefer to use **nado** など (or **nanka** なんか) instead of **o**, as in (7) above. There are many other expressions in Japanese that help make statements less direct and less specific, such as **mo** も, **-tari** たり, **bakari** ばかり, and **hodo** ほど (Kunihiro, p. 37), and these are the words that lend Japanese its particular flavor.

Na⌐gara ながら *while; even though*

Nagara ながら is used to express two actions occurring simultaneously. The subject of the two actions must be one and the same.

EXAMPLE:
(1) **Watashi wa itsumo shinbun o yomi-nagara asagohan o taberu.**
私はいつも新聞を読みながら朝ご飯を食べる。
I always eat breakfast while reading the paper.

When the subjects are different, the sentence becomes ungrammatical. In that case, **aida** 間 must be used instead.

EXAMPLE:
(2) **Watashi wa tsuma ga shinbun o yonde iru aida** (not ***yominagara** 読みながら) **hirune o shite-ita.**
私は妻が新聞を読んでいる間昼寝をしていた。

Nagara みながら has another meaning, i.e., "even though." In this case, too, the same subject must hold for both clauses.

EXAMPLE:

(3) **Jon wa Nihongo ga heta nagara, itsumo isshōkenmei hanasō to suru.**
ジョンは日本語が下手ながら、いつも一生懸命話そうとする。
John always tries hard to speak Japanese even though he is not good at it.

The same-subject rule does not apply, however, in the case of some idiomatic expressions, especially **zannen-nagara** 残念ながら "regrettably" (lit., "even though it is regrettable"), as in

EXAMPLE:

(4) **Zannen-nagara, Nihon-chīmu wa makete shimatta.**
残念ながら、日本チームは負けてしまった。
Regrettably, the Japanese team lost.

Of these two uses of **nagara** ながら, the first one is far more common, appearing both in speech and writing. The latter use, i.e., "although," is basically a written expression. One of the few exceptions would be **zannen-nagara** 残念ながら, which could be used in speech as a set phrase.

Na⌐ka 中 *in, inside*

English-speaking students of Japanese tend to overuse **naka** 中. They should remember that **naka**, which means "in," is probably not used as often as English "in." The reason is because Japanese has **ni** に and **de** で, which, by themselves, can mean "in," as in

EXAMPLES:

(1a) **Tarō wa Nihon ni** (not ***Nihon no naka ni** 日本の中に) **sunde iru.**
太郎は日本に住んでいる。
Taro lives in Japan.

(1a) **Kyōshitsu de benkyō-shita.**
教室で勉強した。
I studied in the classroom.

Kyōshitsu no naka de 教室の中で would be allowed only if it contrasts with **kyōshitsu no soto de** 教室の外で "outside the classroom," as in

EXAMPLE:

(2) A: **Kyōshitsu no soto de benkyō-shita n desu ka.**
教室の外で勉強したんですか。
Did you study outside the classroom?

B: **Iie, ame ga futte ita node, (kyōshitsu no) naka de benkyō-shita n desu yo.**
いいえ、雨が降っていたので、(教室の)中で勉強したんですよ。
No, I studied in the classroom because it was raining

To repeat, **naka** 中 "in" is often omitted unless the speaker has a reason to emphasize the idea of "in" in contrast with other location words such as **soto** 外 "outside," **ue** 上 "on top," and **shita** 下 "under."

Nakanaka なかなか *quite, rather*

Nakanaka なかなか, when used with words of positive meanings, signifies "quite" or "rather."

EXAMPLE:

(1) **Koko no sushi wa nakanaka oishii desu ne.**
ここの寿司はなかなかおいしいですよ。
This restaurant serves pretty good sushi, doesn't it?

When used this way, **nakanaka** なかなか is very much like other intensifiers such as **totemo** とても, **taihen** たいへん, and **hijō ni** 非常に. The difference, first of all, is that **totemo**, **taihen**, and **hijō ni** may be used with words of negative meanings while **nakanaka** may not.

EXAMPLES:

(2a) **Kono hon wa totemo/taihen/hijō ni tsumaranai.**
この本は とても/たいへん/非常に つまらない。
This book is very uninteresting.

(2b) **Koko no ryōri wa totemo/taihen/hijō ni mazui.**
ここの料理は とても/たいへん/非常に まずい。
This restaurant serves very bad food.

Second, when **nakanaka** なかなか is used with words of positive meanings, it implies, unlike **totemo/taihen/hijō ni** とても/たいへん/非常に, that the speaker feels something is better than expected. In that sense, **nakanaka** is similar to **zuibun** ずいぶん.

EXAMPLE:

(3) **Sumisu-san, Nihongo ga nakanaka/zuibun jōzu ni narimashita ne.**
スミスさん、日本語が なかなか/ずいぶん 上手になりましたね。
Mr. Smith, your Japanese has improved a lot!

There is a slight difference, however, between **nakanaka** なかなか and **zuibun** ずいぶん, in that the latter shows a greater surprise than **nakanaka**. Moreover, since **nakanaka** could sound a little condescending, you should probably avoid using it when giving a compliment to a higher-status person.

EXAMPLE:

(4) **Sensei, zuibun (?nakanaka) tenisu ga otsuyoi n desu ne.**
先生、ずいぶん（？なかなか）テニスがお強いんですねえ。
Professor, you're a very good tennis player, indeed!

Nakanaka...nai なかなか...ない, on the other hand, means "not easily," as in

EXAMPLE:

(5) **Nihongo wa, ichi-nen dake no benkyō de wa nakanaka jōzu ni narumai.**
日本語は、一年だけの勉強ではなかなか上手になるまい。
Japanese cannot be easily mastered in just one year.

Naku 泣く, 鳴く *to cry, weep*

English has a group of verbs that describe different ways tears come out, such as "cry," "weep," "sob," "whimper," and "wail." In Japanese, different types of crying are often expressed by adding onomatopoetic adverbs to the basic verb **naku** 泣く.

EXAMPLES:

(1a) **oioi naku**
おいおい泣く
to sob

(1b) **mesomeso naku**
めそめそ泣く
to whimper

(1c) **ēnēn to naku**
えーんえーんと泣く
to wail

Naku written 鳴く is used for animals making sounds. In Japanese, different sounds made by different animals are expressed by onomatopoetic adverbs while, in English, different verbs are used for sounds made by different animals.

EXAMPLES:

(2a) **Neko wa nyānyā naku.**
猫がニャーニャー鳴く。
*Cats meow. (lit., cats go **nyānyā**.)*

(2b) **Ushi wa mōmō naku.**
牛はモーモー鳴く。
*Cows moo. (lit., cows go **mōmō**.)*

(2c) **Karasu wa kākā naku.**
からすはカーカー鳴く。
*Crows caw. (lit., crows go **kākā**.)*

(2d) **Suzume wa chunchun naku.**
すずめはチュンチュン鳴く。
*Sparrows chirp. (lit., sparrows go **chunchun**.)*

Nakunaru 亡くなる *to pass away*

Shinu 死ぬ is the most direct way of saying "to die," as in **Shinu no wa iya da** 死ぬのはいやだ。 "I don't want to die." However, just as English speakers often say "pass away," avoiding the word "die," Japanese speakers frequently use **nakunaru** 亡くなる (lit., "to disappear") as a euphemism for **shinu**. **Nakunaru** is usually used in reference to people outside the speaker's family, but it may be used in reference to one's own relatives, too.

EXAMPLES:

(1) **Tamura-san no otō-san ga nakunatta to kiite odoroita.**
田村さんのお父さんが亡くなったと聞いて驚いた。
I was surprised to hear Mr. Tamura's father is dead.

(2) **Chichi ga nakunatte sugu sōshiki ga atta.**
父が亡くなってすぐ葬式があった。
Immediately after my father died, there was a funeral.

However, **nakunaru** 亡くなる is never used in reference to oneself. Use **shinu** 死ぬ in that case.

EXAMPLE:

(3) **Watashi ga shindara** (not *nakunattara 亡くなったら) **kodomo-tachi wa dō suru darō.**
私が死んだら子供たちはどうするだろう。
What would happen to my children if I died?

The honorific form of **nakunaru** 亡くなる is **onakunari ni naru** お亡くなりになる, a term which should never be used in reference to one's own family.

EXAMPLE:

(4) **Kono tabi wa otōto-san ga onakunari ni natta sō de...**
この度は弟さんがお亡くなりになったそうで...
I'm sorry to hear that your younger brother has passed away. (lit., This time I hear that your younger brother has passed away...)

Namae 名前 *name*

In a broad sense, **namae** 名前 may mean either "full name," "family name," or "given name," as in

EXAMPLES:

(1) **Kare no namae wa**   (a) **Tanaka Taro**   **da.**
彼の名前は   田中太郎   だ。
His name is   *Taro Tanaka.*

                              (b) **Tanaka**
                                   田中
                                   Tanaka.

                              (c) **Tarō**
                                   太郎
                                   Taro.

In a narrow sense, however, **namae** 名前 means "given name" only.

EXAMPLE:

(2) **Kare no myōji wa Tanaka de, namae wa Tarō da.**
彼の名字は田中で、名前は太郎だ。
His family name is Tanaka, and his given name is Taro.

Na¹n da なんだ *What!; Why!*

Nan da なんだ ordinarily means "What is it?", as in

EXAMPLE:

(1) **Kore wa nan da.**
これはなんだ。
What is this?

Nan da なんだ, however, is sometimes used not as an interrogative but rather as an exclamation of surprise, disappointment, or disgust. For example, suppose you hear some noise at the door and open it, expecting a visitor, but find only a stray cat. In that case, you are likely to say.

EXAMPLE:

(2) **Nan da, noraneko ka.**
なんだ、野良猫か。
Why, it's a stray cat! (implication: *To my disappointment, I find only a stray cat.*)

Na⌐n no hi 何の日 *what kind of day*

Nan no hi 何の日 literally looks like "what day," but it does not really mean that. In English, if one asks "What day is today?", it normally means "What day of the week is today?" In Japanese, on the other hand, if you want to know the day of the week, you must ask **Kyō wa naniyōbi desu ka** 今日は何曜日ですか, not **Kyō wa nan no hi desu ka** 今日は何の日ですか. **Kyō wa nan no hi desu ka** is used only when you are wondering whether today is any special day. Suppose you are walking along the street in Kyoto with a Japanese friend and suddenly see a long procession. You wonder what the procession is commemorating and ask your friend **Kyō wa nan no hi desu ka**, and your friend would say, for example, **Kyō wa Gion Matsuri desu yo** 今日は祇園祭ですよ ("Today is Gion Festival Day").

Na⌐o⌐su 直す *to correct, to repair, to cure*

Naosu 直す basically means "to make [something] right" and is used to mean "to repair, to correct, to cure."

EXAMPLES:

(1) **terebi (tokei, kuruma, etc.) o naosu**
テレビ(時計、車、etc.)を直す
to repair a TV (*watch, car*, etc.)

(2) **machigai (sakubun, bun, etc.) o naosu**
間違い(作文、文、etc.)を直す
to correct errors (*compositions, sentences*, etc.)

(3) **byōki (byōnin, kaze, etc.) o naosu**
病気(病人、風邪、etc.)を治す
to cure an illness (*sick person, cold*, etc.)

Thus, **naosu** 治す has a much wider range of usage than either **shūri-suru** 修理する or **shūzen-suru** 修繕する, both of which can only mean "to repair." **Shūri-suru** or **shūzen-suru** can therefore replace **naosu** in (1) above, but not in (2) or (3). **Shūri-suru** and **shūzen-suru** are synonymous and can be used more or less interchangeably. Tokugawa and Miyajima (p. 194) suggest, however, that **shūzen-suru** might sound a little more dated than **shūri-suru**.

Na⌐ra⌐u 習う *to study, to take lessons*

Although **narau** 習う is often equated with "learn" by American students of Japanese, it is more like "study" in the sense that it does not imply mastery as does "learn." (1) and (2) below are therefore correct, but (3) is not.

EXAMPLES:

(1) **Uchi no musume wa ima piano o naratte-imasu.**
うちの娘はいまピアノを習っています。
My daughter is taking piano lessons.

(2) **Eigo wa roku-nen mo gakkō de naraimashita ga, jōzu ni narimasen deshita.**
英語は六年も学校で習いましたが、上手になりませんでした。
I studied English for six years in school, but I never became good at it.

(3) ***Aoki-san wa san-nen Amerika ni ita aida ni eigo o hitori de ni naraimashita.**
*青木さんは三年アメリカに行った間に英語を一人でに習いました。
Mr. Aoki learned English without effort during his three-year stay in America.

To make (3) correct, **naraimashita** 習いました must be replaced by **oboemashita** 覚えました "learned" (see OBOERU).

EXAMPLE:

(4) **Aoki-san wa san-nen Amerika ni ita aida ni eigo o hitori de ni oboemashita.**
青木さんは三年アメリカに行った間に英語を一人でに覚えました。

A student of mine once wrote sentence (5) below, with the intended meaning "It goes without saying that Japanese too can learn English."

EXAMPLE:

(5) ***Nihonjin de mo eigo ga naraeru koto wa iu made mo nai.**
*日本人でも英語が習える事は言うまでもない。

Of course, he should have used **oboerareru** 覚えられる "can learn" instead of **naraeru** 習える "can take lessons."
　　Narau 習う and **benkyō-suru** 勉強する are often interchangeable, as below.

EXAMPLE:

(6) **Daigaku de Nihongo o naratte-imasu (or benkyō-shite-imasu).**
大学で日本語を習っています（勉強しています）。
I am studying Japanese in college.

There are, however, at least three differences between the two verbs. First of all, **narau** 習う implies the presence of a teacher while **benkyō-suru** 勉強する does not.

EXAMPLES:

(7) **Nihongo o naratte-imasu.**
日本語を習っています。

(8) **Nihongo o benkyō-shite-imasu.**
日本語を勉強しています。

Although both (7) and (8) mean "I am studying Japanese," the speaker in (7) is presumably taking a course somewhere or taking lessons from a tutor, while the speaker in (8) might be just trying to teach himself.
　　Second, **narau** 習う has to have an object while **benkyō-suru** 勉強する does not. Sentence (9) is therefore incorrect unless preceded by a sentence that specifies the object of studying, while sentence (10) is correct by itself.

EXAMPLES:

(9) ***Nishio-san wa naratte-imasu.**
*西尾さんは習っています。
Mr. Nishio is studying [what?].

(10) **Nishio-san wa benkyō-shite-imasu.**
西尾さんは勉強しています。
Mr. Nishio is studying.

Third, **narau** 習う may be used for academic subjects as well as nonacademic skills, while **benkyō-suru** 勉強する is normally reserved for academic subjects only. When **benkyō-suru** is used for nonacademic skills, it connotes a very serious endeavor. In (11), for example, one would most normally use **narau**. If, however, **benkyō-suru** were used, it would connote that the speaker was taking lessons from a master carpenter perhaps with a view to making an occupation of carpentry. If carpentry is meant to be a hobby, the use of **benkyō-suru** would indicate a very serious hobby. **Narau** has no such connotation.

EXAMPLE:
(11) **Daiku-shigoto o naratte-imasu.**
　　 大工仕事を習っています。
　　 I am taking lessons in carpentry.

Narubeku なるべく *as . . . as possible; if possible*

Narubeku なるべく is used as follows, and is usually replaceable by **dekiru dake** できるだけ.

EXAMPLES:
(1a) **Shukudai wa narubeku/dekiru dake hayaku yaru koto ni shite-iru.**
　　 宿題は なるべく/できるだけ 早くやることにしている。
　　 I make it a rule to get my homework done as soon as possible.
(1b) **Ashita no pātī ni wa, narubeku/dekiru dake kite kudasai ne.**
　　 あしたのパーティーには、なるべく/できるだけ 来てくださいね。
　　 Please come to tomorrow's party if at all possible.

There is a slight difference in connotation between **narubeku** なるべく and **dekiru dake** できるだけ, however. According to *Effective Japanese Usage Guide* (pp. 474–476), **dekiru dake** is more like "to one's utmost ability" and is therefore more emphatic than **narubeku**.

Another difference between the two expressions is that **dekiru dake** できるだけ may modify a noun by using **no** whereas **narubeku** なるべく is not used that way.

EXAMPLE:
(2)　 **Anata no tame nara, dekiru dake** (not *****narubeku** なるべく) **no koto wa shimasu.**
　　 あなたのためなら、できるだけのことはします。
　　 If it's for you, I'll do the best I can.

Naruhodo なるほど *I see*

Naruhodo なるほど means "I see" in the sense of "I see what you say is right." It is most often used as a response to an explanation given by someone. The implication is "Why didn't I think of it?"

EXAMPLE:
A: **Kono mado ga akanai n desu ga.**
　　 この窓が空かないんですが。
　　 I can't seem to open this window.
B: **Kō sureba ii n desu yo.**
　　 こうすればいいんですよ。
　　 This is all you have to do.

A: **Aa, naruhodo.**
ああ、なるほど。
Oh, I see.

Nebō-suru 寝坊する *to oversleep; to sleep late*

In English, one may say "I slept late" to mean "I overslept." American students who come to a morning class late may make the mistake of translating "I slept late" into **Osoku nemashita** 遅く寝ました to mean "I overslept." They should actually say:

EXAMPLE:
(1) **Nebō-shite osoku narimashita.**
寝坊して遅くなりました。
I was late because I overslept.

Osoku nemashita 遅くなりました has its own meaning, i.e., "I went to bed late," as in

EXAMPLE:
(2) **Yūbe osoku neta node, kesa hayaku okiraremasen deshita.**
ゆうべ遅く寝たので、けさ早く起きられませんでした。
Because I went to bed late last night, I wasn't able to get up early this morning.

Neru 寝る *to go to bed, to sleep, to fall asleep, to lie down*

Neru 寝る has three meanings: "to go to bed," as in example (1) below; "to sleep, to fall asleep," as in (2); and "to lie down," as in (3).

EXAMPLES:
(1) **Maiban jūichi-ji-goro nemasu.**
毎晩11時頃寝ます。
I go to bed about 11 o'clock every night.
(2) **Maiban hachi-jikan nereba jūbun deshō.**
毎晩8時間寝れば十分でしょう。
If you sleep eight hours a night, it should be enough.
(3) **Nenagara hon o yomu to me ni yoku arimasen yo.**
寝ながら本を読むと目によくありませんよ。
If you read lying down, it's not good for your eyes.

For each of these meanings, there is a synonym for **neru** 寝る: **toko ni hairu** とこに入る "to get into one's bed," **nemuru** 眠る "to sleep, to fall asleep," and **yoko ni naru** 横になる "to lie down." But **neru** 寝る has a much wider range of meaning than any of these.

Ni˩chibei 日米 *Japan-U.S.*

In English, one normally says "U.S.-Japan relations," "U.S.-Japan Peace Treaty," etc., putting U.S. before Japan. In Japanese, it is the other way around. One must say **Nichibei-kankei** 日米関係 (lit., "Japan-U.S. relations"), **Nichibei-Heiwajōyaku** 日米平和条約 (lit., "Japan-U.S. Peace Treaty"), etc. It seems that we want to place our countries first in our respective languages.

Nigate 苦手 *weak point*

Nigate 苦手 is similar to **heta** 下手.

EXAMPLE:

(1) **Watashi wa sukī ga nigate/heta da.**
私はスキーが 苦手/下手 だ。
I am not good at skiing.

Nigate 苦手, however, is not the same as **heta** 下手. Whereas **heta** is an objective description, **nigate** is more subjective. For example, in sentence (1) above, **nigate** implies that the speaker is not only a poor skier but is not too fond of the sport or is embarrassed to talk about it. If someone is **heta** at skiing, he can still like it. There is even a proverb, **Heta no yokozuki** 下手の横好き, meaning "There are people who are crazy about something without being good at it." On the other hand, if someone is **nigate** at something, he cannot possibly like it; in the above proverb, therefore, **heta** may not be replaced by **nigate**.

Nigate is sometimes used with respect to one's attitude toward someone, as in

EXAMPLE:

(2) **Watashi wa Yoshida-san no yō na hito wa nigate** (not *heta 下手) **da.**
私は吉田さんのような人は苦手だ。
I find it hard to deal with someone like Mr. Yoshida.

Nigate 苦手 used in this sense is naturally not a synonym for **heta** 下手.

Nigiri 握り *a kind of sushi*

Usually a Japanese noun does not change its meaning whether or not it is preceded by an honorific prefix **o**. For example, **sushi** 寿司 and **osushi** お寿司 refer to the same object, the only difference being the **o**-version sounds more polite. With **nigiri**, however, the same cannot be said. **Nigiri** 握り is short for **nigirizushi** 握り寿司, i.e., a small oblong chunk of sushi rice topped with a slice of fish. **Onigiri** おにぎり, on the other hand, refers to a rice ball with things like a pickled plum inside and often covered with **nori** のり, a sheet of dried black seaweed. If you want to eat **nigiri**, you go to a sushi restaurant, but if you want an **onigiri**, you either make one yourself or go to a Japanese-style non-sushi restaurant.

Ni⌈ho⌉n 日本 *Japan*

I am sure students of Japanese sometimes wonder about the difference between the two common ways of referring to Japan in Japanese: **Nihon** and **Nippon**.

Before and during World War II, the Japanese government promoted the pronunciation **Nippon** 日本 rather than **Nihon** 日本. The reason was apparently that **Nippon** sounds more lively and powerful than **Nihon** because it contains a plosive sound. Japanese athletes representing their country at sporting events such as the Olympics often wear uniforms with **Nippon** printed on them in **romaji** ローマ字, never **Nihon**. Certainly **Nippon** is better suited to cheering than is **Nihon**. Strangely, however, in daily conversation, **Nihon** seems to be preferred by most speakers of Japanese.

Ni⌐honji⌐n 日本人 *a Japanese*

In English, "Japanese" means both "a Japanese person" and "the Japanese language." **Nihonjin** 日本人, on the other hand, only means "a Japanese." (**Nihongo** is of course the word for "the Japanese language.") In fact, **Nihonjin** has a very narrow meaning, i.e., "a Japanese national." A Japanese-American, therefore, is not a **Nihonjin**. Japanese who have emigrated to other countries and have acquired citizenship in those countries—as well as their offspring, such as **nisei** and **sansei**—are referred to as **Nikkeijin** "person[s] of Japanese origin."

When **Nihonjin** is written in kanji (i.e., 日本人), the last character is the one for **hito** 人. Since **hito** is not an honorific expression, **Nihonjin** is not either. Upon meeting a Japanese-looking stranger, therefore, it is not courteous to use **Nihonjin desu ka** 日本人ですか to mean "Are you a Japanese?" It is better to ask **Nihon no kata desu ka** 日本の方ですか, using **kata** 方, the honorific counterpart of **hito**.

Nihon-shiki 日本式 *Japanese-system/style*

Nihon-shiki 日本式 and **Nihon-fū** 日本風 (or **wafū** 和風) may both be translated "Japanese-style." Their uses overlap somewhat, but not completely.

Nihon-shiki is basically for contraptions, systems, and such, as in

EXAMPLE:
(1) **Nihon-shiki no toire wa, shagamanakereba naranai.**
日本式のトイレは、しゃがまなればならない。
A Japanese-style toilet requires squatting.

Nihon-fū (or **wafū**) **no toire** 日本風（和風）のトイレ calls up a different image. It could very well be a Western-style toilet, but the walls may be covered with Japanese wallpaper or the window might look **shoji**-style. In sentence (1), therefore, **Nihon-fū** would not be suitable.

EXAMPLE:
(2) **Amerika no kōkō ni wa, Nihongo no kurasu o Nihonshiki/fū no ojigi de hajimeru tokoro mo aru.**
アメリカの高校には、日本語のクラスを日本式/風のおじぎではじめることろもある。
In some American high schools, Japanese-language classes begin with Japanese-style bowing.

In sentence (2), **Nihon-shiki no ojigi** 日本式のおじぎ is a bow that strictly follows the Japanese school tradition, whereas **Nihon-fū no ojigi** 日本風のおじぎ could be any bow as iong as it is similar to the Japanese bow.

Ni kanshite に関して *concerning*

Ni kanshite に関して means "concernng" and is used adverbially only, as in

EXAMPLE:
(1) **Nichibei-seifudaihyō wa, Nichibei-bōeki ni kanshite hageshii giron o shita.**
日米政府代表は、日米貿易に関して激しい議論をした。
The representatives of the U.S. and Japanese governments vehemently argued about U.S.-Japan trade.

Ni kanshite に関して must be replaced by **ni kansuru** に関する when used adjectivally, modifying a noun. If you wish to use **ni kanshite** adjectivally, you must insert **no** before the following noun, as in

EXAMPLE:

(2) **Nichibei-seifudaihyō wa, Nichibei-bōeki ni kansuru (or kanshite no) kaigō o hiraita.**
日米政府代表は、日米貿易に関する(関しての)会合を開いた。
The representatives of the U.S. and Japanese governments held a meeting that con-cerned U.S.-Japan trade.

Ni kanshite に関して is a formal written form and is not used in normal speech. In conversation or less formal written Japanese, **ni tsuite** について should be used, as in

EXAMPLE:

(3) **Sensei, Amerika no gikai ni tsuite setsumei-shite kudasai.**
先生、アメリカの議会について説明してください。
Professor, please explain the U.S. Congress to us.

Ni⌈ku⌉ 肉 *flesh; meat*

In English, "meat" and "flesh" are two different words, but in Japanese, **niku** 肉 takes care of both meanings.

EXAMPLES:

(1) **Ano hito wa hone bakari de, niku ga nai.**
あの人は骨ばかりで、肉がない。
He is all bones and no flesh.
(2) **Konogoro no kodomo wa sakana yori niku no hō ga suki desu.**
このごろの子供は魚より肉の方が好きです。
Kids these days prefer meat to fish.

Ninki 人気 *popularity*

Ninki 人気 by itself means "popularity," not "popular." If you wish to say someone or some-thing is popular, therefore, you must say **ninki ga aru** 人気がある (lit., to have popularity).

EXAMPLE:

(1) **Sakkā wa ninki ga aru.**
サッカーは人気がある。
Soccer is popular.

To say "to become popular," use **ninki ga deru** 人気がでる, not **ninki ni naru** 人気に なる.

EXAMPLE:

(2) **Nihon de sakkā no ninki ga deta (not *ninki ni natta 人気になった) no wa sūnen mae datta to omou.**
日本でサッカーの人気がでたのは数年前だったと思う。
I think it must have been several years ago that soccer became popular in Japan.

Ninki 人気 may be attached to other nouns to create compound nouns such as **ninki-sakka** 人気作家 "popular novelist."

EXAMPLE:

(3) **Murakami Haruki wa konogoro ninkisakka ni natta.**
村上春樹はこのごろ人気作家になった。
Haruki Murakami has lately become a popular novelist.

(See also HAYARU and SAKAN.)

Ninshin-suru 妊娠する *to become pregnant*

In English, one "becomes pregnant" but, in Japanese, one "does pregnancy."

EXAMPLE:

(1) **Tanaka-san wa okusan ga ninshin-shita** (not **ninshin ni natta* 妊娠になった) **sō da.**
田中さんは奥さんが妊娠したそうだ。
I hear Mr. Tanaka's wife is pregnant.

There are many other expressions in Japanese that do not require **naru** なる although their English counterparts use "become." For example,

English	Japanese
become angry	**okoru** 怒る
become fat	**futoru** 太る
become hungry	**onaka ga suku** おなかが空く
become old	**toshi o toru** 年を取る
become popular	**ninki ga deru** 人気がでる
become thirsty	**nodo ga kawaku** のどが渇く

Nite-iru 似ている *to be similar; look alike; resemble*

Nite-iru 似ている comes from the dictionary form **niru** 似る, but the latter is rarely used.

EXAMPLES:

(1) **Kankokugo no bunpō wa Nihongo no bunpō ni nite-iru to iwareru.**
韓国語の文法は日本語の文法に似ていると言われる。
Korean grammar is said to be similar to Japanese grammar.

(2) **Hanako wa hahaoya ni amari nite-inai.**
花子は母親にあまり似ていない。
Hanako does not resemble her mother very much.

As a modifier in prenoun position, either **nite-iru** 似ている or **nita** 似た may be used, as in

EXAMPLE:

(3) **Nihon ni wa, Fujisan ni nite-iru/nita yama ga kekkō ōi.**
日本には、富士山に 似ている/似た 山が結構多い。
In Japan, there are quite a few mountains that look like Mt. Fuji.

Ni yoru to によると *according to*

Ni yoru to によると means "according to," and is used as follows:

EXAMPLES:

(1a) **Tenkiyohō ni yoru to, kyō wa ame ga furu sō da.**
天気予報によると、今日は雨が降るそうだ。
According to the weather forecast, it's going to rain today.

(1b) **Buraun-san ni yoru to, Shikago no fuyu wa kanari samui rashii/yō da.**
ブラウンさんによると、シカゴの冬の冬はかなり寒い らしい/よう だ。
According to Mr. Brown, winter in Chicago is pretty cold.

As the above examples show, when **ni yoru to** によると is used, the sentence normally ends with **sō da** そうだ, **rashii** らしい, or **yō da** ようだ whereas, in English, there is no need for the addition of expressions such as "it seems," "it looks like," or "it sounds like." **Ni yore ba** によれば is synomymous with **ni yoru to** and is used in exactly the same way. **Ni yotte** によって, however, is different in meaning and must not be confused with **ni yoru to**. Although **ni yotte** is sometimes translated as "according to," it could mean "according to" only in the sense of "in accordance with," as in

EXAMPLE:

(2) **Akunin wa hōritsu ni yotte sabakareru beki da.**
悪人は法律によって裁かれるべきだ。
Villains should be tried in accordance with the law.

In (1a) and (1b), therefore, **ni yotte** によって cannot replace **ni yoru to** によると.

(See also NI YOTTE below.)

Ni yotte によって *depending on; by means of; because of; by*

Ni yotte によって has different meanings, but the most common is "depending on," as in

EXAMPLE:

(1) **Nihongo no akusento wa chihō ni yotte kanari chigau.**
日本語のアクセントは地方によってかなり違う。
The Japanese accent varies considerably, depending on the region.

The other uses are mainly for written or formal Japanese. For example, one of the meanings, "by," is used in written passive sentences, as in

EXAMPLE:

(2) **Nihon wa Amerika no guntai ni yotte senryō-sareta.**
日本はアメリカの軍隊によって占領された。
Japan was occupied by American troops.

In conversation, **ni yotte** によって is normally replaced by **ni** に alone. Sentence (2), therefore, becomes **Nihon wa Amerika no guntai ni senryō sareta** 日本はアメリカの軍隊に占領された。

Noboru 登る *to climb*

In English, it is perfectly all right to use "climb" as a transitive verb, as in "I climbed Mt. Fuji." In Japanese, on the other hand, climbing Mt. Fuji takes the particle **ni** に, not **o** を.

EXAMPLE:

(1) **Fujisan ni** (not ****o** を) **nobotta.**
富士山に登った。
I climbed Mt. Fuji.

In certain situations, **o** を could be used instead of **ni** に, but the connotation would be different.

EXAMPLE:

(2) **Ano saka o nobotte iku hito ga miemasu ka.**
あの坂を登って行く人が見えますか。
Can you see the person going up that slope?

Ni に is used when the goal is the main concern while **o** is used when the process is the issue, e.g., in sentence (1), the speaker is talking about the experience of reaching the top of Mt. Fuji, whereas the speaker of sentence (2) is talking about someone who is in the process of going uphill.

No⌐mu 飲む *to drink*

Although **nomu** 飲む is often equated with "drink," it actually means "to take something orally without chewing" (Suzuki, p.19). It is therefore used in reference not only to drinks but also to medicine taken orally and cigarette smoke. It may correspond to other English verbs besides "drink," depending on the object.

EXAMPLES:

(1) **bīru o nomu**
ビールを飲む
to drink beer
(2) **kusuri o nomu**
薬を飲む
to take medicine
(3) **tabako o nomu**
タバコを飲む
to smoke [a cigarette]
(4) **tsuba o nomu**
つばを飲む
to swallow saliva

No⌐ro⌐i のろい *slow*

Unlike **osoi** 遅い (see OSOI), which means both "late" and "slow," **noroi** のろい can only mean "slow." When **osoi** is used in the sense of "slow," however, there is still a difference in connotation between the two words.

EXAMPLE:

(1) **Ano hito wa aruku no ga**
あの人は歩くのが

(a) **osoi.**
遅い。

(b) **noroi.**
のろい。

He walks slowly.

Sentence (1a) is just an objective statement, whereas (1b) implies that the speaker disapproves of that person's slowness (Tokugawa and Miyajima, p. 72).

Noru 乗る *to get on, to get into [a vehicle]*

While, in English, prepositions following "get" vary, depending on the means of transportation (e.g., "get on the bus," "get into a cab"), in Japanese, the particle used with **noru** 乗る is always **ni** に, no matter what type of vehicle is in question.

EXAMPLES:

(1a) **kuruma** (or **takushī**) **ni noru**
車(タクシー)に乗る
to get into a car (or *taxi*)

(1b) **basu** (or **densha**) **ni noru**
バス(電車)に乗る
to get on a bus (or *train*)

Noru 乗る usually refers to the act of getting on or into a vehicle.

EXAMPLE:

(2) **Kisha ga demasu kara, hayaku notte-kudasai.**
汽車が出ますから、早く乗ってください。
The train is leaving; please get on board immediately.

To refer to the act of traveling by some means of transportation, say **notte iku** 乗って行く. The particle used is still the same, that is, **ni** に.

EXAMPLE:

(3) **Mainichi kaisha made basu ni notte ikimasu.**
毎日会社までバスに乗って行きます。
Every day I take the bus to the office.

If, however, **notte** 乗って is deleted from sentence (3), the particle has to be changed to **de** で.

EXAMPLE:

(4) **Mainichi kaisha made basu de ikimasu.**
毎日会社までバスで行きます。
Every day I go to the office by bus.

Nozomu 望む *to hope*

In English, "to hope" is a very common verb. If we look up "hope" in an English-Japanese dictionary, we find "corresponding" Japanese verbs such as **nozomu** 望 and **kibō-suru** 希望する. It is true that these Japanese verbs mean "to hope," but they are written expressions not used in speech. For example, how would you say "I hope we'll have good weather tomorrow" in Japanese? The dictionary might suggest **Ashita tenki ga ii koto o nozomimasu** あした天気がいいことを望みます, which is the direct translation of the English. But no one would say that in daily conversation. More normally, one would use an entirely different structure such as

EXAMPLES:
(1a) **Ashita ii tenki da to ii nā.**
あしたいい天気だといいなあ。
lit., It'll be nice if the weather is good tomorrow.
(1b) **Ashita ii tenki da to ii desu ne.**
あしたいい天気だといいですね。
lit., It'll be nice if the weather is good tomorrow, won't it?

In other words, instead of directly saying "I hope...," Japanese speakers normally say the equivalent of "It'll be nice if..." in conversation. "I hope so" does not become **Sō nozomimasu** そう望みます, but rather **Sō da to ii desu ne** そうだといいですね (lit., "It'll be nice if it's so").

Nu'gu 脱ぐ *to take off [clothing]*

Whereas the act of putting on clothing requires various verbs such as **kiru** 着る, **kaburu** かぶる, and **haku** はく, depending on what one puts on, the act of taking off clothing is often taken care of by one verb, **nugu** 脱ぐ.

EXAMPLES:
(1a) **uwagi o kiru**
上着を着る
to put on a jacket
(1b) **uwagi o nugu**
上着を脱ぐ
to take off a jacket
(2a) **bōshi o kaburu**
帽子をかぶる
to put on a hat
(2b) **bōshi o nugu**
帽子を脱ぐ
to take off a hat
(3a) **kutsu o haku**
靴をはく
to put on shoes
(3b) **kutsu o nugu**
靴を脱ぐ
to take off shoes

Other verbs meaning "to put on [clothing]" however, do not match up with **nugu** 脱ぐ, but with **toru** 取る or **hazusu** はずす instead.

EXAMPLES:
(4a) **nekutai o shimeru** (or **suru**)
ネクタイをしめる(する)
to put on a tie

(4b) **nekutai o toru**
ネクタイを取る
to take off a tie
(5a) **tokei o hameru** (or **suru**)
時計をはめる(する)
to put on a [wrist] watch
(5b) **tokei o toru** (or **hazusu**)
時計を取る(はずす)
to take off a [wrist] watch
(6a) **megane o kakeru**
眼鏡をかける
to put on glasses
(6b) **megane o toru** (or **hazusu**)
眼鏡を取る(はずす)
to take off glasses

Nu⌐ru⌐i ぬるい *lukewarm*

Nurui ぬるい is as a rule used with reference to liquids to mean "not hot enough." That is why (1b) is wrong.

EXAMPLES:
(1a) **nurui kōhī** (**ocha**, **ofuro**, etc.)
ぬるいコーヒー(お茶、お風呂、etc.)
lukewarm coffee (tea, bath, etc.)
(1b) ***nurui gohan** (**supagettī**, **piza**, etc.)
*ぬるいご飯(スパゲッティー、ピザ、etc.)
lukewarm rice (spaghetti, pizza, etc.)

Sometimes, **nurui** ぬるい means "not cold enough" in reference to liquids.

EXAMPLE:
(2) **nurui bīru**
ぬるいビール
lukewarm beer

When used figuratively, "lukewarm" means "half-hearted," as in "a lukewarm handshake." On the other hand, **nurui** ぬるい, when used figuratively, does not mean "half-hearted," but "not strict enough."

EXAMPLE:
(3) **Sonna nurui yarikata wa dame da.**
そんなぬるいやり方はだめだ。
Such a measure is not strict enough and is therefore no good.

This figurative use of **nurui** ぬるい, however, is probably not as common as **tenurui** 手ぬるい, which also means "not strict enough."

O⌈boe⌉ru 覚える *to commit something to memory, to learn*

Oboeru 覚える means "to commit something to memory," and therefore "to learn."

EXAMPLES:
(1) **Hayaku Nihongo o oboe-tai desu.**
早く日本語を覚えたいです。
I'd like to learn Japanese as soon as possible.
(2) **Mainichi kanji o gojū mo oboeru no wa muri deshō.**
毎日漢字を五十も覚えるのは無理でしょう。
It might be too difficult to learn 50 Chinese characters a day.

To express the idea of "retaining something that has been committed to memory," one has to say **oboete-iru** 覚えている rather than **oboeru** 覚える. American students of Japanese often make the error of identifying **oboeru** with "remember" and make sentences such as (3), but (3) is a misrepresentation of (4), and cannot mean "I don't remember his name."

EXAMPLES:
(3) ****Ano hito no namae wa oboemasen.**
*あの人の名前は覚えません。
(4) **Ano hito no namae wa oboete-imasen.**
あの人の名前は覚えていません。
I don't remember his name.

Sentence (3) can be correct only in the sense of "I won't (i.e., I refuse to) commit his name to memory."

Oboeru 覚える cannot mean "to bring back from memory," either. For that one needs **omoidasu** 思い出す (see OMOIDASU).

Ocha o ireru お茶を入れる *to make tea*

"Make tea" is not **ocha o tsukuru** お茶を作る, but **ocha o ireru** お茶を入れる.

EXAMPLE:
(1) **Koi ocha o ippai irete** (not ****tsukutte** 作って) **kudasai.**
濃い茶を一杯入れてください。
Please make me a strong cup of tea.

Ocha o tsukuru お茶を作る would mean "to grow tea," as in **Shizuoka-ken ni wa ocha o tsukutte-iru nōka ga ōi** 静岡県にはお茶を作っている農家が多い "In Shizuoka Prefecture, there are lots of farmers who cultivate tea."

The intransitive counterpart of **ireru** 入れる is **hairu** 入る, and it is used just as often when talking about making tea, as in

EXAMPLE:
(2) **Ocha ga hairimashita kara dōzo.**
お茶が入りましたからどうぞ。
Tea is ready (lit., Tea has been made). Please have some.

Although it is possible to say **Ocha o iremashita** お茶を入れました (lit., "I just made tea"), Japanese speakers often prefer the intransitive version, treating the occasion as something that just happened rather than as something they themselves brought about. This is true with many other transitive-intransitive verbs, as well. (See Alfonso, p.885.)

Odaiji ni お大事に *Please take care [of yourself]*

Odaiji ni お大事に is an expression of sympathy directed to someone who is ill or whose family member is ill. Although its literal meaning is "Take care of yourself," it is uttered in the same spirit as the English expression "I hope you (he, she, etc.) will get well soon."

EXAMPLE:

A: **Konogoro koshi ga itakute komatte-iru n desu.**
このごろ腰が痛くて困っているんです。
I've been bothered by a lower-back pain lately.

B: **Ikemasen nē. Odaiji ni.**
いけませんねえ。お大事に。
I'm sorry to hear that. Please take care of yourself.

In English, "Take care" is sometimes used as a farewell meaning "Good-by." **Odaiji ni** お大事に, on the other hand, is not used as a farewell unless the speaker knows that either the addressee or a member of the latter's family is ill.

O⌈fu⌉ro お風呂 *bath*

Ofuro お風呂, which is more often used than the plain form **furo** 風呂, means "bath" or "bathtub." "Take a bath" is **ofuro ni hairu** お風呂に入る or **ofuro o abiru** お風呂を浴びる. Sometimes **oyu** お湯 meaning "hot water" (see OYU) is used instead of **ofuro**, as in **oyu ni hairu** お湯に入る. "Get out of the bath" is either **ofuro o** (or **kara**) **deru** お風呂を (or から) 出る, or **ofuro kara agaru** お風呂から上がる. The reason **agaru** 上がる (lit., "to go up") is used is that, in Japan, after a bath one steps up from the bathroom to the anteroom where one's clothing was removed and left before the bath.

Ofuro お風呂 does not refer to a room with a bathtub. Such a room is **ofuroba** お風呂場 (lit., "bath place") or, if it is a Western-style bathroom with a Western-style bathtub, **basurūmu** (from English "bathroom").

In English, "bathroom" serves as a euphemism for "toilet" and is used even when there is no bathtub in the room (e.g., "May I use your bathroom?"). **Ofuro** お風呂, on the other hand, can never be used to mean "toilet." For that purpose, say **otearai** お手洗い or **toire** トイレ (from English "toilet").

EXAMPLE:

Chotto oterai (or toire) o haishaku-sasete-kudasai.
ちょっとお手洗い（トイレ）を拝借させてください。
Please let me use your bathroom.

O⌈gen⌉ki desu ka お元気ですか *Are you well? How are you?*

Although **Ogenki desu ka** お元気ですか "Are you well?" is sometimes taught in Japanese language textbooks for English speakers as the "equivalent" of "How are you?", the frequency of its usage is far below that of "How are you?" One does not indiscriminately direct the question **Ogenki desu ka** to everyone one encounters. In English, "How are you?" has almost been reduced to the status of a greeting, and it often serves merely as another way of saying "Hi!" **Ogenki desu ka**, on the other hand, has remained a genuine question and is reserved for someone one has not seen for a long time.

O⌐hayō gozaima⌐su おはようございます *Good morning!*

Ohayō gozaimasu おはようございます is a greeting exchanged between persons (whether or not they are members of the same family) when they meet in the morning. It may be shortened to **Ohayō** おはよう in addressing a close friend, or a person lower in status. The original meaning of **Ohayō gozaimasu** was "It is early" (with a connotation of respect and politeness); this greeting is therefore most appropriate in. the early morning. At 11 A.M., for example, one is more likely to say **Konnichi wa** こんにちは "Good day!" (see KON-NICHI WA).

Unlike "Good morning!", which, on formal occasions, may be used as a farewell in the morning, **Ohayō gozaimasu** おはようございます can never be used in parting.

Ōi [O⌐oi] 多い *many, much*

Ōi 多い means "a lot," in terms of both numbers and quantities.

EXAMPLES:
(1) **Konogoro wa ame ga ōi.** (quantity)
このごろは雨が多い。
It's been raining a lot lately.
(2) **Nyūyōku ni wa gaikokujin ga ōi.** (number)
ニューヨークには外国人が多い。
In New York, there are many foreigners.

O⌐kaeri-nasa⌐i お帰りなさい *Welcome home!*

Okaeri-nasai お帰りなさい (lit., "You've come home") is the standard response to **Tadaima** ただいま (see TADAIMA). Its closest English equivalent would be "Welcome home!" or "I'm glad you're home again," but whereas these English expressions are reserved for special occasions, **Okaeri-nasai** is a set phrase used every day.

In rapid, less careful speech, **Okaeri-nasai** お帰りなさい regularly becomes **Okaen-nasai** お帰んなさい. A higher-status family member speaking to a lower-status member (e.g., a father speaking to a child) sometimes shortens the greeting to **Okaeri** お帰り.

Okaeri-nasai お帰りなさい is also used in non-family situations—for example, when talking to an in-group person (e.g., to a person working for the same company) who has just returned from an outing or trip. In this case, **Okaeri-nasai** is never shortened to **Okaeri** お帰り.

Okage-sama de おかげさまで *thanks to you*

Okage-sama de おかげさまで, meaning "thanks to you," is often used even when the person addressed has nothing to do with the event in question. In (1), a student who has just passed a college entrance examination is talking to a teacher who helped him prepare for it; thus the addressee does have a connection with the happy event. In (2), however, speaker A has not contributed at all to the good health of B's family.

EXAMPLES:
(1) **Okage-same de pasu-shimashita.**
おかげさまでパスしました。
Thanks to your help, I passed.

(2) A: **Otaku no mina-san ogenki desu ka.**
お宅の皆さんお元気ですか。
Is everybody in your family in good health?

    B: **Hai, okage-sama de.**
はい、おかげさまで。
Yes, thank you (lit., thanks to you).

In cases like (2), **Okage-sama de** おかげさまで is like saying "I appreciate your concern" or "Thank you for asking."

    As Jorden (1, p. 3) states, **Okage-sama de** おかげさまで "always accompanies, or itself implies, favorable or pleasant information."

O⌐ka⌐shi お菓子 *confectionery*

Okashi お菓子, or its plain form, **kashi** 菓子, is a generic term for cake, sweets, and candy, whether Japanese or Western. A distinction can be made between Japanese sweet things and Western ones by calling the former **wagashi** 和菓子 (lit., "Japanese **kashi**"), and the latter **yōgashi** 洋菓子 (lit., "Western **kashi**").

    Wagashi 和菓子 and **yōgashi** 洋菓子 can each be divided into subcategories. The most popular type of **wagashi** is **mochigashi** 餅菓子 (i.e., **mochi**-based **kashi**) while the most popular type of **yōgashi** is undoubtedly **kēki** ケーキ "cake [baked Western style]."

Okazu おかず *food to eat with rice*

If you look up **okazu** おかず in a Japanese-English dictionary, you find strange explanations such as "subsidiary articles of diet" and "an accompanying dish." The reason is because there is no equivalent idea in English-speaking cultures and therefore no exact English translation. A typical Japanese dinner always includes rice as the staple, and that is why rice is called **shushoku** 主食 (lit., "main food") in Japanese. Along with rice, one may have vegetables, fish, or meat. Those non-rice items are what is called **okazu** おかず. In a typical Japanese family, the following conversation often takes place in the late afternoon between a child who just got home from school and his/her mother, who is preparing dinner:

EXAMPLE:

Child: **Konban no okazu nāni.**
    今晩のおかずなあに。
    lit., What's this evening's okazu?

Mother: **Tenpura yo.**
    天ぷらよ。
    It's tempura.

    In normal English, one might just ask "What's today's dinner?" because what is **okazu** おかず to a Japanese is actually conceived of as dinner itself by English speakers for, in English-speaking cultures, bread, which is considered to play the same role as rice, is in truth just something that goes with the main course, not vice versa.

Ō⌐ki⌐i [O⌐oki⌐i] 大きい *big; large*

Although **ōkii** 大きい means "big/large," it does not follow that **ōkii** can modify any nouns that its English counterparts can. For example, **ōkii** does not modify **shokuji** 食事 "meal" or any kind of meal such as **asagohan** 朝ご飯 ("breakfast"), **hirugohan** 昼ご飯 ("lunch"), or **bangohan** 晩ご飯 ("dinner"). For example,

EXAMPLE:

(1) *Ōkii asagohan o tabeta.
     *大きい朝ご飯を食べた。
     I had a big breakfast.

To make the above Japanese acceptable, one would have to say **Asagohan o takusan tabeta** 朝ご飯をたくさん食べた。(lit., "I ate a lot for breakfast.").

For weather-related words such as **ame** 雨 ("rain"), **kaze** 風 ("wind"), **yuki** 雪 ("snow"), etc., use compounds with the prefix **ō-** 大, rather than use the full adjective **ōkii** 大きい, as in

EXAMPLES:

(2a) **ōame** (not *ōkii ame 大きい雨)
      大雨
      a big rainfall
(2b) **ōkaze** (not *ōkii kaze 大きい風)
      大風
      a big wind
(2c) **ōyuki** (not *ōkii yuki 大きい雪)
      大雪
      a big snowfall

Ōkii 大きい often becomes **ōki na** 大きな (not *ōkii na 大きいな) when placed before a noun.

EXAMPLE:

(3) **ōkii** (or **ōki na**) **hon**
     大きい（大きな）本
     a big book

Shibata, 1970 (pp. 20–21), states that Tokyoites feel more comfortable with **na** な while Osakaites are more likely to use **-i** い than **na** な. Morita (p. 118), on the other hand, distinguishes **ōkii** 大きい from **ōki na** 大きな, saying that **ōkii** is for concrete objects and **ōki na** for abstract nouns, citing such examples as

EXAMPLES:

(4) **ōkii ie** (**hito, machi**, etc.)
     大きい家（人、町、etc.）
     a big house (person, town, etc.)
(5) **ōki na jiken** (**seikō, shippai**, etc.)
     大きな事件（成功、失敗、etc.）
     a big event (success, failure, etc.)

It is quite doubtful, however, how many speakers of Japanese really observe these distinctions. My guess is that to most Japanese **ōkii** 大きい and **ōki na** 大きな are simply interchangeable.

Ōki na 大きな is like one word in that **ōki** 大き and **na** な are inseparable. Although **ōki** is listed as a **na**-noun by Jorden (2, p. 368), it is quite different from other **na**-nouns such as **kirei** きれいな "pretty, clean" (see KIREI). **Kirei** きれい, for example, can be used without a following **na**, as in

EXAMPLES:

(6) **Kirei desu nē.**
きれいですねえ。
Isn't it pretty!

(7) **Heya o kirei ni shite kudasai.**
部屋をきれいにしてください。
Please tidy up your room.

Ōki 大き, on the other hand, can never be used without **na** + following noun.

With regard to sound or voice level, **ōkii** (or **ōki na**) **koe** 大きい（大きな）声 "a loud voice" (lit., "a big voice") is a common expression. Similarly, "to make the sound [of a TV, radio, etc.] louder" is **ōkiku-suru** 大きくする (lit., "to make big").

EXAMPLE:

(8) **Rajio ga kikoenai kara, motto ōkiku-shite.**
ラジオが聞こえないから、もっと大きくして。
I can't hear the radio very well. Will you turn it up? (lit., Will you make it bigger?)

O⌐kona⌐u 行なう *to do, conduct, carry out, administer*

Okonau 行なう "to do" is a synonym for **suru** but is much more formal and, as a rule, used in writing only. When used in speech, it is restricted to formal occasions such as announcements and speeches.

EXAMPLE:

(1) **Nigatsu jūgonichi ni nyūgakushiken o okonau.**
二月十五日に入学試験を行なう。
We shall hold an entrance examination on February 15.

More informally, one would say

EXAMPLE:

(2) **Nigatsu jūgonichi ni nyūgakushiken o shimasu.**
二月十五日に入学試験をします。
We'll give an entrance exam on February 15.

Because of its nature, **okonau** 行なう is most likely used with nouns denoting formal events and functions, and not with colloquial expressions. In Sentence (3) below, **okonau** would be out of place because **minna de** みんなで and **kakekko** かけっこ are colloquial expressions.

EXAMPLE:

(3) **Minna de kakekko o suru** (not *okonau 行なう) **yo.**
みんなでかけっこをするよ。
We're having a foot race for everyone.

Okonau 行なう would sound fine, however, if used with formal words describing the same event, as in

EXAMPLE:
(4) **Zen'in de tokyōsō o okonaimasu.**
全員で徒競走を行ないます。
We shall hold a foot race for everyone.

Since **zen'in de** 全員で and **tokyōsō** 徒競走 are more formal expressions, the whole tone of the sentence allows the use of **okonaimasu** 行ないます in this case.

The passive form of **okonau** 行なう, i.e., **okonawareru** 行なわれる, is often used, although also restricted to formal speech or writing, to mean that "something is a common practice," as in

EXAMPLE:
(5) **Gendai no Nihon no wakamono no aida ni wa, chapatsu to iu hen na shūkan ga okonawarete-iru.**
現代の日本の若者の間には、茶髪という変な習慣が行なわれている。
Among today's Japanese youth, a fad called chapatsu (i.e., hair dyed brown) has become a common practice.

Okonawareru 行なわれる is not normally replaceable by the passive form of **suru** する, i.e., **sareru** される。

Oʼkoʼru 怒る *to become angry; to scold*

There is no adjective in Japanese that means "angry." Japanese has a verb **okoru** 怒る, which by itself means "become angry." Don't therefore say ***okoru ni naru** 怒るになる or ***okotte ni naru** 怒ってになる. Just use **okoru** 怒る without **naru** なる, as in

EXAMPLE:
(1) **Yamamoto-san wa yoku okoru.**
山本さんはよく怒る。
Mr. Yamamoto gets angry often.

To express the idea of "be angry," rather than "become angry," use the **te-iru** ている form of **okoru** 怒る, as in Sentence (2) below.

EXAMPLE:
(2) **Yamamoto-san wa totemo okotte-iru.**
山本さんはとても怒っている。
Mr. Yamamoto is very angry.

English speakers may describe their own anger by saying, "I'm angry!!" Don't translate this, however, directly into Japanese by saying ***Watashi wa okotte-iru** 私は怒っている, because **okoru** 怒る, as a rule, is not used in reference to the speaker. Instead say something like (3a) or (3b).

EXAMPLES:
(3a) **Hara ga tatsu nā!**
腹が立つなあ！
I'm boiling inside!

(3b) **Shaku ni sawaru nā!**
しゃくにさわるなあ。
(lit., Something is irritating my temper!)

Okoru 怒る is sometimes used as a synonym for **shikaru** 叱る in the sense of "to scold." There are, however, two main differences. First, **shikaru** takes the particle **o**, whereas **okoru**, when used to mean "to scold," takes **ni** に.

EXAMPLE:
(4) **Nihon no kyōshi wa yoku seito**   **ni okoru.**
日本の教師はよく生徒   に怒る。
    o shikaru.
    叱る。
Japanese teachers often scold their students.

Second, **okoru** 怒る means "to scold angrily," while **shikaru** 叱る can refer to all manners of scolding including scolding gently and tenderly. In sentence (5), therefore, **shikaru** is correct, but **okoru** is not.

EXAMPLE:
(5) **Oya wa, toki ni wa ko o yasashiku shikaru** (not *****okoru** 怒る) **koto mo hitsuyō da.**
親は、時には子をやさしく叱ることも必要だ。
It is sometimes necessary for parents to scold their children gently.

Oko-san お子さん *your child*

When you talk about your own child or children, say **kodomo** 子供 or **uchi no ko[domo]** うちの子(ども), but to refer to a child or children of someone whose status calls for deference in speech, say **oko-san** お子さん. Unfortunately **oko-san** sounds very much like **oku-san** 奥さん, meaning "your wife." One has to distinguish them by pronouncing **oko-san** without an accent and **oku-san** by placing an accent on the first syllable, i.e., o⌐ku-san (see OKU-SAN).

EXAMPLES:
(1) **Oko-san wa ogenki desu ka.**
お子さんはお元気ですか。
How is your child?
(2) **Oku-san wa ogenki desu ka.**
奥さんはお元気ですか。
How is your wife?

O⌐ku-san 奥さん *your wife*

Oku-san 奥さん means "your (or someone else's) wife." Until the end of World War II, **oku-san** was used exclusively for the wives of men of average or higher-than-average social status. Women married to men of below-average social status such as merchants and farmers used to be called **okami-san** おかみさん. After the war, however, **okami-san** came to be thought of as a somewhat discriminatory term. As a result, even wives who would have been called **okami-san** in prewar years are often addressed as **oku-san** nowadays.

When talking to a teacher or superior, it would be more appropriate to say **oku-sama** 奥様 rather than **oku-san**.

O⌐medetō gozaima⌐su おめでとうございます *Congratulations!*

Omedetō gozaimasu おめでとうございます is a very convenient set phrase that may be used to congratulate a person on any happy occasion, be it his birthday, his wedding, or some success he has achieved. **Omedetō gozaimasu** may be used by itself or together with a word or words referring to a specific occasion.

EXAMPLES:

(1) **Otanjōbi omedetō gozaimasu.**
お誕生日おめでとうございます。
Happy birthday!

(2) **Gokekkon omedetō gozaimasu.**
ご結婚おめでとうございます。
Congratulations on your wedding!

(3) **Akachan ga oumare ni natte, omedetō gozaimasu.**
赤ちゃんがお生まれになって、おめでとうございます。
Congratulations on having a new baby!

If the word preceding **omedetō** おめでとう is a noun, as in (1) and (2), no particle is used in Japanese that might correspond to "on" in English. If the preceding word is inflected, use the gerund form. In (3), for example, **natte** なって is the gerund form of **naru** なる. (See also AKEMASHITE OMEDETŌ GOZAIMASU.)

O⌐moida⌐su 思い出す *to bring back from memory*

English "remember" means both (a) "to retain something in the memory" (as in "You should always remember your wife's birthday"), and (b) "to recall" (as in "I suddenly remembered I had some homework"). In Japanese, these two meanings are represented by two different verbs. Meaning (a) is represented by **oboete-iru** 覚えている (see OBOERU), and meaning (b) by **omoidasu** 思い出す. In the following examples, therefore, **omoidasu** is correct in (1), but not in (2).

EXAMPLES:

(1) **Shukudai ga aru koto o kyū ni omoidashita.**
宿題があることを急に思い出した。
I suddenly remembered that I had some homework.

(2) ***Okusan no otanjōbi wa omoidashita hō ga ii desu yo.**
＊奥さんのお誕生日は思い出した方がいいですよ。
You should remember your wife's birthday.

In sentence (2) above, **omoidashita** 思い出した should be replaced by **oboete-ita** 覚えていた.

O⌐moiko⌐mu 思い込む *to be under the wrong impression*

Omoikomu 思い込む is to hold an incorrect belief.

EXAMPLE:

(1) **Amerikajin ni wa Nihongo ga oboerarenai to omoikonde-iru Nihonjin ga ōi.**
アメリカ人には日本語が覚えられないと思い込んでいる日本人が多い。
There are a lot of Japanese who are under the erroneous impression that Americans cannot learn Japanese.

Shinjikomu 信じ込む is quite similar to **omoikomu** 思い込む and may be used in sentence (1) above. **Kangaekomu** 考え込む, however, is not a synonym for **omoikomu** despite the fact that **omou** 思う and **kangaeru** 考える are synonyms. **Kangaekomu** means "to be deep in thought," as in

EXAMPLE:
(2) **Sensei wa gakusei ni muzukashii shitsumon o sarete kangaekonde** (not *omoikonde 思い込んで) **shimatta.**
先生は学生に難しい質問をされて考え込んでしまった。
The teacher sank deep in thought when he was asked a difficult question by a student.

O⌐mo⌐u 思う *to think*

Omou 思う can represent one's judgment, realization, expectation, decision, belief, intention, wish, doubt, etc., but not analytical thinking. It is for this reason that, whereas examples (1) through (3) are correct, (4) and (5) are not.

EXAMPLES:
(1) **Sō omoimasu.** (judgment)
そう思います。
I think so.
(2) **Ano hito wa kitto kuru to omou.** (belief)
あの人はきっと来ると思います。
I think he'll definitely come.
(3) **Kyō wa hayaku neyō to omou.** (intention)
今日は早く寝ようと思う。
I think I'll go to bed early today.
(4) *Kono mondai o yoku omotte-kudasai. (analytical thinking)
*この問題をよく思ってください。
Please consider this problem carefully.
(5) *Kare ga naze sonna koto o shita no ka, ikura omotte mo wakaranai. (analytical thinking)
*彼がなぜそんなことをしたのか、いくら思ってもわからない。
No matter how much I rack my brains, I cannot figure out why he did such a thing.

For analytical thinking, **kangaeru** 考える is the verb to be used (see KANGAERU).

Omou 思う is used when the object of thinking is mentioned (or at least clearly implied). **Omou**, therefore, is most commonly preceded by **o** を or **to** と.

EXAMPLES:
(6) **Ima chotto haha no koto o omotte-iru n desu.**
いまちょっと母のことを思っているんです。
I'm just thinking of my mother.
(7) **Watanabe-san wa ii hito da to omou.**
渡辺さんはいい人だと思う。
I think Mr. Watanabe is a very nice person.

One very common error made by students of Japanese is to use a **desu/masu** です/ます form before to **omoimasu** 思います, as in (8a) and (8b).

EXAMPLES:

(8a) *Sō desu to omoimasu.

　　*そうですと思います。

　　I think that's the case.

(8b) *Kyō wa ame ga furimasen to omoimasu.

　　*今日は雨が降りませんと思います。

　　I don't think it'll rain today.

Before **to omoimasu** と思います, always use a plain form. Sentence (8a) should be **Sō da to omoimasu** そうだと思います, and (8b) should be **Kyō wa ame ga furanai to omoimasu** 今日は雨が降らないと思います.

The reason so many students make these errors when talking to a higher-status person such as their teacher is that they erroneously believe they can make the whole statement more polite by using a **desu/masu** です/ます form before **to omoimasu** と思います. They must remember that the clause preceding **to omoimasu** represents what the speaker is thinking. One's thought is basically what one says to oneself, i.e., it is like a monologue. One need not be formal when speaking to oneself. Hence, no **desu/masu** form before **to omoimasu**.

Other verbs of thinking behave the same way. Never use **desu-masu** before such expressions as **to kangaemasu** 考えます "I think," **to sōzō shimasu** と想像します "I imagine," etc., even though those verbs themselves may be in the **-masu** form.

Now, observe (8b) again. The English translation makes the main verb "think" negative, i.e., "I don't think it'll rain today." Note the correct Japanese version is not *Kyō wa ame ga furu to omoimasen 今日は雨が降ると思いません but **Kyō wa ame ga furanai to omoimasu** 今日は雨が降らないと思います, making the verb **furu** 降る, rather than **omou** 思う, negative.

Another mistake involving **omou** may occur when a student who has just seen a film or read a book is asked by a Japanese person, **Dō deshita ka** どうでしたか? ("How was it?"). The answer often comes out as *Omoshirokatta to omoimashita おもしろかったと思いました, using two **-ta** forms because of the incorrect association with the English "I thought it was fun," which uses two past tense forms. Say **Omoshiroi to omoimashita** おもしろいと思いました instead, because **Omoshirokatta to omoimashita** literally means "I thought it had been fun."

Onaji 同じ *the same*

Onaji 同じ is a noun but behaves much like an adjective (such as **ōkii** 大きい and **chiisai** 小さい) in that it can modify a noun without **na** な or **no** の in between.

EXAMPLE:

(1)　**onaji hito** (not *onaji no hito 同じの人 or *onaji na hito 同じな人)

　　同じ人

　　the same person

Otherwise it is like any other noun in that it is followed by **ja** (or **de wa**) **arimasen** じゃ（では）ありません in negative sentences.

EXAMPLE:

(2)　**Onaji ja arimasen.**

　　同じじゃありません。

　　It isn't the same.

This hybrid nature comes from the fact that **onaji** 同じ was an adjective at one time. In fact, its **ku** く form is still used in written Japanese, revealing its origin.

EXAMPLE:
(3) **Iwate-ken wa Aomori-ken to onajiku Tōhoku ni ichishite-iru.**
岩手県は青森県と同じく東北に位置している。
Iwate Prefecture, like Aomori Prefecture, is located in the Tohoku region.

Onaka おなか *stomach*

The Japanese equivalent of "I am hungry" is normally **Onaka ga suita** おなかが空いた, which literally means "My stomach has gotten empty," i.e., "I've become hungry." This interesting difference between the English and the Japanese supports the theory that very often English expressions using stative verbs correspond to Japanese expressions using verbs that basically mean "to become such-and-such" or "to do such-and-such" (Kunihiro, pp. 88–89). Other examples are:

EXAMPLES:
(1) **Nodo ga kawaita.**
のどがかわいた。
I am thirsty. (lit., My throat has gotten dry.)
(2) **Kinō kekkon-shita.**
きのう結婚した。
He was married yesterday. (lit., He married yesterday.)
(3) **Ima sugu ikimasu.**
いますぐ行きます。
I'll be there in a minute. (lit., I'll go in a minute.)
(4) **Ashita itsutsu ni naru.**
あした五つになる。
He will be five tomorrow. (lit, He'll become five tomorrow.)
(5) **Fuyu ga owatta.**
冬が終わった。
Winter is over. (lit., Winter has ended.)
(6) **Haru ga kita.**
春が来た。
Spring is here. (lit., Spring has come.)
(7) **Shinda.**
死んだ。
He is dead. (lit., He has died.)

Another version of **Onaka ga suita** おなかが空いた is **Hara ga hetta** 腹がへった, which also means "I'm hungry." Although usually explained as a vulgar expression, **Hara ga hetta** is acceptable if used by men among close friends and associates on informal occasions.

O⌐negai-shima⌐su お願いします *lit., I [humbly] request*

Onegai-shimasu お願いします is the humble form of the verb **negau** 願う meaning "to request" and is used very often in all sorts of request-making situations. For example, when one goes into a store and doesn't see the shopkeeper or any salesclerk, one can call out **Onegai-shimasu!** meaning "Hello!" (lit., "I [humbly] request [your service]"). Even if you see someone working for the store, you can still say **Onegai-shimasu** to attract his attention.

You can say **Onegai-shimasu** also when you ask for specific items of your choice at a store, a restaurant, etc.

EXAMPLES:

(1) **Kono ringo o mittsu onegai-shimasu.**
このリンゴを三つお願いします。
I'd like three of these apples, please. (lit., I [humbly] request three of these apples.)

(2) **Sukiyaki o onegai-shimasu.**
すき焼きをお願いします。
I'd like sukiyaki. (lit., I [humbly] request sukiyaki.)

In the examples above, **onegai-shimasu** お願いします may be replaced by **kudasai** ください (lit., "please give me") without causing any change in meaning, the only difference being that the **onegai-shimasu** versions are a little more polite.

During election campaigns, all candidates shout out **Onegai-shimasu!** repeatedly instead of calmly discussing relevant issues. With **Onegai-shimasu!** and humble bows, they are of course soliciting votes from their constituents.

When one entrusts something to someone else, e.g., "when submitting papers such as application forms ... in a government office, bank, and the like" (Mizutani and Mizutani, 1, p. 59), one often says

EXAMPLE:

(3) **Kore o onegai-shimasu.**
これをお願いします。
Please take care of this for me. (lit., I request this.)

Suppose you go to see someone with a request. You present him with the request, he says, "All right," and you engage in small talk briefly. Now, what would you say to conclude the conversation? The best thing to say would be

EXAMPLE:

(4) **Ja onegai-shimasu.**
じゃお願いします。
Well then, please take care of it for me.

What you are really saying is "I ask that you kindly comply with the request I have just made." This parting remark serves as an act of confirmation.

O⌐nna⌐ 女 *female*

Onna 女 "female" corresponds to **otoko** 男 "male" (see OTOKO). **Onna** corresponds to **otoko, onna-no-ko** 女の子 "girl" to **otoko-noko** 男の子 "boy," **onna-no-hito** 女の人 "woman" to **otoko-no-hito** 男の人 "man," and **onna-no-kata** 女の方 "lady" to **otoko-no-kata** 男の方 "gentleman."

In somewhat vulgar Japanese, **onna** sometimes means "paramour," as in **kare no onna** 彼の女 "his woman."

Oˈriˈru 降りる, 下りる *to go down, to get off*

Oriru 下りる meaning "to go down" takes the particle **o** when the place where the act of going down occurs is mentioned as in

EXAMPLE:

(1) **kaidan (yama, saka**, etc.) **o oriru**
階段(山、坂、etc.)を下りる。
to go down the stairs (mountain, slope, etc.)

This is also true of **oriru** 降りる meaning "to get off, to get out of [a vehicle]."

EXAMPLES:

(2a) **basu** (or **densha**) **o oriru**
バスを(電車)を降りる。
to get off the bus (or *train*)

(2b) **kuruma** (or **takushī**) **o oriru**
車(タクシー)を降りる。
to get out of the car (or *taxi*)

In example (2) above, **kara** から "from, out of" could be used instead of **o** を, but **o** is more common.

Oshieru 教える *to teach, to tell, to inform*

Oshieru 教える basically means "to impart [something, e.g., information, to someone]." Although it is often equated with "teach," it does not always correspond to that.

EXAMPLES:

(1) **kodomo ni sūgaku o oshieru**
子供に数学を教える
to teach children mathematics

(2) **hito ni eki e iku michi o oshieru**
人に駅へ行く道を教える
to tell a person the way to the station

(3) **hito ni kikai no tsukaikata o oshieru**
人に機械の使い方を教える
to show a person how to use a machine

When the idea of "to someone" is expressed, the particle **ni** に is used as in the three examples above. When **oshieru** 教える is used in the sense of "teach" (and not "tell" or "show"), however, the person being taught might become the direct object with the attachment of **o** instead of **ni**.

EXAMPLE:

(4) **Kodomo o oshieru no wa muzukashii.**
子供を教えるのは難しい。
It is difficult to teach children.

In this case, the subject being taught becomes irrelevant.

O⌐shi⌐i 惜しい *regrettable; disappointingly close*

Oshii 惜しい has two basic uses. First, it is used in a situation when something comes very close to being achieved but fails to do so, as in

EXAMPLE:

(1) **Oshii tokoro de makete shimatta.**
惜しいところで負けてしまった。
I lost after coming very close to winning.

Second, it is used when something or someone very precious is lost, as in

EXAMPLE:

(2) **Oshii hito o nakushita.**
惜しい人をなくした。
It is regrettable that we lost such a precious person.

Osoi 遅い *slow, late*

Osoi 遅い means both "slow" and "late." This probably indicates that, in the Japanese speaker's mind, slowness and lateness are closely connected. After all, if you travel slowly, you get to your destination late!

Sometimes, **osoi** 遅い might cause ambiguity as in the case of **osoi kisha** 遅い汽車, which can mean either "a late train" or "a slow train," but usually this kind of ambiguity disappears with sufficient contextual information, as in

EXAMPLE:

(1) **Asa roku-ji shuppatsu ja haya-sugiru n desu ga, motto osoi kisha wa arimasen ka.**
朝六時出発じゃ早すぎるんですが、もっと遅い汽車はありませんか。
Leaving at six in the morning would be too early. Aren't there later trains?

However, **osoku** 遅く, the adverbial form of **osoi** 遅い, only means "late," and not "slowly" (Morita, p. 130).

EXAMPLE:

(2) **Kesa wa osoku okimashita.**
けさは遅く起きました。
This morning I got up late.

To express the meaning of "slowly," use **yukkuri** ゆっくり (see YUKKURI).

EXAMPLE:

(3) **Motto yukkuri** (not *osoku 遅く) **tabeta hō ga ii desu yo.**
もっとゆっくり食べた方がいいですよ。
You should eat more slowly.

Otaku お宅 *your home*

While **taku** 宅 meaning "my home" or "my husband" is not used very often, its honorific counterpart **otaku** お宅 is used all the time to refer to the house of someone (most often the addressee) whom the speaker wishes to treat with deference.

EXAMPLES:

(1) **Uchida-sensei no otaku no denwa-bangō wa nan-ban deshō ka.**
内田先生のお宅の電話番号は何番でしょうか。
What's Professor Uchida's home phone number?

(2) **Ashita no ban chotto otaku ni ukagatte mo yoroshii desu ka.**
あしたの晩ちょっとお宅に伺ってもよろしいですか。
May I visit your house for a little while tomorrow evening?

(3) **Are wa otaku no obotchan desu ka.**
あれはお宅のお坊ちゃんですか。
Is that your son? (lit., Is that the son of your home?)

In recent years, **otaku** お宅 has come to be used increasingly more frequently as the politer version of **anata** あなた "you," as in

EXAMPLE:

(4) **Otaku wa dochira ni osumai desu ka.**
お宅はどちらにお住まいですか。
Where do you live?

O'toko' 男 *male*

Otoko 男 "male" by itself is a plain term and often carries a derogatory tone when used in reference to a specific person, especially in speech (though generally not in written Japanese). **Otoko-no-hito** 男の人 "man" has no such connotation.

EXAMPLES:

(1) **Ano otoko wa iya na yatsu da na.**
あの男はいやなやつだな。
Isn't that guy nasty?

(2) **Ano otoko-no-hito wa shinsetsu desu nē?**
あの男の人は親切ですねえ。
Isn't that man kind?

In sentence (1), **otoko** 男 is more appropriate than **otoko-no-hito** 男の人 because of **iya na yatsu** いやなやつ "a nasty guy," which carries a negative value. In (2), on the other hand, **otoko** would sound a little strange unless the speaker wished to convey the idea that he himself is decidedly of higher status than the man he is talking about.

To make **otoko-no-hito** even more polite, **otoko-no-kata** 男の方 "gentleman" should be used.

EXAMPLE:

(3) **Ano otoko-no-kata wa donata deshō ka.**
あの男の方はどなたでしょうか。
Who could that gentleman be?

In English, "man" sometimes means "human being," as in "Man is mortal." **Otoko** 男 (and **otoko-no-hito** 男の人) cannot be so used. **Ningen** 人間 is the word for that.

In somewhat vulgar Japanese, **otoko** 男 sometimes means "lover," as in

EXAMPLE:

(4) **Toshiko wa otoko ni suterareta.**
とし子は男に捨てられた。
Toshiko was left by her lover.

O⌈tōto⌉ 弟 *younger brother*

In Japanese, there is no genuine equivalent of "brother." While in English one can talk about one's brother without indicating who is older, in Japanese one generally talks about one's **ani** 兄 "older brother" (see ANI) or **otōto** 弟 "younger brother."

Otōto 弟, first of all, means "younger brothers in general."

EXAMPLE:

(1) **Nihon de wa otōto wa ani no meshita da.**
日本では弟は兄の目下だ。
In Japan, younger brothers are of lower status than older brothers.

Second, **otōto** 弟 refers to one's own younger brother when one is talking to an outsider.

EXAMPLE:

(2) **Otōto ga yatto Tōdai ni hairimashita.**
弟がやっと東大に入りました。
My younger brother has finally gotten into Tokyo University.

When talking to someone about his brother, use **otōto-san** 弟さん.

EXAMPLE:

(3) **Otōto-san ga Tōdai ni ohairi ni natta sō desu ne.**
弟さんが東大にお入りになったそうですね。
I hear your younger brother has gotten into Tokyo University.

When talking to someone about a third person's brother, use **otōto-san** 弟さん (though **otōto** 弟 is also possible if, for example, you are talking to a member of your family about the younger brother of a close friend of yours).

EXAMPLE:

(4) **Yamanaka-san no otōto-san wa ima Amerika-ryūgaku-chū desu.**
山中さんの弟さんはいまアメリカ留学中です。
Mr. Yamanaka's younger brother is studying in America now.

An older brother or an older sister addresses his/her younger brother not as **otōto** but by his given name.

EXAMPLES:

(5) **Saburō,**　　　　(a) **gohan da yo.** (an older brother speaking)
三郎、　　　　　　　　ご飯だよ。
　　　　　　　　　　(b) **gohan yo.** (an older sister speaking)
　　　　　　　　　　　　ご飯よ。

Saburo, it's dinner time!

Otsuri おつり *change*

Otsuri おつり corresponds to "change" in a limited way.

EXAMPLE:

(1) **Sen-en-satsu o dashitara, nihyaku-en otsuri ga kita.**
千円札を出したら、二百円おつりが来た。
I gave them a 1,000-yen bill and received 200 yen in change.

"Change" can also refer to money given in exchange for an equivalent of higher denomination. For example, if you wish to exchange a 1,000-yen bill for the same amount in coins, you can say in English

EXAMPLE:

(2) I need change for a 1,000-yen bill.

This kind of change is not **otsuri** おつり. The Japanese equivalent of (2) would be

EXAMPLE:

(3) **Sen-en-satsu o komakaku shi-tai n desu ga.**
千円冊をこまかくしたいんですが。
lit., I'd like to make a 1,000-yen bill smaller.

"Change" can also mean "small coins," as in

EXAMPLE:

(4) I always carry some change in my pants pocket.

This kind of change is not **otsuri** おつり but **kozeni** 小銭 (lit., "small money"). In short, "change" is much broader in meaning than **otsuri**. **Otsuri** おつり may be used only in reference to a balance of money returned at the time of purchase.

Owaru 終わる *to end*

Owaru 終わる can be either transitive, as in (1), or intransitive, as in (2).

EXAMPLES:

(1) **Kurasu ga owatta.** (intransitive)
クラスが終わった。
The class ended.

(2) **Kurasu o owatta.** (transitive)
クラスを終わった。
I ended the class.

Owaru 終わる has, however, a transitive counterpart, **oeru** 終える, which cannot be used intransitively.

EXAMPLE:

(3) **Kurasu o oeta.**
クラスを終えた。
I ended the class.

Although to me, (2) and (3) have no difference in meaning except that (3) may sound a little more bookish than (2), **oeru** 終える connotes, according to Morita (p. 386), "consciously ending something."

O⌐yasumi-nasa⌐i お休みなさい *Good night!*

Oyasumi-nasai お休みなさい is a farewell one directs to a person who is already in bed or is about to go to bed. It is therefore most commonly heard late in the evening. For example, you say **Oyasumi-nasai** at the time of leaving someone's home after spending an evening there. Unlike English "Good night!", **Oyasumi-nasai** may not be used as one leaves the office at 5 P.M. That would be too early for **Oyasumi-nasai**, which literally means "Sleep well!"

O⌐yo⌐gu 泳ぐ *to swim*

The most common verb for "swimming" is **oyogu** 泳ぐ.

EXAMPLE:

(1) **Kyō wa atsui kara pūru e oyogi ni ikō.**
    今日は暑いからプールへ泳ぎに行こう。
    It's so hot today. Let's go swimming in the pool.

Another word for "swimming" is **suiei** 水泳, but it is mostly used as a noun. **Suiei-suru** 水泳する might be found in dictionaries, but it is actually rarely used. "I'm not good at swimming" can be said in two different ways, as in (2a) and (2b).

EXAMPLES:

(2a) **Boku wa suiei ga heta da.**
     ぼくは水泳が下手だ。

(2b) **Boku wa oyogu no ga heta da.**
     ぼくは泳ぐのが下手だ。

When the sport of swimming is meant, **suiei** is the only word used, as in

EXAMPLE:

(3) **Tomu wa oyogu no ga jōzu na node, kōkō no suiei-chīmu ni haitta.**
    トムは泳ぐのが上手なので、高校の水泳チームに入った。
    Tom joined his high school's swimming team since he was a good swimmer.

Incidentally, as the English translation for sentence (3) indicates, it is quite common in English to say "He is a good swimmer" instead of "He is good at swimming." In Japanese, on the other hand, the counterpart of the latter is the norm. For example,

EXAMPLE:

(4) English: *Betty is a wonderful singer.*
    Japanese: **Betī wa uta ga subarashiku jōzu da.**
    ベティーは歌がすばらしく上手だ。
    (lit., Betty is good at singing.)

In (4) above, it is possible to say in Japanese **Betī wa subarashii shingā da** ベティーはすばらしいシンガーだ, which is the exact translation of "Betty is a wonderful singer." **Betī wa subarashii shinga da** would be possible only in reference to a professional or professional-level singer. It won't be used to describe an amateur who happens to sing well.

Oyu お湯 *hot water*

Oyu お湯 (or the less often used plain form **yu** 湯) means "hot water." In English, "water" may be hot or cold. In Japanese, on the other hand, water is called either **mizu** 水 "cold water" (see MIZU) or **oyu**, depending on its temperature. Although **oyu** by itself (i.e., without an accompanying modifier) can refer to hot water, to mean "really hot water," it is perfectly correct and not redundant to say

EXAMPLE:
atsui oyu
熱いお湯
really hot water

Sometimes, **oyu** お湯 is used in place of **ofuro** お風呂 (see OFURO) to mean "bath" (but not "bathtub").

Ra⌈ku⌉ 楽 *easy; comfortable*

Whereas **yasashii** やさしい "easy" is the opposite of **muzukashii** 難しい "difficult," **raku** 楽 is the opposite of **tsurai** つらい (see TSURAI). **Yasashii** focuses on the lower degree of difficulty, while **raku** stresses the comfortable ease with which something can be handled. For example,

EXAMPLE:
(1) **Amerikajin no naka ni wa, mukashi no hō ga kurashi ga raku datta to iu hito ga iru.**
アメリカ人の中には、むかしの方が暮らしが楽だったと言う人がいる。
There are some Americans who say life used to be easier before.

If you compare (2a) and (2b) below, both of which mean "It was an easy job," the difference between **yasashii** やさしい and **raku** 楽 should become clear.

EXAMPLES:
(2a) **Yasashii shigoto datta.**
やさしい仕事だった。
(2b) **Raku na shigoto datta.**
楽な仕事だった。

In (2a), the focus is on the fact that the job was not difficult, i.e., the degree of difficulty was very low. In (2b), on the other hand, the focus is on the fact that the job was handled comfortably and that no exertion was necessary, though the degree of difficulty may, in fact, have been high.

Renshū 練習 *practice, training, exercise*

Renshū 練習 is most typically used as follows:

EXAMPLE:
(1) **Kanji wa nando mo kaku renshū o shinai to oboerarenai.**
漢字は何度も書く練習をしないと覚えられない。
Kanji can't be learned unless you practice writing them over and over.

In a Japanese-English dictionary, one of the translations given for **renshū** 練習 could be "exercise," but **renshū** means "exercise" only in the sense of "task for practicing/training," not in the sense of "physical exercise for the sake of health." Sentence (2) below is correct, but sentence (3) is not.

EXAMPLES:
(2) **Renshū-mondai no nai bunpō no kyōkasho wa amari yaku ni tatanai.**
練習問題のない文法の教科書はあまり役に立たない。
Grammar textbooks without exercises (lit., practice problems) are not very useful.
(3) ***Mainichi renshū-suru no wa karada ni yoi.**
*毎日練習するのは体に良い。
It's good for your health to exercise every day.

For sentence (3), **renshū-suru** 練習する must be replaced by **undō-suru** 運動する.

Ri˥ka 理科 *science*

Rika 理科, meaning "science," is used as the name of a subject in elementary through high school covering a broad spectrum including biology, chemistry, and physics.

EXAMPLE:
(1) **Jirō wa kōkō de Eigo wa dekita ga rika wa dame datta.**
次郎は高校で英語はできたが理科はだめだった。
Jiro was good in English but not in science in high school.

When one talks about science in general, apart from school curricula, one must use the term **kagaku** 科学, not **rika** 理科.

EXAMPLE:
(2) **Kagaku** (not ***rika** 理科) **no shinpo wa todomaru tokoro o shiranai.**
科学の進歩はとどまるところを知らない。
The progress of science is never-ending.

(See also KAGAKU.)

Ri˥kai-suru 理解する *to comprehend*

Rikai-suru 理解する meaning "to comprehend" is a transitive verb. Unlike **wakaru** 分かる, which takes **ga**, it therefore takes **o**.

EXAMPLE:
(1) **Nihonjin wa Nihon o rikai-suru gaikokujin wa amari inai to omotte-iru.**
日本人は日本の理解する外国人はあまりいないと思っている。
The Japanese feel that there are few foreigners who understand Japan.

Another difference is that while **wakaru** 分かる is an everyday expression, **rikai-suru** 理解する is a written form.

While **wakaru** 分かる does not represent a controllable action and cannot therefore take a potential form (not ***wakareru** 分かれる), **rikai-suru** 理解する is considered to represent a controllable action and can take a potential form, i.e., **rikai-dekiru** 理解できる.

EXAMPLE:

(2) **Konna yasashii koto de mo rikai-dekinai** (not *wakarenai 分かれない) **hito ga iru rashii.**
こんなやさしいことでも理解出来ない人がいるらしい。
There are apparently some people who cannot even understand such a simple thing as this.

(See also WAKARU.)

Roku ni ろくに *hardly; not well; not enough*

Roku ni ろくに is often translated as "hardly." Don't forget, however, that **roku ni** is regularly accompanied by a negative expression (i.e., **-nai** ない) unlike "hardly," which is by itself negative and is not accompanied by another negative word.

EXAMPLE:

(1) **Hiroshi wa roku ni jugyō ni denai.**
弘はろくに授業に出ない。
Hiroshi hardly ever goes to class.

From this example alone, **roku ni** ろくに might be considered synonymous with **metta ni** めったに "rarely," as in

EXAMPLE:

(2) **Hiroshi wa metta ni jugyō ni denai.**
弘はめったに授業に出ない。
Hiroshi rarely goes to class.

There are differences between **roku ni** ろくに and **metta ni** めったに, however. First, **metta ni** is objective while **roku ni** is subjective and evaluative. In sentence (1) above, the speaker is indicating that it is undesirable that Hiroshi does not attend class often enough, whereas, in sentence (2), the speaker is merely reporting the infrequency of Hiroshi's attendance. Second, while **metta ni** is a frequency word, **roku ni** is a degree word. In sentence (3) below, therefore, only **roku ni** would be acceptable.

EXAMPLE:

(3) **Watashi wa Supein no koto wa roku ni** (not *metta ni めったに) **shiranai.**
私はスペインのことはろくに知らない。
I hardly know anything about Spain.

Roku ni ろくに is different not only from **metta ni** めったに but from "hardly" as well, in that the latter is not evaluative. In (3) above, the English is a mere reporting of the fact while the Japanese version implies that the speaker feels embarrassed or humiliated about the fact.

Rōnin 浪人 *masterless samurai; high school graduate not yet in college*

Rōnin 浪人 originally meant "masterless samurai." We often see those tough guys in samurai movies such as some famous Kurosawa films.

Students who graduate from high school but fail to get into college are somewhat like "masterless samurai" in that they have no place to belong to. They have thus come to be called **rōnin** 浪人, as in

EXAMPLE:

Takashi wa ima rōnin-chū de, yobikō de benkyō-shite-imasu.

孝はいま浪人中で、予備校で勉強しています。

Takashi is a ronin now studying at a cram school.

High school graduates who spend one year as **rōnin** 浪人 are called **ichinen-rōnin** 一年浪人, or **ichirō** 一浪 for short. Those who spend two years in that status are, as you might easily guess, **ninen-rōnin** 二年浪人, or **nirō** 二浪.

Ru˥su 留守 *not at home*

Rusu 留守 should not be explained as "out," "away," or "absent" but more specifically as "not at home."

EXAMPLES:

(1) **Kinō Tomita-san no uchi ni denwa o shimashita ga rusu deshita.**
きのう富田さんのうちに電話をしましたが留守でした。
I called Mr. Tomita's home yesterday, but he was not at home.

(2) **Sekkaku yotte-kudasatta no ni rusu o shite, shitsurei shimashita.**
せっかく寄ってくださったのに留守をして、失礼しました。
I'm sorry I wasn't home when you kindly stopped by my house.

The following example is a dialogue once written by a student of mine who identified **rusu** 留守 with "absent."

EXAMPLE:

(3) A: **Nakamura-san wa kinō kaisha ni kimashita ka.**
中村さんはきのう会社に来ましたか。
Did Mr. Nakamura come to work yesterday?

B: **Iie, rusu deshita.**
*いいえ、留守でした。
No, he was absent.

To express the idea of "No, he was absent," this student should have written one of the following alternatives:

EXAMPLES:

(4a) **Iie, kimasen deshita.**
いいえ、来ませんでした。
No, he didn't come.

(4b) **Iie, yasumi deshita.**
いいえ、休みでした。
No, he was absent.

(4c) **Iie, kekkin-shimashita.**
いいえ、欠勤しました。
No, he missed work.

Ryōhō 両方 *both*

Ryōhō 両方, meaning "both," is mostly used for non-human objects. Very often it is accompanied by **-tomo** とも.

EXAMPLES:
(1) A: **Sushi to tenpura to dotchi ga suki desu ka.**
     寿司と天ぷらとどっちが好きですか。
     Which do you like better, sushi or tempura?
     B: **Ryōhō(-tomo) suki desu.**
     両方(とも)好きです。
     I like them both.
(2) A: **Takanohana to Wakanohana to dotchi ga suki desu ka.**
     貴乃花と若乃花とどっちが好きですか。
     Whom do you like better, Takanohana or Wakanohana?
     B: **Ryōhō(-tomo) suki desu.**
     両方(とも)好きです。
     I like them both.

Although what 2B says is not entirely wrong, it is probably more natural to use **futari-tomo** 二人とも (**-tomo** in this case being obligatory) in reference to two persons. **Dotchi mo** どっちも or **dochira mo** どっちも would also be correct whether what is being talked about is human or non-human.

Ryokō-suru 旅行する *to travel*

Ryokō-suru 旅行する refers to traveling done by humans. In English, it is possible to say, for example, "Light travels faster than sound"; in Japanese, on the other hand, one would have to use an entirely different expression and say **Hikari no sokudo wa oto no sokudo yori hayai** 光の速度は音の速度より速い "The speed of light is faster than that of sound."

"Travel" basically means "to move (or go) from place to place"; therefore it can even refer to daily commuting, as in "I have to travel quite a distance to get to my office every day." **Ryokō-suru** 旅行する, on the other hand, implies a specially planned trip for business or for pleasure, and cannot be used for daily commuting.

Sa⌈bishi⌉i さびしい, 淋しい, 寂しい *lonely, lonesome*

Sabishii さびしい, 淋しい, 寂しい means "lonely" but only with regard to the speaker.

EXAMPLE:
(1) **Haha ga shinde sabishiku-natta.**
     母が死んで淋しくなった。
     I am lonely now that my mother is dead. (i.e., I miss my mother now that she is dead.)

As is the case with other adjectives of feelings such as **kanashii** 悲しい "sad" and **ureshii** うれしい "glad," **sabishii** さびしい must be used with **-garu** がる, **-sō** そう, **-yō** よう, **-rashii** らしい, etc., when the subject is someone other than the speaker.

EXAMPLES:

(2a) **Tanaka-san wa, gārufurendo ga ryokō-chū na node, sabishigatte-iru.**

田中さんは、ガールフレンドが旅行中なので、寂しがっている。

Mr. Tanaka is feeling lonely (lit., is showing signs of being lonely) because his girl-friend has gone on a trip.

(2b) **Tanaka-san wa sabishi-sō da.**

田中さんは寂しそうだ。

Mr. Tanaka looks lonely.

Sabishii 寂しい can be used with reference to such things as places, too, as in

EXAMPLE:

(3) **Koko wa zuibun sabishii machi da.**

ここはずいぶん寂しい町だ。

This is a very lonesome town.

In idiomatic Japanese, **sabishii** 寂しい is sometimes almost synonymous with **kanashii** 悲しい "sad," but the implication is that the speaker misses something.

EXAMPLE:

(4) **Wafukusugata no josei ga kieteiku no wa sabishii.**

和服姿の女性が消えて行くのは寂しい。

I am sad kimono-clad women are gradually disappearing.

(i.e., I miss those kimono-clad women.)

Sabishii 寂しい appears in some interesting expressions such as **fu-tokoro ga sabishii** 懐が寂しい "I have little money at the moment" (lit., "My pocket is lonely") and **kuchi ga sabishii** 口が寂しい (or **kuchisabishii** 口寂しい) "I'd like to put some food in my mouth" (lit., "My mouth is lonely"). **Sabishii** has another version, i.e., **samishii** さみしい.

Sagasu さがす *to look for*

Don't confuse **sagasu** さがす "to look for" with **mitsukeru** 見つける "to find." For example, in the following sentence, looking for a job is not difficult. What is difficult is finding a job.

EXAMPLE:

(1) **Watashi wa daigaku o sotsugyō-shite mo shigoto o mitsukeru** (not *sagasu さがす) **no wa muzukashii darō to omou.**

私は大学を卒業しても仕事を見つけるのは難しいだろうと思う。

I'm afraid it'll be difficult to find (not *look for) *a job even if I graduate from college.*

Sagasu さがす is for concrete things, not for abstract things such as happiness and peace. For those things, use **motomeru** 求める "to seek."

EXAMPLE:

(2) **Ooku no hito ga kōfuku o *sagashite-iru**

 　　　　　　　　heiwa o motomete-iru

多くの人が　　幸福を探している
　　　　　　　平和を求めている

A lot of people are seeking happiness/peace.

Saikin 最近 *recently; lately*

Saikin 最近 may be used in reference to either (a) a current state that has continued since a recent point of time, as in sentence (1), or (b) an event that occurred at a recent point of time, as in sentence (2).

EXAMPLES:

(1) **Nihongo wa saikin gairaigo ga ōsugiru.**
日本語は最近外来語が多すぎる。
Lately, too many loanwords are being used in Japanese.

(2) **Suzuki-san wa saikin hon o dashita.**
鈴木さんは最近本を出した。
Mr. Suzuki recently published a book.

Saikin 最近 used in the sense of sentence (1) may be replaced by **konogoro** このごろ, as in

EXAMPLE:

(3) **Nihongo wa konogoro gairaigo ga ōsugiru.**
日本語はこのごろ外来語が多すぎる。
Lately, too many loanwords are being used in Japanese.

Saikin 最近 in the sense of sentence (2), however, may not be replaced by **konogoro** このごろ.

EXAMPLE:

(4) ***Suzuki-san wa konogoro hon o dashita.**
*鈴木さんはこのごろ本を出した。

In other words, **konogoro** このごろ may not be used in reference to a single action. It may be used, however, if the action repeats itself over a sustained period of time, as in

EXAMPLE:

(5) **Suzuki-san wa konogoro yoku hon o dasu.**
鈴木さんはこのごろよく本を出す。
Nowadays, Mr. Suzuki often publishes books.

According to Morita (p. 160, vol. 2), the time span covered by **saikin** 最近 is much longer than that covered by **konogoro** このごろ. Thus, in sentence (6) below, **saikin** is fine, but **konogoro** probably is not.

EXAMPLE:

(6) **Nihonjin ga yōfuku o kiru yō ni natta no wa, Nihon no nagai rekishi kara mireba saikin (?konogoro) no koto da.**
日本人が洋服を着るようになったのは、日本の長い歴史からみれば最近（？このごろ）のことだ。
In terms of Japan's long history, it was only recently that the Japanese started wearing Western clothes.

What is important about **saikin** 最近 is that it means "recent" or "recently" as viewed from the present, and never from a point of time in the past, and there it clearly differs from English "recent." In English, for example, sentence (7) is correct.

EXAMPLE:

(7) *When I visited Mr. Suzuki ten years ago, he gave me a book he had recently published.*

In this sentence, "recently" means "a little while before," not "a little while ago." **Saikin** 最近, on the other hand, cannot be used to mean "a little while before" and must be replaced by such expressions as **chotto mae ni** ちょっと前に, as in

EXAMPLE:

(8) **Jūnen mae ni Suzuki-san o tazunetara, chotto mae ni** (not **saikin* 最近) **dashita hon o kureta.**
十年前に鈴木さんを訪ねたら、ちょっと前に出した本をくれた。
When I visited Mr. Suzuki ten years ago, he gave me a book he had recently published.

Sakan 盛ん *prosperous, thriving*

Sakan 盛ん is basically for something that is prospering or thriving, as in

EXAMPLE:

(1) **Nihon de ichiban sakan na supōtsu wa yakyū darō.**
日本でいちばん盛んなスポーツは野球だろう。
The most thriving sport in Japan is probably baseball.

In this sense, **sakan** 盛ん is quite similar to **ninki ga aru** 人気がある, which also could be used in sentence (1). There is, however, a slight difference between them in connotation. **Sakan** implies "strong businesswise," while **ninki ga aru** simply means "popular with a lot of people." See (2a) and (2b) below.

EXAMPLES:

(2a) **Nihon no zōsengyō wa mukashi hodo sakan de wa nai.**
日本の造船業は昔ほど盛んではない。
The Japanese shipbuilding industry is not as thriving as before.

(2b) **Nihon no zōsengyō wa mukashi hodo ninki ga nai.**
日本の造船業は昔ほど人気がない。
The Japanese shipbuilding industry is not as popular as before.

(2a) means shipbuilding in Japan is not as strong as before, while (2b) means high school or college graduates in Japan do not wish to go into the shipbuilding business as eagerly as before.

In some cases, **sakan** 盛ん simply cannot be replaced by **ninki ga aru** 人気がある. For example,

EXAMPLE:

(3) **Senzen no Amerika de wa, jinshusabetsu ga sakan datta** (not **ninki ga atta* 人気があった).
戦前のアメリカでは、人種差別が盛んだった。
In prewar America, racial discrimination was rampant.

(See also HAYARU and NINKI.)

Sakaya 酒屋 *saké store*

A **sakaya** 酒屋 is a saké store but sells beer and whiskey as well. It is quite different from an American liquor store, however. At a **sakaya**, liquor is only one of the many items sold. Most of the merchandise is groceries such as sugar, canned food, and miso. The **sakaya** is a relic from another time and is disappearing, though.

Sakaya 酒屋 should not be confused with **sakaba** 酒場, a kind of bar.

Sake 酒 *saké, liquor*

Sake 酒 (or, more politely, **osake** お酒) can refer to either (a) Japanese rice wine, or (b) alcoholic beverages generally. In (1) below, **sake** is used with meaning (a), while in (2) it has meaning (b).

EXAMPLES:
(1) **Osake wa arimasen ga bīru wa arimasu.**
お酒はありませんがビールはあります。
We don't have saké, but we have beer.
(2) **Ano hito wa sake mo tabako mo nomimasen.**
あの人は酒もタバコも飲みません。
He neither drinks liquor nor smokes.

To avoid this confusion, however, **nihonshu** 日本酒 "Japanese rice wine" is sometimes used for meaning (a), and **arukōru** アルコール (lit., "alcohol") for meaning (b), as in

EXAMPLES:
(3) **Kyō wa nihonshu ni shimashō.**
今日は日本酒にしましょう。
Let's have saké today.
(4) **Ano hito wa arukōru ni tsuyoi desu nē.**
あの人はアルコールに強いですねえ。
He can certainly hold his liquor, can't he!

Sakka 作家 *writer, novelist*

A **sakka** 作家 is a fiction writer and most commonly a novelist. The word is used with reference to a person's occupation as a writer (or novelist).

EXAMPLE:
(1) **Kawabata wa Ninon no daihyō-teki na sakka datta.**
川端は日本の代表的な作家だった。
Kawabata was a representative writer (or novelist) of Japan.

Sakka 作家 cannot be used with regard to the authorship of a specific book. In (2) below, **sakka** is wrong; it has to be replaced by **sakusha** 作者 "the author of a specific work of fiction."

EXAMPLE:
(2) **Kono shōsetsu no sakusha** (not *****sakka** 作家) **wa Mishima desu.**
この小説の作者は三島です。
The author of this novel is Mishima.

(See also CHOSHA and SHŌSETSUKA.)

Sakunen 昨年 *last year*

The most common word for last year is **kyonen** 去年, which is used commonly both in speech and writing. When one wishes to be very formal, however, one may switch to **sakunen**. There is no difference in meaning, only in the degree of formality. See the following pairs of expressions referring to years.

	Normal	**Formal**
the year before last	**ototoshi** 一昨年	**issakunen** 一昨年
last year	**kyonen** 去年	**sakunen** 昨年
this year	**kotoshi** 今年	**konnen/honnen** 今年/本年
next year	**rainen** 来年	**myōnen** 明年
the year after next	**sarainen** 再来年	**myōgonen** 明後年

Sa⌐ma⌐zama 様々 *various*

The most common word for "various" is **iroiro** いろいろ. **Samazama** 様々, a more formal expression, could be used almost synonymously. In (1) below, for example, both would be correct.

EXAMPLE:

(1) **Nihon ni wa iroiro/samazama na hōgen ga aru.**
日本には いろいろ/様々な 方言がある。
In Japan, there are various kinds of dialects.

There is, however, a slight difference between these two words. **Iroiro** いろいろ means "many different kinds," and sometimes "many" is emphasized over "different," as in

EXAMPLE:

(2) **Iroiro arigatō gozaimasu.**
いろいろありがとうございます。
Thank you for the many (different) things you did for me.

This use of **iroiro** いろいろ cannot be replaced by **samazama** 様々, which always focuses on "different" rather than "many." That is why **iroiro** and **samazama** can even be used together, as in

EXAMPLE:

(3) **Nihon ni wa iroiro samazama na hōgen ga aru.**
日本にはいろいろ様々な方言がある。
In Japan, there are many different kinds of dialects.

Sa⌐mu⌐i 寒い *cold*

Samui 寒い "cold" represents a sensation of coldness perceived throughout the whole body.

EXAMPLE:

(1) **Kyō wa samui.**
今日は寒い。
It's cold today.

Samui 寒い is never used in reference to solids or fluids. Examples (2) and (3) below are therefore incorrect.

EXAMPLES:

(2) *samui te
     *寒い手
     lit., cold hand

(3) *samui jūsu
     *寒いジュース
     lit., cold juice

In such cases, **samui** 寒い has to be replaced by **tsumetai** 冷たい (see TSUMETAI).
Some nouns may be modified by either **samui** or **tsumetai**.

EXAMPLES:

(4a) **samui kaze**
     寒い風
     cold wind

(4b) **tsumetai kaze**
     冷たい風
     cold wind

There is, however, a slight difference between (4a) and (4b). (4a) represents the cold wind as something affecting one's whole body, whereas (4b) represents the coldness of the wind as it affects one's skin, one's face, or one's hands only.

-San さん *(suffix attached to a name)*

-San さん most commonly follows a person's family name (or family name plus given name) to function somewhat like "Mr.," "Mrs.," or "Miss," as in **Tanaka-san** 田中さん or **Tanaka Ichirō-san** 田中一郎さん. Unlike "Mr.," "Mrs.," and "Miss," however, **-san** is not used when addressing a person higher in status than the speaker. For example, a company employee speaking to his boss does not use **-san** but rather uses the latter's title as a term of address, e.g., **shachō** 社長 "company president," **buchō** 部長 "department chief," or **kachō** 課長 "section chief." A student speaking to his teacher does not as a rule use **-san** either but calls him or her **sensei** 先生 (see SENSEI) instead.

    -San さん may also be attached to given names alone. This is the case when one addresses cousins, maids, neighbors' children, etc. (e.g., **Tarō-san** 太郎さん, **Michiko-san** 美智子さん). **-San** may be added to occupation names to address, or refer to, people in certain occupations. Carpenters, gardeners, bakers, for example, are often called **daiku-san** 大工さん (lit., "Mr. Carpenter"), **uekiya-san** 植木屋さん (lit., "Mr. Gardener"), and **pan'ya-san** パン屋さん (lit., "Mr. Baker"), respectively. **-San** is also used with kinship terms in addressing one's relatives if the addressee is higher in status than the speaker, e.g., **otō-san** お父さん "father," **okā-san** お母さん "mother," **oji-san** おじさん "uncle," and **oba-san** おばさん "aunt." When one addresses one's own children, grandchildren, or younger siblings, one uses their names without **-san** さん, although **-chan** ちゃん (the diminutive variant of **-san**) may sometimes be used.

    -San さん is never used by itself, nor is it ever used in reference to oneself.

Sanpo 散歩 *walk, stroll*

Sanpo 散歩 is a noun meaning "a walk" or "a stroll," and **sanpo-suru** 散歩する is the corresponding compound verb meaning "to take a walk (or stroll)." **Sanpo** only refers to a leisurely walk for exercise or for pleasure, and should not be used when a specific destination is mentioned or when some business is involved. If one walks to the office, for example, it is not a **sanpo**.

EXAMPLE:
(1) *Maiasa kaisha made sanpo-shimasu.
     *毎朝会社まで散歩します。
     I take a walk to the office every day.

This sentence has to be rephrased, for example, like the following:

EXAMPLE:
(2) **Maiasa kaisha made aruite ikimasu.**
     毎朝会社まで歩いて行きます。
     I walk to the office every day.

Sa⌐yonara⌐ さよなら *Good-by*

Sayonara さよなら (or, more formally, **Sayōnara** さようなら) is the most common farewell that may be used at any time of the day. However, it carries a rather informal tone and therefore does not go well with **keigo** 敬語 (respect language). An adult is unlikely to say **Sayonara** さよなら or **Sayōnara** さようなら to a person of much higher status. For example, an employee would normally use **Shitsurei-shimasu** 失礼します (lit., "Excuse me [for leaving]") as he parts with his boss.

   Sayonara さよなら is not appropriate for all occasions of leavetaking. For example, it cannot be used when one leaves one's own home (**Itte-mairimasu** 行ってまいります is the correct expression then) or when one sees off a member of one's own household (**Itte-irasshai** 行っていらっしゃい is the set phrase for that occasion) (see ITTE-MAIRIMASU and ITTE-IRASSHAI).

Seichō-suru 成長する *to grow*

English "grow" may refer not only to the growth of persons, animals, plants, and inanimate objects but also to an increase in the number of something. **Seichō-suru** 成長する, on the other hand, may never refer to an increase in the number of something. The use of **seichō-suru** is therefore correct in sentences (1) and (2) below but not in sentence (3).

EXAMPLES:
(1) **Kodomo wa jūdai ni kyūgeki ni seichō-suru.**
     子供は十代に急激に成長する。
     Children grow rapidly in their teens.
(2) **Nihon-keizai wa 60-nendai kara 70-nendai ni kakete ōkiku seichō-shita.**
     日本経済は60年代から70年代にかけて大きく成長した。
     The Japanese economy grew markedly during the 1960s and the 1970s.
(3) *Sen-kyūhyaku-hachijū-nendai ni Amerika no Nihongo no gakuseisū wa zuibun seichō-shita.
     *1980年代にアメリカの日本語の学生数はずいぶん成長した。
     In the 1980s, the number of Japanese-language students in America grew a lot.

In sentence (3) above, "grew in number" should be **fueta** 増えた.

　　Seichō-suru 成長する, unlike "grow," is basically a written expression. Sentence (1) above, for example, should be rephrased in speech as follows:

EXAMPLE:

(4)　**Kodomo wa jūdai de sugoku ōkiku naru/se ga nobiru.**
　　子供は十代ですごく大きくなる/背が伸びる。
　　Children grow a lot taller in their teens.

Se˥ifu 政府 *government*

In English, "government" may refer to any level of government. You can talk about a city government, a state government, or a federal government. In Japanese, on the other hand, **seifu** 政府 is generally reserved for a national government only. It is therefore correct to say **Nihon-seifu** 日本政府 "the Japanese government" or **Amerika-seifu** アメリカ政府 "the American government" but not, for example, **ken-seifu 県政府 (lit., "prefectural government"). **Kenchō** 県庁 "prefectural office" is used instead.

　　Along the same lines, English speakers often make the following error in Japanese:

EXAMPLE:

(1)　***Ano hito wa seifu ni tsutomete-imasu.**
　　*あの人は政府に勤めています。
　　That person works for the government.

　　In (1) above, the English version is of course correct, but the Japanese, its direct translation, is not. Japanese has other ways of expressing the same idea, as in (2a) and (2b).

EXAMPLES:

(2a) **Ano hito wa kanchō ni tsutomete-imasu.**
　　あの人は官庁に勤めています。
　　That person works for a government office.

(2b) **Ano hito wa kanryō/kōmuin desu.**
　　あの人は 官僚/公務員 です。
　　That person is a government employee.

　　Also, Japanese speakers normally would prefer being more specific, e.g.,

EXAMPLE:

(3)　**Ano hito wa Monbu-Kagakushō (Zaimushō, Gaimushō ...) ni tsutomete-imasu.**
　　あの人は文部科学省(財務省、外務省...)に勤めています。
　　That person works for the Ministry of Education, Culture, Sports, Science and Technology (Finance, Foreign Affairs, etc.).

Seikatsu 生活 *life*

Seikatsu 生活, **inochi** 命, and **jinsei** 人生 are all translated as "life," but each is different. **Seikatsu** means "life" in the sense of "making a living."

EXAMPLE:

(1)　**Bukka ga takai to seikatsu** (not **inochi 命, **jinsei 人生) **ga kurushiku naru.**
　　物価が高いと生活が苦しくなる。
　　When prices are high, life (i.e., making a living) becomes tough.

Inochi 命 is what sustains life within living things, as in

EXAMPLE:

(2) **Itō-san wa mada wakai noni kekkaku de inochi** (not *seikatsu 生活, *jinsei 人生) **o otoshita.**
伊藤さんはまだ若いのに結核で命を落とした。
Mr. Ito lost (lit., dropped) his life because of TB despite his young age.

Jinsei 人生 is human existence in the sense of "a course of life," as in

EXAMPLES:

(3a) **Jinsei** (not *seikatsu 生活, *inochi 命) **wa yonjū kara to iwarete kita.**
人生は四十からと言われてきた。
It has always been said that life begins at forty.

(3b) **Kare no jinsei** (not *inochi 命) **wa mijime datta.**
彼の人生はみじめだった。
His life was miserable.

In (3b) above, **jinsei** 人生 may be replaced by **seikatsu** 生活, but the meaning of the sentence would change. (3b) means "His life from beginning to end was a miserable one," i.e., "he was never happy throughout his life." On the other hand, **Kare no seikatsu wa mijime datta** 彼の生活はみじめだった would seem to focus on a particular period of his life. For example, he grew up happily in the country, but then he moved to Tokyo to enter college and, while there, he had no money and had to live a very sad life.

Se¹ito 生徒 *student, pupil*

In English, a person attending almost any kind of school from elementary school to college and beyond may be called a student. In Japanese, on the other hand, **gakusei** 学生 (see GAKUSEI) and **seito** 生徒, both meaning "student," are fairly clearly distinguished from each other, the former being reserved mostly for college and university students, and the latter for younger students in nursery school through high school. The line of demarcation is somewhat blurred, however, high school students sometimes being referred to as **gakusei**.

Students taking private lessons are not **gakusei** 学生 but **seito** 生徒 regardless of age. For example, a housewife taking piano lessons from a tutor is his **seito**. Note the difference between the two words.

EXAMPLE:

Ano piano no sensei ni wa seito ga takusan aru. Gakusei mo, shufu mo, komodo mo iru.
あのピアノの先生は生徒がたくさんある。学生も、主婦も、子供もいる。
That piano teacher has lots of private students—[college] students, housewives, and children.

Se¹izei せいぜい *at the most*

Seizei せいぜい means "at the most," as in

EXAMPLE:

(1) **Watashi wa bīru o nonde mo, seizei ippai da.**
私はビールを飲んでも、せいぜい一杯だ。
I can drink only one glass of beer at the most.

The implication in the above case is "even if I put in all my effort."

EXAMPLE:

(2) **Kare no nenshū wa seizei niman-doru darō.**

化rの年収はせいぜい二万ドルだろう。

His annual income must be at the most $20,000.

In sentence (2), **seizei** せいぜい could imply either "even with his best effort" or "even if I'm trying to give it the highest possible estimate."

Se⌐kai 世界 *world*

If you look up "world" in an English-Japanese dictionary, you will find at least three words: **sekai** 世界, **yononaka** 世の中, and **seken** 世間. **Sekai** in a broad sense is the physical world that spreads all over the globe, as in

EXAMPLE:

(1) **Sekai** (not ***yononaka** 世の中, ***seken** 世間) **-jū o ryokō-shite mitai.**

世界中を旅行してみたい。

I'd like to travel all over the world.

Sekai 世界 in a much narrower sense may refer to a particular segment of society, as in

EXAMPLE:

(2) **Gakusha no sekai** (not ***yononaka** 世の中, ***seken** 世間) **wa, ii koto bakari de wa nai.**

学者の世界は、いいことばかりではない。

The world of academics is not all pleasant.

Yononaka 世の中 means "this general world where we live" but not the kind of geographical world consisting of almost 200 countries. For example,

EXAMPLE:

(3) **Toshi o toru to yononaka** (not ***sekai** 世界, ***seken** 世間) **ga iya ni naru hito ga iru.**

年を取ると世の中がいやになる人がいる。

Some people, as they grow old, become tired of the world (not in the sense of international politics or anything like that, but rather in terms of what happens around them in daily life in general).

Seken 世間 is very close to **yononaka** 世の中 but much narrower in scope.

EXAMPLE:

(4) **Konna koto o suru to, seken** (not ***sekai** 世界, ***yononaka** 世の中) **ni taishite hazukashii.**

こんな事をすると、世間に対して恥ずかしい。

If I do something like this, I'll be too embarrassed to face the world (i.e., the people around me).

Se⌐ma⌐i 狭い *narrow, small in area*

Semai 狭い is the opposite of **hiroi** 広い "wide" (see HIROI). As is the case with **hiroi**, **semai** is used both one-dimensionally as in example (1) and two-dimensionally as in (2).

EXAMPLES:

(1) **semai michi** (**mon, toguchi**, etc.)
狭い道(門、戸口、etc.)
narrow road (gate, doorway, etc.)

(2) **semai heya** (**niwa, kuni**, etc.)
狭い部屋(庭、国、etc.)
small (i.e., limited in space) room (yard, country, etc.)

When used two-dimensionally, **semai** 狭い is similar in meaning to **chiisai** 小さい "small," but these two adjectives are different in focus. **Chiisai** is simply "small in size," whereas **semai** signifies "not spacious enough for a particular purpose." Even a **chiisai** room may not be **semai** if occupied by someone without furniture, while even an **ōkii** 大きい "large" room could become **semai** if used for a huge banquet (Suzuki, p. 80). One might say that **semai** carries a negative connotation while **chiisai** doesn't.

Senjitsu 先日 *the other day*

Senjitsu 先日 is probably used most often in greetings, as in the following:

EXAMPLES:

(1) **Senjitsu wa gochisō-sama deshita.**
先日はごちそうさまでした。
Thank you for the treat the other day.

(2) **Senjitsu wa dōmo arigatō gozaimashita.**
先日はどうもありがとうございました。
Thank you for what you did for me the other day.

In Japan, when two people meet after a few days (perhaps up to a week or two), each tries to remember in words what favor the other person did for him the last time they met. Even if the other person might not have done any favor at all, one often acknowledges the last meeting by saying something less specific such as

EXAMPLE:

(3) **Senjitsu wa dōmo shitsurei-shimashita.**
先日はどうも失礼しました。
lit., I was rude the other day.

This expression is used even when the speaker did nothing rude at all. It is merely the Japanese way of saying "It was good to see you (or talk to you) the other day." In fact, (3) is a good example of how Japanese speakers have a tendency to apologize where English speakers would express happiness or pleasure (e.g., "It was good to see you," "I enjoyed talking to you," "Your party was simply great," etc.).

If one wishes to be even less specific than (3) above, one can simply say

EXAMPLE:

(4) **Senjitsu wa dōmo.**
先日はどうも。

This could be an abbreviation of either (2) or (3). Precisely because of its vagueness, this expression is considered very convenient and is used quite frequently.

Senjitsu 先日 is a formal expression and should be replaced by **kono-aida** この間 in informal speech (see KONO-AIDA).

Senpai 先輩 *lit., one's senior*

If a person enters, and graduates from, the same school or college that you do, but ahead of you in time, even by one year, he is a **senpai** 先輩 to you, and you don't refer to him as a **tomodachi** 友達 "friend" (see TOMODACHI). Men observe these terminology rules much more rigidly than women do. Suppose Tanaka and Suzuki, both men, graduated from the same high school or college, with Tanaka graduating a year or two before Suzuki. If they meet, Tanaka will call Suzuki either **Suzuki** 鈴木 or **Suzuki-kun** 鈴木君, but Suzuki will address Tanaka as **Tanaka-san** 田中さん. (In this particular instance, women's speech might be called more democratic than men's. If Tanaka and Suzuki above were both women, they would call each other **Tanaka-san** and **Suzuki-san**.)

Being a **senpai** 先輩 thus gives one higher status in Japanese human relations, but at the same time this is accompanied by "noblesse oblige." It is tacitly understood in Japanese society that **senpai** are supposed to look after the well-being of their **kōhai** 後輩 "juniors," especially if they used to belong to the same athletic team in school or college. In fact, high school or college athletic teams in Japan are often coached by **senpai** who volunteer their service free of charge. (See also KŌHAI.)

Se⌈nse⌉i 先生 *teacher*

Sensei 先生 has two uses. First of all, it means "teacher."

EXAMPLE:

(1) **Ano hito wa kōkō no sensei da sō da.**
あの人は高校の先生だそうだ。
I hear he is a high-school teacher.

Second, it is used as a respectful term of address for people in certain professions, e.g., teachers, doctors, dentists, writers, lawyers, and politicians.

EXAMPLE:

(2) **Sensei, ashita wa gotsugō ga yoroshii deshō ka.**
先生、あしたはご都合がよろしいでしょうか。
Would tomorrow be convenient for you?

This second use of **sensei** 先生 is impossible to translate into English because there is no equivalent. (It is for this reason that the translator of Soseki Natsume's novel *Kokoro* ここ ろ used the Japanese word **sensei** throughout the English version for the elderly gentleman who is called **sensei** and otherwise remains nameless in the original.) In situations such as (2) above, the English speaker would use the name of the addressee, e.g., "Dr. (or Mr., Mrs., Miss) Miller, would tomorrow be convenient for you?"

There is another word, **kyōshi** 教師, which also means "teacher," but there are several differences between this word and **sensei**. First of all, **kyōshi** does not refer to anyone but teachers. Second, it is never used as a term of address. Third, the word **sensei** carries with it a connotation of respect and is therefore not used in reference to oneself. When a teacher mentions his occupation to someone else, he should say, for example,

EXAMPLE:

(3) **Kōkō no kyōshi** (not *sensei 先生) **o shite-imasu.**
高校の教師をしています。
I am a high-school teacher.

Fourth, except when one is referring to oneself, **kyōshi** 教師 is mostly a written form. It is not a conversational expression like **sensei** 先生 and is rarely used by children.

Se⌐nshu 選手 *a player (selected to play a sport)*

Senshu 選手 is often translated as "player," but one must be careful not to equate the two. First, a "player" can be a player of anything, e.g., a tennis player, a chess player, a piano player, etc., while **senshu** normally refers only to athletes. Second, a **senshu** is someone selected to play a certain sport while a player can be anyone who plays something. See the difference between (1a) and (1b).

EXAMPLES:

(1a) **Tarō wa tenisu no senshu da.**
太郎はテニスの選手だ。
Taro is a varsity tennis player.
(1b) **Jon wa tenisu o suru.**
ジョンはテニスをする。
John is a tennis player.

Sentence (1a) means "Taro is a member of his school's tennis team," whereas (1b) is just another way of saying "John plays tennis."

Sentaku 洗濯 *washing*

Sentaku 洗濯 means "washing, laundering," and it becomes a compound verb with the addition of **suru** する, i.e., **sentaku-suru** 洗濯する, meaning "to wash, to launder." **Sentaku** refers only to washing clothes, linens, etc. and is, in this sense, quite different from **arau** 洗う "to wash," which may refer to washing anything. In sentence (1), therefore, either **sentaku-suru** or **arau** would be all right, but in (2), **arau** would be the only correct verb.

EXAMPLES:

(1) **Ato de kutsushita o sentaku-suru** (or **arau**) **tsumori desu.**
あとでくつ下を洗濯する(洗う)つもりです。
I plan to wash some socks later.
(2) **Te o arai-nasai** (not *sentaku-shinasai 洗濯しなさい).
手を洗いなさい。
Wash your hands.

English "wash" does not always require an object. For example, in "Monday is the day we wash," "wash" by itself means "wash clothes" and doesn't need an object. In Japanese, on the other hand, although **sentaku-suru** 洗濯する does not always need an object, **arau** does. In the following example, therefore, only (a) would be correct.

EXAMPLE:

(3) **Getsuyō ga**	(a) **sentaku-bi**	**desu.**
月曜が	洗濯日	です。
	(b) ***arau hi**	
	*洗う日	

Monday is our wash day.

Se¹nzo 先祖 *ancestor*

There are two main words in Japanese meaning "ancestor": **senzo** 先祖 and **sosen** 祖先. **Senzo** sounds more personal and usually refers to one's own family ancestors, especially fairly recent (i.e., going back only a few generations). For example, a **butsudan** 仏壇 "family Buddhist altar" is dedicated to one's **senzo**, or more politely, **gosenzo-sama** ご先祖様 "dear ancestors," i.e., one's deceased parents, grandparents, and perhaps great grandparents. **Sosen** is a more impersonal term; thus there is no such expression as ***gososen-sama** *ご祖先様 to refer to one's own "dear" ancestors. **Sosen** connotes going back much farther and is therefore preferred to **senzo** when, for example, one talks about the ancestors of the Japanese race, as in

EXAMPLE:

Nihonjin no sosen (?senzo) ga doko kara kita ka to iu koto wa, ima demo tokidoki mondai ni sareru.
日本人の祖先（？先祖）がどこから来たかと言うことは、いまでも時々問題にされる。
Where the ancestors of the Japanese race originally came from is still argued about at times.

Shibai 芝居 *play*

Shibai 芝居 means a "play" in the sense of "theatrical performance" or "show."

EXAMPLES:
(1) **Kyō wa shibai o mi ni ikimashō.**
今日は芝居を見に行きましょう。
Let's go and see a play today.
(2) **Are wa ii shibai deshita yo.**
あれはいい芝居でしたよ。
That was a good play.

Shibai 芝居 may also mean "playacting, putting on an act."

EXAMPLE:
(3) **Hontō ni naite-iru n ja arimasen. Shibai desu yo.**
本当に泣いているんじゃありません。芝居ですよ。
She isn't really crying. She's just faking it.

Dramas one reads are usually not **shibai** 芝居 but **gikyoku** 戯曲 (although when a **gikyoku** is performed on stage, it is referred to as a **shibai**).

EXAMPLE:

(4) **Chēhofu no gikyoku** (not *shibai 芝居) **wa zuibun yonda ga, shibai wa mada mita koto ga nai.**
チェーホフの戯曲はずいぶん読んだが、芝居はまだ見たことがない。
I've read a lot of dramas by Chekhov, but I've never seen any of them performed.

"Drama" in the sense of "theater arts" is not **shibai** 芝居 but **engeki** 演劇.

EXAMPLE:

(5) **Ano hito wa daigaku de engeki o senkō-shite-imasu.**
あの人は大学で演劇を専攻しています。
He is majoring in theater arts in college.

An amateur play staged by young students, especially elementary-school children, is usually called **geki** 劇 rather than **shibai** 芝居.

EXAMPLE:

(6) **Uchi no ko wa kondo gakugeikai de geki ni deru sō desu.**
うちの子は今度学芸会で劇に出るそうです。
Our child says he'll be in a play at the school's art festival.

When **geki** 劇 is used in compounds, however, there is no connotation of amateurishness. For example, **kageki** 歌劇 "opera," **shūkyōgeki** 宗教劇 "religious play," etc., just represent different categories of plays.

Plays written and produced for radio or TV are called **dorama** ドラマ (from English "drama")—more specifically, **rajio-dorama** ラジオドラマ (lit., "radio drama") or **terebi-dorama** テレビドラマ (lit., "TV drama").

Shibaraku-buri しばらくぶり *for the first time after a long while*

Shibaraku しばらく and **shibaraku-buri** しばらくぶり are often confused by students of Japanese, but they are not the same. **Shibaraku** means "for a while," as in

EXAMPLE:

(1) **Shibaraku koko de omachi kudasai.**
しばらく ここでお待ちください。
Please wait here for a while.

Just as in the case of English "for a while," the time span referred to as **shibaraku** しばらく could be either long or not so long; only the context determines the actual length.

Shibaraku-buri しばらくぶり, on the other hand, means "for the first time after a long while" and is never used unless the time span is long. It is thus synonymous with **hisashi-buri** 久しぶり, as in

EXAMPLE:

(2) **Kyōwa**	**shibaraku-buri**	**ni/de Nihon-eiga o mita.**
今日は	しばらくぶり	に/で 日本映画を見た。
	hisashi-buri	
	久しぶり	

Today I saw a Japanese film after a long time.

When you see someone after many months or years, you may exchange the following greeting, which is a standard formula used quite often:

EXAMPLE:

(3) **(O)hisashi-buri** | **desu ne.**
(お)久しぶり | ですね。
Shibaraku-buri
しばらくぶり
We haven't seen each other for a long time.

When the person you meet in such a situation is a good friend with whom you speak informally, just say

EXAMPLE:

(4) **Shibaraku!**
しばらく！
Haven't seen you for a while!

In this case, **-buri** ぶり is omitted. Note that **-buri** in **hisashi-buri** 久しぶり, however, can never be left out, i.e., "**hisashi** 久し" by itself can never be used.

Shigoto 仕事 *work, job*

Shigoto 仕事 means "job" or "work."

EXAMPLES:

(1a) **Jon wa daigaku o sotsugyō-shite sugu shigoto ga mitsukatta.**
ジョンは大学を卒業してすぐ仕事が見つかった。
John found a job right after he graduated from college.

(1b) **Kyō wa kaisha de shigoto ga nakute taikutsu-shite-shimatta.**
今日は会社で仕事がなくて退屈してしまった。
Today I was bored at the office because there was no work to do.

In English, one may say "I just came home from work" to mean "I just came home from the office." In Japanese, however, **shigoto** 仕事 cannot replace **kaisha** 会社 "company; office."

EXAMPLE:

(2) **Ima kaisha** (not *__shigoto__ 仕事) **kara kaette kita tokoro desu.**
いま会社から帰って来たところです。
I just came home from the office.

An American once said to me **Shigoto kara denwa o kakemasu** 仕事から電話をかけます。 to mean "I'll call you from my office." This sentence is also wrong. **Shigoto** 仕事 in this context must be replaced by **kaisha** 会社, **ginkō** 銀行 "bank," **daigaku** 大学 "university," **kenkyūjo** 研究所 "institute," etc., depending on where one works; otherwise just use **tsutomesaki** 勤め先 "place where one is employed."

Shi⌈kata ga na⌉i 仕方がない *cannot be helped*

Shikata ga nai 仕方がない, or **shikatanai** 仕方ない, is almost always equated with "cannot be helped," as in

EXAMPLE:

(1) **Byōki no toki ni gakkō o yasumu no wa shikata ga nai.**
病気の時に学校を休むのは仕方がない。
Missing school when one is ill is something that can't be helped.

This expression, however, has other uses. For example, it may mean "useless" when preceded by **te mo** ても.

EXAMPLE:

(2) **Imasara sonna koto o itte mo shikata ga nai.**
いまさらそんな事を言っても仕方がない。
It's useless to say that kind of thing now.

Or it may mean "unbearably" when preceded by **te** て.

EXAMPLE:

(3) **Atsukute shikata ga nai kara, pūru e ikō to omou.**
暑くて仕方がないから、プールへ行こうと思う。
It's unbearably hot (lit., It's so hot and there's nothing we can do about it); I think I'll go to the pool.

It also means "hopeless" when it directly modifies a noun.

EXAMPLE:

(4) **Aitsu hontō ni shikata ga nai/shōganai yatsu da.**
あいつは本当に仕方がない/しょうがない やつだ。
He's a really hopeless guy.

Shi⌈kaku⌉ 四角 *square*

Shikaku 四角 literally means "four-cornered [shape]." It follows, therefore, that the word may refer not only to squares but to rectangular shapes as well. When one has to make a distinction between the two, one may say **seihōkei** 正方形 for "a square" and **chōhōkei** 長方形 for "a rectangular shape."

Shi⌈ke⌉n 試験 *examination*

Don't translate "take an examination" directly into Japanese and say *shiken o toru *試験を取る (lit., "to take an examination"). The correct expression is **shiken o ukeru** 試験を受ける (lit., "to receive an examination").

EXAMPLE:

(1) **Miyata-kun wa Tōdai no nyūgaku-shiken o ukeru sō da.**
宮田君は東大の入学試験を受けるそうだ。
I hear Miyata will be taking the entrance examination for Tokyo University.

Unlike English "examination," **shiken** 試験 does not normally refer to examination papers. A sheet of paper with examination questions is called **shiken-mondai** 試験問題 before the answers are written in, and **tōan** 答案 (lit., "answer draft") afterward.

EXAMPLES:

(2) Teacher: **Ima shiken-mondai** (not *shiken 試験) **o tsukutte-iru n desu.**
いま試験問題を作っているんです。
I'm preparing an exam.

(3) Teacher: **Tōan** (not *shiken 試験) **o takusan shirabe-nakucha naranai n desu.**
(after exams) 答案をたくさん調べなくちゃならないんです。
I've got to read lots of exams.

Sh⌐inji⌐ru 信じる *to believe*

English "believe" is sometimes used very lightly, just to signify "think," as in

EXAMPLE:

(1) I believe (or think) I'll have lunch now.

Shinjiru 信じる cannot be used in this manner; it is a much weightier word, as in

EXAMPLE:

(2) **Watashi no iu koto o shinjite kudasai.**
私の言う事を信じてください。
Please believe what I say.

Shinjiru 信じる has another version, **shinzuru** 信ずる, but this latter verb is more formal and is basically a written form.

EXAMPLE:

(3) **Kirisuto o shinzuru mono wa Kurisuchan de aru.**
キリストを信ずる者はクリスチャンである。
A person who believes in Christ is a Christian.

Shinkansen 新幹線 *the New Trunk Line; the train which runs on the New Trunk Line*

Shinkansen 新幹線, the so-called Bullet Train, literally means "New Trunk Line." The word may refer to either the line or the train.

EXAMPLES:

(1a) **Shinkansen wa rokujū-nendai ni kaitsū-shita.**
新幹線は60年代に開通した。
The Shinkansen opened in the 60s.

(1b) **Kondo no Kyōto-yuki no Shinkansen wa nan-ji ni demasu ka.**
今度の京都行きの新幹線は何時に出ますか。
What time is the next Shinkansen leaving for Kyoto?

This kind of ambiguous usage is quite common in Japanese and is seen widely. English tends to be a little more specific. Compare the Japanese and the English versions below.

EXAMPLE:

(2) **Kondo no Nikkō wa ku-ji ni demasu.**
今度の日航は9時に出ます。
The next Japan Airlines flight leaves at 9 A.M.

Shi⌈ntai-shōga⌉isha 身体障害者 *physically-handicapped person*

Just as English has become very sensitive about the use of discriminatory expressions such as "blind," "deaf," "mute," "cripple," etc., so has Japanese. Although the Japanese public in general still remains insensitive, the media have become extremely careful not to use any discriminatory terms. In fact, more and more neutral-sounding new words are being coined for this purpose. For example, a deaf person used to be called **tsunbo** 聾, but the official term these days is **rōsha** 聾者, which sounds much less offensive. **Shintaishōgaisha** 身体障害者 is another fairly new word meaning "physically-handicapped person." Since it is such a long word consisting of five kanji, it is often shortened to **shinshōsha** 身障者 or **shōgaisha** 障害者.

Shiritsu 私立 *private*

In a Japanese-English dictionary, **shiritsu** 私立 is always translated as "private," but this is actually very misleading because the idea of "private" is expressed only by the first kanji of the two, and not by the second, which is 立, meaning "established" or "founded." A private university is a privately-established university, so it is **shiritsu-daigaku** 私立大学 A private property, however, is a privately-owned, not privately established, property, so you must call it **shiyū-zaisan** 私有財産 (lit., "privately-owned property"), not **shiritsu-zaisan** 私立財産. A private hospital room is called **koshitsu** 個室 (lit., "individual room").

 Shiritsu-daigaku 私立大学 "private university" and **shiritsu-daigaku** 市立大学 "municipal university" (lit., city-founded university) are unfortunately pronounced the same. To make the distinction clear in speech, the former is often pronounced **watakushi-ritsu** (私立), giving a **kun** reading to the first kanji 私, which is normally given an **on** reading in this context. **Shi** 市 in 市立大学, too, is pronounced sometimes with its **kun** reading, i.e., **ichi** (市), for the sake of differentiation.

Shiru 知る *to get to know*

Shiru 知る is a very strange verb. To express the idea of "I don't know," we use the non-past negative, as in

EXAMPLE:

(1) **Shirimasen.** (or **Shiranai.**)
知りません。(知らない。)
I don't know.

However, to express the idea of "I know," we must use the **-te-iru** form, as in

EXAMPLE:

(2) **Shitte-imasu.** (or **Shitte-iru.**)
知っています。(知っている。)
I know. (lit., I am in the state of having gotten to know.)

In other words, for some reason, we never use **Shirimasu** 知ります (or **Shiru** 知る) to mean "I know," nor do we usually use **Shitte-imasen** 知っていません (or **Shitte-inai** 知っていない) to mean "I don't know." (Although we occasionally hear **Shitte-imasen** or **Shitte-inai**, they are not common expressions.) The reason "I know" is **Shitte-iru** 知っている is because **shiru** is a punctual verb meaning "to get to know," and not a stative verb meaning "to know." **Shitte-iru**, therefore, literally means "I am in the state of having gotten to know." The question still remains, however, why **Shitte-inai** 知っていない (lit., "I am not in the state of having gotten to know") is not as common an expression as **Shiranai** 知らない in the sense of "I don't know." No other verb behaves quite like this.

English "I don't know" does not always correspond to **Shirimasen** 知りません (or **Shiranai** 知らない) in Japanese; it sometimes corresponds to **Wakarimasen** 分かりません (or **Wakaranai** 分からない). For the difference between these two Japanese expressions, see WAKARU.

Shisō 思想 *thought; idea; ideology*

English "thought" and "idea" are words that can be used in daily speech, e.g., "I'll give it some thought," "That's a good idea," etc. **Shisō** 思想, on the other hand, is a more technical, academic, philosophical term, as in

EXAMPLES:
(1a) **Kanto no shisō**
カントの思想
Kant's ideology
(1b) **kindai-shisōshi**
近代思想史
modern intellectual history

For "I'll give it some thought," therefore, just say **Chotto kangaete mimasu** ちょっと考えてみます. For "That's a good idea," say **Ii kangae da** いい考えだ, or even **Ii aidia da** いいアイデアだ, but not ***Ii shisō da** いい思想だ.

Shitamachi 下町 *lower town; downtown*

Shitamachi 下町 literally means "lower town" and refers mostly to the low-lying areas of Tokyo, such as Asakusa, Kanda, and Shiba, where, during the Edo period, the townspeople (mainly merchants) resided. This is the home of genuine **Edokko** 江戸っ子 "Edoites," the speakers of **shitamachi** speech, which is known for its lack of distinction between **hi** ひ and **shi** し. (Incidentally, in the Japanese version of *My Fair Lady*, Eliza Doolittle speaks this sort of **shitamachi** speech as the Japanese equivalent of Cockney.)

To equate **shitamachi** 下町 with English "downtown" is absolutely erroneous. For one thing, any good-sized town has a downtown section, whereas **shitamachi** is used almost exclusively in reference to Tokyo. For another, **shitamachi** is not as frequently used in Japanese as "downtown" is in English. The English speaker talks about going downtown, eating downtown, or shopping downtown. That is all part of everyday language. The Japanese counterparts of these expressions, however, do not ordinarily contain the word **shitamachi**. Even in Tokyo, which has a section called **shitamachi**, one does not use, for example, ***Kyō wa shitamachi e ikimashō** 今日は下町へ行きましょう to mean "Let's go downtown today." Instead, one would refer to specific sections of Tokyo, as in **Kyō**

wa Ginza e ikimashō 今日は銀座へ行きましょう "Let's go to the Ginza today," **Kyō wa Shinjuku de eiga o mimashita** 今日は新宿で映画を見ました "I saw a movie in Shinjuku today," or **Shibuya de shokuji o shimashita** 渋谷で食事をしました "I ate [at a restaurant] in Shibuya." The word **shitamachi** is used primarily to describe a person's background, as in **Ano hito wa shitamachi-sodachi desu yo** あの人は下町育ちですよ "He grew up in shitamachi."

Shi⌈tsu⌉rei-shimasu 失礼します *Excuse me*

Shitsurei-shimasu 失礼します and **Shitsurei-shimashita** 失礼しました both become "Excuse me" in English, but they should be clearly distinguished. **Shitsurei-shimasu** means "I am going to commit an act of rudeness" while **Shitsurei-shimashita** means "I have committed an act of rudeness." The former, therefore, should be used to mean "Excuse me" for something you are about to do—for example, before going into your teacher's office. The latter, on the other hand, should be used to mean "Excuse me" for something you have already done, such as having bothered the addressee.

  Shitsurei-shimasu 失礼します and **Shitsurei-shimashita** 失礼しました are also used in situations that English speakers do not normally consider worth apologizing for. For example, Japanese say **Shitsurei-shimasu** when invited into someone's home. We regularly say **Shitsurei-shimasu** as a farewell instead of **Sayonara** さよなら when parting with someone higher in status than we are. It is normal for us to say **Senjitsu wa shitsurei-shimashita** 先日は失礼しました when we see someone with whom we have done something recently, e.g., dining out together. The English equivalent in such a case would not be "I'm sorry for what I did the other day," but rather "It was good to see you the other day." In informal conversation, both **Shitsurei-shimasu** and **Shitsurei-shimashita** become **Shitsurei** 失礼.

Shokuji 食事 *meal*

In English, you can say either "have a meal" or "eat a meal." In Japanese, however, use **shokuji o suru** 食事をする (lit., "do a meal") or, more formally, **shokuji o toru** 食事を取る (lit., "take a meal"), but not *__shokuji o taberu__ 食事を食べる.

  Gohan ご飯, when used in the sense of "meal," on the other hand, takes **taberu** 食べる, and not **suru** する or **toru** 取る. See the example below.

EXAMPLE:
Gohan mō tabeta (not *__shita/totta__ した/取った)**?**
ご飯もう食べた？
Have you eaten yet? (lit., Have you eaten a meal yet?)

Shōsetsu 小説 *novel, short story*

A **shōsetsu** 小説 is a work of fiction, be it a novel or a short story. In other words, the Japanese language does not generally make a distinction between novels and short stories. When it is necessary to do so, however, one can use the term **chōhen-shōsetsu** 長編小説 (lit., "long **shōsetsu**") for novels and **tanpen-shōsetsu** 短編小説 (lit., "short **shōsetsu**") for short stories.

Shōsetsuka 小説家 *novelist*

Shōsetsuka 小説家 means "novelist" or "writer of short stories." Thus it has a narrower range of meaning than **sakka** 作家, which, although it most often means "novelist," can also refer to playwrights (see SAKKA, also CHOSHA).

Shōˈtai-suru [Shoˈotai-suru] 招待する *to invite*

Shōtai-suru 招待する "to invite" is a formal expression and is usually used with expressions denoting formal affairs.

EXAMPLE:

(1) **hito o kekkonshiki (en'yūkai, kaiten-iwai, etc.) ni shōtai-suru**
人を結婚式（園遊会、開店祝い、etc.）に招待する
to invite a person to a wedding (a garden party, the opening of a store, etc.)

In daily conversation, especially in reference to less formal affairs, **yobu** よぶ is the verb used.

EXAMPLE:

(2) **Kinō wa Ishida-san no uchi e yūshoku ni yobareta n desu.**
きのうは石田さんのうちへ夕食によばれたんです。
Yesterday I was invited to dinner at the Ishidas.

Yobu よぶ implies that the person invited comes to where the inviter is. On the other hand, if you wish to ask someone to go somewhere with you, use **sasou** 誘う to mean "Let's go to such-and-such a place."

EXAMPLE:

(3) **tomodachi o eiga (shibai, ongakukai, etc.) ni sasou**
友達を映画（芝居、音楽会、etc.）に誘う
to ask a friend out to a movie (play, concert, etc.)

Shuˈjutsu 手術 *(surgical) operation*

Shujutsu 手術 refers to "surgical operation," and not any other kind of operation. "Be operated on" is formally **shujutsu o ukeru** 手術を受ける (lit., "receive an operation").

EXAMPLE:

(1) **Satō-san wa raigetsu i no shujutsu o ukeru koto ni natte-iru.**
佐藤さんは来月胃の手術を受けることになっている。
Mr. Sato is scheduled to have a stomach operation next month.

"To operate on someone" is **shujutsu o suru** 手術をする, as in

EXAMPLE:

(2) **Gekai wa shujutsu o suru no ga senmon da.**
外科医は手術をするのが専門だ。
Surgeons specialize in operating.

Colloquially, however, **shujutsu o suru** 手術をする is often used to mean the same as **shujutsu o ukeru** 手術を受ける.

EXAMPLE:

(3) **Satō-san wa raigetsu i no shujutsu o suru n datte.**
佐藤さんは来月胃の手術をするんだって。
I hear Mr. Sato is going to have a stomach operation next month.

In informal speech, **shujutsu** 手術 is frequently pronounced **shujitsu** just as **Shinjuku** 新宿 is often pronounced **Shinjiku**.

Shu˥mi 趣味 *hobby; taste*

Shumi 趣味 has two meanings. First, it is something one does for fun in one's spare time, as in

EXAMPLE:

(1) **Watashi no shumi wa dokusho to supōtsu desu.**
私の趣味は読書とスポーツです。
My hobbies are reading and sports.

Second, **shumi** 趣味 means "ability to see and enjoy what is good in art, manners, etc.," as in

EXAMPLE:

(2) **Yoshida-san no kite-iru mono wa, itsumo shumi ga ii.**
吉田さんの着ている物は、いつも趣味がいい。
Ms. Yoshida's clothes always show good taste.

Shūsen 終戦 *end of the war*

August 15 is commemorated in Japan as **Shūsen Kinenbi** 終戦記念日 "the day to commemorate the end of World War II." What is interesting is the fact that the Japanese rarely use the word **haisen** 敗戦 "defeat (in war)" because it hurts their egos too much to admit the war ended in Japan's surrender. Hence **shūsen** 終戦, which they can swallow more easily. Although some people criticize this hypocrisy, it may not be a bad practice. After all, **shūsen** is not a lie. The war did end that day.

Shushō 首相 *prime minister*

In English, "prime minister" and "premier" may refer to the same person. In Japanese, there are **shushō** 首相 and **sōridaijin** 総理大臣, but the former is used more frequently than the latter. **Sōridaijin** is often shortened to just **sōri** 総理.

EXAMPLE:

Kyō shushō/sōri (daijin) wa Igirisu no shushō to kaidan no yotei da sō da.
今日 首相/総理（大臣）はイギリスの首相と会談の予定だそうだ。
I hear the premier is scheduled to have a meeting with the prime minister of England today.

Interestingly, **sōri (daijin)** 総理（大臣） is rarely used in reference to the prime minister of a foreign nation.

Sō[Sō'o] desu そうです *That's right*

Sō desu そうです meaning "That is so" and its negative counterpart **Sō ja arimasen** そうじゃ ありません meaning "That isn't so" are most normally used in response to a question that ends with a noun + **desu ka** ですか (or **ja arimasen ka** じゃありませんか).

EXAMPLES:

(1)　A:　**Are wa Tanaka-san desu ka.**
　　　　あれは田中さんですか。
　　　　Is that Mr. Tanaka?
　　　B:　**Hai, sō desu.**
　　　　はい、そうです。
　　　　Yes, it is.

(2)　A:　**Are wa Suzuki-san desu ka.**
　　　　あれは鈴木さんですか。
　　　　Is that Mr. Suzuki?
　　　B:　**Iie, sō ja arimasen. Tanaka-san desu yo.**
　　　　いいえ、そうじゃありません。田中さんですよ。
　　　　No, it isn't. It's Mr. Tanaka.

　　In response to a question that ends with an adjective + **desu ka** ですか or a verb + **ka** か, don't use **Sō desu** そうです but repeat the same adjective or verb instead.

EXAMPLES:

(3)　A:　**Sore wa oishii desu ka.**
　　　　それはおいしいですか。
　　　　Is that delicious?
　　　B:　**Ee, oishii desu yo.**
　　　　ええ、おいしいですよ。
　　　　Yes, it is [delicious].

(4)　A:　**Takano-san wa eigo ga wakarimasu ka.**
　　　　高野さんは英語が分かりますか。
　　　　Does Mr. Takano understand English?
　　　B:　**Ee, wakarimasu yo.**
　　　　ええ、分かりますよ。
　　　　Yes, he does (lit., he understands).

The above does not apply to **Sō desu nē** そうですねえ or **Sō desu ka** そうですか.

EXAMPLES:

(5)　A:　**Kore wa oishii desu nē.**
　　　　これはおいしいですねえ。
　　　　This is delicious, isn't it!
　　　B:　**Sō desu nē.**
　　　　そうですねえ。
　　　　It is, isn't it!

(6)　A:　**Takada-san wa yoku nomimasu nē.**
　　　　高田さんはよく飲みますねえ。
　　　　Mr. Takada drinks a lot, doesn't he!

B: **Sō desu nē.**
そうですねえ。
He does, doesn't he!

(7) A: **Kore wa oishii desu yo.**
これはおいしいですよ。
This is delicious, you know.

B: **Sō desu ka.**
そうですか。
Oh, is it?

(8) A: **Takada-san wa yoku nomimasu yo.**
田中さんはよく飲みますよ。
Mr. Takada drinks a lot, you know.

B: **Sō desu ka.**
そうですか。
Does he?

Incidentally, Japanese **sō** そう has etymologically nothing to do with English "so," although they sound alike and have similar meanings. Japanese **sō** is traceable to its older version **sayō** 左様, which has survived in the farewell **Sayōnara** さようなら "Goodby," which literally meant "If it is so [then we must part]." (See also SŌ DESU KA.)

Sō¹ [So¹o] desu ka そうですか *Is that so?*

Sō desu ka そうですか "Is that so?" is a standard response to someone's statement.

EXAMPLE:

(1) A: **Kinō Fujisan ni nobotte-kimashita.**
きのう富士山に登ってきました。
Yesterday I went climbing Mt. Fuji.

B: **Sō desu ka.**
そうですか。
Is that so?

Since **Sō desu ka** そうですか is just a response and not a real question (though it looks like a question, with **ka** か at the end), pronounce it with a falling intonation. If it is pronounced with a rising intonation, it becomes a genuine question meaning "Is what you've just said really so?" You would then sound as though you were questioning the other person's credibility.

Also remember that, in Japanese, **Sō desu ka** そうですか is probably used much more often than "Is that so?" in English. The reason is that **Sō desu ka** does not have many variants, while "Is that so?" does. Consider the following examples in English:

EXAMPLES:

(2) A: He's a great athlete.
B: Is he?

(3) A: My wife left for Europe yesterday.
B: Did she?

(4) A: Mr. Smith can speak Japanese, you know.
B: Can he?

All the responses above would be **Sō desu ka** そうですか in Japanese.

Sō desu ka そうですか does have a few variants, however, one being **Hontō desu ka** 本当ですか (lit., "Is that a truth?"). **Hontō desu ka**, as explained by Jorden (1, p. 29), "indicates livelier interest and greater surprise." It should, like **Sō desu ka**, be pronounced with a falling intonation unless you wish to indicate doubt.

Su⌈go⌉i すごい *terrific*

Sugoi すごい used to be nothing more than an adjective, as in

EXAMPLES:

(1a) **Ano josei wa sugoi bijin da.**
あの女性はすごい美人だ。
That woman is a striking beauty.

(1b) **Sugoi ame da ne.**
すごい雨だね。
Isn't this an awful downpour!

Nowadays, in colloquial Japanese, it is sometimes used as an adverb as well, as in (2).

EXAMPLE:

(2) **Kono kēki sugoi oishii ne.**
このケーキすごいおいしいね。
Doesn't this cake taste great?

In traditional speech, **sugoku oishii** すごくおいしい used to be the norm. Even today, **sugoi** すごい as an adverb is still substandard, but it is becoming quite common among young people speaking casually.

Su⌈ki⌉ 好き *to like*

Although **suki** 好き is a **na**-noun and not a verb, it often corresponds to the English verb "like." It is probably used more commonly in reference to things than persons.

EXAMPLE:

(1) **Wakai hito wa sakana yori niku no hō ga suki desu.**
若い人は魚より肉の方が好きです。
Young people like meat better than fish.

Although **suki** 好き may be used concerning people, as in (2) below, other expressions such as **ii** いい "good, nice" are probably used more frequently, as in (3), to express the same idea.

EXAMPLES:

(2) **Kimi no otō-san ga suki da.**
君のお父さんが好きだ。
I like your father.

(3) **Kimi no otō-san ii hito da ne.**
君のお父さんいい人だね。
lit., Your father is a nice man.

This is, I suspect, due to Japanese speakers' preference for describing a person objectively over mentioning their subjective feelings toward him. In fact, **suki** 好き used with reference to a person often means more than just "like." It means "love."

EXAMPLE:
(4) Man: **Kimi ga suki da.**
君が好きだ。
I love you.
Woman: **Watashi mo anata ga suki yo.**
私もあなたが好きよ。
I love you too. (For Japanese expressions of love, see AISURU.)

Suki 好き, unlike English "like," cannot refer to momentary liking. American students of Japanese misuse the word when they ignore this distinction. In English, one can say, for example,

EXAMPLE:
(5) I liked the movie I saw yesterday.

In Japanese, on the other hand, **suki** 好き cannot be used in such a context.

EXAMPLE:
(6) ***Kinō mita eiga ga suki datta.**
*きのう見た映画が好きだった。
lit., I liked the movie I saw yesterday.

Instead, one would have to say something like

EXAMPLE:
(7) **Kinō mita eiga wa yokatta (or omoshirokatta).**
きのう見た映画はよかった（面白かった）。
The movie I saw yesterday was good (or fun).

Suki 好き refers to liking something over a longer period of time, for example:

EXAMPLES:
(8) **Eiga ga suki desu.**
映画が好きです。
I like movies.
(9) **Kinō mita yō na eiga ga suki desu.**
きのう見たような映画が好きです。
I like movies such as the one I saw yesterday.

Su⌐ko⌐shi 少し *a little, a few, some*

Unlike **sukunai** 少ない "little, few," **sukoshi** 少し has no negative overtone.

EXAMPLES:
(1) **Mada okane ga sukoshi aru.**
まだお金が少しある。
I still have a little money.

(2) **Kinō wa ōki na hon'ya e itta no de, sukoshi hon o katta.**
きのうは大きな本屋へ行ったので、少し本を買った。
Since I went to a large bookstore yesterday, I bought some books.

Since **sukoshi** 少し itself does not carry a negative connotation, in order to convey the idea of "not many" with **sukoshi**, one has to place the word in negative constructions, such as **shika ... nai** しか...ない.

EXAMPLE:

(3) **Kyō wa gakusei ga sukoshi shika konakatta.**
今日は学生が少ししか来なかった。
Only a few students came today.

Sentence (3) is very similar in meaning to (4).

EXAMPLE:

(4) **Kyō kita gakusei wa sukunakatta.**
今日来た学生は少なかった。
The number of students who came today was small.

Note that in order to express the same idea, **sukoshi** 少し has to be placed in a negative sentence, whereas **sukunai** 少ない, which carries a negative overtone, does not (see SUKUNAI).

Su⌈ku⌉nai 少ない *little, few*

Sukunai 少ない is the opposite of **ōi** 多い "much, many" (see ŌI) and carries the negative overtone of "not much, not many."

EXAMPLES:

(1) **Nihon ni wa yuden ga sukunai.**
日本には油田が少ない。
Japan has few oil fields.

(2) **Mochigane mo sukunaku-natta.**
持ち金も少なくなった。
I don't have much money left with me.

As is the case with **ōi** 多い, **sukunai** 少ない cannot directly modify a noun that follows. For example, ***sukunai hon** 少ない本 does not normally mean "few books." Therefore, to express "I have few books," one cannot say

EXAMPLE:

(3) ***Sukunai hon o motte-imasu.**
*少ない本を持っています。

The above sentence should be changed, for example, to

EXAMPLE:

(4) **Watashi ga motte-iru hon wa sukunai desu.**
私が持っている本は少ないです。
lit., The books I have are few.

The combination **sukunai hon** 少ない本 can occur, however, in environments such as (5), where the item that is scarce is not the **hon** 本 "book" but something else.

EXAMPLE:

(5) **Kore wa goshoku no sukunai hon desu.**
これは誤植の少ない本です。
This is a book with few misprints.

Su⌈mimase⌉n すみません *I'm sorry; thank you.*

Sumimasen すみません is basically a form of apology. If a student is scolded by his/her teacher, the best thing to do is to bow, saying **Sumimasen** ("I'm sorry").

Sumimasen is increasingly used as an expression of thanks, too. If someone gives you a gift, you accept it with a bow, saying **Dōmo sumimasen** どうもすみません ("Thank you very much"). Although purists are against this use—saying that a word of apology should not be used to express gratitude—it is so common nowadays that no one can stem the tide. The reason this has happened is because in the minds of Japanese people, apologizing and thanking are very similar. The Japanese apologize when they have done something wrong and feel they have to repay for that; they express gratitude when someone does something for them for which they feel they have to repay. Both involve the feeling of owing something to someone.

Incidentally, in English, it is perfectly in accordance with decorum to say "Pardon me?" or "I beg your pardon?" when one fails to catch what someone has just said. However, do not translate this into *Sumimasen? すみません? when you are speaking Japanese. The most common expression in that case would be **Ha?** は? in formal speech, and **E?** え? in informal speech. In other words, if you want a higher-status person to repeat, say **Ha?**, and if you want a friend to repeat, say **E?** Even though this **Ha?** unfortunately sounds somewhat like English "Huh?", it is a polite expression which is totally acceptable. You must not feel shy about using it.

Sumō 相撲 *sumo wrestling; sumo wrestler*

Sumō 相撲 means both "sumo wrestling," as in (1), and "professional sumo wrestler," as in (2).

EXAMPLES:

(1) **Sumō wa, suru supōtsu to iu yori, miru supōtsu da.**
相撲は、するスポーツというより、見るスポーツだ。
Sumo is a spectator sport rather than a participatory sport.

(2) **Chiyonofuji wa rippa na sumō datta.**
千代の富士は立派な相撲だった。
Chiyonofuji was a great sumo wrestler.

In the second sense, **sumō** 相撲 may be replaced by **sumōtori** 相撲取り (lit., "person who does sumo"), **rikishi** 力士, or **osumōsan** お相撲さん. Of these three, the last one is the most colloquial version.

Su⌐mu 住む *to live [somewhere]*

Sumu 住む is usually translated as "live" (in the sense of "to reside"), but it does not function exactly like "live." For example, **Nihon ni sumimasu** 日本に住みます, literally "I live in Japan," does not actually mean "I live in Japan." To express "I live in Japan," one must use the gerund form.

EXAMPLE:

(1) **Nihon ni sunde-imasu.**
日本に住んでいます。
I live in Japan.

Nihon ni sumimasu 日本に住みます would only mean "I am going to live in Japan."

English "live" means both "to reside" and "to be alive." **Sumu** 住む, however, does not cover this second meaning. In Japanese, this meaning is expressed by another verb, **ikiru** 生きる.

EXAMPLE:

(2) **Chichi wa mō nakunarimashita ga, haha wa mada ikite-imasu** (not *sunde-imasu 住んでいます).
父はもう亡くなりましたが、母はまだ生きています。
My father is already dead, but my mother is still living.

Suru する *to do*

In English, "do" is both a real verb, as in (1), and an auxiliary verb used in place of another verb, as in (2), where "do" replaces the verb "drink."

EXAMPLES:

(1) I do my homework every day.
(2) My wife drinks coffee, and I do too.

Japanese **suru** する, on the other hand, functions only as a real verb and cannot by itself function in replacement of another verb. **Suru** is therefore correct in sentence (3) but not in (4).

EXAMPLES:

(3) **Mainichi shukudai o suru.**
毎日宿題をする。
I do my homework every day.
(4) **Kanai mo kōhī o nomu shi, watashi mo nomu** (not *suru する).
家内もコーヒーを飲むし、私も飲む。
My wife drinks coffee, and I drink coffee too.

Suru する as a verb, however, has a great variety of uses, many of which do not correspond to the uses of English "do."

EXAMPLES:

(5) **Aoi kao o shite-iru.** (appearances)
青い顔をしている。
He looks pale. (lit., He is doing a pale face.)

(6) **Isha o shite-iru.** (occupations)
医者をしている。
He is a doctor. (lit., He is doing a doctor.)

(7) **Yoku seki o suru.** (physiological phenomena)
よく咳をする。
He often coughs. (lit., He often does a cough.)

(8) **Nekutai o shite-iru.** (certain items to wear)
ネクタイをしている。
He is wearing a necktie. (lit., He is doing a necktie.)

(9) **Mainichi tenisu o suru.** (activities)
毎日テニスをする。
He plays tennis every day. (lit., He does tennis every day.)

In addition to functioning as a transitive verb, as in the above sentences, **suru** する is also used as an intransitive verb, as in the following:

EXAMPLES:

(10) **Hen na oto ga suru.**
変な音がする。
I hear a strange sound.

(11) **Nan ni suru?** (at a restaurant, asking a family member)
何にする？
What will you have?

Suru する is an extremely convenient word in that it can create new verbs by being attached to nouns. This is particularly the case with the ever-increasing number of verbs based on loanwords, e.g., **hassuru-suru** ハッスルする "to hustle" (i.e., "to move about briskly") and **taipu-suru** タイプする "to type" (Morita, pp. 248–55).

Suwaru 座る *to sit down*

"Sitting down" in general is **suwaru** 座る whether one sits on a floor or in a chair. There is another verb (**koshi**) **kakeru** (腰)掛ける, which means "sit down (in a chair, on a bench, sofa, etc.)" but not "sit down on a floor." In the following examples, therefore, **koshika-keta** 腰掛けた is correct in (1a), but not in (1b).

EXAMPLES:

(1a) **Sofā ni suwatta** (or **koshikaketa**).
ソファーに座った（腰掛けた）。
I sat down on the sofa.

(1b) **Tatami ni suwatta** (not *****koshikaketa** 腰掛けた).
畳に座った。
I sat down on the tatami.

Suwaru 座る is a verb expressing the momentary action of sitting down. **Suwatte-iru** 座っている, therefore, does not mean "someone is in the process of sitting down," but rather "someone is in the state of having sat down," i.e., someone is in a sitting position. **Koshikakeru** 腰掛ける also is a momentary verb and is used likewise.

EXAMPLE:

(2) **Asoko ni suwatte-iru** (or **koshikakete-iru**) **hito wa Ōyama-san ja nai deshō ka.**
あそこに座っている（腰掛けている）人は大山さんじゃないでしょうか。
Isn't that Ms. Oyama sitting over there?

(See also KAKERU.)

Su⌐zushi¹i 涼しい *[pleasantly] cool*

In English, "cool" does not always refer to a pleasant temperature. **Suzushii** 涼しい, on the other hand, always does. **Suzushii** therefore may be construed as corresponding to "pleasantly cool" rather than "cool" by itself.

Another important difference between "cool" and **suzushii** is that **suzushii** may not modify nouns that represent solids and fluids, whereas "cool" may. Of the following examples, therefore, (1) and (2) are correct, but (3) and (4) are not.

EXAMPLES:

(1) **suzushii kaze**
涼しい風
a [pleasantly] cool wind
(2) **suzushii tenki**
涼しい天気
[pleasantly] cool weather
(3) ***suzushii nomimono**
*涼しい飲み物
something cool to drink
(4) ***tēburu no suzushii hyōmen**
*テーブルの涼しい表面
the cool surface of the table

To make (3) and (4) correct, one would have to use **tsumetai** 冷たい "cold" (see TSU-METAI) instead of **suzushii** 涼しい.

Like other temperature-related adjectives such as **samui** 寒い "cold" (see SAMUI), **atatakai** 暖かい "warm" (see ATATAKAI), and **atsui** 暑い "hot" (see ATSUI), **suzushii** 涼しい is closely connected with the change of seasons in Japan. **Suzushii** is tied with **aki** 秋 "fall," just as **samui** "cold" and **fuyu** 冬 "winter," **atatakai** "warm" and **haru** 春 "spring," and **atsui** "hot" and **natsu** 夏 "summer" are inseparable pairs. **Suzushii** is most appropriately used when there is a pleasant drop in temperature following a hot day or a hot season. One says **Suzushii desu nē** 涼しいですねえ "Isn't it nice and cool!" when, for example, there is a cool breeze at the end of a hot summer day, or when there is a nice cool day after the long hot summer months. In this sense, **suzushii** is different from "cool," which represents a temperature range between "cold" and "warm" and may be used regardless of preceding temperatures.

Tabako たばこ, タバコ *cigarette*

Since **tabako** たばこ, タバコ came into Japanese from Portuguese so long ago (i.e., in the 16th century), the fact that it was originally a foreign word is no longer felt very strongly. That is the reason **tabako** is often written in hiragana (as たばこ) instead of in katakana (タバコ), which is used for more recent loanwords.

    Tabako たばこ, タバコ originally meant "tobacco," but nowadays it usually refers to cigarettes, since they are the most common form of smoking material now.

    The verb for "to smoke [a cigarette, tobacco, a cigar, etc.]" is **nomu** のむ (lit., "to swallow") or **sū** 吸う (lit., "to inhale").

EXAMPLE:

Anmari tabako o nomu (or **sū**) **no wa karada ni yokunai.**
あんまりタバコをのむ（吸う）のは体によくない。
Smoking too much is not good for the health.

Ta⌐bemo⌐no 食べ物 *food*

The difference between **tabemono** 食べ物 and "food" is that **tabemono** implies "prepared food" while the English equivalent does not. For example, uncooked rice is "food" but not **tabemono**. In English, you go to the supermarket to buy groceries or food. In Japanese, on the other hand, you go to the supermarket to buy **shokuryōhin** 食料品 (or **shokuhin** 食品) "groceries," not **tabemono**.

EXAMPLES:

(1) A: **Donna tabemono ga suki desu ka.**
      どんな食べ物が好きですか。
      What kind of food do you like?
    B: **Yappari sushi desu ne.**
      やっぱり寿司ですね。
      Sushi (as might be expected).

(2) **Nihonjin wa mainichi no yō ni shokuryōhin** (not ***tabemono** 食べ物) **o kai ni iku.**
    日本人は毎日のように食料品を買いに行く。
    Japanese people go grocery shopping almost every day.

Ta⌐be⌐ru 食べる *to eat*

Taberu 食べる means "to eat," but there are at least two usage differences between **taberu** and "eat." First, as a rule, one "eats" soup in English but "drinks" it in Japanese.

EXAMPLE:

(1) **Nihon no inaka de wa maiasa misoshiru o nomu** (not ***taberu** 食べる).
    日本の田舎では毎朝味噌汁を飲む。
    In rural areas in Japan, they have (lit., drink) miso soup every morning.

    Second, in English, one may either "have" or "eat" a meal. In Japanese, one "does" a meal.

EXAMPLE:

(2) **Nihonjin wa futsū mainichi san-do shokuji o suru/toru** (not ***taberu** 食べる).
    日本人は普通毎日三度食事をする/取る。
    Japanese usually have (lit., do) three meals a day.

(However, if **gohan** ご飯 is used instead of **shokuji** 食事 to mean "meal," **taberu** 食べる is the correct verb, as in **Mō gohan o tabemashita** もうご飯を食べました "I've already eaten a meal.")

Tabitabi たびたび, 度々 *often, frequently*

Tabitabi たびたび is synonymous with such words as **yoku** よく and **shibashiba** しばしば.

EXAMPLE:

(1) **Nihon de wa tabitabi (yoku, shibashiba) jishin ga aru.**
日本ではたびたび(よく、しばしば)地震がある。
They often have earthquakes in Japan.

Of these three, **yoku** よく is the most commonly used, **tabitabi** たびたび comes in second, and **shibashiba** しばしば is definitely reserved for writing. **Tabitabi** and **shibashiba** are nothing more than frequency words, but **yoku** can mean other things such as "well" (see YOKU). The following sentence is correct with any of the three words, but **yoku** may imply more than **tabitabi** and **shibashiba**.

EXAMPLE:

(2) **Nihonkai-engan wa tabitabi (shibashiba, yoku) yuki ga furu.**
日本海沿岸はたびたび(しばしば、よく)雪が降る。
Along the Japan Sea, it often snows.

While **tabitabi** たびたび and **shibashiba** しばしば simply refer to the frequency of the snowfalls, **yoku yuki ga furu** よく雪が降る may imply "it snows a lot" as well as "it often snows."

-Tachi たち *(pluralizing suffix)*

-Tachi たち is a pluralizing suffix.

EXAMPLE:

(1) **gakusei-tachi**
学生たち
students

It may not be attached to nouns representing inanimate objects, nor is it added to nouns referring to animate beings other than humans. Therefore, (2) and (3) below are incorrect.

EXAMPLES:

(2) **hon-tachi*
*本たち
books
(3) **inu-tachi*
*犬たち
dogs

The use of **-tachi** たち is often not obligatory. It is dropped when its absence does not make the meaning of the sentence unclear.

EXAMPLE:

(4) **Kodomo** (not **Kodomo-tachi* 子供たち) **ga futari imasu.**
子供がふたりいます。
I have two children.

-Tachi たち is different from the pluralizing suffix, "-s," in English in that it often means "and [the] others."

EXAMPLES:

(5) **Tanaka-san-tachi ga kita.**
田中さんたちが来た。
Mr. Tanaka and the others (not *the Tanakas*) *have arrived.*

(6) **Hayaku chichi-tachi ni kore o mise-tai.**
早く父たちにこれを見せたい。
I'd like to show this to my father and the others (i.e., *my mother and/or the other members of my family*) *at once.*

Ta⌈daima⌉ ただいま *I'm home!*

Tadaima ただいま is a greeting used by a person who has just come home. In other words, it is an announcement of one's arrival at home. **Tadaima** is an abbreviation of **Tadaima kaerimashita** ただいま帰りました (lit., "I have returned just now"). Although this original sentence is still sometimes used on formal occasions, among family members it is almost always shortened to **Tadaima**, and most speakers are not even conscious of the original meaning of the word (i.e., "just now"), especially because the accent has changed. In the original sentence, the word is accented on the second syllable, whereas when used alone to mean "I'm home!" the accent shifts to the last syllable.

   Tadaima ただいま is used every time one arrives home from school, work, shopping, or other outings, and the other members of the family respond to it by saying **Okaeri-nasai** お帰りなさい meaning "Welcome home!" (see OKAERI-NASAI).

Taihen たいへん, 大変 *very, terrible, tremendous*

Taihen たいへん, like **totemo** とても (see TOTEMO), means "very."

EXAMPLE:

(1) **Kono natsu wa taihen** (or **totemo**) **atsukatta.**
この夏はたいへん（とても）暑かった。
This summer was very hot.

Taihen たいへん used in this sense sounds more formal than **totemo** とても, which is relatively colloquial.

   Taihen 大変 is sometimes used by itself or with **da** だ to mean "Something terrible has happened!" It is like an interjection.

EXAMPLE:

(2) **Taihen da! Kaban o wasureta!**
大変だ！カバンを忘れた！
Good heavens! I forgot my briefcase!

   When **taihen** 大変 modifies a noun, **na** な comes in between. As a noun modifier, **taihen na** 大変な (somewhat like English "tremendous") may have either a good or a bad connotation, depending on the context.

EXAMPLES:

(3) **taihen na gochisō**
大変なごちそう
a tremendous feast

(4) **taihen na atsusa**
大変な暑さ
tremendous heat

Taiken 体験 *experience*

Keiken 経験 is the most frequently used word for "experience," as in

EXAMPLES:

(1a) **Ano kaisha wa, keiken no jūbun na hito shika yatowanai sō da.**
あの会社は、経験の十分な人しか雇わないそうだ。
That company hires only people with sufficient experience, I hear.

(1b) **Gaikokujin ni Nihongo o oshieta keiken ga arimasu ka.**
外国人に日本語を教えた経験がありますか。
Have you had any experience in teaching Japanese to foreigners?

Taiken 体験 also means "experience," but it emphasizes the fact that something was experienced "with one's own body," i.e., firsthand.

EXAMPLE:

(2) **Sensō o taiken-shite miru to, sensō no kowasa ga wakaru yō ni naru.**
戦争を体験してみると、戦争の怖さが分かるようになる。
By experiencing war firsthand, one begins to understand its horrors.

Keiken 経験 could be used in (2), too, but then the sentence would just mean "by living through war," whereas **taiken** 体験 would bring up more vivid images of bombings and other horrors.

Taisetsu 大切 *important*

Taisetsu 大切 is quite similar to **daiji** 大事.

EXAMPLE:

(1) **Ichiban taisetsu (or daiji) na hito wa jibun no hahaoya da to omotte-iru hito wa ōi darō.**
いちばん大切（大事）な人は自分の母親だと思っている人は多いだろう。
I'm sure there are lots of people who think their mother is the most important person.

As the above example indicates, **taisetsu** 大切 (or **daiji** 大事) is subjective, i.e., important to a particular person. In other words, if someone is **taisetsu** to you, you consider him/her dear to your heart. **Taisetsu** (or **daiji**) **na mono** 大切（大事）なもの is something you cherish.

Jūyō 重要 also means "important," but it is objective rather than subjective and signifies "important in terms of a specific role," as in

EXAMPLE:

(2) **Mishima Yukio wa, Shōwa no bungakushi-jō jūyō** (not ***taisetsu/daiji** 大切/大事) **na sakka de atta.**
三島由紀夫は、昭和の文学史上重要な作家であった。
Yukio Mishima was an important writer in terms of the literary history of the Showa period.

Since sentence (2) concerns Mishima's importance in terms of his role in the literary history of Showa, **jūyō** 重要 is more appropriate than **taisetsu/daiji** 大切/大事.

Taisetsu and **daiji** are often used with **ni suru** にする, but **jūyō** is never used that way, e.g.

EXAMPLE:

(3) **Ningen wa karada o taisetsu/daiji** (not ***jūyō** 重要) **ni shinakereba ikenai.**
人間は体を 大切/大事 にしなければいけない。
One must take care of oneself (lit., one's body).

Ta⌐ka⌐i 高い *expensive, high, tall*

Takai 高い meaning "expensive" is the opposite of **yasui** 安い"inexpensive."

EXAMPLE:

(1) **Anmari takai kara, kaemasen.**
あんまり高いから、買えません。
I can't buy it because it's too expensive.

Regarding height, **takai** 高い means "high" or "tall." When used in this sense, **takai** is the opposite of **hikui** 低い "low, short."

EXAMPLES:

(2) **takai tana**
高い棚
high shelf

(3) **Hikōki ga takai tokoro o tonde-iru.**
飛行機が高いところを飛んでいる。
There's an airplane flying high up in the sky.

(4) **takai yama**
高い山
high mountain

(5) **Asoko ni mieru ki wa zuibun takai desu nē.**
あそこに見える木はずいぶん高いですねえ。
The tree we can see over there is very tall, isn't it!

To describe someone as being tall, we usually use **se ga takai** 背が高い (lit., "the height is tall") instead of **takai** 高い by itself.

EXAMPLE:

(6) **Jonson-san wa se ga takai.**
ジョンソンさんは背が高い。
Mr. Johnson is tall. (lit., Mr. Johnson's height is tall.)

To the surprise of English speakers, **takai** 高い is also used in reference to some parts of the face when they protrude more than normal.

EXAMPLES:

(7) **takai hana**
高い鼻
long nose (lit., high nose)

(8) **takai hōbone**
高いほお骨
protruding cheekbones (lit., high cheek bones)

Takusan たくさん *a lot, enough*

Takusan たくさん means "a lot" in the sense of "a great number" or "a great amount."

EXAMPLES:

(1) **Asoko ni hito ga takusan iru.**
あそこに人がたくさんいる。
There are a lot of people over there.

(2) **Hon o takusan kaita.**
本をたくさん書いた。
I wrote a lot of books.

When **takusan** たくさん precedes a noun, **no** の is required in between.

EXAMPLE:

(3) **Takusan no hon o kaita.**
たくさんの本を書いた。
I wrote a lot of books.

The pattern used in (3), however, is not as common as that used in (1) and (2), where **takusan** たくさん follows a noun with a particle in between.

Takusan たくさん also means "enough." When used in this sense, it is often preceded by **mō** もう "already."

EXAMPLES:

(4) **Sore dake areba, takusan desu.**
それだけあれば、たくさんです。
If I have that much, it should be enough.

(5) **Konna hanashi wa mō takusan da.**
こんな話はもうたくさんだ。
I don't want to hear that kind of thing any more. (lit., I've already had enough of this kind of talk.)

Takusan たくさん meaning "enough" does not normally precede a noun. (See also ŌI).

Ta⌐ni⌐ 谷 *valley*

Although **tani** 谷 is usually equated with English "valley," there is definitely a difference between the two. A valley can be either quite narrow or fairly wide, often corresponding to what one might call a **bonchi** 盆地 "basin" in Japanese. A **tani**, on the other hand, is always a very narrow space between mountains with no or little flat area to speak of.

Ta⌐no⌐mu 頼む *to request; ask (a favor)*

English "ask" has two basic meanings: "request," as in "I asked him to help me," or "inquire," as in "I asked him about his job." Japanese **tanomu** 頼む, on the other hand, may be used for "request," but not for "inquire."

EXAMPLES:
(1) **Watashi wa, tasukete kureru yō ni to kare ni tanonda.**
私は、助けてくれるようにと彼に頼んだ。
I asked him to help me.
(2) **Watashi wa, kare no shigoto ni tsuite kiita** (not *tanonda 頼んだ).
私は、彼の仕事について聞いた。
I asked him a question about his job.

Ta⌐noshi⌐i 楽しい *happy, enjoyable*

An experience one enjoys makes one feel **tanoshii** 楽しい.

EXAMPLES:
(1) **Gakusei-seikatsu wa tanoshii.**
学生生活は楽しい。
Student life makes me happy. (or I'm enjoying student life.)
(2) **Tomodachi to hito-ban-jū nondari hanashitari-shite tanoshi katta.**
友達と一晩中飲んだり話したりして楽しかった。
I was happy to spend the whole night drinking and talking with my friend.
(or I enjoyed drinking and talking with my friend all night.)

Tanoshii 楽しい refers to a sustained state of happiness. To express a momentary state of joy, use **ureshii** うれしい "glad, joyous."

EXAMPLE:
(3) A: **Shiken ni pasu-shita toki wa donna kimochi deshita ka.**
試験にパスした時はどんな気持ちでしたか。
How did you feel when you passed the exam?
  B: **Ureshikatta** (not *tanoshikatta 楽しかった) **desu.**
うれしかったです。
I was happy.

Tanoshii 楽しい represents a sense of happiness due to one's own experience. Simply receiving the news of a happy event, for example, does not make one **tanoshii**.

EXAMPLE:
(4) **Betonamu-sensō ga owatta nyūsu o kiite ureshikatta** (not *tanoshikatta 楽しかった).
ベトナム戦争が終わったニュースを聞いてうれしかった。
I was happy to hear the news that the Vietnam War was over.

Tanoshii 楽しい, as a rule, refers to the speaker's happy feeling, and no one else's. That is why sentence (5) is right while (6) is wrong.

EXAMPLES:
(5) **Watashi wa mainichi tanoshii.**
私は毎日楽しい。
I am happy every day.

(6)   *Kojima-san wa mainichi tanoshii.
      *児島さんは毎日楽しい。
      Mr. Kojima is happy every day.

In Japanese, one just cannot make a definite statement like (5) about someone else's feeling unless one is a novelist manipulating a character in a novel. To convey the idea of "Mr. Kojima is happy every day" in Japanese, one would have to say one of the following:

EXAMPLE:

(7)   **Kojima-san wa mainichi**   (a)   **tanoshi-sō da.**
      児島さんは   楽しそうだ。

                                         (b)   **tanoshii rashii.**
                                                楽しいらしい。

                                         (b)   **tanoshii yō da.**
                                                楽しいようだ。

      Mr. Kojima looks (or *seems*) *happy every day.*

This is true of other adjectives of emotion, such as **kanashii** 悲しい "sad," **sabishii** 寂しい "lonely," and **ureshii** うれしい "happy."

Ta⌈ore⌉ru 倒れる *to fall (over); collapse*

Taoreru 倒れる may be used for either animate beings that are standing or inanimate objects, as in

EXAMPLES:

(1a) **Densha no naka de, mae ni tatte-ita hito ga kyū ni taoreta node bikkuri-shita.**
      電車の中で、前に立っていた人が急に倒れたのでびっくりした。
      I was surprised on the train when someone standing in front of me suddenly collapsed.

(1b) **Taifū de ki ga nan-bon mo taoreta.**
      台風で木が何本も倒れた。
      A lot of trees fell because of the typhoon.

   Korobu 転ぶ is also translated as "fall," but it is used only for animate beings that are in motion, e.g., walking, running, etc.

EXAMPLE:

(2)   **Yuki no hi wa, subette korobu** (not *taoreru 倒れる) **hito ga ōi.**
      雪の日には、滑って転ぶ人が多い。
      On a snowy day, lots of people slip and fall.

   In sentence (2), **taoreru** 倒れる, which refers to the falling of someone who is standing, cannot be used.

Ta⌉shika たしか, 確か *certain; if I remember correctly*

When **tashika** 確か is used as a **na**-adjective, it means "sure, certain, definite."

EXAMPLES:

(1a) **Sore wa tashika na koto da.**
      それは確かな事だ。
      That's a sure thing.

(1b) **Tōkyō no natsu ga mushiatsui no wa tashika da.**
東京の夏が蒸し暑いのは確かだ。
It is certain that summer in Tokyo is muggy.

When **tashika** たしか is used as an adverb, the meaning changes to "if I remember correctly."

EXAMPLE:
(2) A: **Tōkyō no jinkō wa dono gurai desu ka.**
東京の人口はどのぐらいですか。
What's the population of Tokyo?

   B: **Tashika issenman gurai da to omoimasu ga.**
確か一千万ぐらいだと思いますよ。
If I remember correctly, it's about 10,100,000.

Don't confuse this adverbial use with **tashika ni** たしかに "certainly."

EXAMPLE:
(3) **Tōkyō wa tashika ni daitoshi da.**
東京はたしかに大都市だ。
Tokyo is certainly a big city.

Tassha 達者 *healthy; skillful*

Tassha 達者 has two meanings. First, it means "healthy," as in

EXAMPLE:
(1) **Goryōshin wa otassha desu ka.**
ご両親はお達者ですか。
Are your parents well?

In this sense, it may be replaced by **(o) genki** (お)元気.
    Second, **tassha** 達者 means "skillful."

EXAMPLE:
(2) **Kobayashi-san wa Eigo ga tassha da.**
小林さんは英語が達者だ。
Mr. Kobayashi is good at English.

In this sense, **tassha** 達者 is synonymous with **jōzu** 上手.

Ta⌐suka⌐ru 助かる *to be saved, relieved, etc.*

Tasukaru 助かる is the intransitive counterpart of **tasukeru** 助ける "to help/to save (someone)" and is used mainly in reference to animate beings. There is no close one-word English equivalent.

EXAMPLES:
(1a) **Sensei ga ashita no shiken o yamete kureru to tasukaru n da keredo.**
先生が明日の試験をやめてくれると助かるんだけれど。
I wish our teacher would cancel tomorrow's exam. (Implication: We would be greatly relieved then.)

(1b) **Ani ga shukudai o tetsudatte kurete hontō ni tasukatta.**
兄が宿題を手伝ってくれて本当に助かった。
My brother helped me with my homework. That was a great help.

When something happens that gives us great relief, we mumble to ourselves:

EXAMPLE:

(2) **Aa, tasukatta!**
ああ、助かった！
Thank heaven!

Ta⌈suke⌉ru 助ける *to help*

Tasukeru 助ける is sometimes used in the sense of **tetsudau** 手伝う "to help [someone] do [something, such as chores]." For example, in sentence (1), either **tasukeru** or **tetsudau** may be used without much difference in meaning.

EXAMPLE:

(1) **Chichi no shigoto o tasukete-imasu** (or **tetsudatte-imasu**).
父の仕事を助けています（手伝っています）。
I am helping my father with his work.

Tasukeru 助ける meaning "to help [someone] do [something]," however, is usually reserved for more than mere chores. A mother who is doing the dishes, for example, is likely to say to her daughter

EXAMPLE:

(2) **Tetsudatte.** (rather than ***Tasukete** 助けて.)
手伝って。
Help me [with the dishes].

Tasukeru 助ける also means "to help" in the sense of "to save, to relieve, to rescue [someone]" or "to spare [someone's life]." **Tetsudau** 手伝う does not have such meanings, as in the following:

EXAMPLES:

(3) **Shinu tokoro o ano hito ni tasukerareta.**
死ぬところをあの人に助けられた。
I was saved (or rescued) by him from certain death.

(4) **Inochi dake wa tasukete-kudasai.**
命だけは助けてください。
Please spare my life.

(5) **Byōki ni kurushimu hitobito o tasukeru no ga isha no tsutome da.**
病気に苦しむ人々を助けるのが医者の務めだ。
It is the doctor's obligation to relieve those suffering from illness.

Likewise, if you are about to be drowned or if you are attacked by a mugger, yell out

EXAMPLE:

(6) **Tasukete!**
助けて！
Help!

If you yelled **Tetsudatte!** 手伝って, no one would come to your rescue!

Ta⌈taka⌉u 戦う *to fight; wage war; do battle*

Tatakau 戦う is a written expression and is not used in normal conversation. It is used for real battles or wars.

EXAMPLE:

(1) **Nihon wa Dainiji-taisen de Amerika o teki to-shite tatakatta.**
日本は第二次大戦でアメリカを敵として戦った。
In World War II, Japan fought the U.S. as its enemy.

Sentence (2) below sounds strange because **tatakau** 戦う is not used in the sense of "to quarrel" or "to have a fist fight."

EXAMPLE:

(2) *****Watashi wa ōki na hito to wa tatakawanai koto ni shite-imasu.**
*私は大きな人とは戦わないことにしています。
It's my policy not to fight big guys.

In this sense, use **kenka o suru** けんかをする "to have a fight" instead.

EXAMPLE:

(3) **Watashi wa ōki na hito to wa kenka o shinai koto ni shite-imasu.**
私は大きな人とはけんかしないことにしています。
It's my policy not to fight big guys.

Ta⌈temo⌉no 建物 *building*

Tatemono 建物 literally means "built thing" and is a generic term for buildings in general, whether they are Japanese style or Western style. **Birudingu** ビルディング (from English "building"), or more often **biru** ビル for short, on the other hand, refers only to large Western-style buildings.

Ta⌈te⌉ru 建てる *to build*

English "build" may be used for all kinds of things: one may build a bridge, house, road, ship, dam, etc. All of these require different verbs in Japanese unless one uses **tsukuru** 作る "make." **Tateru** 建てる "build," however, has a limited use. You can say **ie/biru/apāto o tateru** 家/ビル/アパートを建てる "build a house/building/apartment house," but for other things such as **hashi** 橋 "bridge," **dōro** 道路 "road," **fune** 船 "ship," and **damu** ダム "dam," you need other verbs such as **kensetsu-suru** 建設する and **kenzō-suru** 建造する.

EXAMPLES:

(1) **hashi/dōro/damu o kensetsu-suru/tsukuru**
橋/道路/ダムを建設する/つくる
build/make a bridge/road/dam

(2) **fune o kenzō-suru/tsukuru**
船を建造する/作る
build/make a ship

Tazuneru 訪ねる, 尋ねる *to visit; inquire*

Tazuneru is written in two different kanji, depending on the meaning. First, if it's written 訪ねる, it means "to visit someone or some place."

EXAMPLES:

(1a) **Ōsaka e itta toki, Yamada-san o tazuneta.**
大阪へ行った時、山田さんを訪ねた。
When I went to Osaka, I visited Mr. Yamada.

(1b) **Watashi wa kyonen 50-nen-buri de Nara o tazuneta.**
私は去年50年ぶりで奈良を訪ねた。
Last year I visited Nara for the first time in fifty years.

Tazuneru 訪ねる is a formal expression. The above sentences would become more colloquial if changed as follows:

EXAMPLES:

(2a) **Ōsaka e itta toki, Yamada-san ni ai ni itta.**
大阪へ行った時、山田さんに会いに行った。
When I went to Osaka, I went to see Mr. Yamada.

(2b) **Watashi wa kyonen 50-nen-buri de Nara e itta.**
私は去年50年ぶりで奈良へ行った。
Last year I went to Nara for the first time in fifty years.

Second, if written 尋ねる, **tazuneru** means "to inquire," as in

EXAMPLE:

(3) **Tanaka-san ni tazune-tai koto ga atte, denwa o kaketa.**
田中さんに尋ねたいことがあって、電話をかけた。
I called Mr. Tanaka to inquire about something.

Tazuneru 尋ねる is also a formal expression. In normal conversation, **kiku** 聞く is used far more often, as in

EXAMPLE:

(4) **Tanaka-san ni kiki-tai koto ga atte, denwa o kaketa.**
田中さんに聞きたいことがあって、電話をかけた。
I called Mr. Tanaka to ask about something.

Te¹nki 天気 *weather*

Don't confuse **tenki** 天気 "weather" with **kikō** 気候 "climate." **Tenki** is short range, while **kikō** is long range. Therefore, **tenki** is correct in (1a), but not in (1b).

EXAMPLES:

(1a) **Kyō no tenki** (not *kikō 気候) **wa hare nochi kumori da sō da.**
今日の天気は晴れのち曇りだそうだ。
They say today's weather will be sunny first and cloudy later.

(1b) **Kariforunia no kikō** (not *tenki 天気) **wa ichi-nen-jū ondan da.**
カリフォルニアの気候は一年中温暖だ。
California's climate is mild throughout the year.

American students of Japanese often make the following errors:

EXAMPLES:

(2a) ***Kyō wa atsui** (or **samui**) **tenki desu nē!**

　　*今日は暑い（寒い）天気ですねえ。

　　Don't we have pretty hot/cold weather today?

(2b) ***Kyō wa tenki ga atsui** (or **samui**) **desu nē!**

　　*今日は天気が暑い（寒い）ですねえ。

　　Isn't the weather pretty hot/cold today?

Unlike Enlish "weather," Japanese **tenki** 天気 basically goes with adjectives like **ii** いい "good" and **iya na** いやな "nasty," and not normally with **atsui** 暑い or **samui** 寒い. Instead of (2a)/(2b) above, say:

EXAMPLE:

(3)　**Kyō wa atsui** (or **samui**) **desu nē!**

　　今日は暑い（寒い）ですねえ。

　　Isn't it pretty hot/cold today?

The polite form of **tenki** 天気 is **otenki** お天気:

EXAMPLES:

(4)　**Kyō wa ii otenki da.**

　　今日はいいお天気だ。

　　We are having nice weather today.

(5)　**Iya na otenki desu nē.**

　　いやなお天気ですねえ。

　　Nasty weather, isn't it!

Interestingly enough, when used without specific modifiers such as **ii** いい "good" or **iya na** いやな "nasty," **tenki** 天気 sometimes means "good weather."

EXAMPLE:

(6)　**Ashita wa otenki ni naru deshō.**

　　あしたはお天気になるでしょう。

　　I think it's going to clear up tomorrow. (lit., It will probably become good weather tomorrow.)

This contrasts with English "weather," which, when used without "good" or "bad" modifying it, might mean "bad weather," as in "We have some weather coming our way."

To 戸 *door*

To 戸 has a wider range of meaning than **doa** ドア (from English "door"), which refers to Western-style doors only. Sliding doors such as those found at the entrance of a Japanese inn are therefore **to**, and not **doa**.

When one talks about doors of all kinds, both Japanese and Western, **to** is the term to be used.

EXAMPLE:

(1)　**Yoru neru mae ni ie-jū no to o kichinto shimete-kudasai.**

　　夜寝る前に家中の戸をきちんと閉めてください。

　　Before you go to bed, be sure to lock all doors in the house.

When one refers specifically to a Western-style door, **doa** ドア is more likely to be used than **to** 戸.

EXAMPLE:

(2) **Doa** (probably not *To 戸) **no nobu ga torete-shimatta.**
ドアのノブが取れてしまった。
The doorknob has fallen off.

Doors of a Western-style vehicle (e.g., **kuruma** 車 "car" or **erebētā** エレベーター "elevator") are also **doa** ドア rather than **to** 戸.

Tōi 遠い *far, distant*

Tōi 遠い can mean "far, distant" in terms of space, time, or relationships.

EXAMPLES:

(1) **Boku no uchi wa eki kara tōi.** (space)
僕のうちは駅から遠い。
My house is far from the station.
(2) **Sore wa tōi shōrai no koto da.** (time)
それは遠い将来の事だ。
That is a matter of the distant future.
(3) **Kare wa boku no tōi shinseki da.** (relationship)
彼は僕の遠い親戚だ。
He is a distant relative of mine.

In example (1) above, **kara** から "from" may be replaced by **made** まで "as far as," as in (4), with only a slight difference in meaning.

EXAMPLE:

(4) **Boku no uchi wa eki made tōi.**
僕のうちは駅まで遠い。
It is a long distance from my house to the station.

There are some interesting uses of **tōi** 遠い.

EXAMPLES:

(5) **Ano hito wa mimi ga tōi.**
あの人は耳が遠い。
He is hard of hearing. (lit., As for him, the ears are far, i.e., All sounds are like faraway sounds to him.)
(6) **Denwa ga tōi desu kara, ōki na koe de hanashite kudasai.**
電話が遠いですから、大きな声で話してください。
Since your voice on the phone is faint (lit., faraway), please talk louder.

To issho ni と一緒に *together with*

American students who have returned to the U.S. after a year's study in Japan often talk about their homestay experience as follows:

EXAMPLE:

(1) **?Nihonjin no hosutofamirī to issho ni sunde-imashita.**
?日本人のホストファミリーと一緒に住んでいました。
I was living with a Japanese host family.

This sentence, however, sounds very strange in Japanese. Basically **to issho ni** と一緒に is used when the two parties involved are on an equal footing. In sentence (2), for example, **to issho ni** is correctly used.

EXAMPLE:

(2) **Nihonjin no tomodachi to issho ni sunde-imashita.**
日本人の友達と一緒に住んでいました。
I was living with a Japanese friend.

When you do a homestay, however, you are a renter/boarder while the host family is the owner of the house. Sentences (3a) and (3b) therefore sound much more natural than sentence (1).

EXAMPLES:

(3a) **Nihonjin no hosutofamirī no ie** (or **tokoro**) **ni sunde-imashita.**
日本人のホストファミリーの家(ところ)に住んでいました。
I was living at the home of a Japanese host family.

(3b) **Nihonjin no ie de hōmusutei o shimashita.**
日本人の家でホームステイをしました。
I did a homestay at a Japanese home.

Tō˺ji [To˺oji] 当時 *in those days*

Tōji 当時, which means "in those days," refers to a period of time in the past—not in the recent past, but rather a number of years ago.

EXAMPLE:

(1) **Watashi wa jūni-sai no toki hatsukoi o shita. Tōji watashi wa chūgaku no ichi-nensei datta.**
私は十二歳の時初恋をした。当時私は中学の一年生だった。
I experienced my first love when I was twelve. In those days, I was a seventh grader.

Since **tōji** 当時 refers to a period of time, but not a point of time, it cannot be used in the following sentence.

EXAMPLE:

(2) **Kōkō-jidai no aru hi, watashi wa Ginza e kaimono ni itta no da ga, sono toki** (not **tōji 当時) **igai na hito ni atta.**
高校時代のある日、私は銀座へ買い物に行ったのだが、その時意外な人にあった。
One day when I was in high school, I went shopping in the Ginza; I bumped into an unexpected person then.

Tōji 当時 is replaceable by **sono koro** その頃 but is more formal than the latter.

To⌈ji⌉ru 閉じる *to close (something)*

For some objects, **shimeru** 閉める cannot be used to mean "to close (something)." **Tojiru** 閉じる must be used instead. Three good examples of those objects are **hon** 本 "book," **me** 目 "eye," and **kuchi** 口 "mouth."

EXAMPLES:

(1) **Hon o tojite** (not *shimete 閉めて) **kudasai.**
本を閉じてください。
Please close your book.

(2) **Zazen no toki wa, me o tojiru** (not *shimeru 閉める) **koto ni natte-iru.**
座禅のときは、目を閉じることになっている。
When you do zazen, *you are expected to close your eyes.*

(3) **Urusai ne. Kuchi o toji-nasai** (not *shime-nasai 閉めなさい).
うるさいね。口を閉じなさい。
You talk too much. Close your mouth.

Tokai 都会 *(big) city*

Tokai 都会 means "city," especially "big city," as in

EXAMPLE:

(1) **Watashi wa inaka yori tokai ni sumi-narete-iru.**
私は田舎より都会に住み慣れている。
I am more used to living in a big city than in a rural area.

Toshi 都市 also means "(big) city," but in speech it is rarely used by itself. Rather, it is more often used as part of a compound, as in

EXAMPLES:

(2a) **kōgyōtoshi** (not *tokai 都会)
工業都市
industrial city

(2b) **toshi** (not *tokai 都会) **keikaku**
都市計画
city planning

Tokei 時計 *watch, clock*

Any kind of timepiece is a **tokei** 時計. Both clocks and watches are usually called **tokei** unless it becomes necessary to make a distinction between them. When it is necessary, however, we say **ude-dokei** 腕時計 "wristwatch," **kaichū-dokei** 懐中時計 "pocket watch," **oki-dokei** 置き時計 (the kind of clock you might find on a mantlepiece), **mezamashi-dokei** 目覚まし時計 "alarm clock," etc.

To⌈ki⌉ 時 *time*

It seems that **toki** 時 tends to refer to a shorter time span than English "time." This is particularly true of the expression **sono toki** その時 (lit., "at that time") as compared with English "at that time." Suppose you have been talking about the early years of Meiji and now want to refer to the scarcity of Japanese who were familiar with English during that period. In English, you can use either (1a) or (1b) to express that idea.

EXAMPLES:
(1) | (a) In those days, | not too many Japanese spoke English.
| (b) At (*or* About) that time, |

In Japanese, on the other hand, **sono toki** その時 "at that time" would not be as appropriate as **sono koro** その頃 "about that time, in those days." (See also KORO.)

EXAMPLES:
(2) | (a) **Sono koro** その頃 | **eigo no dekiru Nihonjin wa sokunakatta.**
| (b) **?Sono toki** その時 | 英語の出来る日本人は少なかった。

Sono toki その時 is not quite appropriate, since the time referred to is a span of several years that is not clearly defined. If, however, the time referred to were more specific, e.g., the time of the departure of the Iwakura Mission for the United States in 1872, **sono toki** would be perfectly correct. (See also JIKAN.)

To⌈ko⌉rode ところで *by the way; incidentally*

Tokorode ところで is used when you change a conversational topic completely. Suppose you have been talking about something and suddenly want to talk about a new topic. **Tokorode** would be the right word to use.

EXAMPLE:
(1) (A and B talk about professional baseball first, but then A feels like talking about something else.)

A: **Jaiantsu makemashita ne.**
ジャイアンツ負けましたね。
The Giants lost, didn't they?

B: **Sō desu ne. Konogoro yoku makemasu ne.**
そうですね。このごろよく負けますね。
Yes, they did. They have been losing a lot of games lately.

A: **Tokorode, B-san. Konogoro gorufu no hō wa dō desuka.**
ところで、Bさん。このごろゴルフの方はどうですか。
On another note, Mr. B., how's your golf game these days?

Sate さて, too, is used to change topics and may be translated as "by the way" or "incidentally," but there are at least two differences between **sate** and **tokorode** ところで. First, **sate** is often used without a preceding conversation, i.e., just to indicate switching to a new action. Suppose you have been watching TV and suddenly decide to take a walk. You may mumble to yourself or someone around you,

EXAMPLE:
(2) **Sate** (not *****Tokorode** ところで) **sanpo ni dekakeyō ka.**
さて散歩に出かけましょうか。
Well, I guess I'll go for a walk now.

Second, **sate** さて indicates the conversation that is to follow is more important than the preceding one. For example, suppose you go to visit someone to talk business. At first, you just exchange small talk for a few minutes, talking about the weather or some timely events. You then wish to indicate the true intention of your visit.

EXAMPLE:

(3) **Sate kyō ukagatta wake wa ...**
さて今日伺ったわけは...
By the way, the reason I came to see you today was ...

In this case, **tokorode** ところで could be used, too, but it would just indicate you are switching to a new topic, whereas **sate** さて signals the fact that the new topic will be more important.

Tomodachi 友達 *friend*

The word **tomodachi** 友達 probably carries more weight in Japanese than "friend" does in English. In other words, becoming a **tomodachi** is much more difficult than becoming a friend. In fact, you almost have to go to school with someone and remain pretty close to him for some time before becoming his **tomodachi**. Even if you go to the same school with someone, you are his **senpai** 先輩 "senior" (see SENPAI) if you are even one class ahead, and his **kōhai** 後輩 "junior" (see KŌHAI) if you are even one class behind. In neither case can you call yourself his **tomodachi**.

When someone graduates from college and starts working, he is surrounded at work by **senpai** 先輩, **kōhai** 後輩, and **dōryō** 同僚 "colleagues at about the same seniority level." But he does not normally call them **tomodachi** 友達. Among them, he might find some **nomi-tomodachi** 飲み友達 "drinking pals," but they are still referred to by that compound rather than simply as **tomodachi**.

Some Americans in Japan ask Japanese how to say "friend" in their language. Upon receiving the answer **tomodachi** 友達, they start calling their Japanese acquaintances **tomodachi** or **watashi no tomodachi** 私の友達. Those few Japanese who know English well enough realize that what these Americans are doing is simply translating "my friend" into Japanese, but others just feel uncomfortable, not knowing how to respond.

Some Americans also make the error of using **ii tomodachi** いい友達 (lit., "good friend") as a direct translation of English "good friend" meaning "close friend." In Japanese, however, **ii tomodachi** does not mean "close friend," but rather "friend who is good, i.e., one who is reliable, faithful, helpful, and exerts good influence on you." "Good friend" in the sense of "close friend" is **shin'yū** 親友. As in the case of **tomodachi**, the Japanese speaker uses this word very sparingly. It is more like "closest friend."

Tōnan 東南 *southeast*

In English, "southeast" can refer to either a location (e.g., Southeast Asia) or a direction (e.g., "if you drive southeast, you'll come to a big river"). In Japanese, for location, **tōnan** 東南 (lit., "eastsouth") is the norm, as in

EXAMPLE:

(1) **Tōnan Ajia**
　東南アジア
Southeast Asia (lit., Eastsouth Asia)

For direction, follow the same pattern as English.

EXAMPLE:

(2) **Nantō no kaze**
南東の風
southeasterly wind

Tonari 隣 *next door, adjacent, adjoining*

Tonari 隣 is used especially when two objects of more or less the same category are in question. When two objects belong to two entirely different categories, **tonari** is not appropriate. Examples (1) and (2) are therefore correct, but (3) and (4) sound very strange.

EXAMPLES:

(1) **Sakanaya wa nikuya no tonari desu.**
魚屋は肉屋の隣です。
The fish market is next to the meat market.

(2) **Uchi no tonari ni Amerikajin no kazoku ga sunde-iru.**
うちの隣にアメリカ人の家族が住んでいる。
An American family is living next door to us (i.e., in the house next to ours).

(3) **?Boku no uchi wa ōki na sakura no ki no tonari desu.**
?僕のうちは大きな桜の木の隣です。
My house is next to a huge cherry tree.

(4) **?Kadan no tonari ni inu ga nete-iru.**
?花壇の隣に犬が寝ている。
There is a dog lying next to the flower bed.

In such cases as (3) and (4), **tonari** 隣 should be replaced by [**sugu**] **yoko** [すぐ]横 "by, at the side of."

In English, a person living next to you is a neighbor, but a person living several doors away is also a neighbor. In Japanese, however, only the former would be a **tonari no hito** 隣の人 (lit., "person next door"), whereas the latter would be a **kinjo no hito** 近所の人 (lit., "person in the neighborhood").

Tori 鳥; 鶏 *bird; chicken*

Tori 鳥, first of all, means "bird."

EXAMPLE:

(1) **Nihon ni iru tori no shurui wa hette-kite-iru.**
日本にいる鳥の種類は減ってきている。
The number of bird species in Japan is decreasing.

Second, **tori** 鶏 is used as an abbreviation of **toriniku** 鶏肉, which means "chicken" (lit., "bird meat").

EXAMPLE:

(2) **Gyū ga takai node, konogoro wa tori bakari tabete-iru.**
牛が高いので、このごろは鶏ばかり食べている。
Since beef is expensive, we've been eating nothing but chicken these days.

Totemo とても *very*

Totemo とても has two basic uses. First, it means "very," as in (1) and (2), where it modifies an adjective and a **na**-noun, respectively.

EXAMPLES:

(1) **Kyō wa totemo samui.**
今日はとても寒い。
It's very cold today.

(2) **Yamada-san wa totemo shinsetsu na hito da.**
山田さんはとても親切な人だ。
Mr. Yamada is a very kind person.

Totemo とても may also modify some verbs.

EXAMPLE:

(3) **Totemo komatta.**
とても困った。
I was quite at a loss.

According to Morita (p. 324), only verbs that describe states may be modified by **totemo**. That is why we cannot use, for example, ***Totemo hataraita** とても働いた to mean "I worked very hard." (To express the idea of "I worked very hard," an entirely different word would have to be used: **Isshōkenmei hataraita** 一生懸命働いた.)

Unlike "very," **totemo** とても meaning "very" cannot be used with a negative word. Compare the following examples:

EXAMPLES:

(4) It is not very cold today.

(5) ***Kyō wa totemo samukunai.**
*今日はとても寒くない。
lit., It is not very cold today.

While (4) is perfectly grammatical, (5) is ungrammatical. Sentence (5) becomes grammatical if **totemo** とても is replaced by **amari** あまり "too" (see AMARI).

EXAMPLE:

(6) **Kyō wa amari samukunai.**
今日はあまり寒くない。
It is not too cold today.

The second use of **totemo** とても is to modify a negative verb or a **na**-noun with a negative meaning to signify "[cannot] possibly" or "[not] by any means."

EXAMPLES:

(7) **Konna muzukashii mondai wa watashi ni wa totemo wakarimasen.**
こんな難しい問題は私にはとても分かりません。
I cannot possibly understand such a difficult problem.

(8) **Sore wa boku ni wa totemo muri da.**
それは僕にはとても無理だ。
I cannot possibly do that.

There are several synonyms for **totemo** とても meaning "very," e.g., **hijō ni** 非常に and **taihen** たいへん. In (1) through (3) above, these two words can be used in place of **totemo**, as in

EXAMPLE:

(9) **Kyō wa hijō ni** (or **taihen**) **samui.**
今日は非常に(たいへん)寒い。
It is very cold today.

Of these three words, **totemo** とても is the most colloquial, **taihen** たいへん is more formal, and **hijō ni** 非常に is the most formal (see TAIHEN).

Totemo とても has a variant, **tottemo** とっても, which is even more colloquial than **totemo** and perhaps more emphatic as well.

Tō˥tō [To˥oto] とうとう *finally, at last, in the end, after all*

Tōtō とうとう is used when something eventually materializes (or fails to materialize) after a long process. It is neutral with regard to the desirability or undesirability of the final outcome.

EXAMPLES:

(1) **Ano genki na Mori-san mo tōtō byōki ni natta.**
あの元気な森さんもとうとう病気になった。
That tough Mr. Mori, too, has finally taken ill.

(2) **Takahashi-san wa nagai aida dokushin datta ga, tōtō kekkon-shita.**
高橋さんは長い間独身だったが、とうとう結婚した。
Mr. Takahashi was a bachelor for a long time, but he finally got married.

(3) **Zuibun matte-ita no ni tōtō kimasendeshita.**
ずいぶん待っていたのにとうとう来ませんでした。
I waited for a long time, but he never showed up (lit., he didn't come after all).

(See also YATTO.)

Tō˥zaina˥nboku [To˥ozaina˥nboku] 東西南北 *lit., east-west-south-north*

In English, the four directions are usually referred to as "north-south-east-west," in that order. In Japanese, however, they follow a different order 東西南北, lit. "east-west-south-north." This particular order was originally introduced from China.

Tsu˥gō ga i˥i 都合がいい *convenient*

Tsugō ga ii 都合がいい "convenient" literally means "circumstances are good" and should be clearly distinguished from **benri** 便利 "convenient." **Benri** means "handy, accessible, convenient to use," while **tsugō ga ii** indicates that "stated conditions are convenient for someone on a particular occasion" (Jorden, 2, p. 185). In sentence (1) only **benri** is correct, whereas in (2) only **tsugō ga ii** can be used.

EXAMPLES:

(1) **Denki-suihanki wa benri** (not *****tsugō ga ii** 都合がいい) **desu nē.**
電気炊飯器は便利ですねえ。
Aren't electric rice cookers handy?

(2) **Pikunikku ga ashita da to tsugō ga ii** (not ***benri** 便利) **n desu ga.**
ピクニックがあしただと 都合がいいんですが。
it would be convenient for me if the picnic were scheduled for tomorrow.

Tsuide ni ついでに *taking the opportunity while doing something else*

Tsuide ni ついでに is used when one takes the opportunity to do something while doing something else.

EXAMPLES:

(1) **Sanpo ni itta tsuide ni, sūpā ni yotte kaimono o shita.**
散歩に行ったついでに、スーパーに寄って買い物をした。
I stopped by the supermarket for some shopping while I was out taking a walk.

(2) Husband: **Chotto tabako o katte kuru yo.**
ちょっとタバコを買って来るよ。
I'm going out to buy cigarettes.

    Wife: **Ja, tsuide ni kore posuto ni irete kite.**
じゃ、ついでにこれポストに入れて来て。
Will you mail this then? (lit., Will you take that opportunity to mail this?)

Don't forget the fact that both actions must be volitional (i.e., intentionally done). Sentences (3a) and (3b) are wrong because, in each of them, one of the events described is involuntary.

EXAMPLES:

(3a) ***Tenki ga yoku-natta tsuide ni sentaku o shita.**
*天気が良くなったついでに洗濯をした。
When the weather improved, I took the opportunity to do the wash.

(3b) ***Sanpo ni itta tsuide ni, omoigakenai hito ni deatta.**
*散歩に行ったついでに、思いがけない人に出会った。
When I went out for a walk, I happened to bump into an unexpected person.

Since, in (3a), **tenki ga yoku-natta** 天気が良くなった "the weather improved" is not a controllable action, **tsuide ni** ついでに may not be used. The sentence must be restated as follows:

EXAMPLE:

(4) **Tenki ga yoku-natta node, sentaku o shita.**
天気が良くなったので、洗濯をした。
Since the weather improved, I did the wash.

In sentence (3b), **tsuide ni** ついでに is inappropriate because bumping into someone is an involuntary event. The sentence must be restated as follows:

EXAMPLE:

(5) **Sanpo no tochū de omoigakenai hito ni deatta.**
散歩の途中で思いがけない人に出会った。
While taking a walk, I bumped into an unexpected person.

Tsu⌈kare⌉ru 疲れる *to become tired*

Americans often forget the fact that **tsukareru** 疲れる by itself means "to become tired," not just "tired." To mean "I became tired," all one has to say is **Tsukareta** 疲れた or **Tsuka-remashita** 疲れました. Try not to create the false equivalent of English "I became tired."

EXAMPLE:

Amari tenisu o shita node tsukaremashita.
あまりテニスをしたので疲れました。

*tsukarete ni narimashita.
*疲れてになりました。
*tsukarete-iru ni narimashita.
*疲れているになりました。

I played so much tennis that I became tired.

(See also NINSHIN-SURU.)

Tsu⌈ma 妻 *wife*

Tsuma 妻 is normally a written form.

EXAMPLE:
bushi no tsuma
武士の妻
the wives of samurai

In conversation, one would use **samurai no oku-san** 侍の奥さん to mean "the wives of samurai."

In spoken Japanese, **tsuma** 妻 is sometimes used to refer to one's own wife, but it sounds formal and somewhat stilted (see KANAI and OKU-SAN).

Tsu⌈mara⌉nai つまらない *uninteresting, insignificant*

Tsumaranai つまらない most often means "dull, uninteresting, no fun."

EXAMPLES:
(1) **Ano eiga wa tsumaranai kara, minai hō ga ii.**
あの映画はつまらないから、見ない方がいい。
That movie is dull; you'd better not see it.
(2) **Kinō no pātī wa tsumaranakatta.**
きのうのパーティーはつまらなかった。
Yesterday's party was no fun.

When used in this sense, **tsumaranai** つまらない is the opposite of **omoshiroi** おもしろい "interesting, fun."

Tsumaranai also means "insignificant" or "trivial."

EXAMPLE:
(3) **Tsumaranai koto de okotte wa ikenai.**
つまらない事で怒ってはいけない。
One should not get angry over trivial matters.

Tsumaranai つまらない meaning "insignificant" often appears as part of the set phrase **Konna tsumaranai mono de shitsurei desu ga** こんなつまらない物で失礼ですが (lit., "Forgive me for such an insignificant gift"), a cliché but nonetheless a still enormously popular expression used by gift givers as they present gifts. English speakers, when first coming across this expression, might feel it is hypocritical of Japanese to call all gifts **tsumaranai**, for some could be quite special or expensive. The reason the Japanese speaker uses this phrase, however, is not because he is hypocritical but because he does not want the receiver to feel obligated.

Although these two meanings of **tsumaranai** つまらない may sound totally unrelated, they are actually not that far apart. Dull things are often trivial and insignificant, and trivial and insignificant things of course fail to interest anyone.

Tsu⌈meta⌉i 冷たい *cold*

Unlike **samui** 寒い, which refers to a sensation of coldness affecting the whole body (see SAMUI), **tsumetai** 冷たい represents a sensation of coldness perceived by the skin only or by a limited portion of one's body. **Tsumetai** is therefore especially appropriate when used in reference to solids and fluids, as in

EXAMPLES:

(1)　**tsumetai jūsu**
　　冷たいジュース
　　cold juice
(2)　**tsumetai te**
　　冷たい手
　　cold hand

When one takes a cold shower, the first sensation perceived by the skin makes one shout **Tsumetai!** 冷たい! If, however, one feels chilled after the cold shower, one might say, shivering, **Samui!** 寒い!

Tsurai つらい *hard to bear*

Tsurai つらい is often quite similar to **kurushii** 苦しい "painful." For example, a tough, demanding job can be described as either **tsurai shigoto** つらい仕事 or **kurushii shigoto** 苦しい仕事. However, while **kurushii** focuses more on physical difficulty, **tsurai** is more mental and psychological. Study the following examples:

EXAMPLES:

(1)　**Kodomo ni shinareru no wa tsurai** (not *****kurushii** 苦しい).
　　子供に死なれるのはつらい。
　　It's hard to lose a child.
(2)　**Kaze o hiite mune ga kurushii** (not *****tsurai.** つらい).
　　風邪を引いて胸が苦しい。
　　I have a cold, and my chest hurts.

Tsurete-iku 連れて行く *to take (someone) along*

In English, one can say both "take someone along" and "take something along." Whether what one takes along is animate or inanimate makes no difference. In Japanese, however, one must use **tsurete-iku** 連れて行く when the object is a person or an animal, but **motte-iku** 持って行く when it is inanimate.

EXAMPLES:

(1) **Kodomo o eiga e tsurete-iku yakusoku o shita.**
子供を映画へ連れて行く約束をした。
I promised to take my child to a movie.

(2) **Kodomo-tachi wa mainichi gakkō e obentō o motte-iku.**
子供たちは毎日学校へお弁当を持って行く。
My children take box lunches to school every day.

Making a distinction between animate beings and inanimate objects is one of the characteristics of the Japanese language, the most basic example being **iru** いる for animate beings versus **aru** ある for inanimate objects.

Tsu⌈tome⌉ru 勤める; 務める; 努める *to become employed; serve as; make efforts*

Tsutomeru has three main meanings, depending on the kanji used. The first one is 勤める, meaning "to become employed," and it usually appears in the **-te** form.

EXAMPLE:

(1) **Takada-san wa ginkō ni tsutomete-iru.**
高田さんは銀行に勤めている。
Mr. Takada works for a bank.

Ginkō ni tsutomete-iru 銀行に勤めている "to work for a bank" should be clearly distinguished from **ginkō de hataraite-iru** 銀行で働いている "to be working at a bank" (see HATARAKU).

Tsutomeru when written 務める means "to serve as," as in

EXAMPLE:

(2) **Yoshida Shigeru wa, nan-nen ni mo watatte shushō o tsutometa.**
吉田茂は、何年にも渡って首相を務めた。
Shigeru Yoshida served as premier for many years.

Tsutomeru when written 努める means "make efforts."

EXAMPLE:

(3) **Gakusei wa bengaku ni tsutomeru beki da.**
学生は勉学に努めるべきだ。
Students should put all their effort into study.

The second and the third uses above, i.e., 務める and 努める, are fairly formal and are not as common as the first, i.e., 勤める. Sentences (2) and (3) would perhaps be more commonly restated as (4) and (5), respectively.

EXAMPLES:

(4) **Yoshida Shigeru wa nan-nen mo shushō datta.**
吉田茂は、何年も首相だった。
Shigeru Yoshida was premier for many years.

(5) **Gakusei wa isshōkenmei benkyō-suru beki da.**
学生は一生懸命勉強するべきだ。
Students should study hard.

Tsū˥yaku [Tsu˥uyaku] 通訳 *the art of interpretation; interpreter*

Tsūyaku 通訳 has two meanings. First, the act of orally translating from one language to another.

EXAMPLE:

(1) **Sumisu-san wa Nihongo ga dekinai kara, Nihon e ittara dare ka tadashii tsūyaku o shite kureru hito ga hitsuyō darō.**
スミスさんは日本語が出来ないから、日本へ行ったら誰か正しい通訳をしてくれる人が必要だろう。
Since Mr. Smith doesn't speak Japanese, he will need someone in Japan who can do accurate interpreting for him.

Second, **tsūyaku** 通訳 means someone whose job is interpreting.

EXAMPLE:

(2) **Nihon ni wa Eigo no dekiru tsūyaku wa ōi ga, Roshiago no dekiru tsūyaku wa sukunai.**
日本には英語の出来る通訳は多いが、ロシア語の出来る通訳は少ない。
In Japan, there are a lot of interpreters who can speak English, but very few who can handle Russian.

For this second meaning, one may also use **tsūyakusha** 通訳者, but this is a formal expression reserved for written language only.

The situation is quite different with **hon'yaku** 翻訳, which means "translation" only, and not "translator." For the latter, one has to use **hon'yakuka** 翻訳家, which means "professional translator," or **yakusha** 訳者 "translator (of a particular piece of writing)."

Uchi うち *home, house*

Uchi うち is quite similar in meaning to **ie** 家 (see IE). For example, in sentence (1) below, **uchi** and **ie** are more or less interchangeable.

EXAMPLE:

(1) **Ano hito wa zuibun ōkii uchi (or ie) o katta.**
あの人はずいぶん大きいうち（家）を買った。
He bought a very large house.

The only difference in this case—at least, to a Tokyoite—is that **uchi** うち is more colloquial, while **ie** is more formal.

There are some situations where **uchi** うち is preferred to **ie** 家 (Matsuo et al., pp. 35–36). For example, when one refers to one's own home, **uchi** is more appropriate.

EXAMPLES:

(2) **Yūbe wa uchi ni imashita.**
ゆうべはうちにいました。
I was at home yesterday.

(3) **Uchi e kaette mo ii desu ka.**
うちへ帰ってもいいですか。
May I go home?

Uchi no うちの (but not *__ie no__ 家の) is often used to mean "my" or "our" when referring to one's own family members or family belongings.

EXAMPLE:

(4) **uchi no musuko (musume, inu, kuruma**, etc.)
うちの息子(娘、犬、車、etc.)
my (or our) son (daughter, dog, car, etc.)

Uchi うち is sometimes used as an abbreviation of **uchi no shujin** うちの主人 "my husband." **Ie** 家 has no such usage.

EXAMPLE:

(5) **Uchi** (not *__Ie__ 家) **wa itsumo kaeri ga osoi n desu.**
うちはいつも帰りが遅いんです。
My husband always comes home late.

Ukagau 伺う *to inquire; visit*

Ukagau 伺う, first of all, is the humble counterpart of **tazuneru** 訪ねる "to visit."

EXAMPLE:

(1) **Sensei, ashita ken'kyūshitsu no hō e ukagatte mo yoroshii deshō ka.**
先生、あした研究室の方へ伺ってもよろしいでしょうか。
Sensei, may I come and see you in the office tomorrow?

Second, **ukagau** 伺う is the humble counterpart of **tazuneru** 尋ねる "to inquire."

EXAMPLE:

(2) **Sensei, chotto ukagaitai koto ga aru n desu ga.**
先生、ちょっと伺いたいことがあるんですが。
Sensei, I have a question I'd like to ask you.

Although **ukagau** 伺う is a humble form to begin with, its humble form also exists, i.e., **oukagai-suru** お伺いする. For example, **ukagatte mo** 伺っても in sentence (1) above could be rephrased **oukagai-shite mo** お伺いしても, and **ukagaitai** 伺いたい in sentence (2) could be replaced by **oukagai-shi-tai** お伺いしたい, respectively. However, **oukagai-suru** is a double humble verb and may thus sound overly polite to some people.

Uˈmaˈi うまい, 上手い; 美味い *skillful; delicious*

Umai has two basic meanings: 上手い "skillful," as in (1), and 美味い "delicious," as in (2).

EXAMPLES:

(1) **Ano hito wa gorufu ga umai.**
あ人はゴルフが上手い。
He is good at golf.

(2) **Kono sakana wa umai.**
この魚は美味い。
This fish is delicious.

In the sense of "skillful," **umai** 上手い is synonymous with **jōzu** 上手, but, according to Tokugawa and Miyajima (p. 54), **umai** is a little more colloquial than **jōzu**.

In the sense of "delicious," **umai** 美味い is synonymous with **oishii** おいしい, but **umai** is used only by men, and in rather informal situations.

U⌐n 運 *luck; fortune*

"Lucky" is **un ga yoi** (or **ii**) 運が良い（いい）, lit., "(my) luck is good"; "unlucky" is **un ga warui** 運が悪い, lit., "(my) luck is bad."

EXAMPLES:

(1) **Anna subarashii josei to kekkon dekita nante, Suzuki-san wa un ga ii.**
あんなすばらしい女性と結婚出来たなんて、鈴木さんは運がいい。
Mr. Suzuki is fortunate to have been able to marry such a wonderful woman.

(2) **Un ga warui koto ni, pikunikku no hi ni ame ni natte shimatta.**
運が悪いことに、ピクニックの日に雨になってしまった。
Unluckily, it started raining on the day of the picnic.

There is a synonym for **un** 運, i.e., **unmei** 運命, which means "destiny, fate." **Unmei** cannot be used in sentences (1) and (2) above, but conversely in sentence (3) below **unmei** cannot be replaced by **un**.

EXAMPLE:

(3) **Sore ga watashi no unmei** (not *****un** 運) **datta no ka mo shirenai.**
それが私の運命だったのかもしれない。
That was perhaps my fate/destiny.

U⌐nte⌐nshu 運転手 *driver*

An **untenshu** 運転手 is a person who operates or drives a vehicle for a living. The English counterpart could be "driver," "motorman," or "engineer," depending on the type of vehicle. **Untenshu** might also mean "chauffeur."

Unless a person operates or drives a vehicle for a living, he cannot be called **untenshu** 運転手. In English, anyone who drives well may be referred to as a good driver. In Japanese, on the other hand, **jōzu na untenshu** 上手な運転手 means "skillful professional driver." If someone who is not a driver by occupation happens to drive well, we say,

EXAMPLE:

Ano hito wa unten ga jōzu da.
あの人は運転が上手だ。
He is good at driving.

U⌐rayamashi⌐i うらやましい *envious; enviable*

Urayamashii うらやましい is "envious/enviable."

EXAMPLE:

(1) **Watashi wa anata ga urayamashii.**
私はあなたがうらやましい。
I am envious of you. (lit., As for me, you are enviable.)

Urayamashii うらやましい has a corresponding verb **urayamu** うらやむ "to envy."

EXAMPLE:

(2) **Hito ga ōki na ie o tateta no o urayande wa ikenai.**
人が大きな家を建てたのをうらやんではいけない。
You mustn't envy someone who has built a big house.

As is the case with adjectives of feelings (see also SABISHII), when the person who is envious is not the speaker, **urayamashii** うらやましい must be changed to a verb, i.e., **urayamashigaru** うらやましがる "to show signs of being envious," or other words such as **rashii** and **yō** must be added, as in

EXAMPLES:

(3a) **Tanaka-san wa Sumisu-san no atarashii konpyūtā o urayamashigatte-iru.**
田中さんはスミスさんの新しいコンピューターをうらやましがっている。
Mr. Tanaka is envious (lit., is showing signs of being envious) of Mr. Smith's new computer.

(3b) **Tanaka-san wa Sumisu-san no atarashii konpyūtā ga urayamashii rashii/yō da.**
田中さんはスミスさんの新しいコンピューターがうらやましい らしい/ようだ。
Mr. Tanaka seems to be envious of Mr. Smith's new computer.

U⌐rusa⌐i うるさい *noisy, fussy, bothersome*

Urusai うるさい most frequently means "noisy."

EXAMPLE:

(1) **Tonari no rajio wa urusai desu nē!**
隣のラジオはうるさいですねえ！
Isn't the radio next door noisy!

Urusai うるさい might also mean "fussy," since a fussy person makes noise by fussing about trivial things.

EXAMPLE:

(2) **Yamamoto-sensei wa komakai koto ni urusai.**
山本先生は細かいことにうるさい。
Professor Yamamoto is fussy about little details.

Urusai うるさい in the sense of "noisy" is often used as a warning to someone who is too noisy. It is extremely interesting that in English an adjective with the opposite meaning, "quiet," would be used in a similar situation.

EXAMPLE:

(3) **Urusai!** (i.e., You're noisy, [so be quiet]!)
うるさい！
Quiet! (i.e., [You're noisy, so be] quiet!)

Urusai うるさい sometimes means "bothersome, annoying" also.

EXAMPLE:

(4) **Kinjo-zukiai ga urusai.**
近所付き合いがうるさい。
Getting along with the neighbors is bothersome.

There is a synonym for **urusai** うるさい, **yakamashii** やかましい. In the sense of "noisy" or "fussy," these two adjectives may be used more or less interchangeably, although **urusai** is the more common word and **yakamashii** can never mean "bothersome." In other words, although **urusai** can be replaced by **yakamashii** in (1), (2), and (3) above, it cannot in (4).

Ushi 牛 *cattle, bull, cow, ox, steer*

Since the English have long been a cattle-raising people, their language is replete with terms referring to different types of bovines such as "cattle," "bull," "cow," "ox," and "steer." The Japanese, on the other hand, have never been a cattle-raising people, and their language reflects this fact by having only one word, **ushi** 牛, to refer to all bovines. When the Japanese speaker must be specific about different types of ushi, he simply adds different prefixes to make compounds, such as **o-ushi** 雄牛 "male ushi," **me-ushi** 雌牛 "female ushi," and **kyosei-ushi** 去勢牛 "castrated **ushi**."

"Beef," however, is not called **ushi** 牛, but **gyū-niku** 牛肉 (**gyū** 牛 being another reading of the *kanji* for **ushi** 牛, plus **niku** 肉 "meat") or simply **gyū**. A loanword, **bīfu** ビーフ (from English "beef"), is also used in the sense of "beef," but usually in compounds such as **rōsuto-bīfu** ローストビーフ "roast beef" and **bīfu-shichū** ビーフシチュー "beef stew."

U⌐tsukushi⌐i 美しい *beautiful*

Although **utsukushii** 美しい is regularly equated with English "beautiful," it is far less conversational than the latter. For example, **utsukushii onna-no-hito** 美しい女の人 "beautiful women" and **utsukushii keshiki** 美しい景色 "beautiful view" are perfectly all right in writing, but a little unnatural in conversation. Most speakers of Japanese would rather say **kirei na onna-no-hito** きれいな女の人 and **kirei na keshiki** きれいな景色 instead.

Utsukushii 美しい basically describes something that is pleasing to the eye or the ear (e.g., **utsukushii hana** 美しい花 "beautiful flower" and **utsukushii ongaku** 美しい音楽 "beautiful music"), and, on limited occasions, to the heart (e.g., **utsukushii hanashi** 美しい話 "beautifully moving story"). It does not have as wide a range of meaning as "beautiful," which is frequently used, especially in colloquial English, to mean "excellent, terrific, super" (e.g., "a beautiful opportunity," "a beautiful plan").

Unlike **kirei** きれい, **utsukushii** 美しい cannot mean "clean." **Kirei**, on the other hand, cannot mean "beautifully moving," as **utsukushii** does.

Wa⌐ka⌐i 若い *young*

Unlike "young," **wakai** 若い cannot be used to describe children. In English, little children may be called young, but **wakai** is used for people who are at least in their upper teens. In other words, until one becomes old enough to become a **wakai hito** 若い人 "young adult," one is simply a **kodomo** 子供 "child," not a ***wakai kodomo** 若い子供.

Although **wakai** 若い as a rule modifies only animate beings such as **hito** 人 "person," it is sometimes used with reference to serial numbers to mean "smaller." For example, 23 is a **wakai bangō** 若い番号 "smaller number" (lit., "young number") in comparison with 24.

Wa⌈ka⌉ru 分かる *to understand*

Wakaru 分かる means "[something] is clear" or "to become clear [to someone]." That is why the particle preceding **wakaru** is **ga** instead of **o**. When **wakaru** is translated into English, however, the most natural equivalent is often either "understand" or "know."

EXAMPLES:

(1) **Nishio-san wa Roshiago ga wakaru.**
西尾さんはロシア語が分かる。
Mr. Nishio understands Russian.

(2) **Ano hito ga naze konakatta ka wakaranai.**
あの人がなぜ来なかったか分からない。
I don't understand (or know) why he didn't come. (lit., Why he didn't come is not clear to me.)

(3) A: **Ima nan-ji deshō ka.**
いま何時でしょうか。
What time is it?

B: **Chotto wakarimasen ga.**
ちょっと分かりませんが。
Sorry, but I don't know. (lit., It's a bit unclear to me.)

Since **wakaru** 分かる means "[something] is *or* becomes clear," it represents an event that is not controllable by the speaker. **Wakaru** consequently cannot take a potential form, i.e., there is no such form as *__wakareru__ 分かれる to mean "[something] can be or become clear."

In example (3) above, **Wakarimasen** 分かりません, meaning "I don't know," may be replaced by **Shirimasen** 知りません, which also means "I don't know." But there is a difference between the two. According to Mizutani and Mizutani (1, p. 57), **Shirimasen** means "I haven't had the chance to get the information," while **Wakarimasen** is used when the speaker feels he should know the answer. Therefore, as a rule, avoid **Shirimasen** as an answer to a question about yourself. For example,

EXAMPLE:

(4) A: **Kondo no shūmatsu ni wa nani o suru tsumori desu ka.**
今度の週末には何をするつもりですか。
What do you plan to do this weekend?

B: **Wakarimasen** (not *__Shirimasen__ 知りません).
分かりません。
I don't know.

Wakarimasen 分かりません in this case implies "I should know the answer but I'm sorry I don't" and is therefore a proper answer, whereas **Shirimasen** 知りません might even indicate "This sort of thing has nothing to do with me," and is therefore inappropriate.

The past-tense form **Wakarimashita** 分かりました often means "I have understood what you just said" (Jorden, 1, p. 78). This usage occurs especially as a response to an explanation or request.

EXAMPLE:

(5) Professor: **Kono tēpu-rekōdā, rabo ni kaeshite-oite-kuremasen ka. Kyō wa rabo ga yasumi dakara, ashita no asa ne.**

このテープレコーダー、ラボに返しておいてくれませんか。今日はラボが休みだから、あしたの朝ね。

Would you mind returning this tape recorder to the lab? The lab is closed today, so do it tomorrow morning, will you?

Student: **Wakarimashita.**

分かりました。

I'll be glad to. (lit., I understood you[r request and will gladly accommodate it].)

(See also SHIRU and RIKAI-SURU.)

Waku 沸く *to boil*

Waku 沸く is normally "to come to a boil," as in

EXAMPLE:

(1) **Oyu ga waita kara, ocha o iremashō.**

お湯が沸いたから、お茶を入れましょう。

Water has boiled. Let's have tea.

Note the expression to be used is **oyu ga waku** お湯が沸く (lit., "hot water boils") and not *mizu ga waku 水が沸く (lit., "cold water boils").

Another use of **waku** 沸く that could be confusing to English speakers is **furo ga waku** 風呂が沸く, as in

EXAMPLE:

(2) **Ofuro ga wakimashita yo.**

お風呂が沸きましたよ。

The bath water has gotten warm enough.

Note that, in this case, the bath water is not really boiling!

Warau 笑う *to laugh*

English has a number of verbs that express different kinds of laugh, such as "giggle," "chuckle," and "guffaw." In Japanese, however, **warau** 笑う is the basic verb, and one adds onomatopoetic adverbs to describe different types of laugh.

EXAMPLES:

(1a) **kusukusu warau**

くすくす笑う

to giggle

(1b) **kutsukutsu warau**

くつくつ笑う

to chuckle

(1c) **geragera warau**

げらげら笑う

to guffaw

Kinds of smiles, too, are expressed in a similar way, i.e., by adding onomatopoetic adverbs.

EXAMPLES:

(2a) **nikotto warau** (or **nikotto-suru**)
にこっと笑う(にこっとする)
to break into a pleasant smile

(2b) **nikoniko warau** (or **nikonikosuru**)
にこにこ笑う(にこにこする)
to smile pleasantly and continuously

(2c) **niyaniya warau** (or **niyaniya-suru**)
にやにや笑う(にやにやする)
to grin

Wareware 我々 *we*

Wareware 我々 is more formal than **watakushi-tachi** 私たち or **watashi-tachi** 私たち, both of which mean the same thing. It is more suited to writing or formal speech.

EXAMPLE:
Wareware wa kuni no tame ni tachi-agaranakereba naranai.
我々は国のために立ち上がらなければならない。
We must rise for the sake of our country.

Waꜛruꜜi 悪い *bad*

Warui 悪い is used not only to refer to things or persons that are "bad," like **warui tenki** 悪い天気 "bad weather" and **warui ko** 悪い子 "a bad child," but is sometimes used to express gratitude, as in sentence (1) below. (When used in this sense, **warui** does not normally precede a noun.)

EXAMPLE:
Kekkō na mono o itadaite warui desu nē.
けっこうな物をいただいて悪いですねえ。
Thank you for giving me such a nice present.

The reason **warui** 悪い is used as an expression of gratitude is probably that Japanese people often feel guilty about a favor done for them. For them, receiving a favor from someone is like having inconvenienced that person, who must have spent time and/or money on it. This guilty feeling is what is behind the expression **Warui desu nē** 悪いですねえ.

Watashi 私 *I*

Watashi 私 (and its even more formal variant, **watakushi**) is a "personal pronoun" used by a speaker to refer to himself. Males hardly ever use it when they are young because they use **boku** instead (see BOKU). They begin using **watashi** immediately after they graduate from college and start working. They use it on formal occasions, especially in talking to people higher in status. Females start using **watashi** (or more colloquially, **atashi**) as children and use it throughout their lives. The frequency of **watashi** in Japanese, however, is minuscule compared with that of "I," "my," and "me" in English, since Japanese speakers, instead of using "pronouns," would rather use the context to make it clear that they are talking about themselves, as in the following example:

EXAMPLE:

Ashita [watashi no] uchi e irasshaimasen ka.
明日[私の]うちへいらっしゃいませんか。
Would you like to come to my house tomorrow?

In this case, while "my" would be obligatory in English, **watashi no** meaning "my" is optional and most likely to be left out in Japanese.

Ya⌐ha⌐ri/Ya⌐ppa⌐ri やはり/やっぱり *as might be expected*

When one listens to interviews on TV or on the radio, one is struck by the frequency of the occurrence of **yahari** やはり or its more colloquial variant, **yappari** やっぱり. For example,

EXAMPLES:
(1) A: **B-san wa donna ryōri ga osuki desu ka.**
      Bさんはどんな料理がお好きですか。
      What kind of cuisine do you like the best?
     B: **Yappari Nihonryōri desu nē.**
      やっぱり日本料理ですねえ。
      Japanese food (as you might expect).
(2) A: **Kondo no harubasho wa dare ga yūshō-suru deshō ka.**
      今度の春場所は誰が優勝するでしょうねえ。
      Who do you think will win the sumo tournament this spring?
     B: **Yappari Yokozuna ja nai desu ka.**
      やっぱり横綱じゃないですか。
      Yokozuna (grand champion), I guess (like everybody else).

Yahari/yappari やはり/やっぱり basically signifies "What I'm saying is nothing unusual. It's something you might be expecting to hear. I'm no different from others." In other words, **yahari/yappari** is used frequently because it suits the typical Japanese mind, which does not wish to be too individualistic.

Ya⌐ku 約 *approximately*

Yaku 約 is attached to a numeral to indicate an approximate number/amount. It is synonymous with **gurai** ぐらい. There are, however, some differences between the two. First, **yaku** sounds more formal than **gurai**. Second, **yaku** must precede a numeral while **gurai** follows, as in

EXAMPLE:
(1) **Nyūyōku ni wa, yaku jū-nen (or jū-nen gurai) sunde-ita.**
      ニューヨークには、約十年(十年ぐらい)住んでいた。
      I lived in New York about ten years.

Another difference is that **yaku** 約 is used only with a number, whereas **gurai** ぐらい does not have to be, as in

EXAMPLE:

(2) **Musuko wa watashi to onaji gurai** (not ***yaku onaji** 約同じ) **no shinchō desu.**
息子は私と同じぐらいの身長です。
My son is about as tall as I am.

Yakyū 野球 *baseball*

A number of sports that used to be called by non-Western names before and during World War II are now called by Western names. For example,

EXAMPLES:

shūkyū 蹴球	→	**sakkā** サッカー	"soccer"
haikyū 排球	→	**barēbōru** バレーボール	"volleyball"
rōkyū 篭球	→	**basukettobōru** バスケットボール	"basketball"

Yakyū 野球 "baseball" is an exception. It still is rarely called **bēsubōru** ベースボール even though most people understand the term. Baseball terms, on the other hand, are mostly loanwords, e.g., **pitchā** ピッチャー "pitcher," **kyatchā** キャッチャー "catcher," **hitto** ヒット "hit," and **fauru** ファウル "foul."

In English, "baseball" and "a baseball" are different, the former being the name of a sport and the latter referring to the ball used for baseball. In Japanese, on the other hand, **yakyū** 野球 simply means "baseball," and in order to refer to a baseball, one has to say **yakyū no bōru** 野球のボール, lit., "a baseball ball."

Ya¹ne 屋根 *roof*

Yane 屋根 is "roof," as in

EXAMPLE:

(1) **Konogoro no Nihon de wa, ao ya aka no yane ga fuete-kita yō na ki ga suru.**
このごろの日本では、青や赤の屋根が増えてきたような気がする。
It seems to me that lately blue or red roofs have increased in Japan.

To refer to the roofs of Western-style buildings such as department stores and hotels, however, use **okujō** 屋上 instead of **yane** 屋根, as in

EXAMPLE:

(2) **Natsu ni naru to, okujō** (not ***yane** 屋根) **ni biagāden o hiraku depāto ga aru.**
夏になると、屋上にビアガーデンを開くデパートがある。
Some department stores open "beer gardens" on their roofs in the summer.

Yaru やる *to do*

Yaru やる, when used in the sense of "to do," is synonymous with **suru** する.

EXAMPLE:

(1) **Ban-gohan no ato de sugu shukudai o**　　　(a) **yaru.**
晩ご飯のあとですぐ宿題を　　　　　　　　　　　　　やる
I do my homework right after dinner.　　　　(b) **suru.**
　　　　　　　　　　　　　　　　　　　　　　　　　する

Both (a) and (b) mean the same thing. The only difference is that **yaru** やる is a little more conversational than **suru** する (Tokugawa and Miyajima, p. 217).

Yaru やる cannot be attached to nouns to form compound verbs, whereas **suru** する can.

EXAMPLE:

(2) **benkyō-suru** (not *benkyō-yaru 勉強やる. However, **benkyō o yaru** 勉強をやる would be acceptable.)
勉強する
to study

Yaru やる and **suru** する are not always interchangeable. **Yaru**, for example, also means "to give [to a lower-status person]," as in **Musuko ni pen o yatta** 息子にペンをやった "I gave my son a pen," but **suru** does not have that meaning. Of the sample sentences given under **suru** (see SURU), (6) and (9) can definitely take **yaru** instead of **suru**, and (7) and (8) can probably take **yaru**, but (5) is definitely unacceptable. Since **yaru** has no intransitive uses, it cannot replace **suru** in (10) and (11).

Ya⌐sashi⌐i やさしい *gentle, easy*

Yasashii やさしい has two meanings: "gentle," as in (1), and "easy," as in (2).

EXAMPLES:

(1) **Ano hito wa yasashii.**
あの人はやさしい。
That person is gentle.

(2) **Ano mondai wa yasashii.**
あの問題はやさしい。
That question is easy.

"Easy" and "gentle" may seem far apart in meaning to English speakers, but they really are not that distant if one stretches one's imagination a little. After all, it is easy to deal with gentle people, and easy problems keep you gentle!

When **yasashii** やさしい means "easy," it is normally not used adverbially. Sentence (3) below is therefore incorrect.

EXAMPLE:

(3) *Kodomo de mo yasashiku dekiru.
*子供でもやさしくできる。
Even children can do it easily.

Yasashiku やさしく in (3) should be replaced by **kantan ni** 簡単に "simply, easily."

EXAMPLE:

(4) **Kodomo de mo kantan ni dekiru.**
子供でも簡単にできる。
Even children can do it easily.

Ya⌈su⌉i 安い *inexpensive*

Yasui 安い "inexpensive" is the opposite of **takai** 高い meaning "expensive."

EXAMPLE:
(1) **Ano mise ni wa takai mono wa aru ga, yasui mono wa nai.**
あの店には高いものはあるが、安いものはない。
That store has expensive things but not inexpensive things.

When **takai** 高い means "high" or "tall," however, the opposite is not **yasui** but **hikui** 低い (see HIKUI).

Yasui やすい means "easy," too, but mainly in the set phrase **Oyasui goyō desu** おやすいご用です "I'll be happy to do that for you" (lit., "That's an easy thing to do"), an expression of willingness to meet someone's request. Ordinarily, **yasashii** やさしい is the word for "easy" (see YASASHII).

Yasui 安い in the sense of "easy" is also used in combination with the stem of a verb, as in **yomi-yasui** 読みやすい "easy to read," **oboe-yasui** 覚えやすい "easy to learn," etc.

Ya⌈sumi⌉ 休み *vacation, absence*

Yasumi 休み comes from the verb **yasumu** 休む meaning "to rest" or "not to work." It therefore corresponds to a wide range of English words such as "absence," "recess," "vacation," "day off," and "holiday."

EXAMPLES:
(1) **Hiru-yasumi ni resutoran e itta.**
昼休みにレストランへ行った。
I went to a restaurant during the noon recess.

(2) **Suzuki-san wa kyō yasumi da ga dō shita n darō.**
鈴木さんは今日休みだがどうしたんだろう。
Mr. Suzuki is absent today. I wonder what's happened to him.

(3) **Kotoshi no natsu-yasumi ni wa doko e ikimasu ka.**
今年の夏休みにはどこへ行きますか。
Where are you going during the summer vacation this year?

(4) **Ashita yasumi o torō to omotte-iru.**
あした休みを取ろうと思っている。
I'm thinking of taking the day off tomorrow.

(5) **Ninon de wa Kurisumasu no hi wa yasumi desu ka.**
日本ではクリスマスの日は休みですか。
Is Christmas Day a holiday in Japan?

In America, "vacation" often indicates "pleasure trip one takes away from work," as in "He is on vacation in Europe." Japanese **yasumi**, on the other hand, does not suggest "trip" by itself. The following is therefore wrong.

EXAMPLE:
(6) *****Shōgakusei no koro, yoku ryōshin to yasumi ni itta koto o oboete-iru.**
＊小学生の頃、よく両親と休みに行ったことを覚えている。

The above sentence was once written by a student of mine to mean "I remember often going on vacation with my parents when I was in elementary school." This student should have written as follows:

EXAMPLE:

(7) **Shōgakusei no koro, yasumi ni naru to, yoku ryōshin to ryokō-shita koto o oboete-iru.**
小学生の頃、休みになると、よく両親と旅行したことを覚えている。
I remember that, in my elementary school days, I often went on a trip with my parents when vacation time came around.

Ya⌐su⌐mu 休む *to rest; to be absent; to go to bed*

The basic meaning of **yasumu** 休む is "to rest."

EXAMPLE:

(1) **Tsukareta kara, chotto yasunde-iru n desu.**
疲れたから、ちょっと休んでいるんです。
I'm resting because I'm tired.

Occasionally, **yasumu** 休む means "to go to bed" or "sleep." In this case, **yasumu** is synonymous with **neru** 寝る.

EXAMPLE:

(2) Mother speaking to a child: **Mō jūichi-ji da kara yasundara** (or **netara**) **dō.**
もう十一時だから休んだら（寝たら）どう。
It's already 11 o'clock. Why don't you go to bed?

Yasumu 休む is also used to mean "to be absent," as in

EXAMPLE:

(3) **Tanaka-san wa, konogoro byōki de kaisha o yasumu koto ga ōi.**
田中さんは、このごろ病気で会社を休むことが多い。
These days, Mr. Tanaka is often absent from the office because of illness.

Be careful not to confuse **kaisha o yasumu** 会社を休む with **kaisha de yasumu** 会社で休む, which would mean "to rest at the office."

Ya⌐tsu やつ, 奴 *guy; fellow*

Yatsu やつ, 奴 means "guy" or "fellow" and is considered a coarse, not refined, expression. It is used mainly by men in informal situations.

EXAMPLE:

(1) **Yoshimoto te kawatteru yatsu da na.**
吉本って変わってる奴だな。
Yoshimoto is a strange guy, isn't he?

Although it is a coarse word, it is not a profanity like English "bastard." However, it does not belong in polite speech just the same.

EXAMPLE:

(2) **Yoshimoto-san to iu kata wa, chotto kawatte-iru kata** (not *****yatsu** 奴) **desu ne.**
吉本さんという方は、ちょっと変わっている方ですね。
Mr. Yoshimoto is a strange person, isn't he?

Yatsu やつ sometimes means "thing," as in

EXAMPLE:

(3) **Motto yasui yatsu ga hoshii n da kedo.**
もっと安いやつが欲しいんだけど。
(customer to a salesclerk) *I'd like a cheaper one.*

Kono yatsu このやつ "this guy," **sono yatsu** そのやつ "that guy," **ano yatsu** あのやつ "that guy (over there)," **dono yatsu** どのやつ "which guy" become **koitsu** こいつ, **soitsu** そいつ, **aitsu** あいつ, **doitsu** どいつ, respectively, as in

EXAMPLE:

(4) **Aitsu (=Ano yatsu) nikurashii yatsu da.**
あいつ（あのやつ）にくらしい奴だ。
He's a detestable guy.

Yatta! やった *"Hurray!"*

Yatta! やった is a frequently used exclamation of joy uttered when something wonderful happens unexpectedly. For example, children might say this when their parents tell them they are taking them on a vacation to Hawaii.

It seems to me that the usage of **Yatta!** has changed over the years. It used to be used only when someone really did something great. For example, when we were at a baseball game and a batter hit a homerun for the team we were cheering for, we probably uttered the exclamation. Nowadays, however, any happy turn of events seems to cause youngsters to yell out **Yatta!**

Yatto やっと *finally*

Although **yatto** やっと and **tōtō** とうとう (see TŌTŌ) are both translated into English as "finally," they are not the same. First of all, **yatto** cannot be used when something fails to materialize. In (1), therefore, only **tōtō** is correct.

EXAMPLE:

(1) **Tegami wa kyō mo tōtō** (not *yatto やっと) **konakatta.**
手紙は今日もとうとうこなかった。
The letter didn't arrive today either, despite all my waiting.

Second, while **tōtō** とうとう is neutral as to the desirability or undesirability of the final outcome, **yatto** やっと is used only when the result is desirable. In sentence (2), therefore, only **tōtō** is correct.

EXAMPLE:

(2) **Hitori, futari to shinde-itte, tōtō** (not *yatto やっと) **minna shinde-shimatta.**
ひとり、ふたりと死んで行って、とうとうみんな死んでしまった。
They died one by one until finally they were all dead.

(In sentence (2) above, **yatto** やっと would be correct if the speaker, for some reason or other, had wanted all of these people to die.)

When **yatto** やっと and **tōtō** とうとう are used with regard to a desirable outcome, they are quite similar, but there is a slight difference in connotation.

EXAMPLE:

(3) **Mai-tsuki chokin-shite-ita okane ga tōtō (or yatto) hyakuman-en ni natta.**
毎月貯金していたお金がとうとう（やっと）百万円になった。
The money that I've been saving every month has finally reached the sum of 1,000,000 yen.

In this case, **tōtō** とうとう signals that the speaker is reporting objectively on the eventual outcome of a particular event; how he feels about the outcome is not the issue. **Yatto** やっと, on the other hand, implies that the speaker has been looking forward to this outcome for some time.

-Yōbi 曜日 *day of the week*

In Japanese, the names of the days of the week all have **-yōbi** 曜日 (or **-yō** for short) at the end, e.g., **nichi-yōbi** 日曜日, **getsu-yōbi**, etc. There is a significant difference in usage between these Japanese terms and their English counterparts, for the Japanese speaker does not seem to use these names as often as the English speaker does the English terms. The reason is that Japanese speakers are often more comfortable referring to a particular day by its date than by its day of the week. For example, while an American might say "I'm getting married two weeks from this Friday," using the name of a day of the week, a Japanese in a corresponding situation would be more likely to refer to the date of the same day and say, for example, **Kongetsu no jūhachi-nichi ni kekkon-shimasu** 今月の十八日に結婚します "I'm getting married on the 18th of this month."

Yobu 呼ぶ *to call*

First, **yobu** 呼ぶ means "to call" in the sense of "to call out" or "to call by name."

EXAMPLE:

(1) **"Morita-san!" to yonda no ni henji o shinakatta.**
「森田さん！」と呼んだのに返事をしなかった。
I called out, "Mr. Morita!" but he didn't answer.

Second, **yobu** 呼ぶ means "to call" in the sense of "to give someone (or something) the name of."

EXAMPLE:

(2) **Nyūyōku wa naze biggu-appuru to yobareru no darō ka.**
ニューヨークはなぜビックアップルと呼ばれるのだろうか。
I wonder why New York is called the Big Apple.

Third, **yobu** 呼ぶ means "to call" in the sense of "to send for" or "to summon."

EXAMPLE:

(3) **Kanai ga byōki ni natta no de, isha o yonda.**
家内が病気になったので、医者を呼んだ。
I sent for the doctor because my wife became ill.

In English, "call" can mean "to telephone" or "to make a short visit." **Yobu** 呼ぶ does not have those meanings. In (4) below, only (b) is correct.

EXAMPLES:

(4a) | *Yobimashita ga,
     | *呼びましたが、

(4b) | Denwa o kakemashita ga,　　　　ohanashi-chū deshita.
     | 電話をかけましたが、　　　　　　お話中でした。
     | *I called that number, but the line was busy.*

For the English sense of "to visit," use **kuru** 来る, not **yobu** 呼ぶ, as in the following sentence.

EXAMPLE:

(5) **Kin'yōbi wa oisha-san ga kuru** (not *yobu 呼ぶ) **hi da.**
金曜日はお医者さんが来る日だ。
Friday is the day when the doctor calls/comes.

Unlike "call," **yobu** 呼ぶ is often used to mean "to invite."

EXAMPLE:

(6) **Ashita Matsuda-san o yūshoku ni yobō.**
あした松田さんを夕食に呼ぼう。
Let's invite Mr. Matsuda [to our house] for dinner tomorrow.

Yo⌐ko⌐su よこす, 寄越す *to give/send over (to me)*

Yokosu よこす means "to give/send over," but the direction of the movement of the object in question must be toward the speaker. Compare (1) and (2) below.

EXAMPLES:

(1) **Yoshida ga hisashiburi ni nengajō o yokoshita.**
吉田が久しぶりに年賀状をよこした。
Yoshida sent me a New Year's card for the first time in many years.

(2) **Konoaida okutta** (not *yokoshita よこした) **hon tsuita?**
この間送った本着いた？
Has the book I sent you the other day arrived?

Yokosu よこす may not be used when the giver/sender is a higher status person.

EXAMPLE:

(3) **Takahashi-sensei ga hisashiburi ni nengajō o kudasatta** (not *yokoshita よこした).
高橋先生が久しぶりに年賀状をくださった。
Professor Takahashi sent me a New Year's card for the first time in many years.

Yo⌐ku よく *often*

Yoku よく, the adverbial form of **yoi** 良い (or **ii** いい), is frequently used to mean "often."

EXAMPLES:

(1) **Yoku eiga e ikimasu.**
よく映画へ行きます。
I often go to the movies.

(2) **Konogoro wa yoku ame ga furu.**
このごろはよく雨が降る。
It often rains these days.

However, **yoku** よく should not be used in the negative. The following sentence is wrong.

EXAMPLE:

(3)   **Yoshimoto-san wa yoku eiga e ikimasen.*
*吉本さんはよく映画へ行きません。
Mr. Yoshimoto does not go to the movies often.

To make (3) correct, **yoku** よく must be replaced by **amari** あまり (see AMARI).

EXAMPLE:

(4)   **Yoshimoto-san wa amari eiga e ikimasen.**
吉本さんはあまり映画へ行きません。
Mr. Yoshimoto does not go to the movies often (lit., much).

Since **yoku** よく is the adverbial form of **yoi** 良い (or **ii** いい) meaning "good," it may be used in the sense of "well."

EXAMPLE:

(5)   **Yūbe wa yoku neta.**
ゆうべはよく寝た。
I slept very well last night.

However, while "well" may be used in the sense of "skillfully," as in "Mr. Smith speaks Japanese very well," **yoku** よく often cannot be used in this sense. Sentence (6) below, for example, is wrong if the speaker wants it to mean "Mr. Smith speaks Japanese very well."

EXAMPLE:

(6)   **Sumisu-san wa Nihongo o yoku hanasu.*
*スミスさんは日本語をよく話す。

This sentence is correct only in the sense of "Mr. Smith often speaks Japanese." The Japanese equivalent of "Mr. Smith speaks Japanese very well" would be, for example,

EXAMPLES:

(7)   **Sumisu-san wa Nihongo o hanasu no ga jōzu da.**
スミスさんは日本語を話すのが上手だ。
lit., Mr. Smith is good at speaking Japanese.

(8)   **Sumisu-san wa Nihongo ga jōzu ni hanaseru.**
スミスさんは日本語が上手に話せる。
lit., Mr. Smith can speak Japanese very well.

Yo'mu 読む *to read*

In English, the following dialogue might very well take place the day after a weekend:

EXAMPLE:

(1)   A: What did you do yesterday?
B: I read all day.

What B means in this conversation is that he read, most likely, a book or books. In other words, in English, you don't have to express what you read. In Japanese, on the other hand, **yomu** may not be used that way.

EXAMPLE:

(2) A: **Kinō wa, donna koto o shita n desu ka.**
昨日は、どんなことをしたんですか。

B: ***Ichinichi-jū yomimashita.**
*一日中読みました。

This dialogue, which is the direct translation of (1), sounds very strange because, in Japanese, B would have to be more specific, as follows:

EXAMPLE:

(3) **Ichinichi-jū hon o yonde-imashita.**
一日中本を読んでいました。
I was reading a book/books all day.

If you don't want to use **hon o** 本を, you can say the following:

EXAMPLE:

(4) **Ichinichi-jū dokusho o shite-imashita.**
一日中読書をしていました。
I read all day (lit., I was doing reading all day).

This expression **dokusho** 読書 is often used when describing hobbies. For example,

EXAMPLE:

(5) A: **B-san no shumi wa?**
Bさんの趣味は？
What are your hobbies?

B: **Tenisu to dokusho desu.**
テニスと読書です。
They are tennis and reading.

Yomu 読む may be used without an object, however, when the object is clear from the context, as in

EXAMPLE:

(6) A: **"Kaze to tomo ni Sarinu" o yonda koto arimasu ka.**
「風と共に去りぬ」を読んだことありますか。
Have you ever read Gone with the Wind?

B: **Ee, ni-kai mo yomimashita yo.**
ええ、二回も読みましたよ。
Yes, I've read it twice.

Yo⌐n 四 *four*

The standard Japanese pronunciation of the kanji for "four" used to be **shi** 四. However, **shi** being homonymous with **shi** 死 "death," the Japanese have started avoiding the pronunciation and using **yon**, the Japanese word for "four." Very few young people nowadays say **jūshi** 十四 to signify "fourteen,"for example. They definitely prefer **jūyon** 十四.

Likewise, the pronunciation of the kanji 七, "seven," which used to be **shichi** 七, has become unpopular because **shichi** includes the sound **shi**. It has thus changed to **nana**, the traditional Japanese word for "seven." There may be another reason for avoiding **shichi**, i.e., it sounds too similar to **ichi** 一, which means "one," because some Japanese speakers, particularly residents of the low-lying section of Tokyo, pronounce **shichi** as **hichi**, which makes the word sound even more like **ichi**.

Also 九, the kanji for "nine," is more often read **kyū** 九 than **ku**, which used to be the standard reading. **Ku** has come to be avoided because it is homonymous with **ku** 苦, which means "suffering."

Yo⌐roko⌐bu 喜ぶ *to rejoice, to be glad*

Yorokobu 喜ぶ, like **ureshii** うれしい, can often be equated with English "be glad," as in

EXAMPLE:
(a) **Kitagawa-san wa sono shirase o kiite yorokonda.**
   北川さんはその知らせを聞いて喜んだ。
   Mr. Kitagawa was glad to hear the news.

There is, however, a crucial difference between **yorokobu** 喜ぶ and **ureshii** うれしい beyond the fact that the former is a verb and the latter an adjective. **Ureshii**, like other adjectives of emotion, refers to the speaker's (or, in questions, the addressee's) state of being glad and does not normally take third-person subjects, whereas **yorokobu**, as a rule, describes a third person's feeling glad and expressing it by speech, attitude, or behavior. Thus, of the following examples, (1) is correct, but (2) is not.

EXAMPLES:
(1) **Kodomo wa yasumi ni naru to yorokobu.**
   子供は休みになると喜ぶ。
   Children are glad when a holiday arrives.
(2) ***Watashi wa yasumi ni naru to yorokobu.**
   *私は休みになると喜ぶ。
   I am glad when a holiday arrives.

In (2), to express the idea intended, **yorokobu** 喜ぶ would have to be replaced by **ureshii** うれしい, as in

EXAMPLE:
(3) **Watashi wa yasumi ni naru to ureshii.**
   私は休みになるとうれしい。
   I am glad when a holiday arrives.

Yorokonde 喜んで, the gerund form of **yorokobu** 喜ぶ, however, may be used in reference to any subject, even the speaker.

EXAMPLE:
(4) **Yorokonde ukagaimasu.**
   喜んで伺います。
   I'll be glad to come [to your place]. (lit., I'll come rejoicingly.)

Yoroshiku よろしく *lit., suitably, favorably, kindly*

When you wish to ask someone to convey your regards to someone else, there are many ways to express that idea in English, such as "Remember me to so-and-so," "Give so-and-so my regards," "Say hello to so-and-so," etc. In Japanese, on the other hand, there is basically only one formula: **daredare** (so-and-so) **ni yoroshiku** 誰々によろしく.

EXAMPLE:

(1) **Okusan ni yoroshiku.**
奥さんによろしく。
Please remember me (lit., [remember me] suitably) to your wife.

Japanese speakers are probably more greeting conscious than English speakers and therefore use this formula more frequently than the latter do similar English expressions.

Yoroshiku よろしく is also a greeting exchanged between two people when introduced to each other for the first time. In this case, **yoroshiku** is usually preceded by **dōzo** どうぞ (see DŌZO).

EXAMPLE:

(2) **Dōzo yoroshiku.**
どうぞよろしく。
How do you do? (lit., Please [treat me] favorably.)

Yoroshiku よろしく is also used when requesting that someone take care of something or someone for you. In this case, the word expressing the thing or person concerned is followed by the particle **o**, as in

EXAMPLE:

(3) **Musuko o yoroshiku onegai-shimasu.**
息子をよろしくお願いします。
lit., Please take care of my son kindly.

This sentence can be used, for instance, when you are talking to a teacher who is just beginning to teach your son. In a similar situation, English-speaking parents might occasionally make a request such as "Please be tough with my son," but they are probably more likely to say something like "I hope my son will do all right." Japanese speakers seem more request oriented than English speakers.

Yōsu 様子 *appearance; state*

Yōsu 様子 "appearance" may not be used to mean "facial features." Use **kao** 顔 instead.

EXAMPLE:

(1) **Indian no kao** (not *****yōsu** 様子) **wa, tokidoki Nihonjin no kao ni nite-iru.**
インディアンの顔は、時々日本人の顔に似ている。
Some American Indians share the same facial features with the Japanese.

Sono Nihonjin no josei wa Amerikajin no yō na yōsu datta その日本人の女性はアメリカ人のような様子だった (lit., "That Japanese woman had the appearance of an American"), therefore, does not really mean "That Japanese woman had American facial features" but rather indicates that she was wearing the kind of clothing an American woman would wear, that she behaved like an American, or that she had the aura of an American.

Yōsu 様子 does not have to be visually perceivable. For example,

EXAMPLE:

(2) **Kare to denwa de hanashita no da ga, nandaka yōsu ga okashikatta.**
彼と電話で話したのだが、なんだか様子がおかしかった。
I talked with him by phone; somehow he sounded as though something were wrong.

Yo¹u 酔う *to get drunk*

"To get drunk" is **you** 酔う or **yopparau** 酔っ払う, the latter indicating a higher degree of intoxication.

EXAMPLE:
(1) **Boku wa you koto wa aru keredo, yopparau koto wa nai yo.**
僕は酔うことはあるけれど、酔っぱらうことはないよ。
I sometimes get a little drunk, but never heavily drunk.

The noun form of **yopparau** 酔っ払う is **yopparai** 酔っ払い "drunkard."

EXAMPLE:
(2) **Tōkyō no eki ni wa, yoru ni naru to, tokidoki benchi ni nete-iru yopparai ga iru.**
東京の駅には、夜になると、時々ベンチで寝ている酔っ払いがいる。
At Tokyo railroad stations at night, there are sometimes drunken men who are lying down on platform benches.

You 酔う, unlike **yopparau** 酔っ払う, may also be used to refer to psychological, not physical, intoxication, as in

EXAMPLE:
(3) **Chīmu no membā wa, zen'in shōri ni yotte-** (not *****yopparatte-** 酔っ払って) **ita.**
チームのメンバーは、全員勝利に酔っていた。
The members of the team were all intoxicated with victory.

Yu⌈bi¹ 指 *finger, toe*

English-speaking students of Japanese usually equate **yubi** 指 with "finger," but **yubi** actually has a much broader range of meaning than "finger" because it may also refer to toes. Although English speakers conceive of fingers and toes as totally unrelated to each other and have two entirely different terms referring to them, Japanese speakers conceive of both as belonging to the same category and have one term for both. When it is absolutely necessary to make a distinction, however, one can do so by saying **te no yubi** 手の指 (lit., "hand **yubi**") and **ashi no yubi** 足の指 (lit., "foot **yubi**"), as in

EXAMPLE:
(1) **Ashi no yubi wa te no yubi yori futokute mijikai.**
足の指は手の指より太くて短い。
Toes are thicker and shorter than fingers.

In English, despite the fact that one can say "There are five fingers on each hand" or "Each hand has five fingers," one does not normally refer to a thumb as a finger (Ogasawara, p. 122). In Japanese, on the other hand, one can point to one's thumb and say, for example,

EXAMPLE:
(2) **Kono yubi ga itai n desu.**
この指が痛いんです。
This finger hurts.

In English, one would probably say in such a case

EXAMPLE:

(3) My thumb hurts.

Yūbin 郵便 *mail*

To mean "to send out mail," the most commonly used verb is **dasu** 出す, as in

EXAMPLE:

(1) Wife to her husband: **Sanpo no tsuide ni, kono tegami o dashite ne.**
散歩のついでに、この手紙を出してね。
If you're going out for a walk, please mail this letter for me.

"To drop a letter into a mailbox" requires another verb, i.e., **ireru** 入れる, as in

EXAMPLE:

(2) **Eki-mae no posuto ni tegami o ireta.**
駅前のポストに手紙を入れた。
I dropped a letter into the mailbox outside the station.

Interestingly, the word **yūbin** 郵便 is not used for e-mail. E-mail is officially called **denshi-mēru** 電子メール "electronic mail," but since it is a little too long, most people just call it **mēru** メール.

EXAMPLE:

(3) **Mēru itadakimashita.**
メールいただきました。
I received your e-mail.

Yūgata 夕方 *dusk*

Although **yūgata** 夕方 is usually equated with English "evening," **yūgata** is actually earlier than evening and shorter as well. It is from about half past four to six or so, about the time Japanese wives are busy preparing dinner. The word **yūgata** evokes a certain picture in most Japanese people's minds: children going home for dinner after having played outside, birds flying home to roost, and the sun about to set in the west. The after-dinner hours are normally not referred to as **yūgata**.

Yūjin 友人 *friend*

Yūjin 友人 means exactly the same as **tomodachi** 友達 but is more formal than the latter.

EXAMPLE:

Gakusei-jidai kara no yūjin (or **tomodachi**) **to iu no wa, ii mono da.**
学生時代からの友人（友達）というのは、いいものだ。
Old friends from one's schooldays are great.

Tomodachi 友達 is sometimes preceded by other nouns to form compounds such as **nomitomodachi** 飲み友達 "drinking pal(s)" and **asobitomodachi** 遊び友達 "playmate(s)." **Yūjin** 友人, on the other hand, is not used that way.

(See TOMODACHI)

Yu⌈kku⌉ri ゆっくり *slowly*

Yukkuri ゆっくり means "slow" or "slowly."

EXAMPLE:

(1) **Mada hayai kara yukkuri arukimashō.**
まだ早いからゆっくり歩きましょう。
It's still early; let's walk more slowly.

There is another word meaning "slow," **osoi** 遅い (see OSOI). In (2) below, both (a) and (b) mean "He eats slowly" (lit., "His way of eating is slow").

EXAMPLE:

(2) **Ano hito wa tabekata ga**   (a) **osoi.**
あの人は食べ方が   遅い。
                                 (b) **yukkuri da.**
                                      ゆっくりだ。

There is, however, a slight difference between (2a) and (2b). While (2a) simply means "He eats slowly," (2b) implies more because **yukkuri** ゆっくり connotes "in a relaxed, leisurely manner." This meaning of **yukkuri** ゆっくり becomes more apparent in the following example:

EXAMPLE:

(3) **Kinō wa kaisha ga yasumi datta kara, ichi-nichi yukkuri yasunda.**
きのうは会社が休みだったから、一日ゆっくり休んだ。
Yesterday I took it easy (lit., rested relaxedly) all day, since I had the day off from work.

Yukkuri-suru ゆっくりする (lit., "to do something slowly") is regularly used in the sense of "to take it easy" or "to relax," especially in the often used invitation **Yukkuri-shite kudasai** ゆっくりしてください meaning "Please stay longer" or "Make yourself at home." A politer version of **Yukkuri-shite kudasai** is **Goyukkuri-nasatte kudasai** ごゆっくりなさってください, which is frequently shortened to **Goyukkuri** ごゆっくり.

Yūmei 有名 *famous*

To express the idea of "famous for something," use **de yūmei** で有名.

EXAMPLE:

(1) **Kamakura wa daibutsu de yūmei desu.**
鎌倉は大仏で有名です。
Kamakura is famous for its great statue of Buddha.

To express the idea of "famous as something," however, use **to-shite yūmei** として有名 instead.

EXAMPLE:

(2) **Kamakura wa daibutsu no aru machi to-shite** (not *de で) **yūmei desu.**
鎌倉は大仏のある町として有名です。
Kamakura is famous as a city with a great statue of Buddha.

To-shite として is not as conversational as **de** で, however. Although (1) and (2) basically say the same thing, (1) is better suited to conversation, and (2) to writing.

Zannen 残念 *regret*

Zannen 残念 "regret" literally means "lingering thought." In other words, it refers to the sense of sorrowful dissatisfaction that lingers on in the mind of someone who realizes that things did not or are not going to turn out according to his wish.

EXAMPLES:

(1) **Araki-san ga issho ni ikarenakute zannen desu.**
荒木さんが一緒に行かれなくなって残念です。
It's too bad Mr. Araki can't go with us.

(2) **Zannen desu ga pikunikku wa toriyame ni narimashita.**
残念ですがピクニックは取りやめになりました。
I am sorry but the picnic has been canceled.

Zannen 残念 should not be used when you feel a sense of guilt about something bad that you have done. For that use **kōkai-suru** 後悔する (see KŌKAI).

EXAMPLE:

(3) **Ano hito no okane o nusunda koto o**　　(a)　*zannen ni omou.
あの人のお金を盗んだことを　　　　　　　　*残念に思う。
　　　　　　　　　　　　　　　　　　　　　(b)　kōkai-shite-iru.
　　　　　　　　　　　　　　　　　　　　　　　後悔している。

By the same token, do not use **zannen** 残念 as an expression of apology. Unlike English "I am sorry," which may be used either as a plain expression of regret (as in the English translation of example (2) above) or as a form of apology (as in "I am sorry I lost your pen"), **zannen** cannot be used for an apology. For that purpose, use **Mōshiwake arimasen** 申し訳ありません "I don't know how to apologize," **Shitsurei-shimashita** 失礼しました "I'm sorry for what I've done," or **Sumimasen** すみません "I'm sorry."

Zasshi 雑誌 *magazine*

In English, "magazine" could be added to the name of a specific magazine, as in "I just bought a *Time* magazine." **Zasshi** 雑誌 has no such usage. You may use the second half of **zasshi** as a suffix, however, as in

EXAMPLE:

(1) **Konshū no Taimu-shi wa, kyō deru hazu da.**
今週のタイム誌は、今日出るはずだ。
This week's Time *magazine is supposed to come out today.*

This usage is quite formal and normally occurs only in writing. In conversation, just say **Taimu** タイム.

To indicate "weekly/monthly/quarterly magazine," use the suffix **-shi** 誌. These words may be used in speech as well as in writing.

EXAMPLE:

(2) **shūkan/gekkan/kikan-shi**
週刊/月刊/季刊誌
weekly/monthly/quarterly magazine

Ze⌐hi ぜひ *by all means; at any cost*

Zehi ぜひ has two basic functions. First, it emphasizes requests. In this case, it is normally accompanied by **-te kudasai** てください, as in

EXAMPLE:

(1) **Ashita no pātī ni wa, zehi irasshatte kudasai.**
あしたのパーティーには、ぜひいらっしゃってください。
Please by all means come to tomorrow's party.

Second, **zehi** ぜひ is used to indicate strong wishes or desires. In this case, it is accompanied by such forms as **-tai** たい and **-(shi) yō** (し)よう.

EXAMPLES:

(2a) **Zehi musuko ni ii daigaku ni haitte morai-tai mono da.**
ぜひ息子にいい大学に入ってもらいたいものだ。
I strongly hope my son gets into a good university.

(2b) **Kondo zehi issho ni gorufu o yarimashō.**
今度ぜひ一緒にゴルフをやりましょう。
Let's be sure to play golf together one of these days.

Zehi ぜひ is not used with negative verbs. Use **zettai ni** 絶対に "absolutely," instead, as in

EXAMPLES:

(3a) **Ashita wa zettai ni** (not *zehi ぜひ) **konaide kudasai.**
あしたは絶対に来ないでください。
Absolutely, please don't come tomorrow.

(3b) **Zettai ni** (not *zehi ぜひ) **sonna eiga wa mi-takunai.**
絶対にそんな映画は見たくない。
I would never wish to see a movie like that.

Ze⌐nbu 全部 *all*

Zenbu 全部 may be used in reference to both animate beings and inanimate objects, but it probably sounds better when used with inanimate objects.

EXAMPLE:

(1) **Nihonjin ga zenbu** (or **Nihonjin no zenbu ga**) **reigitadashii wake de wa nai.**
日本人が全部（日本人の全部が）礼儀正しいわけではない。
Not all Japanese are courteous.

Zenbu 全部 is correct in this sentence, but **min(n)a** probably sounds a little more natural, as in

EXAMPLE:

(2) **Nihonjin ga mi(n)na** (or **Nihonjin no mi(n)na ga**) **reigitadashii wake de wa nai.**
日本人がみ（ん）な（日本人のみ（ん）なが）礼儀正しいわけではない。
Not all Japanese are courteous.

In other words, **zenbu** 全部 goes better with inanimate objects while **mi(n)na** み(ん)な can refer equally to animate beings or inanimate objects. In (3) below, for example, **zenbu** is definitely odd, while **minna** みんな sounds perfectly all right.

EXAMPLE:

(3) A: **Gokazoku wa ogenki desu ka.**
ご家族はお元気ですか。
Is your family doing well?

　　B: **Okagesamade, mi(n)na** (not *****zenbu** 全部) **genki desu.**
おかげさまで、み(ん)な元気です。
They're all doing well, thanks.

With inanimate objects, either **zenbu** 全部 or **mi(n)na** み(ん)な will do, as in

EXAMPLE:

(4) **Kanji o zenbu/mi(n)na oboeru nante fukanō da.**
漢字を全部/み(ん)な覚えるなんて不可能だ。
It's impossible to learn all kanji.

Zenzen 全然 *[not] at all*

Zenzen 全然, as a rule, is used only in negative environments.

EXAMPLES:

(1) **Zenzen wakarimasen.**
全然分かりません。
I don't understand at all.

(2) **Zenzen muzukashiku arimasen.**
全然難しくありません。
It's not at all difficult.

Zenzen 全然 is also used with words of negative orientation (though they are not negative in form). In this case, the English equivalent is "completely."

EXAMPLES:

(3) **Zenzen chigaimasu.**
全然違います。
It's completely wrong (or different).

(4) **Zenzen shippai da.**
全然失敗だ。
It failed completely.

In informal conversation, **zenzen** 全然 is sometimes used as an intensifier with the meaning of "very," as in

EXAMPLE:

(5) **zenzen ii**
全然いい
very good

This last use, however, is rather slangy and is not recommended.

Zuibun ずいぶん *very, quite, a lot*

Zuibun ずいぶん as an intensifier is often quite similar in meaning to **totemo** とても "very."

EXAMPLES:

(1) **Kinō wa zuibun** (or **totemo**) **atsukatta.**
きのうはずいぶん(とても)暑かった。
Yesterday was very hot.

(2) **Nihon wa gasorin ga zuibun** (or **totemo**) **takai.**
日本はガソリンがずいぶん(とても)高い。
In Japan, gasoline is very expensive.

Jorden (1, p. 117) points out that **zuibun** ずいぶん and **totemo** とても have different distributions. For example, whereas both **zuibun** and **totemo** occur before **takai** "high, expensive," only **totemo** can occur before **ii** いい "good."

Zuibun ずいぶん perhaps reflects the speaker's sentiment or subjective judgment while **totemo** とても does not. For example, in (1) and (2) above, the versions with **totemo** seem like objective statements whereas the versions with **zuibun** seem to imply the speaker's surprise, disgust, etc.

It is probably because of this subjective implication that in exclamations such as (3) below, **zuibun** ずいぶん is more appropriate than **totemo** とても.

EXAMPLE:

(3)   (a) **Zuibun**   **ōkiku-natta nē.**
       ずいぶん   大きくなったねえ。
     (b) **?Totemo**
       ?とても
How you've grown! (lit., How big you've gotten!)

Zutto ずっと *all through; by far*

Zutto ずっと has two main uses. First, it signals an uninterrupted state or period of time, as in

EXAMPLE:

(1) **Jūni no toki kara, zutto Eigo o benkyō-shite-imasu.**
十二の時から、ずっと英語を勉強しています。
I've been studying English (without stopping) ever since I was twelve.

Second, it is used to compare two things with a large degree of difference.

EXAMPLE:

(2) **Amerika wa, Nihon yori zutto ōkii.**
アメリカは、日本よりずっと大きい。
America is a lot bigger than Japan.

Don't use **zutto** ずっと, however, when the difference is not in degree but in style or in kind. Use other adverbs such as **zuibun** ずいぶん.

EXAMPLE:

(3) **Eigo to Nihongo wa zuibun** (not *zutto ずっと) **chigau.**
英語と日本語はずいぶん違う。
English and Japanese are a lot different.

Bibliography

Alfonso, Anthony. *Japanese Language Patterns*, I & II. Tokyo: Sophia University, 1966.

Backhouse, A. E. *The Japanese Language: An Introduction*. Melbourne: Oxford University Press, 1993.

Bunka-cho (Agency for Cultural Affairs). *Gaikokujin no tame no Kihongo Yorei Jiten* (A Dictionary of Basic Words for Foreigners). Tokyo: Bunka-cho, 1971.

Hattori, Shiro. *Eigo Kiso-goi no Kenkyu* (A Study in the Basic Vocabulary of English). Tokyo: Sanseido, 1968.

Hirose, Masayoshi, and Shoji, Kakuko, eds. *Effective Japanese Usage Guide (Nihongo Tsukaiwake Jiten)*. Tokyo: Kodansha, 1994.

Ikegami, Yoshihiko. *Imi no Sekai* (The World of Meaning). Tokyo: Nihon Hoso Shuppan Kyokai, 1978.

Jorden, Eleanor Harz. *Beginning Japanese*. 2 vols. New Haven and London: Yale University Press, 1963.

Keene, Donald. *"Nihongo no Muzukashisa"* (The Difficulty of Japanese). In *Watashi no Gaikokugo* (My Foreign Language), edited by Tadao Umesao and Michio Nagai, pp. 154–63. Tokyo: Chuokoronsha, 1970.

Kindaichi, Haruhiko, ed. *Meikai Nihongo Akusento Jiten* (A Clearly Explained Dictionary of Japanese Accent), 6th ed. Tokyo: Sanseido, 1962.

Kunihiro, Tetsuya. *Kozoteki Imiron* (Structural Semantics). Tokyo: Sanseido, 1967.

Kuno, Susumu. *The Structure of the Japanese Language*. Cambridge, Mass., and London: MIT Press, 1973.

Kurokawa, Shozo. *Nihongo to Eigo no Aida* (Between Japanese and English). Tokyo: Natsumesha, 1978.

Makino, Seiichi, and Tsutsui, Michio. *A Dictionary of Basic Japanese Grammar*. Tokyo: The Japan Times, 1986.

———. *A Dictionary of Intermediate Japanese Grammar*. Tokyo: the Japan Times, 1995.

Maruya, Saiichi. *Nihongo no tame ni* (For the Japanese Language). Tokyo: Shinchosha, 1974.

Matsui, Emi. *Eisakubun ni okeru Nihonjinteki Ayamari* (Japanese-like Errors in English). Tokyo: Taishukan, 1979.

Matsuo, Hirou, et al. *Ruigigo no Kenkyu* (A Study of Synonyms). Report no. 28 by Kokuritsu Kokugo Kenkyujo (The National Language Research Institute). Tokyo: Shuei Shuppan, 1965.

Miura, Akira, *English Loanwords: A Selection*. Tokyo and Rutland, Vt.: Charles E. Tuttle, 1979.

———. *Japanese Words and Their Uses, I*. Tokyo: Charles E. Tuttle. 1983.

———. *Japanese Words and Their Uses, II*. Tokyo and Rutland, Vt.: Charles E. Tuttle. 2002.

Miura, Akira, and McGloin, Naomi H. *Goi* (Vocabulary). Tokyo: Aratake Shuppan, 1988.

Miyoshi, Hiroshi. *Nichi-Ei Kotoba no Chigai* (Differences Between Japanese and English Expressions). Tokyo: Koronsha, 1978.

Mizutani, Osamu, and Mizutani, Nobuko. *Nihongo Notes*, 1. Tokyo: The Japan Times, 1977.

————. *Nihongo Notes*, 2. Tokyo: The Japan Times, 1979.

Morita, Yoshiyuki. *Kiso Nihongo* (Basic Japanese), I, II, III. Tokyo: Kadokawa Shoten, 1977, 1980, 1984.

Nakamura, Akira. *Sensu Aru Nihongohyoogen no Tame ni* (For Sensible Japanese Expressions). Tokyo: Chuokoronsha, 1994.

Ogasawara, Rinju. *"Eigo-jisho to Nichi-Ei Goi no Hikaku"* (A Comparison of the Japanese and English Vocabularies Through English-Language Dictionaries). In *Nichi-Eigo no Hikaku* (A Comparison of Japanese and English), edited by Kenkyusha, pp. 115–39. Tokyo: Kenkyusha, 1978.

Ohno, Susumu, and Shibata, Takeshi, eds. *Goi to Imi* (Words and Meanings). *Iwanami Koza: Nihongo* (Iwanami Course: The Japanese Language), 9. Tokyo: Iwanami Shoten, 1977.

Petersen, Mark. *Zoku Nihonjin no Eigo* (English of the Japanese). Tokyo: Iwanami Shoten, 1990.

Sandness, Karen. "The Use of *Kare* and *Kanojo*." *Journal of the Association of Teachers of Japanese* 10, no. 1 (March 1975), pp. 75–86.

Shibata, Takeshi. *"Ikite-iru Hogen"* (Living Dialects). In *Modern Japanese for University Students*, 2, 3rd ed., compiled by the Japanese Department, International Christian University, pp. 20–25. Tokyo: International Christian University, 1970.

Shibata, Takeshi, et al. *Kotoba no Imi* (The Meanings of Words), 2. Tokyo: Heibonsha, 1979.

Shogakkan, ed. *Tsukaikata no Wakaru Ruigo-Reikaijiten* (A Dictionary of Synonyms with Explanatory Examples). Tokyo: Shogakkan, 1994.

Soga, Matsuo, and Matsumoto, Noriko. *Foundations of Japanese Language*. Tokyo: Taishukan, 1978.

Suzuki, Takao. *Japanese and the Japanese*. Translated by Akira Miura. Tokyo, New York, and San Francisco: Kodansha International, 1978.

Tokugawa, Munemasa, and Miyajima, Tatsuo. *Ruigigo Jiten* (A Dictionary of Synonyms). Tokyo: Tokyodo, 1962.

Yanafu, Akira. *Hon'yaku to wa Nani ka* (What Is Translation?).Tokyo: Hosei University Press, 1976.

Index

This index includes all the main entries as well as a few hundred more words and expressions that appear in the text explanations. The main entries are in boldface italics type while the other words are in boldface type. Page numbers in boldface type show where the words appear as main entries. An English–Japanese index follows the Japanese–English index.

Japanese–English

English–Japanese

a.m. *gozen* **58–59**
about (indicating time) *-goro* **58**
about (indicating weight) *-gurai* **59**
absence (day off) *yasumi* **285–286**
according to *ni yoru to* **188**
actually *hontō wa* **79**
adjacent *tonari* **267**
adjoining *tonari* **267**
administer *okonau* **198–199**
admirable *erai* **50–51**; *kanshin* **115–116**
advice *chūi* **39**
a few *sukoshi* **243–244**
after (time particle) *ato* **27**
after all *tōtō* **269**
afternoon *gogo* **56**
after-school school ("cram" school) *juku* **105**
ago *mae* **153–154**
a little *chotto* **38–39**
a little (quantity) *sukoshi* **243–244**
all *minna* **162**; *zenbu* **298–29**
all of you *mina-san* **162**
a lot *ippai* **89**; *takusan* **254**; *zuibun* **300**
all right *daijōbu* **40**
all through *zutto* **300**
already *mō* **169**
ancestor *senzo* **230**
and so on *nado* **174–175**
and the like *nado* **174–175**
answer (*n*) *henji* **73**; *kotaeru* **142**
appearance *yōsu* **293**
approximately *yaku* **282–283**
approximately (indicating time) *-goro* **58**
approximately (indicating weight) *-gurai* **59**
approximate time *koro* **141**
Are you well? *Ogenki desu ka* **194**
around *mawari* **158–159**
art of interpretation *tsūyaku* **274**
ashamed *hazukashii* **71–72**
as might be expected *yahari/yappari* **282**
as (much/soon) as possible *narubeku* **182**
ask (a favor) *tanomu* **255**
ask (a question) *kiku* **127–128**
at all *zenzen* **299**
at any cost *zehi* **298**
at last *tōtō* **269**
attend *deru* **46**
attention *chūi* **39**
at the most *seizei* **225–226**
author *chosha* **38**
awful *iya* **98**

awkward *mazui* **159**

baby (sb else's) *akachan* **14**
bad *warui* **281**
bad-tasting *mazui* **159**
baseball *yakyū* **283**
bath *(o)furo* **12, 194**
be *iru* **91**
be able to *dekiru* **43–44**
be absent *yasumu* **286**
beard *hige* **75**
be at a loss *komaru* **137**
beautiful *kirei* **129–130**; *utsukushii* **278**
because of *ni yotte* **188**
become angry *okoru* **199–200**
become congested *komu* **137–138**
become crowded *komu* **137–138**
become employed *tsutomeru* **273–274**
become fashionable *hayaru* **70–71**
become fat *futoru* **53**
become popular *hayaru* **70–71**
become pregnant *ninshin-suru* **187**
become tired *tsukareru* **271**
be different *chigau* **36–37**
be found *mitsukaru* **166–167**
begin (something) *hajimeru* **65**
beginning *hajime* **65**
beginning (something) *hajimete* **66**
be glad *yorokobu* **292**
be impressed *kanshin-suru* **115–116**
be in no position to (do something) *-kaneru*
　113
be incorrect *chigau* **36–37**
believe *shinjiru* **234**
be relieved *tasukaru* **257–258**
be saved *tasukaru* **257–258**
be similar *nite-iru* **187**
be surprised *bikkuri-suru* **32**
before *mae* **153–154**
better of two poor options *mashi* **157**
be under the wrong impression *omoikomu*
　201–202
be visible *mieru* **161**
big *ōkii* **197–198**
bird *tori* **267**
birthplace *furusato* **53**; *kokyō* **136**
blue *aoi* **19**
body *karada* **117**
boil *waku* **280**
borrow (from someone) *kariru* **118**

eat (M vulgar) *kuu* **147–148**
economic(al) *keizaiteki* **122**
eject out of the mouth *haku* **67**
embarrassed *hazukashii* **71–72**
embarrassing *hazukashii* **71–72**
encourage *hagemasu* **61**
end *owaru* **210–211**
end of the war *shūsen* **239**
enjoyable *tanoshii* **255–256**
enough *takusan* **254**
enter *hairu* **64**
entirely *mattaku* **158**
enviable *urayamashii* **276–277**
envious *urayamashii* **276–277**
even though *nagara* **175**
evening *ban* **30**
evening meal *ban-gohan* **30**
every *mai* **154**
everyone *mina-san* **162**; *minna* **162**
examination *shiken* **233–234**
excessively *amari* **15–16**
Excuse me (for doing something rude)
  Shitsurei-shimasu **237**
exercise *renshū* **212–213**
exist *aru* **21–22**; *iru* **91**
expect *kitai-suru* **131**
expensive *takai* **253–254**
experience *taiken* **252**
experience, to have had the *koto ga aru*
  143–144
extremely *kiwamete* **132**

fact *koto* **143**
factory *kōba* **133**
fall (= autumn) **aki 248**
fall (over) *taoreru* **256**
fall asleep *neru* **183**
fall colors (lit., red leaves) *kōyō* **144**
family *kazoku* **121**
famous *yūmei* **296**
far *tōi* **262–263**
fast *hayai* **70**
father *chichi* **35–36**
favorably *yoroshiku* **292–293**
feather *hane* **68**
feel relieved *hotto-suru* **81–82**
fellow *yatsu* **286**
female *onna* **205**
few *sukoshi* **243–244**; *sukunai* **244–245**
fight *tatakau* **259**
finally *tōtō* **269**; *yatto* **287–288**
find (out) *mitsukeru* **167**

finger *yubi* **294–295**
first of all *mazu* **159**
first time *hajimete* **66**
first time after a long while *shibaraku-buri*
  231–232
flesh *niku* **186**
food *tabemono* **249**
food to eat with rice *okazu* **196**
foot *ashi* **24**
for the first time *hajimete* **66**
foreigner *gaijin* **54**
fortune *un* **276**
four *yon* **291–292**
frequently *tabitabi* **250**
friend *tomodachi* **266**; *yūjin* **295**
from *kara* **116–117**; *mae* **153–154**
full-fledged *ichininmae* **84**
fussy *urusai* **277–278**

gain weight *futoru* **53**
gentle *yasashii* **284**
get drunk *you* **294**
get into (a vehicle) *noru* **190**
get married *kekkon-suru* **123–124**
get off *oriru* **206**
get on (a vehicle) *noru* **190**
get to know *shiru* **235–236**
gift *miyage* **167–168**
give (to me) *yokosu* **289**
go *iku* **87–88**
go back *modoru* **170–171**
go down *oriru* **206**
good *ii* **84**
Good-by *Sayonara* **223**
Good day! *konnichi wa* **139**
Good morning! *Ohayō gazaimasu* **195**
Good night! *Oyasumi-nasai* **211**
go out *dekakeru* **42**; *deru* **46**
go to bed *neru* **183**; *yasumu* **286**
go up *agaru* **13**, **194**
government *seifu* **224**
graduate *deru* **46**
grass *kusa* **147**
great *erai* **50–51**
green *midori* **161**
grow *seichō-suru* **223–224**
guest *kyaku* **148–149**
guy *yatsu* **286**

handicapped person (physically) *shintai-*
  shōgaisha **235**
happening *jiken* **101**

happiness *kōfuku* 134
happy *kōfuku* 134; *tanoshil* 255–256
Happy New Year! *Akemashite omedete gozaimasu* 14
hard to bear *tsurai* 272
hardly *roku ni* 214
have *aru* 21–22, 273
have had the experience of doing *koto ga aru* 143–144
having good exposure to the sun *hiatari ga ii* 74–75
he *kare* 117–118
head *atama* 25–26; *kubi* 145–146
healthy *genki* 55–56; *jōbu* 103; *tassha* 257
hear *kiku* 127–128
Hello *Moshimoshi* 172
help *tasukeru* 258–259
here and there *achikochi* 12
high school graduate not yet in college *rōnin* 214–215
high *takai* 253–254
hobby *shumi* 239
home *ie* 84; *katei* 119; *otaku* 207–208; *uchi* 274–275
home village/town *furusato* 53; *kokyō* 136
hot (weather, liquid, etc.) *atsui* 26, 29, 248, 261
hot water *oyu* 212
hour *jikan* 100–101
house *ie* 84; *uchi* 274–275
How about? *ikaga desu ka?* 86–87
How are you? *ikaga desu ka?* 86–87; *Ogenki desu ka* 194
"Hurray!" *Yatta* 287
Hurry home! *Itte-irrasshai* 97

I (lit., humbly) request *onegai-shimasu* 204–205
I *boku* 33; *watashi* 281–282
idea *shisō* 236
ideology *shisō* 236
if I remember correctly *tashika* 256–257
if possible *narubeku* 182
I humbly accept *Itadakimasu* 95
ill *byōki* 34–35
I'm home! *Tadaima* 251
I'm leaving *Itte-mairimasu* 97
important *taisetsu* 252–253
I'm sorry *sumimasen* 245
in *naka* 176
incidentally *tokorode* 265–266
in compensation for (to make up for) *kawari* 120

inexpensive *yasui* 285
inform *oshieru* 206
in good spirits *genki* 55–56
injury *kega* 121–122
inquire *tazuneru* 260; *ukagau* 275
inside *naka* 177
insignificant *tsumaranai* 271–272
instead of *kawari* 120
instruction *kyōju* 150–151
interest *kyōmi* 151–152
interpreter *tsūyaku* 274
in the end *tōtō* 269
in those days *tōji* 263
invite *shōtai-suru* 238
Is anybody home? *Gomen-kudasai* 57
I see *naruhodo* 182
Is that so? *sō desu ka* 241–242
(it) costs (time) *kakaru* 108–109
(it) takes (time) *kakaru* 108–109

Japan *Nihon* 184
Japanese (person) *Nihonjin* 185
Japanese-style *Nihon-shiki* 185
Japanese system *Nihon-shiki* 185
Japan-U.S. *Nichibei* 183
job *shigoto* 232
join *hairu* 64
junior *kōhai* 135
just like *marude* 156–157

keep *mamoru* 155–156
kimono *kimono* 128–129
kindly *yoroshiku* 292–293
Korea *Chōsen* 37

large *Okii* 197–198
last year *sakunen* 221
late *osoi* 207
lately *saikin* 218–219
laugh *warau* 280
learn *oboeru* 193
leave *deru* 46
leave out *habuku* 60
lecture *kōgi* 134–135
leg *ashi* 24
lend (to someone) *kasu* 118–119
lie down *neru* 183
life *inochi* 89; *seikatsu* 224–225
lightning *kaminari* 111
like (want to) *mitai* 165–166; (is fond of) *suki* 242–243
liquor *sake* 220

perfect *kanzen* 116
person *hito* 77–78
phone (*v*) *denwa o kakeru* 45–46
phrase *monku* 171
physically-handicapped person *shintai-shōgaisha* 235
picture *e* 49
play *asobu* 24–25; *shibai* 230–231
player (in a sport) *senshu* 229
pleasantly cool *suzushii* 248
please (asking a favor/request) *dōzo* 49
Please take care (of yourself) *Odaiji ni* 194
point in time *jikoku* 101–102
poor *binbō* 32–33; *mazushii* 160
popularity *ninki* 186–187
population *jinkō* 102
practice *renshū* 212–213
praiseworthy *erai* 50–51; *kanshin* 115–116
present (*n*) *miyage* 167–168
pretty *kirei* 129–130
prices *bukka* 33–34
prime minister *shushō* 239
private (*adj*) *shiritsu* 235
professor *kyōju* 150–151
prosperous *sakan* 219
protect *mamoru* 155–156
pupil *seito* 225
put on (lower part of body) *haku* 66
put on (on hand/finger) *hameru* 67
put on (the head) *kaburu* 106
put on (the upper body) *kiru* 130

question (*n*) *gimon* 56
quite *kekkō* 122; *nakanaka* 177; *zuibun* 300

rather *nakanaka* 177
read *yomu* 290–291
really *hontō ni* 79
Really? *Hē?* 72–73
receive *morau* 171–172
recently *kono-aida* 139; *saikin* 218–219
regret *kōkai* 135–136; *zannen* 297
regrettable *oshii* 207
rejoice *yorokobu* 292
remember correctly, if I *tashika* 256–257
rent (from someone) *kariru* 118
rent (to someone) *kasu* 118–119
repair *naosu* 180
request (a favor) *tanomu* 255
resemble *nite-iru* 187
rest *yasumu* 286
return *kaeru* 106–107; *modoru* 170–171

reverse *gyaku* 60
rice (cooked) *gohan* 57; *meishi* 161
rice (uncooked) *kome* 137
river *kawa* 120
robust *jōbu* 103
rock *iwa* 98
roof *yane* 283

saké *sake* 220
saké store *sakaya* 220
same *onaji* 203–204
samurai (masterless) *rōnin* 214–215
savings *chokin* 37
say *iu* 97
school *gakkō* 54; (after school) *juku* 105
science *kagaku* 107; *rika* 213
scold *okoru* 199–200
scratch *kaku* 109–110
season *kisetsu* 131
see (sb) *au* 28–30; (stg) *miru* 164–165
self *jibun* 99–100
self-supporting *ichininmae* 84
send over (to me) *yokosu* 289
senior *senpai* 228
serious *majime* 155
serve as *tsutomeru* 273–274
serving (of food) *ichininmae* 84
shameful *hazukashii* 71–72
she *kanojo* 114–115
shopping *kaimono* 107–108
short *mijikai* 161–162
short story *shōsetsu* 237
should *hō ga ii* 78–79
shower *abiru* 12
shy *hazukashii* 71–72
sibling *kyōdai* 149–150
sick *byōki* 34–35
sightseeing *kenbutsu* 124–125
sister (younger) *imōto* 89
sit down *kakeru* 109; *suwaru* 247–248
skillful *tassha* 257; *umai* 275–276
sleep *neru* 183
sleep late *nebō-suru* 183
slow *noroi* 189–190; *osoi* 207
slowly *yukkuri* 296
small (in area) *semai* 227
socks *kutsushita* 147
some *sukoshi* 243–244
Sorry *Dōmo* 47; *Gomen-nasai* 58
southeast *tōnan* 266–267
spacious *hiroi* 76
speak *hanasu* 67–68

spring **haru** 248
square (shape) *shikaku* 233
state *yōsu* 293
steer (castrated bull) *ushi* 278
stick it out *ganbaru* 54–55
still *mada* 152
stomach *onaka* 204
store *mise* 165
stroll *sanpo* 223
strong *jōbu* 103
student *gakusei* 54; *seito* 225
study *benkyō* 31; *benkō-suru* 31–32; *narau*
   180–182
suffix (attached to a name) *-chan* 33, 222;
   -kun 146; *-san* 222
suffix (pluralizing) *-tachi* 250–51
suitably *yoroshiku* 292–293
summer **natsu** 248
sumo wrestler *sumō* 245
sumo wrestling *sumō* 245
sun *hi* 73–74
sun, having good exposure to *hiatari ga ii*
   74–75
supervisor *kantoku* 116
sure *kitto* 131–132
surgical operation *shujutsu* 238–239
sushi (kind of) *nigiri* 184
sweet *amai* 15
sweetheart *koibito* 135
swim *oyogu* 211

take (someone) along *tsurete-iku* 272–273
take (time) *kakaru* 108–109
take a bath *abiru* 12
take lessons *narau* 180–182
take off (clothing) *nugu* 191–192
taking the opportunity *tsuide ni* 270
tall *takai* 253–254
taste *shumi* 239
teach *oshieru* 206
teacher *sensei* 228–29
telephone (*n*) *denwa* 44–45
tell *hanasu* 67–68; *oshieru* 206
tell you the truth *jitsu wa* 102–103
terrible *taihen* 251–252
terrific *sugoi* 242
Thank you *Arigatō gozaimasu* 20–21;
   sumimasen 245
Thanks *Dōmo* 47
thanks to you *okage-sama* 195–196
Thank you for your work *Gokurō-sama* 57
that (directional) *are* 19–20

That's fine *kekkō desu* 123
That's right *sō desu* 240–241
theater *gekijō* 55
the other day *kono-aida* 139; *senjitsu*
   227–228
these days *konogoro* 140
thick (for flat objects) *atsui* 27–28
thing *koto* 143
think *kangaeru* 113; *omou* 202–203
this *kore* 140–141
this coming *kondo no* 138
thought *shisō* 236
thriving *sakan* 219
throughout *-jū* 104–105
thunder *kaminari* 111
time *jikan* 100–101; *toki* 264–265
time (point in) *jikoku* 101–102
today *kyō* 149
toe *yubi* 294–295
together *issho* 93–95
together with *to issho ni* 262
toilet *benjo* 31; *otearai* 31, 194
tomorrow *ashita* 24, 105
too (much) *amari* 15–16, 268, 290
totally *mattaku* 158
training *renshū* 212–213
travel *ryokō-suru* 216
tremendous *taihen* 251–252
troublesome *mendō* 160
truly *hontō ni* 79; *mattaku* 158
try one's best *ganbaru* 54–55
turn back *modoru* 170–171

uncooked rice *kome* 137
understand *wakaru* 279–280
uninteresting *tsumaranai* 271–272
university *daigaku* 40
unpleasant *iya* 98
unreasonable *muri* 174
unwise *mazui* 159
use *mochiiru* 169–170
usual *fudan* 51
utilize *mochiiru* 169–170

vacation *yasumi* 285–286
valley *tani* 254
various *iroiro* 90–91; *samazama* 221
very *taihen* 251–252; *totemo* 268–269;
   zuibun 300
violent *hageshi* 61–62
visit *tazuneru* 260; *ukagau* 275
visitor *kyaku* 148–149

vomit *haku* **67**

wage war *tatakau* **259**
waist *koshi* **141–142**
walk (*v*) *aruku* **22–23**; (*n*) *sanpo* **223**
want (something) *hoshii* **80–81**
war, end of *shūsen* **239**
warm (pleasantly) *atatakai* **26**
washing *sentaku* **229–230**
wasteful *mottainai* **172**
watch *miru* **164–165**
watch (time piece) *tokei* **264**
water (cold) *mizu* **168**; (hot) *oyu* **212**
we *wareware* **281**
weak point *nigate* **184**
wealthy (person) *kanemochi* **112–113**
wear (on hand/finger) *hameru* **67**; (on lower part of body) *haku* **66**; (on the head) *kaburu* **106**; (on the upper body) *kiru* **130**
weather *tenki* **260–261**
weed *kusa* **147**
weep *naku* **177–178**
Welcome (to our place)! *Irrasshai* **90**
Welcome home! *Okaeri-nasai* **195**
well *genki* **55–56**
What! *Nan da* **179–180**
what kind (of) *donna* **48**

what kind of day *nan no hi* **180**
What kind of person? *donna hito* **48–49**
When? *Itsu* **95–96**
while (*conj*) *nagara* **175**
whiskers *hige* **75**
who? *dare* **41–42**
Why! *nan da* **179–180**
wide *hiroi* **76**
wife *kanai* **111**; *oku-san* **200**; *tsuma* **271**
win *katsu* **120**
window *mado* **153**
wing *hane* **68**
winter **fuyu** **248**
without fail *kanarazu* **111–112**
woman *fujin* **51**; *josei* **104**; *joshi* **104**
word *monku* **171**
work *hataraku* **69–70**; *shigoto* **232**
world *sekai* **226**
write *kaku* **109–110**
writer *sakka* **220**; (of a particular piece of writing) *hissha* **77**

yes *ee* **50**; *hai* **62–64**, **73**, **142**
you *anata* **17**, **115**, **128**, **208**; *kimi* **128**
You are welcome *Dō itashimashite* **47**
younger brother *otōto* **209**
younger sister *imōto* **89**